Pragmatic Prophet
The Life of Michael Robert Zigler

Pragmatic Prophet

The Life of Michael Robert Zigler

(November 9, 1891–October 25, 1985)

Donald F. Durnbaugh

BRETHREN PRESS
Elgin, Illinois

PRAGMATIC PROPHET: THE LIFE OF MICHAEL ROBERT ZIGLER
by Donald F. Durnbaugh

Copyright © 1989 On Earth Peace Assembly, Inc., Church of the Brethren
General Board

Brethren Press, 1451 Dundee Avenue, Elgin, Illinois 60120

Cover design by Jeane Healy
Edited and typeset by Dave and Neta Jackson

Library of Congress Cataloging-in-Publication Data

Durnbaugh, Donald F.
    Pragmatic prophet: the life of M. R. Zigler / Donald F. Durnbaugh.
        p.   cm.
    Bibliography: p.
    Includes index.
    ISBN 0-87178-715-6 : $24.95
    1. Zigler, M. R.   2. Church of the Brethren—United States—Clergy—
Biography.   3. Pacifists—United States—Biography.   4. Ecumenists—
United States—Biography.   I. Title.
BX7843.Z54D87   1989
286'.5'092—dc20
[B]   89-34973
                                                                    CIP

ISBN 0-87178-715-6
Manufactured in the United States of America

For Hedda
(Proverbs 31: 28-29)

CONTENTS

■ PREFACE

"A well-written life is almost as rare as a well-spent one," said Thomas Carlyle. Echoing the sentiment, the biographer Lytton Strachey, who revolutionized the craft with his racy *Emininent Victorians,* wrote: "It is perhaps as difficult to write a good life as to live one." To try to capture completely the essence of any one personality, let alone a person with so many facets to his character and so many achievements to his credit as Michael Robert Zigler, is virtually impossible. Errors of commission and omission are inevitable, to say nothing of distortions of perspective. No doubt this is why an eighteenth century writer suggested that the fear of what a biographer might do to one's posthumous reputation added a new terror to the contemplation of mortality.

This book was written because M. R. Zigler repeatedly asked that it be done. He had, indeed, talked to other writers who were interested in writing his life history. One of them, Inez Long, succeeded in bringing to print *One Man's Peace: A Story of M. R. Zigler* (1983), based on her long acquaintance with her subject and many hours of interviews in the weeks of writing. As a work of biographical fiction, with invented but well-grounded dialogue, it has handsomely served its purpose, to relate the Zigler saga to a wide readership. It was understood that a longer and documented volume, emphasizing M. R. Zigler's contribution to the Church of the Brethren and the larger world church, should be produced later. This is here attempted.

The On Earth Peace Assembly, the creation of which took so much of Zigler's energies in his last decade of life, commissioned this volume. I was given complete freedom of interpretation, for which I am grateful. I also gladly acknowledge the aid of the Brethren Press for undertaking to

ix

publish the book, the American Theological Association for a research grant, the administration and board of Bethany Theological Seminary for approving a sabbatical leave, and the administrators of the J. Omar Good Fund of Juniata College for an appointment as Visiting Distinguished Professor of Evangelical Christianity for the academic year 1988-1989, which provided time to complete the manuscript.

My gratitude is especially extended to Geraldine Zigler Glick and Robert S. Zigler, M. R. Zigler's daughter and son, for unrestrained access to their father's papers and the use of family photographs. Harold D. Smith, executive director of On Earth Peace, facilitated the use of Zigler materials at New Windsor, Maryland. The curators and archivists of a score of archives and libraries were invariably helpful and knowledgable. I am further indebted to the large number of friends and associates of M. R. Zigler who shared in conversations, more formal interviews, and letters their memories of this unusual and outstanding personality.

As one associated in many endeavors with M. R. Zigler since arriving in Europe with the first group of Brethren Volunteer Service workers in 1949, I have both the advantage and potential bias of close relationship with my subject. In occasionally finding it necessary to point out some human weaknesses of M. R. Zigler, I find comfort in recalling that the hero of this story always welcomed vigorous challenge. His largeness of spirit allowed him to rise above criticisms, to enjoy a hearty laugh at recognized foibles, and to press on in his life crusade to bring peace on earth and good will among all people.

Donald F. Durnbaugh
Huntingdon, Pennsylvania,
December, 1988

PROLOGUE

It was August, 1983, during the final days of the sixth international assembly of the World Council of Churches at Vancouver, Canada. Conference officers gave special recognition to the oldest person present—M. R. Zigler, aged ninety-one. He was one of the very few church leaders yet living who had been present at the landmark conferences held in the summer of 1937 at Oxford and Edinburgh (from which sprang the modern ecumenical movement) and at the foundational assembly of the World Council of Churches at Amsterdam in 1948. He seized the opportunity to appeal once again for Christians to stop killing other Christians— the indispensable first step, to his way of thinking, on the path to world peace. Pointing out his lifelong affiliation with an historic peace church, the Church of the Brethren, the nonagenarian speaker urged delegates in the colorful assembly to rededicate themselves to the cause of peace. The entire assembly rose in spontaneous ovation for the life and work of the veteran peace activist.

The incident well represents the main strands merging into the fabric of the life of Michael Robert Zigler. Born in the rolling hills of the Shenandoah Valley, M. R. Zigler's entire career was dedicated to service in his church, to work with other communions, and to the preservation or restoration of peace. Along the nearly ninety-four years granted him, these three themes were pursued so creatively, so expansively, so aggressively, yet so sensitively, that he became for thousands of friends, both within the Brethren fold and especially outside it, the representative figure of the Church of the Brethren in the twentieth century.

M. R. Zigler had the gift of friendship; he had the intuitive, yet consciously crafted, knack of the right spoken or written word, the right gesture, and the right act of encouragement to bond other people—both younger or older—to him for life. His tenacious drive and exuberant manner exasperated his colleagues at times, but no one could stay at odds for long with such a determinedly cordial figure.

This is evidenced by the outpouring of affection and respect that showered over him at turning points in his life, such as when he retired in

1948 from an executive position at denominational offices in Elgin, Illinois, to take the position of Brethren representative in Europe. Most overpoweringly did these expressions come to him as he lay shattered in a hospital bed in far-off Västervik, Sweden, in late summer and fall, 1958. This followed the devastating traffic accident that took the lives of his beloved wife Amy and a Swedish couple in another car, and left him near death. As many as forty cables, cards, and letters a day reached the hospital, as news of the tragedy spread around the world. In his time of need hundreds of people, whose lives he had touched, remembered the many ways in which they felt indebted to him as they expressed their concerns for his recovery.

"Mr. Brethren," as he was called, was the soul of the Brethren Service story. He moved his isolated church into the modern world of conciliar cooperation and gave a valiant witness for peace in thousands of settings in and out of season. A bewildering number of organizational affiliations, a hectic schedule that broke his sturdy health more than once, constant travel, heavy pressures—through all these ran an essential core of commitment that remained stable throughout his near century of activity. During his lifetime, service through his church, the claims of peace, and the unity of all Christians remained fixed lodestars in his complicated universe. From the pleasant Zigler farm near Broadway, Virginia; to the cluttered office in Elgin, Illinois; to the spacious apartment in Geneva, Switzerland; to the room in the New Windsor Center, Maryland; to his bedroom back in Broadway, in all of the chapters of his life, M. R. Zigler knew one goal—serving the Prince of Peace through his church.

1

BIRTH AND EARLY LIFE

SIXTY-ONE YEARS AFTER leaving home in 1911, M. R. Zigler found himself speaking twice a day to an interested audience in the spacious farm house where he was born in Broadway, Virginia. The house, which received state and national ranking as an historic site in 1971, had been lovingly restored by its present owner Samuel D. Lindsay and his late wife Pauline. To celebrate this recognition, the Lindsays initiated a week-long gathering (July 16-23, 1972) of descendants of the families connected with the structure and the surrounding community. They called the restored building the Tunker House and often showed visitors through it.[1]

For ninety years it had been owned by the Zigler family, including Michael Zigler, the father of M. R. Zigler. Before the Ziglers, it had been the property of the Yount family. Into this family came the noted Brethren convert and church statesman, Peter Nead, who married Elizabeth Yount in 1825. The Younts had originally come to Virginia from Pennsylvania, settling near Broadway in 1794. Their first dwelling, a rude wood cabin, was built in 1819 across the creek from the present brick house. Until the nearby Linville Creek meetinghouse was constructed in 1830, the Yount home had housed the meetings of the local Brethren. This was made possible by hanging hinged partitions between the living room and dining room/kitchen. The partitions were raised to create a larger area for church gatherings. The house was even the site for the 1832 Annual Meeting of the Brethren.[2]

Thus, those assembling at the Tunker House in 1972 were reminded of the long Brethren heritage the house could claim. The Younts and the Ziglers were names to be reckoned with among Brethren, not only in Virginia but also nationally. Peter Nead was the most influential Brethren writer/theologian of the nineteenth century; M. R. Zigler the most noted Brethren spokesman and leader of the twentieth century. In addition, just down the road from the Tunker House sat the home of John Kline, the beloved nineteenth century Brethren leader and martyr of 1864. All three of these noted figures were recognized in the displays in the venerable rooms of the Tunker House, with memorabilia, furniture, photographs, and records of historic importance.[3]

The Zigler family, which had also come to Virginia from Pennsylvania, was linked through marriage with important Brethren families of the Shenandoah valley—the Wamplers, Millers, Klines, Bowmans, Shirkys, and others. In this historic setting, M. R. Zigler recalled some of the noted personalities associated with his birthplace, aiding his recollections by intensive research. He happily reminisced about his early years. They were idyllic in his memory.

Early Life

Michael Robert Zigler was the rather imposing name given to the tiny sixth child of Michael Zigler (1843-1926) and Mary Jane Knupp (or Knopp) Zigler (1850-1904). (A seventh child, Mary, died when only three years old.) At birth on November 9, 1891, the baby was not expected to live. He was a puny youngster, born two months prematurely and weighing under three pounds. The thighs of the infant were smaller around than his mother's thumb, and he had to be carried on a pillow and fed with an eye-dropper. He had colic and cried for seven months. The condition was so precarious that his continued existence was widely considered a miracle. Zigler later wrote: "Especially older people would say this to me again and again. This seemed to leave an impression on me that there must have been some reason for my survival."[4]

Two women from the neighborhood assisted the weakened mother. One, Alice Madden, was black and an occasional hired servant in the Zigler household. Some say she nursed the tiny infant at her own breast. Her son, Sam, later became a favored playmate of young Robert. Many years later, M. R. Zigler looked for the grave of Alice Madden. He found it in the Linville Creek Brethren cemetery and donated $150 for a respectable headstone. It was most unusual for congregations in the South to permit burials of Negroes in church graveyards, let alone provide plots without cost. But the Brethren made a notable exception to the rule. In 1980, with the assistance of Sam Lindsay, Zigler placed a memorial in the cemetery for the unnamed graves of black people.[5]

The shaky start of the infant may have been responsible for his relatively poor hearing and the severe asthma attacks that plagued him for most of his life. He was not as strong physically as other Zigler children and was thus spared some of the drudgery of farm work. Later, when he grew to a stature of six feet, he was occasionally accused of laziness when working or engaged in athletics; he would start strongly but then run out of energy. His relative age also set him apart; he was much younger than the rest of his siblings. Their names were Elizabeth Catharine, Edgar Allen, Benjamin Calvert, John Abraham, and Sarah Edna (Sadie). Sadie, who looked after Zigler like a mother, was nine years older. In his recollection, the older sister and the three older brothers were "old enough to be my parents and their children were more like my brothers and sisters."[6]

Named *Michael* for his father, the family called him *Robert* because there was another Michael Zigler in the neighborhood. Although *Michael Robert Zigler* was his full name, Michael was never used; he preferred to be called *Bob* by his contemporaries. When he began work in 1919 in the church offices, he used the more formal initials, *M. R.*, perhaps to add dignity to his comparative youth. For a brief time he was called *Zig* by colleagues in the YMCA in 1917-1918, but this never caught on in family or church circles.

Parents

M. R. Zigler always looked back on his childhood as a veritable paradise. "I do not know how I could have had a better life from 1891 to 1911. . . . As I think of my life on the farm, there was never an incident that made me feel like leaving home. . . ."[7] The one shadow on this happy life occurred in 1904 when he was thirteen years old. It was then that his mother died at the age of fifty-three. It did not come unexpectedly. She had been an invalid suffering from rheumatism for several years and had been operated on twice at John Hopkins University Hospital in Baltimore for what the boy understood were tumors. For many months young Robert was assigned to keep her company, as she lay in her livingroom sickbed. A window was enlarged to admit more light, and flowers were bunched around the opening to make her confinement more pleasant. Robert kept a continual fire in the stove to warm her, and he spent much time reading to her from the Bible. In this way he memorized many passages from the

New Testament. Biographies of many outstanding personalities recount the importance of their mothers' expectations; it is not hard to imagine that these hours were formative for this young man.[8]

Perhaps a greater influence, however, came from Robert's father, Michael H. Zigler. Born on September 14, 1843, he was the seventh son of John and Catherine Hoover Zigler. He was in the fifth generation from the familial ancestor Phillip Ziegler, probably born in 1734, who arrived in Pennsylvania in 1746 from the Bernese area of Switzerland. In 1770 he and his wife Regina were listed as members of the Brethren congregation of Little Swatara. A grandson, John Zigler (1787-1856), moved from Lebanon County, Pennsylvania, to Virginia in 1812; his wife Elizabeth was a sister of Elder John Kline. According to family lore, it was this man (a miller as well as tanner and farmer) who shortened the spelling, omitting the first "e." Lack of space in a device used to print names on narrow flour sacks was the reason. His son, also named John Zigler (1809-1898), was the father of Michael Zigler (1843-1926) and the purchaser of the Yount/Nead farm and tannery in 1858.[9]

Michael Zigler carried on both enterprises until 1890, when economic circumstances made the tannery unprofitable. He was known as a forward looking man in the community. Particularly devoted to the local Brethren congregation, he served as deacon for over fifty years at a time when that was an important office. Not only were deacons responsible to care for the needy in the community, they were also charged with preserving unity in the church. To pursue this task, they visited each member family once a year to see if all were still in harmony and unity with other members of the congregation. This deacons' visit took place before the annual love feast—the Brethren re-enactment of the events of the Upper Room as described in the thirteenth chapter of John's gospel. This high point in the church year could only be celebrated "decently and in order" if all members were adhering to their rigorous baptismal vows. Strained relations within the immediate family or the larger church had to be resolved or the love feast could not take place. At times, individual members were asked to refrain from participation because of unresolved tensions.

Michael Zigler was also known for his concern for young people. He favored the introduction of Sunday schools when that was still frowned on by Virginia Brethren. The elders followed the traditional thinking that it had not been done before, and—if it were introduced—it would take away the parents' God-given responsibility to instruct their own children. The Sunday school, nevertheless, was finally introduced, for the summer only, in Linville Creek, in time for Robert to profit from it. He later recalled his embarrassment at one point in not being able to identify to the teacher's satisfaction the cedars of Lebanon. Michael Zigler also pioneered with a Sunday evening organization for the youth called the Christian Workers.[10]

The father had other interests. He was passionately taken by the singing school movement, influenced so prominently by the *Harmonia Sacra* music emanating from nearby Singer's Glen under a Mennonite, Joseph Funk. Once prominent in the valley, this movement was for a time under church ban. Yet, the singing schools were not to be suppressed, and Zigler was given major credit for their revival. In a glowing obituary after his death on January 4, 1926, a local journalist noted in the headline: "Zigler Funeral Attracts Throng: Many Old Folk Song Leaders and Others Pay Last Tribute to County Man," continuing: "Particularly noticeable in the audience was the large number of song leaders and lovers of the Old Folks' songs, found in the *Harmonia Sacra*. . . . Scores who had often sung these same melodies under the leadership of him whose voice was stilled, sang in sympathy their last tribute to him." They had gathered—in such numbers that they overflowed the large meetinghouse—from several counties to celebrate the life of one beloved for his "fine Christian character, his charming personality, and joyous, kindly disposition."[11]

The obituary in the *Gospel Messenger* echoed these sentiments: "Bro. Zigler loved the church and was always interested and active in all that concerned it. He was charitably disposed, liberal minded, and optimistic. . . . He was called the 'father of the old folks' sing' so common in the Valley of Virginia. For the last few years his sight had failed so that he could not see to read but that did not hinder his singing. He was so familiar with the songbook that he would select from memory and lead the songs. He will be missed not only in the homes of his children . . . but in the many churches where he was a familiar figure."[12]

A final evidence of his public spirit was his involvement in developing a Brethren retirement home. It was he who made the motion in the district meeting of 1892 to establish the institution. Curiously, but also showing his leadership, he moved its dissolution, when conditions had so changed that the home was no longer needed.[13]

Early Influences

Parental church activism was not the only formative influence in the life of the youngest son. Two other favorite practices were also important.

Michael Zigler intentionally invited visiting church leaders to his home for hospitality, either for the typically generous Sunday meals or, just as likely, for overnight stays. Thereby, young Robert Zigler personally met many of the leading figures in the brotherhood. At the 1972 meeting, M. R. Zigler recalled in loving detail the names and characters of nearly fifty such outstanding personalities. The words of these visitors around the table or in the parlor were carefully monitored by young Zigler and a deep attachment to the church grew within him. Later he confessed that he sometimes would hide behind furniture to listen longer to the discussion of church matters, when other younger family members were sent out of the room.[14]

Quite often he was assigned the task of caring for the personal needs of those staying overnight, or for several weeks for those on extended preaching missions. He recalled especially his encounters with Andrew Hutchinson, the blind preacher, who had memorized the entire New Testament and much of the Old Testament. Another, George B. Holsinger, the song leader and hymn composer, made a vivid impression by treating the lad's asthmatic condition. Although Mary Jane Zigler was known as a healer, and often treated neighbors for their complaints, she never found anything to alleviate her son's asthma. When Holsinger returned from a church meeting to find the ailing youngster coughing and unable to rest, he rubbed his chest and head in such a way that relief came quickly. Robert was so impressed that for years he carried with him a picture of Holsinger, found on the letterhead stationery of a note from the musician.[15]

The second practice of Michael Zigler was to take his son along when he visited other congregations, especially when it was time for District Meeting. He wanted him to be exposed to the best of the Brethren leadership in that day of the unsalaried, nonprofessional "free ministry." Local congregations called a number of leaders, with seniority based on length of service. Elders, ministers of the first and second degrees, and deacons made up the body of church officers. At this time women were not allowed to be active publicly in the church, with very few exceptions, although it was known that some privately gave directions to their husbands once safely home.

From all of these influences, Robert developed a deep love for the church and wanted to serve it. Becoming a missionary was an early goal. He was impressed when I. S. Long and other Valley personalities announced their appointment to the mission fields. In 1953 when M. R. Zigler visited the Brethren mission field in India, he recalled the challenge of I. S. and Nettie Long to the Linville Creek congregation to awaken to its missionary responsibility. Foreign missions became the "first great work" of the church in the decade when Zigler was maturing.

The Zigler Farm

In later life, M. R. Zigler recalled in detail his life on the farm. His were the typical patterns of farm boys at the turn of the century. Activities centered around the rhythm of seasons—tilling and planting in springtime, harvesting in summer and fall, lumbering and preparation in the winter. Except for visits to neighboring congregations for church functions, few trips were made. Once a year, he was permitted to go along on the wagon to Harrisonburg, twelve miles away. He remembered distinctly in later years what a change rubber tires made in buggy riding, to say nothing of the excitement when the first automobiles were introduced in 1902. The early boyhood of a man who went on to become a seasoned world traveler was lived in a narrow but nurturing circle.

The 125-acre farm was divided into six fields and a lush meadow. The crop rotation featured corn, wheat, and pasture in the limestone rich topsoil, which was not deep because of the underlying slate rock, but it had been well maintained. The usual number and kind of livestock were present—fowl, swine, and cows. Some timber was sold as a cash crop. Once a week Saylor Wampler, a merchant from Timberville, sent a wagon to collect eggs and butter; later when a cheese factory was brought into the village, the Ziglers delivered milk for cheese instead of making butter.[16]

The immediate neighbors were Abraham Shank, a Mennonite bishop; grandfather John Zigler, in retirement; and those occupying the John Kline farm. A lane in north-south alignment ran directly through the farm, with access from five gates. In the center of the meadow under a large oak tree was a strongly flowing spring, which by gravity supplied water for the house and farm. It was fed to the spring house for cooling purposes, with the surplus piped to the watering trough for animals. Overflow from this trough was then diverted to the barn and to the tannery. The spring also supplied water to a fishpond. Two other springs on the farm provided water for livestock. This rich supply of free-flowing water was a beneficial resource for the active farm.

The tannery operated by his grandfather and father was closed down in 1890, so the young Robert never saw it in action. What he did know of the idle plant was its lingering pungent odor from the raw hides brought for

7

treatment. Besides the tannery building itself, there were some fifteen vats, a lime house, a well, and a large bark shed. This contained large quantities of bark brought by wagon and mule teams from Brocks Gap mountain. In the tannery, the first floor contained special vats for treating various sorts of leather, with all necessary tools and supplies. Space on the second floor had been used for rolling the hides over and over by hand to produce the desired supple leathers, which were then hung in driers.

South of the tannery plant was a large bank barn, built on the Swiss-German model. On the ground level were areas divided for livestock, consisting ordinarily of six milk cows, steers, calves, and occasionally hogs. Necessary bins stood handy for feeding the stock. On the second floor were large areas for hay, fodder, and a spacious granary for oats, barley, and wheat. There was also room for seeds selected for the next year's crops. Between the hay mows stood the wagons and other farm machinery. Near the barn were located the horse stable, machine shed, hog pen and fertilizer building, chicken house, and other outbuildings.

The old Zigler homestead was used as a summer kitchen and a spring house; its two-story structure featured forty-feet-long logs; the spring-fed water kept milk cool; other food requiring cooling was also placed there. On the second floor was the area where smoked meats were stored. Sausages, spare ribs, tenderloin, pigs-feet and the like were kept in lard-covered crocks. "From the ceiling would hang wonderful cured hams and filled bladders with sausage or pudding meat, also wonderful slabs of bacon," all previously hickory smoked.[17]

On the second floor of the spring house were also stored equipment used for weaving—spinning wheels, clock reels, wool shears, and tools for the preparation of flax. Women in the Zigler household created clothes for the family, comforters, quilts, and even carpets from raw materials. "My mother was capable of shearing the sheep, carding the wool, and doing everything else through to the making of a suit. Of course, they had certain names for that kind of a homemade suit, but we wore them, and she made many suits," Zigler recalled.[18]

The Zigler farm also boasted an ice house; this was a simple log structure without doors, which was half-filled by saw dust to accept blocks of ice cut from the pond during the winter. When covered by more saw dust and a plank roof, the well-insulated ice house kept ice through the hot summers. Buckets of ice-cooled lemonade provided welcome refreshments in the fields, a desired treat for sweaty farm laborers. Ice was also used to make ice cream in hand-turned freezers.

The inevitable woodpile loomed large in the life of Zigler as a boy, for splitting logs was a commonly assigned chore. Wood of different sizes was always needed for heating, cooking, and washing purposes. On Saturdays, old wooden rails were often used to fire the outdoor bake oven. The wood lot of eight acres, in a separate location three miles away, was carefully monitored so that in winter deadwood or damaged trees could be harvested. The best portions were converted into planks to be sold, the next best shaped for railroad ties, and the remainder used on the farm. Wood had to be dried carefully on a systematic basis for best results.

The Zigler house itself was relatively spacious for its time; the first floor had a living room, kitchen-dining room, and a parlor. The parlor was used only for courting and Sunday afternoon music-making, with organ playing and singing. Although the Brethren forbade organs in the meeting-houses, by this time they were permitted in individual homes. When George B. Holsinger visited, he taught the Zigler children the rudiments of playing.[19]

Sleeping rooms were upstairs; the only heating on the second floor during the winter was from stove pipes which ran through the rooms from the first floor on their way to outside vents. All of the bedrooms had extra beds in them to accommodate guests. M. R. Zigler recalled that his bedroom was "too cut off and cold to be a study room." Sometimes in the winter, bricks were heated on the kitchen stove to warm the chilly bedclothes. One small but neat room was set aside for tramps; although Michael Zigler was very hospitable, he did not allow such travelers to sleep in the barn—the usual practice—for fear of fire. Large porches on the east side of the house, one on each floor, added comfort and could be pressed into duty for sleeping places during clement weather.[20]

The basement stored the products of the garden and orchard; the family tried to keep on hand food sufficient for two years' consumption. It had two entrances, one from inside and one from the outside. Near this latter entrance was a bin filled with wood ashes used to produce lye; this corrosive substance was required for creating homemade soap. In the cool, dry basement there were bins for apples, potatoes, carrots, turnips, celery, endive, onions, and cabbage. Green tomatoes were buried in the dirt floor of one part of the basement. Three barrels contained sweet cider.

Inside a large (but no longer used) fireplace were built-in shelves to hold glass jars filled with canned produce from the large garden. Once, a combination of the heavy jars and rotten shelve boards resulted in catastrophe. The shelves collapsed on the cement floor, breaking the jars and spilling their contents. Glass splinters made recovery of the food impossible. The financial loss was valued at $300, a substantial amount in those days. The women who had worked so hard canning in the late summer and fall wept bitterly and expressed fear that there would not be enough food to last the winter.

A large wood stove was the center of the kitchen's activities. Family pets snoozed under it, unless the heat for cooking was too intense, in which case they retired to a couch positioned behind the stove. Late in life in his memoirs, Zigler wrote that the stove was "the center of attraction in the combination kitchen and dining room. Nearly always there was something cooking on the stove with fragrance. Equipment was available for different size pots and pans, skillets, long, short and round ones, large and small. Often all four plates [of the stove top] were in use in preparing the meal."[21]

The most detailed description he gave of any of the rooms was devoted to the kitchen, where so much of the family's time was spent. In his mind's eye, he ranged around the room, indicating where furniture was placed and what it contained, starting with the couch behind the cook stove:

> Beginning clockwise with the couch in the corner was the sink for the washing of dishes furnished with homemade soap and two large pans, one for the hot soapy water and the other for rinsing. Underneath [there was] space for garbage and cleaning materials and wash clothes. Then follows a table where a large pan was used to care for the dishes to be wiped dry. From the table to the door to the south was a very large cupboard with a shelf for many items like books, pencils, mail for the day, [and] gloves. Above this shelf [was] space for dishes. . . . The top shelf of the two was given over to medicines, spices, and the Sunday dishes. Below the shelf were two areas, one of sugar, vinegar bottles, salt, flour, crackers. This cupboard came from Pennsylvania with the migration of John Zigler to Virginia about 1812.[22]

He also recalled that it was the kitchen/dining room which served as a gathering place for the community youth, where they were permitted by his father to play boisterously. Tables were pushed back and he said: "Now you've got the kitchen. Do anything you want." Young Zigler had the habit of inviting his friends to have a "jamboree," as it was one place where they could have their own fun.[23]

Farm families in Virginia ate well, and the women in the family worked hard to supply their menfolk with plentiful meals. Breakfast came only after morning chores were completed, which usually took up to two hours. A typical breakfast included oatmeal, cream of wheat, Virginia ham, tenderloin or bacon, red gravy, bread and biscuits, and cottage cheese. Winter meals featured *pawn haas* with pudding or hominy, hot cakes, and jellies. Quite often pie was also served at breakfast.

Lunchtime could include roast beef, steaks, chicken, with mashed potatoes, gravy, and accompanying dishes. Sometimes the evening meals were left-overs, or fried mush and milk, or potato cakes. On special occasions, such as Thanksgiving and Christmas, these menus were varied by stewed or fried oysters and fancy crackers and topped off with mince pie.

The Zigler farm was known as a choice place to find good meals. When thrashers were in the community, they would arrange their work so that they could arrive there for the main meal. The workers told Robert that "this was the place they wanted to come to eat." Plenty of chicken, ham, and noodles had to be prepared to satisfy these hungry men. At the time of the Love Feast at Linville Creek congregation, scores would come from the Brocks Gap, Greenmount, and Flat Rock congregations. Visitors liked to leave their horse teams at the Ziglers' and walk to the meetinghouse. It was not unusual to have forty women sleeping in the house and a similar number of men sleeping in the barn during these occasions. It was also the custom for those from Brocks Gap attending court day at Harrisonburg to stop off at the Ziglers' for the night.[24]

Indeed, the Ziglers ate well and were noted for their hospitality. They were not wealthy but still had a sufficiency despite their openhandedness. Michael Zigler liked to say their farm could provide all the family needed to survive for a year, with the exception of a sackful of salt. M. R. Zigler never forgot his boyhood years spent on the farm and returned to the area as often as he could.

NOTES

1. The week's events were recorded and published in an illustrated volume: Joseph B. Yount III, ed., *Tunker House Proceedings, 1972* (Waynesboro, VA: author, 1973); see also the special issue of *Brethren Life and Thought*, 19 (Winter, 1974) and the [Harrisonburg, VA] *Daily News Record* (July 25, 1972).
2. *The Brethren Encyclopedia* (1983-1984), 1505; Roger E. Sappington, *The Brethren in Virginia* (Harrisonburg, VA: Committee for Brethren History in Virginia, 1973), 99-100; Joseph B. Yount III, "The Tunker House at Broadway, Rockingham County, Virginia," *Brethren Life and Thought*, 33 (Spring, 1988): 112-121.

3. *Messenger* (Nov. 1, 1972): 6-7.

4. "M. R. Zigler's Memoirs: Introduction," 1.

5. *Proceedings* (1973), 146-147; Samuel D. Lindsay to D. F. Durnbaugh, June 13, 1987; Samuel D. Lindsay to M. R. Zigler, June 5, 1980.

6. Jesse Ziegler, with Daniel P. Ziegler, *The Ziegler Family Record* (Royersford, PA: author, 1906), 51-52; Zigler family Bible; "Memoirs: Introduction," 1.

7. *Proceedings* (1973), 17.

8. *Proceedings* (1973), 35.

9. Ziegler, *Family Record* (1906), 7ff.

10. *Proceedings* (1973), 36.

11. [Harrisonburg, VA] *Daily News-Record* (?), an undated clipping.

12. *Gospel Messenger* (Feb. 26, 1926): 94.

13. Sappington, *Virginia* (1973), 224, 423. Curiously, M. R. Zigler is not mentioned in this district history,

14. *Proceedings* (1973), 118-119, 199-205.

15. *Proceedings* (1973), 119, 200.

16. "M. R. Zigler Homestead," unpubl. essay.

17. "Homestead," 8.

18. *Proceedings* (1973), 196.

19. *Proceedings* (1973), 120.

20. "Homestead," 4.

21. "Homestead," 3.

22. "Homestead," 4.

23. *Proceedings* (1973), 194.

24. "Homestead," 5.

2

CHURCH, SCHOOL, AND ADOLESCENT YEARS

H IS HAPPY HOME AND SUPPORTIVE FAMILY were significant early agents in shaping Robert Zigler's view of the world, but there other influences as well. These included the local Brethren congregation, the local schools, and striking personalities with whom he came into contact during his formative years.

Linville Creek Church

The church loomed large in the life of M. R. Zigler from the very beginning because of the intense and dedicated involvement of his parents with the Brethren. The Linville Creek meetinghouse was within easy walking distance; it was built on land donated by Elder John Kline. Sunday preaching services were held there once each month. It was uncommon at that time for church services to be held every Sunday at each meeting-house; most church districts had several meeting places with alternate meeting times. Linville Creek itself had no fewer than thirteen meeting points. However, on the Sundays when no services were held nearby, it was the custom for church members to pay visits among themselves. Long discussions on the leading church issues fascinated the adults and some of the young people. Occasionally young Zigler would be taken on horseback by his father to a distant meetinghouse to worship; as he had to ride on the back of his father's saddle, he found it less than pleasant.[1]

A contemporary, Weldon T. Myers, later penned an excellent characterization of the Linville Creek meetinghouse and the manner of the services at the turn of the century:

To begin with, it was to me as a boy the largest building in the world. It was bigger than a barn, that is longer and wider, but not as high. The vast auditorium had no rooms or subdivisions. There was a basement entered from the outside, but no stairway from above. Down there I suppose they stored surplus furniture, and had their dishes for communion and stoves for cooking. The cavernous auditorium was heated by two wood-consuming stoves with long iron legs standing on thick wooden blocks. They stood in the aisles, about two thirds of the way from the entrance doors to the pulpit.

. . . The entrance doors opened on the east side. There were two double doors, the south one for the women, the north one for the men. Before the men's door, three or four stone steps led up to a broad landing also of limestone. The women had a much broader landing which was guarded by a sort of hand railing. The steps here were of wood and likewise the landing. The purpose of this spacious platform was to allow the women plenty of room for gathering for greetings and gossip before entering and after adjournment! They mostly wore long black skirts, and black bonnets. Younger women, also having bonnets, but shorter skirts, sometimes halfway to the high shoe-tops, indulged in white and blue and pink; and once in a while a fashionable young woman displayed a worldly hat.

The grand old church itself was perfectly plain, like the collarless coats which the strict order of the Brethren prescribed for the ministry and for all who fulfilled their promise of loyalty and obedience. . . . The architecture was straight, plain, without curves or ornament. No decorations appeared outside or inside. The outer walls were painted for protection against the weather, and brown was selected as the sober autumn color, which did make the great building comely and impressive in the autumn as it stood under and among the scattered old white and red oaks. . . .

The interior of the building was constructed of yellow pine, which paint brush never touched. The pulpit was a straight, long reading desk stretching from one aisle to the other along the west wall. Between this counter-like pulpit and the wall extended the preachers' bench of equal length. Preachers were plentiful, being without salary and elected from time to time by the congregation. . . . Some who were voted in became great preachers, others failed to develop but took their turn in the pulpit to encourage drowsiness among the older members of the congregation.

Each end of the auditorium was built up from the floor into "raised seats" as they were called, like bleachers in a stadium. These outlook positions were favored by the young people before they joined the church. A young man would take his girl and sit high for sight seeing. The couple could look over the valley, at right angles to the worshiper, men with long hair and beards, and women in bonnets or lace caps ("prayer covering"), over to the opposite hill. But in ordinary services a boy would not take his girl. At big meetings it was done frequently.

14

The grand old edifice was a church without a steeple, or a bell. But it represented the people who built it and worshipped there. It was plain, simple, practical, economical, honest, frank, open-minded, unsophisticated, home-made, countrified; dependable, democratic, generous, hospitable; without mystery and without guile. Sentiment grew up around it, like remembered music.[2]

When prayer was called for, all members knelt, facing the benches, often with head in hands. Zigler recalled the consternation of the elders when a minister, A. B. Miller, called on his congregation to stand for prayer instead of kneeling. He was a college-educated man, pastor at Staunton, Virginia, and one of the first salaried ministers among the Virginia Brethren. He was called before the district meeting, and D. C. Flory, founder of Bridgewater College and a stalwart preacher, spoke with his booming voice on the point, ranging for twenty minutes through both Old and New Testaments to identify examples where prayer in the kneeling posture was recorded.[3]

There was great interest when visiting ministers attended services, because by venerable tradition, they were offered the first "liberty" of preaching. A few visitors were kept from speaking, if they were deemed to be too liberal in thought or lifestyle. On one occasion, such a visitor, denied the pulpit, was given the freedom of the local Baptist church building, and mounted a successful revival service there.

Even when he became an old man, M. R. Zigler still remembered the impact upon him that a number of elders had made as preachers. Some were known for their eloquence; others were known for their wonderful voices and were often called on to pray at the crowded Love Feasts, when several hundred members communed and up to a thousand observers watched. Zigler often referred to them as passion plays, not unlike the famed productions at Oberammergau in Bavaria.

Zigler followed the worship services with interest. This is his description of a typical service at Linville Creek as he was growing up:

The Sunday worship service generally opened with the singing of a hymn that everyone knew by heart and led by someone spontaneously. After the hymn, the elder of the church would take the position on the bench in back of the table and then the ministers would follow according to the time they were elected to the ministry. Then the elder would announce a hymn as the deacons would take their position on the opposite side of the table and sometimes the deacons were asked to read the scripture. . . . Prayers were always concluded with the

15

Lord's Prayer and if this was omitted, then we stayed in the kneeling position until another minister prayed the Lord's Prayer.... After prayer, another hymn [followed] and by that time each of the ministers behind the table were given a chance to preach. The congregation waited for the group to decide who would speak at this particular service.

I personally appreciated it when they agreed that maybe the youngest minister in the group ministry should speak. For me as a lad, he was my hero, but I feel that I had a tremendous respect for the older ministers and I listened to their messages with considerable interest. It must be remembered that these ministers were not paid, and were all farmers until the year about 1910, when the principal of the high school, a member of the Church of the Brethren, was selected to the ministry.[4]

Community was a strong element in the Brethren at that time. It was expressed in several ways. One was the winsome practice of fellowship and hospitality, which tended to attract newcomers to the church. "They seemed to intend to build a community of people friendly with their neighbors with a strong pattern of Brotherhood among the members of the congregation," said Zigler. Members reached out to others in time of need, illness, or personal tragedy. It was understood that neither life insurance nor fire insurance were necessary. If the immediate family could not cope with an emergency, the larger church community would see that needs were met. Older people would be cared for by family or by the church. In cases of sickness, the neighbors would rally around with loving care, in cases of a burned building, the community would rebuild.

So with this understanding of church, at the early age of ten Robert Zigler asked for baptism. At first the elders thought that he was too young, but his persistence won the day. His later comment was: "I chose to join the Church of the Brethren on my own and I was too young. They didn't want to take me in at ten. Seems to me all my life I've been on the edge of doing something that I had to fight for." The baptism was performed on June 24, 1901, by Elder J. F. Driver of the Timberville congregation, assisted by Elder J. P. Zigler of Linville Creek. The site of the baptism was the bridge that crossed the Linville Creek near the old blacksmith shop, at the foot of the hill where Elder Daniel Hays lived. After Robert was baptized he went to all of the children he played with and urged them to join the church, too. Most waited until there was a revival to do so.[5]

Robert understood that baptism meant that he would no longer be able to go his own way in lifestyle and manner of religious pursuit. He was now placing himself in the framework of church discipline, still practiced faithfully and sometimes rigorously among the Brethren. This, however, did not prevent him from occasionally wearing fashionable attire, but he knew that the church officers would soon ask for an explanation. The elders tended to exercise patience toward this energetic chap whom they trusted would later develop greater seriousness and dedication to the call of the church.

He recalled what happened the first time he wore a necktie to a church function after becoming a member. This occurred at a time when the rigid enforcement of the distinctive garb was being called into question:

> There for a while I thought I was pretty stylish that afternoon, and J. P. Zigler, the elder of the church, who had performed the baptism that afternoon, I think, saw this tie and came to me. They would always see those things so quickly! He said, "Robert, what are you doing with that tie?" I replied, "My mother said that I could. My father didn't say that I couldn't, but I know he didn't want me to." Then he said, "You know, we're depending on you to be a deacon." Well, my father was a deacon, and I knew all the problems that he had to help solve and the deacons' visits that he had to make, and I didn't think I ever wanted to be a deacon, so that didn't help anything very much and probably helped me to keep the tie on.[6]

Another Virginian, William M. Beahm, commented that the mark of a wise elder was to know what to oversee and what to overlook.

Black Neighbors

As Robert Zigler was so much younger than his brothers and sisters, he rarely could play with them; their interests were different and, when at home, they were busy with chores. Therefore, Robert spent a great deal of time playing with Sam Madden, son of Alice Madden, the black woman who had cared for him as a baby. She had married Ned Madden and lived in a nearby log house, where many of the Ziglers had earlier dwelt. Alice Madden worked for the Ziglers and commonly brought her son along. Sam would help Robert with his chores, especially chopping wood, a never-ending task. They made a game of it, seeing who could split the most logs in the shortest time. When lunchtime came, young Zigler would take meat from the crock, fry it, and prepare gravy. He was disturbed that Sam Madden always insisted on carrying his plate to the back porch, refusing to sit down at the table, so strong was the local custom of separation.

Frequently Robert went over to the Madden's cabin in the evening to

17

continue playing with Sam but also to hear the stirring stories that Alice Madden told. Many of these were of the experiences of her people during slavery: "Sam and I would keep on asking her for new stories and we always asked her for repeats. She kept on talking for hours. . . . [It] was amazing how many stories she had and how Sam and I sat there on the floor and never let her rest. . . . I don't think I came home many nights before they would call across the field that it was time for me to get back and go to bed."[7]

Although the Brethren were well known in the area for their long-standing opposition to slavery—and well remembered the suffering their position brought them before, during, and after the Civil War—not all racial issues had been settled by the liberation of the slaves. A painful question, for example, was presented by the church's custom of the "salutation" or "holy kiss," exchanged by brother to brother and sister to sister upon meeting and again during the Love Feast. Some Negroes joined the Linville Creek congregation, and Zigler recalled seeing them dressed in Brethren plain garb. Several families attended church services regularly, always sitting in the back row even when there were empty benches ahead of them. The question posed to the Brethren was how the salutation should be exchanged with them. "The idea of kissing a Negro would have broken the whole fabric of the Brethren community during that time" was Zigler's mature recollection of the problem. It was understood that breaking the accepted social pattern of the day could have precipitated violence from outsiders.

The compromise solution to the problem was that white members of the congregation were expected to clasp the hands of the black members, and then kiss their hands. Zigler was told later that his mother took the initiative to usher the Negro sisters into the kitchen during the Love Feast, where they then practiced the washing of each other's feet and exchanged the handkiss. "Anyway, the Brethren tried to keep the salutation of the Holy Kiss which meant the comradeship of loyalty to the church. I knew that my mother had a very warm heart for all those colored people because they would come here often." Mary Zigler was often called upon by her black neighbors for medical attention.[8]

Education

Schooling was also part of Zigler's life. For him it meant attendance at the academy at Broadway. The academy had its origin in a community-based endeavor of 1859 with predominant Brethren leadership by John Kline and others; they intended it to develop as a Brethren college, but that was not to be. It was first called Cedar Grove Academy and was located on ground donated by John Kline. Its early directors were educators of more than local renown. Unfortunately, the outbreak of the Civil War soon brought on its demise, although the building was later used as the site of the public school at Broadway.[9]

School was held in a one-room building close to the blacksmith's shop, located about one-half mile from the Zigler farm. Robert started at an earlier age than usual and was allowed to stay because the teacher "put up" with him, as he later recalled it. Attendance was not expected for most of the year as is now the rule. Instead, the academy scholars went to school for at most several months each year. Farm families of the time needed the help of every possible pair of hands on the labor-intensive farms; schooling could wait. Teachers were given licenses to teach after graduation from high school, and often their pupils were larger than they were, which made for discipline problems. Zigler later recalled that teaching was better by the time he reached high school. He had little to say about his early schooling, other than that it was typical for the day, no better and no worse.

Bob Zigler, as he was commonly called as an older youth, graduated in 1910 from the Broadway High School with five other classmates. One of them called the group together for a reunion in 1964; all six graduates were still living at an average age of seventy-six. One had become a prosperous lawyer in Texas, but all of the others, except Zigler, had stayed in the local area in farming, business, and teaching. The newspaper coverage of the reunion hailed M. R. as the "globetrotter," listing his achievements as a church leader in an international setting.[10]

This time of adolescence does not loom large in Zigler's later recollections. Having joined the church at an early age, he was caught up in that world while also remaining open to the impact of the surrounding culture. This was starkly revealed in his reactions to the brief but nationally-shaping Spanish-American War of 1898. Although the church taught nonresistance and nonparticipation in secular affairs, the Brethren were in a process of change. No longer isolated German-speaking dissenters, they were increasingly involved in community affairs and even political activity. Tradition-minded elders continued to preach noninvolvement, but not all members were heeding the message, particularly not the young people.

Robert Zigler was not immune to the excitement in the country at the time of the Spanish American War. He recalls having portraits of the leading United States military figures posted on his bedroom walls, including admirals Dewey, Schley, and Sampson; Admiral Dewey was the hero of the naval struggle off the Philippines during the brief skirmishes which brought the USA into the ranks of imperialist nations. And this was a lad whose life-long hero was Elder John Kline of the neighboring farm, a martyr for his Brethren belief in nonresistance to violence and the prior allegiance of Christians to the church rather than to the state. An older brother, not yet a member of the Brethren, brought his mother to tears by expressing his wish to enlist in the Navy.[11]

Early Influences

In 1962, M. R. Zigler was asked to name some books that had most influenced him. His first reaction was typical: "A list of books? I never read a book in my life. I wouldn't want to clutter up my mind that way!" But upon reflection, he did mention several. These included: the diary of Elder John Kline; the travel books by Elder D. L. Miller; a biography of Adoniram Judson, the admired pioneer Baptist missionary to Burma in the nineteenth century; *Pilgrim's Progress*, the classical Puritan allegory by John Bunyan; and *The Manhood of the Master* by the liberal pastor Harry Emerson Fosdick.[12]

The mention of John Kline is not surprising, given the location of the Kline farm next to the Zigler homestead and the gravestone marking the resting place of Kline in the local Linville Creek church cemetery. Brethren in the Valley loved to talk about the noble character and achievements of the Civil War martyr. Late in life Zigler initiated a reprint of the diary of Kline, eager as he was to keep the peace testimony of the beloved figure alive in the minds and hearts of contemporaries. His boyhood hero remained a guide for him throughout his life.[13]

D. L. Miller was one of the visiting church dignitaries given hospitality at the Zigler home. Unlike many of these guests, the Illinois-based writer and missions advocate visited only once, but his influence was extended through his many books describing travel to mission fields. He was credited with broadening the horizons of the parochial-minded Brethren during the heyday of his activity in the latter decades of the nineteenth century and the first decades of the twentieth century. His world vision for the church had powerful results for the Brethren.[14]

The young Zigler felt this. He recalled that Miller's "books, well bound

20

leather with gold lettering and gold page edging, were always present in the library of our home, and it was always a thrill to page through the volumes for pictures and descriptions of places he visited." Later, when he took up his responsibilities at Elgin, Miller was an elder statesman for the boards of the church. He urged Zigler to work hard to build up home congregations so that they could underwrite a more expansive world ministry. "It was great to be with a man who has much to do with the beginning of Foreign Missions and the publication interests of our church. He reminded me of John Kline's ministry in the United States as he saw the same goal on a world level. He had great dreams for the future."[15]

Through Miller and especially through hearing I. S. Long—the first Brethren missionary from Virginia to go the Indian mission field—Zigler was challenged to become a missionary himself. He was supported in this by the inspiration of early American missionaries who went abroad; preeminent in this group was Adoniram Judson, whose untiring and dangerous exploits in Burma were publicized by his wife. The allegory of the righteous Christian seeking to survive the dangers of his journey to the promised land in Bunyan's *Pilgrim's Progress* fit in well with Zigler's early call to dedicate his life to missions. The Fosdick book, with its portrayal of the life of Jesus Christ as a pattern for emulation fit in well with his developing liberal theology.

This listing of books was extended by a statement late in life of those who had been heroes to him in his youth. They included Dr. John S. Flory, writer and president of Bridgewater College, and Dr. John W. Wayland, historian and professor at Bridgewater College. Both Flory and Wayland were Virginians who were among the first Brethren from the Valley to earn doctorates at the University of Virginia. Both attained distinguished records there academically and socially, serving as editors of university periodicals and winning awards. When they returned to their home areas, they were given great respect as local youths who had made good in the broader world. Both were concerned to raise the educational and vocational sights of the members of the Church of the Brethren, using the college as the mechanism. Their vision is revealed in the chapters they wrote for the bicentennial volume for the church, which appeared in 1908. Wayland's urge for reform outran the pace the denomination was willing to accept, leading to his resignation at Bridgewater College and subsequent long career at James Madison University in Harrisonburg.[16]

There were other heroes to the youthful Zigler. These included Dr. Heber Hays and the four Myers brothers—John, Weldon, Walter, and

21

Harold. Significantly, all of these, like Flory and Wayland, were young men of the community who went off for higher education and important vocational achievement. As they came back to their homes in the summer, they communicated wider possibilities to the farm youths around Broadway, making them less willing simply to continue in the agricultural pursuits of their parents and ancestors.[17]

The last two names mentioned as significant by Zigler were his next oldest sister, Sadie, who cared for him after the death of Mary Zigler, and I. S. Long, the missionary from Virginia. Of course, he had heard news of mission activity before Long took up the missionary cause. The difference was that Long and his wife Effie were the first to volunteer from the Northern District of Virginia and were members of the nearby Mill Creek congregation. Zigler remembered the day of the visit by the Longs:

> I. S. Long preached at Timberville Church on this morning, and in the evening ... he was scheduled for Linville Creek congregation. I remember that he came late with his wife, known as Effie Long, for the service and we had already been having congregational singing. I remember that I was encouraged to go in the church and wait for the coming of this new type of churchmanship, a Foreign Missionary, but I would not leave the driveway where the horse and buggy would have to pass to hitch the horse at the post reserved for the coming of our guest. Finally he came. I watched them get out of their vehicle and walk towards the church. I raced into the church that was crowded and took my place as usual by my father on the Deacons bench, which was just opposite to the spot where I. S. Long would speak. . . . Being a very young person, I. S. Long, having finished his college and [being] trained to speak, gave me a new picture of what the church ought to be and convinced me that in order to do that type of work that I would have to prepare myself for the future, for at that moment I made a commitment to work for the Church of the Brethren, even though I never felt I would be capable. However, I never lost the vision.[18]

Although not mentioned in either of the two foregoing lists, Elder H. C. Early ranked at or near the top of people influential in M. R. Zigler's life. He considered Early to be the most eloquent preacher of all those he heard and as the most outstanding churchman, the "prince among all of them who came" to enjoy the hospitality of the Zigler home. In a long tribute to Early, M. R. Zigler quoted with approval the judgment of Early's churchmanship by fellow Virginian John Flory: "Certainly no one equaled him in influence or ability in this field. For a quarter of a century he was a member or chairman of every important conference committee to consider matters of church polity, readjustment, and organization."[19]

Elder Early was also a leading evangelist for the Brethren, serving in this field for forty years. A pastor and a home missions advocate, he was held by many, including Zigler, to be the "most outstanding minister of the Church of the Brethren following the Civil War." And it was Early who was predominantly responsible for the call to serve the church in its Elgin offices which came to M. R. Zigler after World War I.[20]

Tramps

After this catalog of eminent professors and ministers, there is an unusual category of people who had an influence upon youthful Robert Zigler. These were the tramps, "knights of the road," who came by the Zigler farm seeking sustenance and shelter for the night. Later in his life a neighbor woman told Zigler that she never knew a day during the lifetime of his mother when there was not a house guest—a tramp, gypsies, black people, friends, or relatives.[21] Tramps were brought into the house, fed, and given a bed in a room set aside for this kind of hospitality. The motivation was simple Christian charity, obeying the injunction to take in the stranger. Why was their presence an influence on Zigler? Because these men, who often were well-educated, repaid their hospitality by reporting events of the broader world, interesting occurrences, news that ordinarily would not reach Broadway, Virginia.

> In those days we did not have many visitors from a distance, and when they came, more than likely they were relatives who would talk about relatives, weather, financial problems, and other usual subjects discussed on such occasions. I knew that when the tramp would be at the dinner table, my father and mother would ask him questions that he would always answer in an unusual and interesting way. We would all join in the conversation at the table and around the fireplace during the evening.

Robert enjoyed asking these visitors questions about the Bible and found that they were able to give well-founded answers. They also had a wealth of stories that they were willing to share, but they were not forward about recounting them, fearing to offend. For the lad, the visits of these outsiders were breaths of fresh air; he found that "the tramp in our home was a delight for me because he would bring the outside world to me. He would stretch my imagination. He taught me how to talk, above all I always felt inspired because we entertained him in our home. to trust the stranger."[22]

23

It could well be that these encounters trained young Zigler in the ability that many people later remarked in him, that is, the ability to talk to anyone, of high or low estate, with equal ease and interest.

NOTES

1. Vernon Miller interview with M. R. Zigler, 3/2.
2. Weldon T. Myers to Agnes Kline, Dec. 1, 1963 (Agnes Kline Papers, Eastern Mennonite College).
3. M. R. Zigler, "Ministry in the Church of the Brethren," unpubl. essay.
4. Zigler, "Ministry," 3-4.
5. Transcript of an address at Camp Woodland Altars, Ohio, July 20, 1977, 15.
6. Joseph B. Yount III, ed., *Tunker House Proceedings*, 1972 (Waynesboro, VA: author, 1973), 83.
7. *Proceedings*, (1973), 155.
8. *Proceedings*, (1973), 158.
9. Paul Haynes Bowman, *Brethren Education in the Southeast* (Bridgewater, VA: Bridgewater College, 1955), 27-29; Roger E. Sappington, *The Brethren in Virginia* (Harrisonburg, VA: Committee for Brethren History in Virginia, 1973), 164-165.
10. [Harrisonburg, VA] *Daily News-Record* (Oct. 27, 1964).
11. *Proceedings* (1973), 68.; M. R. Zigler, "To Work for Peace Through the Churches," *Messenger* (Nov. 21, 1968): 2-3, 5.
12. *Gospel Messenger* (Aug. 25, 1962): 18.
13. Benjamin Funk, *Life and Labors of Elder John Kline, the Martyr Missionary* (Elgin, IL: Brethren Press, 1963).
14. Bess Royer Bates, *Life of D. L. Miller* (Elgin, IL: Brethren Publishing House, 1921); Harvey L. Long, "One Who Led," *Brethren Life and Thought*, 17 (Autumn, 1972): 213-222; *Proceedings* (1973), 200.
15. M. R. Zigler, "People I Met Along the Way . . .," unpubl. essay.
16. *Proceedings* (1973), 110-118; Francis F. Wayland, "John Walter Wayland," *Brethren Encyclopedia* (1983-1984), 1323; D. L. Miller, ed., *Two Centuries of the Church of the Brethren* (Elgin, IL: Brethren Publishing House, 1908).
17. *Proceedings* (1973), 17, 37.
18. Zigler, "People I Met," 2.
19. *Proceedings*, (1973), 82.
20. *Proceedings*, (1973), 84.
21. Samuel D. Lindsay to D. F. Durnbaugh, June 1987.
22. *Proceedings*, (1973), 162-171.

3

BRIDGEWATER COLLEGE

BRIDGEWATER COLLEGE played a large role in shaping the course of the Brethren in Virginia. Founded as an academy in 1880 and reorganized on a collegiate level in 1889, it sought to preserve young people for the church, to create an atmosphere that would guard their "moral and spiritual condition." Dr. John S. Flory, leading educator and historian of Brethren higher education, described its influence as "exerted for the most part, silently, and . . . accomplished . . . by transforming our ideals, broadening our interests, clarifying our views, elevating our standards, directing our aims, and cultivating our emotions and sympathies."[1]

Professor Flory has already been mentioned as one who had profound influence on M. R. Zigler in his youth. Flory was entertained in the Zigler home after preaching at a local church; his conversation at the table so impressed young Robert that it "created a determination . . . that at all costs" he "would seek an education beyond the Broadway High School." Later, Flory approached the youth while he was plowing a cornfield to encourage him to enroll at the college; he simply invited Robert and told him that he felt he had "what it took to get a college education." The young man had already had some contact with the school. As a teenager he had visited a Bible institute held at the college; he recalled that the visit had given him a "real insight into the college itself and the meaning of college education."[2]

Robert Zigler was also challenged by the actions of some older community men who had gone off to college—the Myers brothers and Heber Hays, as already indicated; Heber Hays went on to a fine academic career at Northwestern University. Robert looked up to them as they returned in the summer with stories of their experiences. The influence of Flory, of these young men (especially of Walter Myers), and an inchoate desire to serve the church, all combined to push him toward further study on the college level.

But after graduation from high school in 1910, Robert waited a year before deciding to go on with college (although he took a course or two at the high school in Broadway). The big decision facing him was whether to take on the farm, which his father offered to him under favorable conditions, or to attend college. Michael Zigler made it a condition of the offer that his son would not take college work. But because Robert had received the somewhat ambivalent vision of serving the church as a missionary or becoming a physician (both of which required training), and because he thought his threatened health might not stand the farming regimen, he turned down his father's generous offer.

This was a fateful decision, because it meant that the home place had to be sold by auction. "And so I remember distinctly the days of the sale and the tears thereof." Michael Zigler then stayed for the rest of his life at the home of his son Edgar in Harrisonburg in the winter and with his daughter Elizabeth in Edom in the summer. He enjoyed traveling, and went to the states of Texas and Washington to visit his other sons, and to Missouri and Kansas to visit the families of his sisters and brother. In later years his eyesight failed, but that did not hinder his love for singing from memory his beloved hymns from the *Harmonia Sacra*.[3]

Bridgewater College

September, 1911, found "M. Robert Zigler" enrolling in Bridgewater College, about twenty miles south of his home in the Valley. At that time, there were seventy students in the college course, and somewhat fewer in other departments. These included the academy, Bible school, school of pedagogy, music school, and business school. The college bulletin issued that fall reported with pride (and some public relations puffery) on the status of the school:

> From the small beginning in 1880, with two teachers and some two dozen students, and with almost no equipment, the work has steadily grown until now six spacious buildings crown "college hill." These are convenient, up-to-date structures, and are modern in their appointments. The buildings are all heated by steam from a central plant and lighted by electricity. The grounds are well elevated and have been carefully graded and terraced. This with a complete

sewerage system insures well-nigh perfect sanitary conditions. The health of the student body is remarkably good. There has not been a case of severe illness for twenty years, and conveniences and safe-guards are better today than ever before.[4]

Despite this attractive picture, living conditions were Spartan at college by today's standards. Students had only cold water for washing and bathing. The college history describes a washroom in the men's residence hall "with floor and walls covered with galvanized metal and a shower head connected to a water line which brought in cold water containing more shivers per gallon than any water ever known to man." Students slept on straw ticks, which they stuffed themselves each fall. By springtime, the ticks had flattened and were resting on or alongside the slats on the bed.[5]

The bulletin continued its prospectus by looking at its educational attainments:

Along with the growth in material equipment the College has also grown in prestige and influence. The courses of study rank with the best of their kind. The college course conforms to the national standards, and is credited by the large universities. The Pedagogical course provides thorough, up-to-date training for teachers. Some of the most successful teachers in Virginia are graduates in this course. Similar standards are maintained in all of the departments. So the college has come to be known as an institution that does thorough, honest work. It ranks with the standard colleges of the State, and its graduates have taken leading rank wherever they have come in competition with those of other institutions.[6]

The bulletin went on to describe the library with "ten thousand well selected volumes" and the "large and enthusiastic missionary society" attracting up to one-third of the entire student body and faculty. The Volunteer Mission Band was composed of those who had "signified their purpose to give themselves to mission work where-ever they may be called." Weekly meetings on campus were augmented by deputation work to congregations in the area. Members also visited the "sick and distressed" of the community, to carry on missionary endeavor while still students. Literary societies at the college organized weekly and special programs; these were intended "to develop self possession before an audience and drill in expression." All these activities were available to the new student from Broadway, and he took full advantage of them.[7]

Remarks addressed by President Flory to the graduates of 1915 reflect the educational philosophy of the school. Flory's challenge (which Zigler heard) on the need for the best abilities of educated men and women to be brought to bear upon the problems of the day, may well have been of formative influence; at any rate, they conformed well with Zigler's own ideals for the future:

> The class of 1915, the largest in the history of Bridgewater College, will, I believe, contribute their quota to this constructive work. You are now launching upon the voyage of your life's career. May it be a successful voyage. As individuals you know what are the influences of a good home. You have inherited strong bodies and clear minds. You have developed by carefully training the powers God has given you. You have ideals, and you have an appreciation of the responsibility of living. Use your powers in the service of God and humanity. Live for others, and, in so doing, make your own lives the truest, the noblest, the most useful. In the altruistic spirit of the twentieth century you will wish to have a large share. And in your unselfish service you will reflect credit upon yourselves and your Alma Mater.[8]

Life at Bridgewater College

The years at Bridgewater College were generally happy ones for Robert Zigler. His energetic, cordial nature and keen intelligence brought him success in classroom and with fellow students. He kept up the friendships made here for the rest of his life. One of his classmates, Dr. Roy Hoover, wrote him in 1980: "It is interesting how close we have remained over the years since college, in spite of the fact that we have been together very little. We have been able to take each other for granted." Zigler stayed closely in touch with the college throughout his life and it, in turn, honored him on several occasions.[9]

Not surprisingly, given the early contacts, Zigler always ranked Dr. John S. Flory in first place among faculty members who were important to him at Bridgewater. At that time professor of English and president of the school, Flory followed his academic success in his doctoral program at the University of Virginia with notable achievement as leader of the college. He brought the relatively young institution to a new level of attainment and respect. A quiet, dignified man, his scholarly interests and abilities were not limited to his specific discipline of English.

His defense of the basic doctrines of the Brethren was persuasive to Zigler as a young college student. He recalled: "While I heard them preached vigorously . . . in Linville Creek Church and was all but

28

convinced of it, I wasn't quite sure until I went to college that the doctrines were all right. . . ." The fact that "Dr. Flory held to the doctrines of the church with all of his education," and further that he "could translate that to the youth of my day" fortified the early church teachings in Zigler's searching mind, particularly in the area of peace: "He inspired me to believe in our peace message and to be against war." Zigler gave this professor credit for stimulating his love of reading and his interest in good books, as well as "appreciation for the literary and historic values of the Bible." Flory remained an adviser for the younger man until Flory's death in 1961, especially when major vocational decisions were being made.[10]

Another strong influence was exerted by former missionary S. N. McCann. He taught Bible and religion and had been recruited for the faculty when he had to return from India because of health problems. In fact, he was the victim of a wasting disease, which often kept him in a state of extreme suffering; he died in 1917. Zigler recalled how McCann persisted in his lecturing even though the pain was so severe he could not hold himself erect: "I can remember him lecturing to us when he was unable to sit up, looking out at us face to face in agony, resting his stomach on his desk, quoting scriptures from A to Z and explaining the Bible in a way we had never heard it explained. . . . I have never gotten over the agony of that man as he lectured to us." He had a brilliant mind and strengthened Zigler's growing interest in volunteering for the mission field in China.[11]

One of the Myers brothers from Broadway—John C. Myers—taught for some years at Bridgewater College. Myers was impatient at Zigler's slow progress in college mathematics and urged him to do well. Myers could also be blunt with him on occasion as Zigler reports: "I was fussing about something . . . [when] he said, 'Bob Zigler, everybody gets exactly what's coming to him. Don't you go around here fussing about not having this or that. If you don't have it, you don't deserve it!'" The student, thus brought up short, never forgot the admonition.[12]

The Intercollegiate Games Controversy

A longstanding issue on campus was whether students should be permitted to engage in intercollegiate athletics. At one time allowed, these athletic contests were banned by the board of trustees in 1909. Nevertheless, students pressed for permission to restore them, while the board, cognizant of denominational attitudes and worried about financial support, remained most reluctant to give in to student pressure. These were years of student

29

petitions, administrative studies, and faculty suggestions, without resolution of the problem. Finally, a student ultimatum in 1916 won grudging approval, as did their concurrent request to wear academic gowns at commencement time.

This was Zigler's later interpretation of the contested activity: "We got together and 90 percent of us decided we'd go to [another college] next year if they didn't let us play. And the board of trustees took up the subject. We had a basketball game scheduled at another high school. An hour before it was to start the trustees came out and said we could play." As the president of the senior class, Zigler played a key role in pushing through these changes in the face of stubborn trustee opposition. This was an early evidence of his willingness to buck the powers-that-be for the sake of goals he found important.[13]

He was brought into the midst of this struggle, however, not simply by his role as student leader but also by his employment. During much of his collegiate career, Zigler was a member of the college's staff. He had been appointed director of athletic activities in 1914 and, as such, stood between the two parties. As athletic director he was also responsible for regularly reporting on accomplishments in the area of athletics. The school periodical, *The Philomathean Monthly*, included in 1915 several short articles from Zigler's pen (among the first he ever had published) which reveal his attitude toward the crisis. His report for May, 1915, revealed:

> The boys have been anxiously waiting for the day when this privilege [of intercollegiate athletics] will be granted them. It has now been five years since the quietus was placed on our athletic spirit and the young men have shown a remarkably good spirit in abiding by that decision. Several times during this period petitions have been sent to the board of trustees, and again this year, as was generally the rule, practically ever student signed a petition for the restoration of intercollegiate ball. We as a student body are waiting anxiously for a reply to which we feel we are entitled.

An essay published a month later began with several paragraphs on the importance of athletics for health and beauty of body; it then continued: "In the session that is closing there has been fine interest in physical work. The tennis tournaments in the fall were interesting. Then during the winter basket ball accompanied by the gymnasium work was entered into with enthusiasm. When spring opened the baseball spirit reappeared with it, which ran at high water mark for some time." Zigler regretted that the board of trustees had not accepted the petition for "contest [intercollegiate] games" and hoped for better fortune in the future.[14]

He was delighted to report in the June, 1916, issue of the journal the resumption of intercollegiate activity, without mentioning the specific methods used to gain it; the reference to prior loss of students because of the absence of athletics may echo the threat of mass defection:

> To the student body, this year is a long looked and long wished for year. Many of the older students, and especially those who leave this year, have returned each senior [year] for several years with the hope and vision that athletics in the true sense of the word would be reinstated in our school life. Our hope and vision have at last been brought to a reality. It is remarkable to how great a degree the student body has been aroused to loyalty to one another and to its Alma Mater.
>
> We know of valuable young men, sons of Alumni and brothers of Alumni, who have gone away from Bridgewater College because of the absence of athletics. To these we send a cordial invitation to come back. It will take several years to make a team as efficient as it was in the days gone, but with the showing that was made by the teams this year without previous training, it is evident that there will be a record made in the future that shall be a credit to our institution and to the men who make the team.[15]

Other Activities

Besides athletics, he participated in one of the literary societies. At the combined program of the two societies at the end of his first year, Robert Zigler is listed in the program as one of the actors in a drama "That Black Cat" by Rawley; his character, "I. B. Queer," played a "Turnpike Tourist." By his account the two societies on campus attracted different groupings of students. One had the preachers and missionaries and the other the "roughnecks"; he chose the latter. (This is somewhat puzzling, because of his often-stated early interest in missionary service.) According to Zigler's account, it was this association that led to his appointment to the position as leader of the campus Young Men's Christian Association. College authorities made Zigler YMCA *vice*-president, hoping to attract his "crowd." But when the YMCA president, a former missionary who had been appointed to control matters, did not return to campus the next fall (1914), the college administration was stuck with Robert Zigler as president.[16]

During this era the "Y" was at the peak of its influence among college-

31

age young people across North America. It was ecumenical, mission-minded, and featured inspiring speakers who toured college campuses. The college groups were at the forefront of forward looking church action; there were high expectations upon student leaders to excel spiritually and intellectually. Zigler felt unworthy to perform the task. His recollection was that he had been reluctant even to attend Sunday school while at Bridgewater for fear that he would not be able to answer all of the questions. Faced with the YMCA question, he made up his mind that he could either resign or shape up; he chose the latter.

Very important in this decision was the contact with leaders of worldwide standing he began to meet as campus YMCA head. At one point he was given three minutes with John R. Mott, the chief executive of the American YMCA and the Protestant leader of highest standing in the world church. A Methodist layman, Mott emerged as the leader of international student groups and went on to become the preeminent figure of the ecumenical movement. After learning something about the Brethren, he encouraged Zigler to "stay with his bunch" and challenge them to greater things for the kingdom of Christ. Robert E. Speer and Sherwood Eddy were other famous figures of international eminence brought to his attention by YMCA involvement.

Zigler secured some special training in running the YMCA program in North Carolina one summer and in Virginia later, which not only gave him more confidence but brought him again into contact with inspiring personalities of national reputation. Interestingly, though college authorities sponsored the YMCA program, they insisted that it be called on campus the Young Men's Christian *Band*; they probably feared that identification with the YMCA would bring criticism on the school as being "unequally yoked with unbelievers," another reflection of the restricted outlook of the church of those years.[17]

Zigler was president of the senior class and was looked up to as a campus leader. He sang for a time in the choir, acted in theatricals, wrote for the school paper, served on the Lyceum Committee, and played basketball, besides attending to his work as athletic director and YMCA president. Despite all this activity, he managed to do well academically, although he later downplayed his scholarship, stating that "I wasn't brilliant in school." He never liked to be thought of as an intellectual. He scored highest in rhetoric, with an average of 97; he received his single lowest term grade, 80, in German. The other courses he took were literature, algebra, Latin, physiology, plane geometry, physics, mathe-

matics, English, geology, French, philosophy, chemistry, zoology, pedagogy, and New Testament exegesis—scoring usually in the high 80s and
low 90s.[18]

Never known as especially musical, Robert did not last long in the
choir. His senior biography lists him as "excommunicated from Glee
Club, May 22, 1915." Another reference in the school paper noted that
"during his Junior year he became so fond of strolling that he even strolled
away, followed by the good wishes of the director, when he should have
been in Operetta practice."[19]

Assessment by Classmates

Robert Zigler was well liked at Bridgewater College. The class history
featured him on the first page:

> Once upon a time not so many years ago, a mother and a father near Broadway
> rejoiced over a wee, tiny baby boy, and though they never suspected what
> honors he has won, Robert Zigler, commonly known as Bob, is now president
> of the 1916 class of Bridgewater College. As he grew to school age, he was
> very religious, always occupying, in church, a place by his father on the
> Deacon's bench, probably foreshadowing his future activity as a member and
> president of the Y. M. C. A. . . . He has always been a sociable fellow and is
> very active in anything that will promote this phase of college life. In Wardo
> [men's dormitory] feasts he is always an important figure and has distin-
> guished himself there as dishwasher.

The admiring tone continued in the formal write-up of graduating
seniors; they were pictured proudly in academic regalia, newly-permitted
in 1916, but were not actually allowed to wear the gowns at graduation;
that happened for the first time in 1917:

> Our President is a born leader. He was elected to that office four years ago by
> receiving the lucky straw and has held that position successfully ever since
> that time. He also takes great interest in all kinds of religious work. He has been
> President of the Y. M. C. A. for the past three years, and is now looking
> forward to the time when he will be elected to the ministry.
> Bob is known and loved by all. It is fortunate that his love affairs have been
> settled, for Leap Year has brought him many feminine admirers. He has also
> made a name for himself as a pugilist, when he and one of his comrades kept
> at bay a crowd of marauding Freshmen, ten fold their number. The Senior class
> wish him well in all of his undertakings.[20]

33

Amy Arnold

As signaled in the senior statement, it was at Bridgewater College that Robert met his future wife, Amy Arnold, one year ahead of him in class. She was petite, vivacious, and pretty, and soon won his heart. The comment in Zigler's writeup in the 1916 paper's senior history noted that "in the fall of his sophomore year he met and learned to love one of the 'Gold Dust Twins'" (an allusion to a popular advertising theme of the day, featuring attractive women). It noted that he became engaged at Lover's Leap on October 5, 1914. The characterization of Amy Arnold in the 1915 school paper remarked about the graduate in pedagogy:

> In appearance Amy is not imposing, reaching almost five feet and a hundred pounds, but because of her sympathetic nature, pleasing disposition, and withal her cheerfulness, this winsome little maiden is one of the most truly liked among us. She has proven her worth as first to cheer the homesick, first to soothe the aching brow. She is familiarly known as one of the "Gold Dust Twins" and "Jeff," the latter because frequently seen with—well, his six feet make a good "Mutt."[21]

"Mutt and Jeff" were a cartoon pair, marked by the tallness of Mutt and the shortness of Jeff. Such remarks give evidence of the way in which higher education was moving the Brethren into the wider, secular society.

A student of that time, Katherine Flory Blough, recalled an incident which further reveals the tendency toward acculturation; it is not known whether Zigler was involved:

> About 1916, when dancing was not allowed at Bridgewater, a bunch of us, six or eight couples were in the old gym dancing to "Onward Christian Soldiers." You'd be surprised what a good dance tune that is. All at once, Dr. John S. Flory, president of the College, opened one of those double doors. He stood in that door, and said, "Gentlemen, this is not the hour for gymnasium." We each then had to leave, one at a time, passing through that one door Dr. Flory was standing in. He looked each of us up and down, never saying a word. And we never heard anything more about it, but Dr. Flory had a well-behaved campus that year. He held it over us and we were all afraid to draw a long breath.[22]

The years 1911 to 1916 at college were good ones for M. Robert Zigler. He had found good friends, direction, and a life companion. The next step was to launch into a career. This venture took surprising turns.

NOTES

1. John S. Flory, "Bridgewater College," in D. H. Zigler, *History of the Brethren in Virginia*, rev. ed. (Elgin, IL: Brethren Publishing House, 1914), 311; quoted by M. R. Zigler in Joseph B. Yount III, ed., *Tunker House Proceedings*, 1972 (Waynesboro, VA: author, 1973), 132. On the history of the college, see also Paul Haynes Bowman, *Brethren Education in the Southeast* (Bridgewater, VA: Bridgewater College, 1955) and Roger E. Sappington, *The Brethren in Virginia* (Harrisonburg, VA: Committee for Brethren History in Virginia, 1973), 165-168, 408-422.
2. *Proceedings* (1973), 133.
3. *Proceedings* (1973), 17, 37.
4. *Bridgewater College Bulletin*, 1 (September, 1911): 1-2.
5. Bowman, *Brethren Education* (1955), 118.
6. *Bulletin*, 1 (September, 1911): 2.
7. *Bulletin*, 1 (September, 1911): 3-4.
8. *The Philomathean Monthly* (June 1915): [5].
9. Dr. Roy Hoover to M. R. Zigler, March 16, 1980.
10. *Proceedings* (1973), 113.
11. *Proceedings* (1973), 138.
12. *Proceedings* (1973), 106.
13. Vernon Miller interview with M. R. Zigler, 3/7.
14. *Philomathean* (May, 1915): 38; (June 1915): 102-103 See also Sappington, *Virginia* (1973), 408.
15. *Philomathean* (June 1916): 63.
16. Miller interview, 3/7.
17. Miller interview, 3/8.
18. Transcript (1911-1916), M. Robert Zigler, Bridgewater College.
19. *Philomathean* (June, 1916): 26, [86].
20. *Philomathean* (June, 1916): 25-26, [86].
21. *Philomathean* (June, 1915): 65; (June, 1916): 26. The class prophecy, written as if in a letter to Zigler in 1930, foresaw the couple happy in their work as missionaries in China, as "a blessing to that heathen land;" they were the first referred to in the letter—*Philomathean* (June, 1916): [43].
22. Katherine Flory Blough, "Waltzes, Wisdom & Watermelons," *Bridgewater* (December, 1980): 2-3, centennial edition.

4

VANDERBILT AND WORLD WAR I

WHILE AT BRIDGEWATER COLLEGE, Robert Zigler was challenged to consider giving his life to the foreign mission program of the Brethren. In order to prepare for this, he decided that additional training in theology was needed. As it happened, a precedent had been established a few years before his graduation by other Bridgewater students who went on to Vanderbilt University for further academic work. Located in Nashville, Tennessee, the university was founded in 1872-1875 with a million dollar gift by the railroad magnate, Cornelius Vanderbilt.

When Vanderbilt broadened its basis in 1914 from sole Methodist Church sponsorship to an interdenominational posture, the School of Religion sought non-Methodist students; to facilitate this, scholarships were established. Several Brethren graduates from Bridgewater had secured these grants, and Zigler applied for one for himself in late February, 1916. About one month later, Dean W. F. Tillett sent an encouraging response: "As you will secure an A. B. degree from Bridgewater College, and, as you are preparing definitely for Christian missionary work in the foreign field, I see no reason why you should not receive one of our free scholarships." According to the provisions of the award, tuition, board, and lodging costs were covered; the only requirement in return was limited work in the university library (little more than one hour per week). The scholarship was to take effect in time for the summer session, beginning on June 15.[1]

Zigler never forgot a statement made by the dean at the opening of school: "We will never have Christianity in America until India and Africa send their product back to us as missionaries." Studies there went well for Zigler. He recalled the teachers as excellent, though quite different from what he was accustomed to in Virginia; a special favorite was a professor of history named Brown, a "very wonderful gentleman." His only disappointment was in a special course in public speaking, which he took in an attempt to cope with a longstanding weakness. He left college with a strong sense of inadequacy in speaking and late in life mentioned often that he never really got to the point where he felt comfortable in addressing a public gathering. "The teacher was so disappointed when I delivered the first time. He thought I was good, you know, the way I could gab around." But after the trial, his conclusion was that there was no hope. His advice was to "have a good point to start with and have something good to end with and don't bother much about what goes in between." In addition to work in the university, Zigler took some courses at the George Peabody College for Teachers, located across the street.[2]

Later as home missions secretary for the Church of the Brethren, Zigler kept up his relationship with the School of Religion. He recalled working in the 1920s with Dean Tillett to bring Brethren ministers from rural areas to Nashville for two weeks of continuing education; all their expenses were paid by a grant from the Rockefeller Foundation. At that time, Tillett confided to Zigler over a dinner that the reason he wanted the Brethren present was because they neither drank nor smoked. Although the dean himself smoked, he said, according to Zigler's recollection: "I wanted enough preachers around that didn't smoke to show these preachers down here they don't have to be smoking cigarettes and biting cigars." During his year of graduate study, Zigler got on well with members of the student body, many of whom were Methodist or Baptist. His memory was that they respected his abstinence, even though they often tried to get him to indulge in alcohol or nicotine. Later, during his residence in Europe where social drinking among Christians was taken for granted, he made a point of abstaining and found that he was respected in this when he explained that it was part of the discipline of his church. (Zigler preserved in his papers a photograph taken at Vanderbilt of a dissipated scene showing himself and other students posed with cigarettes in their mouths around a table bearing bottles of strong drink. The caption indicates that it was a scene from a temperance play.)[3]

A postcard from his father to "M. Robert Zigler" has been preserved from this year. The text is brief: "I wrote you last Monday. Are you in receipt of it? Fine weather today. All are well, your Papa. Harrisonburg,

Va., 4. 30. 17."[4] This was shortly after the United States entered the war raging in Europe. President Woodrow Wilson had won reelection in 1916 in part through his pledge to keep the country out of the conflict, despite the efforts of a strong Anglo-American lobby urging American intervention. The resumption of unrestricted submarine warfare and revelation of German diplomatic maneuvers involving Mexico are credited with prompting Wilson's shift in policy and the subsequent appeal to Congress to declare war.

YMCA Service

All students of the history of the Brethren at this juncture agree that the church had not prepared its members for the demands which US participation in World War I brought upon them. The denomination still held to its nonresistant principles by long-standing custom, but it had done little to keep this teaching in the forefront. Brethren had changed over the decades from being members of a withdrawn, German-speaking, agriculturally-based sect to being citizens fully involved in society and educated in public schools. They had become active in social movements such as temperance and had begun to call for assertive government action to solve social problems. They had, in fact, become so involved in society that many of their leaders believed that it was no longer possible to follow a disengaged, nonparticipating posture in regard to public affairs. This being the case, the old and strict answer of complete rejection of military service seemed no longer appropriate to some leaders. They began to take the line that young Brethren men might well serve in the army or navy if this could be done as noncombatants.

H. C. Early, one of the most influential of the church leaders of that generation, wrote to the chairman of the Peace Committee: ". . . I have not come to the point where I can recommend to our young men to refuse noncombatant service and take the consequences." He continued: "My judgment is that they should obey the government as far as it can be done without violation to their conscience." Many of the young Brethren caught up in 1917-1918 in the cogs of the vast conscription machine had a hard time drawing the line beyond which they should not go—reporting to the military camp, obeying the first military orders, performing clean-up chores, wearing the uniform, and on to actual military training and combat. They thus reflected the mixed signals received from the church leadership.[5]

One of the most complete accounts of this period of Brethren history was written by J. M. Henry, at that time a pastor in Washington, D. C., and a member of the Peace Committee. He explained the two major positions of church counselors. One group advised "the drafted young men to have absolutely nothing to do with the military machine, and refuse to do any kind of service," arguing "that there could be no such thing as non-military service as long as the government . . . regimented life and directed all physical force, including the lives of people, to prosecute war to the end of killing and defeating the enemy." The other group advised "the young men to be loyal citizens of the government and accept noncombatant service, as long as it did not violate the individual conscience."[6]

The US government compounded the difficulties by its slowness in defining what noncombatant service should entail. The Selective Service Law itself, issued on May 18, 1917, exempted from military service those found to be members of "any well recognized religious sect or organization . . . whose existing creed or principles forbid its members to participate in war in any form. . . ." However, the same section set forth that no person so exempted "shall be exempted from service in any capacity that the President shall declare to be noncombatant." It was not until March, 1918, that a presidential order was released that spelled out the boundaries of noncombatant service. These were then so broadly defined that many conscientious objectors could not accept service, because this participation aided the direct military cause quite directly.[7]

In the meantime, full-scale conscription had begun in September, 1917, resulting in hundreds of young men from Brethren families or of Brethren membership faced with the task of reporting to the military camps and there taking stands on how far their consciences would allow them to obey the military commands. For many, wearing the uniform was the first objectionable step; for others it was work around the camp on seemingly innocuous clean-up details. Although the directives from the Selective Service administration were slow in coming, they had two tendencies: one was to require military officials to respect the consciences of objectors; the second was to operate in such a way as to persuade as many objectors as possible to accept full military service by use of tact and convincing logic. The instincts, and resultant actions, of many noncommissioned and commissioned officers in the camps were to attempt to break the resistance of the objectors by ridicule, punishment, or outright brutality.

Camp visitors organized by the denomination sought to bring spiritual

counsel and support to the Brethren drafted into the military. The experience of the visitors in the camps varied from courteous reception to
outraged rejection. They were themselves as mixed in their counsel as the
general church leadership, and some of the young men they visited
resented their advice. One of the visitors, D. H. Zigler, reported in the
Gospel Messenger (November 3, 1917) on what he found in Camp Lee,
Virginia: "Evidence showed that a few of the Brethren were in training for
the trenches. A few others had yielded in part, because of threats. Some
had endured the sorest persecution, because they refused, to the last, to
take up arms and be trained for the army. Almost every indignity
conceivable was heaped upon them." These men, reported Zigler, "were
afterwards placed in a servitude almost equal to imprisonment."[8]

Because he was a theological student, rather than a ministerial student,
M. R. Zigler was not exempted from the draft. Instead of waiting for the
call of the government, he volunteered for the work of the YMCA, which
developed an ambitious program of service in the military cantonments.
Many seminary students and university students in religion departments
were recruited for the enlarged program. It is probable that this was the
way that Zigler learned of the possibility. His earlier activity in college
with YMCA work and advanced training over several summers stood him
in good stead in this case. After some difficulty with his draft board, with
the support of the national office of the YMCA he was able to secure this
assignment in lieu of military service. The final notice of deferment in
Class 5C was issued on January 11, 1918.[9]

The first step in the process of becoming a YMCA secretary serving the
military was a period of training for several months in the summer of 1917,
at the Black Mountain YMCA Center located in North Carolina. There he
met many outstanding religious leaders, including William Jennings
Bryan, Robert E. Speer, and John R. Mott. Following these weeks, he
reported to his demanding new assignment at the huge training base for the
United States Marine Corps at Parris Island, off Beaufort, South Carolina.
This was to be his base of operations for more than two years.

Zigler's experience there loomed large in his self-understanding and
future direction for the rest of his life. He often spoke of the time there as
the catalyst for his dedication to peace; he was conscious of the paradox,
that an assignment oriented toward maintaining the morale of thousands
of young men being trained to kill should be the motivation for giving his
life to the cause of restraining the impulse toward war. Again and again,
as he spoke to large and small audiences about peace, he would state that

it was his YMCA job on Parris Island that was formative in his career as a crusader for peace.

Life on Parris Island

When Zigler arrived on the base, there were few solid structures. The new recruits, who eventually numbered up to 10,000 at a time, were sheltered in tents. No machinery was used in the upkeep of roads; instead masses of men were detailed to carry and spread crushed oyster shells to construct roads and paths. In three months time, raw recruits were pushed through intensive drills in military life, shooting, bayonet practice, and indoctrination. Noncommissioned officers drove the raw recruits unmercifully in stressful and exhausting exercises to break their wills and remold them into the marine pattern. They swore outrageously at their charges; they made recruits scream as they plunged bayonets in the sawdust-filled dummies taking the place of the future enemies. Zigler watched as the trainees developed "killing eyes." [10]

Zigler became friendly with a Major Edwin Denby, a former lawyer from Evansville, Indiana, who had originally enlisted in the Marines as a private to win a large wager. His task was to lecture each new class of recruits for three hours, stressing three points: (1) the meaning of the US Marine Corps; (2) the purpose of the war; and (3) how to be a good soldier ready to die. Zigler never forgot the effectiveness of this orientation and longed for an equally effective orientation for peacemakers.

Other YMCA secretaries found this experience had quite the opposite effect than increasing pacifist ideals. Some YMCA secretaries developed a rationale for their support of the brutal bayonet drills and the actual use of bayonets in battle. Pointing to the anxiety experienced by many recruits during their first drill, Dr. Henry B. Wright, formerly a professor at Yale Divinity School and then a camp director for the YMCA with the US Army, wrote:

> Sick at heart and haunted by uncertainty, your lad and my lad stand on the night of that initial experience at the parting of the ways of fatalism and faith. . . . But in the hour of soul crisis the [YMCA] Secretary can turn and say with quiet certainty to your lad and my lad, I would not enter this work till I could see Jesus himself sighting down a gun barrel and running a bayonet through an enemy's body. At first I shrank from associating Jesus with the bayonet and essayed to place in His hands the sword the use of which He himself sanctioned. But soon I reflected that the sword, which is today only an article

of adornment, was in His day the most terrible weapon of mutilation and destruction known and that the modern bayonet is no more dreadful an implement since it is simply the sword attached to the rifle.[11]

Zigler was assigned to the reception barracks where all of the new men came. He said that other staff members disliked this assignment but that he had the gift of feeling at home no matter where he was put. Train loads of raw recruits, grist for the military machine, arrived each day to be put through the grueling process of the boot camp. His task was to organize recreation for about 500 men each night, provide for wholesome entertainment, and assist the perplexed. The commanding officer demanded that all new recruits write home to alleviate the worries of their parents. Many of the recruits were poorly educated and needed help in writing.[12]

Although younger than most of the YMCA workers on the island, it was not long until he was asked to become the general secretary for the Y's work there, eventually responsible for administering the energies of thirty-seven staff members. He made good as an administrator, although there were complexities and problems. One was that the Roman Catholics wished to introduce their own care for troops of their persuasion. Prior to this the YMCA had offered services to those of both Protestant and Catholic affiliation, as well as to those with no religious adherence. The Knights of Columbus, a Catholic lay organization, came and requested their own facilities, which Zigler gladly made possible. But tensions remained.

Once he was traveling in Pullman accommodations by train from Savannah, Georgia, to Washington, D. C., when he overheard two marines from Parris Island talking to a businessman about their experiences. They were Roman Catholics and alleged that the Catholic work was dominant on the island and that the YMCA work was weak and insignificant. When the man left, Zigler identified himself as head of the YMCA program and challenged the accuracy of their stories. He said that if they did not find the man and correct their falsehoods, he would report them to the military when he returned to Parris Island. On checking with the businessman the next morning, he found that the two marines had fulfilled their promise.[13]

YMCA workers ran canteens for the military in Europe. To subsidize their program, they charged for food and other items supplied in the canteens. This policy was soon reported back to the United States, where it outraged public opinion. Americans had donated money to the YMCA and now the agency was charging their boys for their donuts and coffee before going into battle! Though there was economic justification for the practice, it created hard feelings against the YMCA, which took years to live down. The effects of the controversy also impinged on YMCA work in the USA and caused problems for Zigler in running his program on Parris Island.

He won his way with the officers, who appreciated his hearty and masculine friendliness. One Sunday evening the commanding officer, whose name Zigler kept confidential, called him to visit his quarters. (According to Marine Corps records, it could have been John T. Myers, Joseph N. Pendelton, or Eli K. Cole, each of whom held the rank of brigadier-general.) The general confided that he was the most lonesome man on the island and asked for prayers. Zigler responded that he usually liked to preach awhile first before praying. What did the general want him to pray about? It was that he would never have to order his men into battle and its inevitable loss of life. But, the officer said, if that eventuality did come, he should pray that the men would fight like hell![14]

It became the pattern that the general would invite Zigler to visit him every Sunday evening, to alleviate his loneliness. Eventually, Zigler was emboldened to tell the general that he was a member of a peace church. The stimulus was his receiving by mail an issue of the *Gospel Messenger* containing articles on peace; he did not wish his orientation to reach the ears of the commandant secondhand. The officer said never to repeat this until he, the general, was dead but that Zigler should stay with the church and work for peace: "Damn you, don't you ever change; you stay right with them!". He never revealed the name of the general, even when he heard of the latter's death, wishing to respect his memory. The same thing happened when he confided to Major Denby that he was a conscientious objector; Denby also charged him never to change. Later, when Denby had become Secretary of the Navy (1921-1924), Zigler visited him in Washington, D. C. Although there might be as many as twenty people waiting to see the high official, when Zigler sent in his card, he would be taken around a back way and the two would talk for over an hour, just as they had on Parris Island.[15]

Zigler's allegiance to the peace teaching of the church was not always firm. In December, 1917, he wrote for advice from the president of Bridgewater College, Dr. John S. Flory. Although Flory agreed that "we owe something to the government under which we live," he disagreed with the suggestion in Zigler's letter that the latter should possibly volunteer as a private in the regular service, even though it went against the "rules of the church." Flory prophetically pointed out:

> I feel that our church has a large place for you when this war is over. There is going to be a need of men and an opportunity for service and an opportunity for preaching a gospel of peace after this over such as the world probably has never known. As a leader of men you can have a foremost place in the work of reconstruction in the Brethren Church. It would be little less than a calamity for you to put yourself in a position in which the church could not use you after the struggle is over.[16]

Late in life Zigler asserted that although he considered himself at that time to be a conscientious objector, "it worried me all the time I was there. And to this day, I don't know if I'd do it that way again." He more than once drew a distinction between being a nonresistant objector, who would not personally fight but did not object to others doing so, and being a pacifist. He asserted that the conversations with the general convinced him to become a pacifist. That is to say, he had thereby dedicated his life to working through the churches to eliminate war.[17]

Zigler always claimed that he never found men in the Marines who really wanted war. They knew what it was and were against it. They were disgusted with the churches for not preventing war. They charged him to convert the churches to the crusade for peace. The motto of Parris Island was: "Where It All Begins." In an ironic way not intended by the USMC, that proved to be prophetic for M. R. Zigler and his peace crusade. He testified hundreds of times that the initiative for his peace endeavors came directly from his experiences with the Marines on Parris Island.

Marriage to Amy Arnold

During this period, M. R. Zigler was corresponding steadily with Amy Arnold, his college sweetheart and fiancee. She had taught school in Virginia and West Virginia since graduation from Bridgewater College in late spring of 1915. Even before finishing her educational work at the college, she was a teacher. Vernon Shirey had been a twelve-year-old in 1911 in the home where Amy Arnold lived while teaching school in Morgan County, Virginia, and her pupil in the Milo School. She was loved by the lad's parents almost as much as their own children, in his recollection. Although small in stature, "Miss Amy commanded respect of the students so that they made no trouble."

She returned to teach at the Milo School in 1915, staying again with the Shirey family. It often happened that Amy Arnold would ask young Vernon to take a letter to the Laurent Post Office, a mile away from the home and across a river; each letter was addressed to "Mr. Robert Zigler, Bridgewater, Virginia." Each time he dropped off such a letter, he brought back one for her with a Bridgewater postmark. After reading in later years of her death, Shirey commented that she "exerted a good influence over the lives of everyone with whom she came into contact."[18]

Amy Laura Arnold and Michael Robert Zigler were married at the Frederick (Maryland) Church of the Brethren on August 10, 1918, by A. B. Miller, the pastor of the Hagerstown Church of the Brethren. The reason for selecting this congregation was that Amy held her membership there at the time. For the honeymoon, they travelled to Washington, D.C., before spending a week camping at Stokesville, Virginia. Zigler returned to Parris Island, while Amy prepared to resume her teaching career near Frederick. In the course of 1919, she joined her husband for a time at Parris Island, but for most of their early married life, they were separated. There were no accommodations for wives on the island, and towns near the cantonment were not appealing.[19]

Those who knew the Ziglers always commented on the tremendous support the petite and quiet Amy Zigler gave to her hulking and boisterous husband. A biographical sketch portrayed her as the "woman who stayed behind." She saw her role as the creator of a home as a "refuge from the whirlwind of her husband's active public life." At this home he "fortified his energy, gathered reinforcements for his sagging dreams and his precarious projects." Amy Zigler kept the home in readiness for him and "all weary church travelers." The Ziglers formed a partnership "in which both understood their need of the other: Bob, an intense, eager pioneer way out ahead; Amy, a composed, patient woman, who invested her time and talents close at hand."[20]

After her death in 1958, she was eulogized as one who possessed the "quiet virtues" of simplicity, modesty, and dignity. "She was mild and unassuming, . . . content to allow others to receive the recognition." She provided the "stability and moral ballast which enthusiasm of vision demands." She was especially noted for her kind and gracious hospitality in the homes she created wherever the church called her husband. When living at Geneva, Switzerland, church leaders from around the world were invited to their apartment and never forgot the warmth of their reception. Dr. Philip Potter, general secretary of the World Council of Churches, and

Archbishop Iakovos of the Greek Orthodox Church are but two of those who paid tribute to her gift of hospitality.[21]

For all of her quietness and often-mentioned sweetness, Amy Zigler thought her own thoughts and formed her own judgments. She also had a tart tongue on occasion. A family friend reported that when the Ziglers once visited the art treasures of Florence, Italy, Amy stood unimpressed before Michelangelo Buonarroti's masterpiece on the Piazzi della Signoria, the giant nude statue of David. Her comment: "He looks just like my M. R. shaving in the morning!"[22]

Amy Arnold Zigler was an important partner over the many decades of service that M. R. Zigler gave to the church and the world. In her own quiet way, she made a significant contribution. Hers was a deep and traditional love, matching his enthusiastic, sometimes awkward, but also heartfelt affection. In 1958 a tragic accident cut short their partnership and once again she proved to be the "woman who stayed behind."

NOTES

1. W. F. Tillett to M. R. Zigler, March 28, 1916, and April 21, 1916.
2. Vernon Miller interview with M. R. Zigler, 3/12.
3. Miller interview, 13a/2-3.
4. Michael Zigler to M. Robert Zigler, April 30, 1917.
5. J. Maurice Henry, *History of the Church of the Brethren in Maryland* (Elgin, IL: Brethren Publishing House, 1936), 527; also quoted in Rufus D. Bowman, *The Church of the Brethren and War*, 1708-1941 (Elgin, IL: Brethren Publishing House, 1944), 173.
6. Henry, *Maryland* (1936), 526; Bowman, *Brethren and War* (1944), 172.
7. Secretary of War, *Statement Concerning the Treatment of Conscientious Objectors in the Army* (Washington, DC: Government Printing Office, 1919), 14. A thorough discussion of the regulations and the Brethren response is found in Bowman, *Brethren and War* (1944), 168-233; see also Roger E. Sappington, *Brethren Social Policy, 1908-1958* (Elgin, IL: Brethren Press, 1971), 38-46, and Albert N. Keim and Grant M. Stoltzfus, *The Politics of Conscience: The Historic Peace Churches and America at War, 1917-1955* (Scottdale, PA: Herald Press, 1988), 32-55.
8. Quoted in Bowman, *Brethren and War* (1944), 177.
9. S. A. Ackley, Executive Secretary of the War Work Council of the YMCA, to M. R. Zigler, July 24, 1917, enclosing copy of a statement for presentation to

the draft board; (War Department) Local Board for the County of Rocking-ham, State of Virginia, to Michael Robert Zigler, January 11, 1918.

10. Miller interview, 4a/1.
11. Ray H. Abrams, *Preachers Present Arms* (New York: Round Table Press, 1933), 69.
12. Miller interview, 4a/2-3, 5a/1.
13. M. R. Zigler, "Understanding the Catholics," unpubl. essay.
14. John J. O'Sullivan and Edgar L. Money, Jr., interview with M. R. Zigler, June 10, 1974, 18 (Stoltzfus Papers, Eastern Mennonite College).
15. Transcript of M. R. Zigler address at Camp Woodland Altars, Ohio, July 20, 1977; O'Sullivan and Money interview, 18; M. R. Zigler, "To Work for Peace Through the Churches," *Messenger* (Nov. 21, 1968): 2-3, 5.
16. John S. Flory to M. R. Zigler, Dec. 10, 1917.
17. O'Sullivan and Money interview, 17-19, 28-31.
18. Vernon H. Shirey to M. R. Zigler, May 27, 1978.
19. M. R. Zigler, "Statement Concerning the Automobile Accident at Västervik, Sweden," unpubl. essay.
20. Inez Long, "Amy Zigler: The Woman Who Stayed Behind," *Gospel Messenger* (June 25, 1960): 14-15, 18; also printed in Inez Long, *Faces of the Faithful* (Elgin, IL: Brethren Press, 1962), 169-173.
21. M. R. Zigler to Inez Long, October 10, 1979; Merlin Garber, "A Tribute to Amy Arnold Zigler," August 24, 1958).
22. Lotte B. Schiff, "A Look-In on the Brethren from Shanghai to New Windsor: Draft notes of an address to be given at [the] New Windsor, Maryland, meeting of the OEP conference, 27/28 XII [July], 1977."

5

THE CALL TO ELGIN
AND ORDINATION

ALTHOUGH M. R. ZIGLER was doing well with his YMCA work, he had not forgotten his interest in serving the church as a missionary. Several college friends were among the Brethren working in the mission field in China (begun in 1908). Zigler corresponded with J. H. B. Williams, the assistant secretary of the denominational General Mission Board in the summer and early fall of 1918, stating that he had not changed his determination to give his life to "the service of the Master in the foreign field." He also reported that he was not in a position to give a definite time for such service as long as the war lasted, a condition understood and accepted by Williams. The latter suggested that Zigler "was to be commended for the service that you are rendering in behalf of the Kingdom and your country."[1]

Zigler expressed interest in getting in a year of study at Yale University to prepare for mission work; he asked if the Board could be of financial assistance to him in that desire. He also asked if the church had a policy for retired workers: "After the laboring days are over what care is taken of the worn out bodies? Will it still be a struggle for life?" In response, he was told that, whereas the Board had no fixed policy of paying educational expenses for preparation for mission service, it had defrayed educational debts for mission candidates, if that debt "stood between them and the field." Again, there was no definite plan of retirement support for "aged or incapacitated brethren and sisters," but in specific cases aid was being given. Williams asserted: "I feel that the church is going to safeguard those who give their all for Christ and the Church, and am hopeful that plans may be inaugurated for this. We are slow in paying our ministers and we are of course[,] largely speaking, to be awakened yet on this."[2]

Fred J. Wampler, a medical missionary in China, was home on leave in the spring of 1919 and pressed Zigler to resign the YMCA position on Parris Island and join the mission team in Asia. Mentioning the intention of Zigler's close friends, Roy and Susie Hoover (Susie Hoover was the sister of Amy), to go to the mission field, Wampler urged: "We are hoping that you and your wife can come to work with us, too. We have some attractive positions there for the right men. From all that I have been able to learn of you and your work, you are about the man that we need for one of our jobs." The area foreseen for M. R. was either evangelistic or YMCA work in China. One specific position thought probable was as a YMCA worker in the Shansi provincial capital of Taiyuanfu, a city of 100,000 inhabitants, with about 5,000 students and 10,000 soldiers present; the mission hoped to reach the latter two groups with the Christian gospel.[3]

Wampler provided detailed advice for the application procedures, with an anticipated appointment occurring at the time of the Annual Conference, to be held at Winona Lake, Indiana, in June. He counselled Zigler not to raise doctrinal differences on the application blank, as some applicants did. The church was moving toward a more liberal position, but not all factions were aware of that, and it could cause difficulties. "One of the best ways to answer the doctrinal sheet that they will send would be to quote them a verse of Scripture in answer to the questions." Indeed the church was in a transitional state, "but, of course, the time has not come yet for the missionaries to express too liberal a view in public on these questions." There would be no problem with this once he was on the mission field itself.[4]

Zigler decided to respond positively to these suggestions and to begin the process leading to appointment as a missionary to China. In May, 1919, he resigned from his YMCA position. R. H. King, executive secretary of the National War Work Council of the YMCA, wrote to express "the high appreciation of this office for the signal service you have rendered," to "note your going with regret," and to extend "best wishes and our confidence that you will make good wherever you go." Likewise, the personnel secretary added his compliments for the "careful statement of business affairs" and for the "splendid work which you have done."[5]

He went to Frederick, Maryland, where Amy Zigler was at the time, with the intention that both would journey on to Winona Lake, Indiana, and the Annual Conference. It was the accepted procedure that all missionaries under appointment were examined by the Standing Committee, before final approval was given. At Frederick they received word of the desperate illness of Amy's mother, Hannah Arnold, who died shortly thereafter; in addition, Amy herself broke out with measles. This meant that they were not able to travel to Indiana and, therefore, were not chosen for service in China. They missed an outstanding conference, with great enthusiasm for the mission program of the church. Over $160,000 was raised for missions, and thirty-two new missionaries were commissioned; ten of these were slated for service in China. The conference sent them off with the stirring Chautauqua salute, the mass waving of clean, white handkerchiefs to wish them "Godspeed."[6]

Zigler contacted Dr. John S. Flory to see if he could do relief work anywhere, but members of the General Mission Board were not interested in that possibility. H. C. Early, the leading Virginia elder and president of the General Mission Board, urged him to take the year in graduate school and prepare for being sent overseas in 1920. Elder Early promised to see to it that any debts incurred would be covered, through gifts of private individuals or interested congregations.[7]

Offer of a Position at Elgin

But events took a different course. Zigler reported the changed circumstances to War Work officials in the YMCA, who were happy to restore him to a staff relationship. Although they had in the meantime appointed someone else as the director of the Camp Parris program, they were not sure that this man would be staying long. At any rate, they needed more staff members there; the associate executive secretary wrote Zigler: "you are well-liked and . . . you will be welcomed back to the Island." His former colleagues were eager for him to return, reporting that his successor was a "weak sister," and that the Knights of Columbus agency work with the Roman Catholic Marines was putting the YMCA work in the shade.[8]

The anticlimactic return to YMCA work did not last long. In late September, 1919, he received a communication from Elder H. C. Early, which left him "not a little shaken." Early offered him the position of Home Missions secretary of the General Mission Board under the supervision of J. H. B. Williams.[9]

The year 1918 had seen sweeping changes in personnel at the Elgin office. Williams became the executive of the General Mission Board in place of Galen B. Royer. I. B. Trout, who had edited Sunday school materials, was released for personal indiscretions that had become public knowledge, to the dismay of the church. He was replaced by the respected president of Mount Morris College, Illinois, J. E. Miller. Another college president, the distinguished Edward Frantz, became the new editor of the denominational periodical, the *Gospel Messenger*, taking the place of the venerable J. H. Moore. A youthful H. Spenser Minnich was recruited as promotional secretary for the Board. The Brethren Publishing House, in whose building the Board rented space, was a nonprofit enterprise, headed by Robert E. Arnold; any funds generated by the House were given to missions. These people, assisted by a few secretaries and printers, represented the entire denominational staff serving a church of perhaps 100,000 members.

The new plan of the Board for the staff was described by Early as calling for the following personnel: "A General Secretary, the position that Williams now holds, who shall have a general supervision of all the Board's work at home and abroad, a Home Secretary, whose duty will be to direct the Board's work in the homeland, and then as the work grows we plan to add an Educational Secretary and also a Financial Secretary."

Work on Home Missions would be with district mission boards to strengthen weak congregations and to establish new ones in "un-occupied territory." The secretary would need to reside at Elgin, Illinois, and work in the offices of the board, located in conjunction with the Brethren Publishing House. A heavy travel schedule was expected. The salary range offered was between $1,200 and $1,500 per year, with travel expenses covered.[10]

Zigler had not been the first choice for the job. It had been earlier offered to Lawrence W. Shultz, an educator connected with Manchester College, who, however, did not accept. Although not explicitly stated, the offer to Zigler came through the influence of Early, who had seen promise in his fellow Virginian. Dr. Flory, president of Bridgewater College, had supported the suggestion, although he did not think highly of Zigler's speaking and preaching ability. Since the work was anticipated to be largely administrative, this was not seen as too much of a handicap. Elder Early commented that the disappointment about going to China might have been because the "Lord kept you from the field this year for this work."

Zigler's response was cautious but positive:

The call to such a position is not a small incident in any man's life. The opportunities are unlimited in that work; the responsibility is hardly to be

51

measured. But on the other hand, if anyone should attempt to put across that program without the help from our Heavenly Father they might just as well not begin it. The work appeals to me. I would love to put my whole soul and might into it if you think that I am needed in that work instead of my own choice. There is nothing of question in my mind except this: Will I be able to place myself so completely under the direction of the Holy Spirit that our work will succeed. If I should take this position and be accepted by the Board I will promise to give the best that is within me.[11]

He asked when the position would begin, feeling a responsibility to the work at the camp on Parris Island until the end of the year. Early responded that the normal process of approval would make that about the earliest possible date in any case. He urged Zigler to accept:

The position, Robert, I consider very good, second only to William's position, which I consider the best in the gift of the church. In fact, I don't know of any position in the church or out that afforded finer opportunities for usefulness, service and sacrifice. This last word may not have an appeal to some, but it must enter into every great life, and not in a small way either. It lies at the foundation of all that's good in human life.

He was thinking particularly, and realistically, of the long absences from home and family such work entailed.[12]

Early's advice was taken very seriously by young Bob Zigler because he considered the older man to be the "most outstanding preacher among the Brethren." He was a man of great dignity and bearing, eloquent in speech, and highly respected in the church, which chose him for its highest positions. He had inspired and impressed students with his addresses at Bridgewater College while Zigler was in residence. The younger man looked to him as a mentor and had the highest estimate of his abilities; he considered him to be a natural leader whom people followed without reservations. If he had been a lawyer, said Zigler, he would have been made chief justice of the Supreme Court. Throughout his life, Zigler looked to him as his chief adviser and stated that he had "perhaps more influence over my life than any other person."[13]

Zigler wrote immediately to Amy for her reaction; he also wrote a number of friends and advisers to secure their counsel. The reactions ranged from dignified to flippant approval. John S. Flory wrote: "I am glad to tell you without reserve that I feel that is a fine opportunity for service. It is opening to you a very important and responsible position in our great church work, a position that demands ability to approach people and do

constructive work on a large scale." His former college roommate Roy
Hoover wrote urging him to accept, with more vehemence than correct-
ness: "You know how badly they need some one in that place with some
pep and some ideas that have been originated since the time of our grand
fathers. I believe that you are the man for the place and that you can
probably do more good there than by going to China your self. You have
the knack of getting around those old birds and not letting them know it,
and you should put it to account. They need a rattle-brained radical like
you who can manage them and keep things greased up well."[14]

Insight on the thinking behind the selection can be gleaned from the
articles printed in the board's promotional periodical, the *Missionary
Visitor*, during the course of the autumn. The October, 1919, issue had this
reference:

> The question of a home mission secretary is likewise still pressing for solution.
> It is easier to create a position than it is to fill it with the right man. . . . In
> addition to the great needs of our Brotherhood for assistance in her home
> problems there press upon us the claims of the regions beyond our homeland—
> the lumber camps of our great forest sections, the sailors along our coasts, the
> overcrowded and under churched of our cities, the Indians on our reservations,
> the settlers of the pioneer districts, the miners, the colored peoples, the
> mountaineers, Mormon territories, and the ever-increasing immigrants. The
> post of this home secretary will be as great as he can make it, for the fields are
> large and the grain is white unto harvest.[15]

J. H. B. Williams wrote a friendly note seconding the invitation to
accept the position, expressing a strong wish that Zigler should visit Elgin
to "see what the office and your humble servant look like." By October 13,
Zigler had secured the approval of his wife to accept the position and had
asked his YMCA superiors for a brief leave in order to travel to Illinois to
discuss the offer. He thought that he could accept a salary of $1,500 per
year, although it meant an immediate drop of $900 from his compensation
from the YMCA. He had also heard of a position opening up for him in the
YMCA headquarters at New York, which would likely pay no less than
$5,000.[16]

At the same time he was continuing to correspond with missionaries
about the China field, one concern was his health, for he had suffered
severe asthma attacks from childhood. Even after he had relocated in
Elgin, they pressed him to accept the YMCA position in China, arguing
that someone else could handle the Elgin work but that he was uniquely

qualified for the work on the mission field. However, by November 5, the General Mission Board had voted solidly for his appointment as Home Missions secretary and he had accepted.[17]

In the kind of move that became typical for him, when Zigler visited Elgin to discuss the position, he first stopped at the YMCA to ask about the reputation of the Brethren in the town, without identifying his own Brethren connections. He learned that they were considered to be good, honest, people but had certain peculiar religious practices. Generally, they enjoyed a favorable reputation.[18]

It had not been that long since the Brethren had arrived in the Chicago suburb, noted for its watch manufacturing. Elgin was chosen in 1899 as the place for production and distribution of the *Gospel Messenger*, previously published at Mount Morris, Illinois. Elgin enjoyed excellent railroad connections and the advantages of the metropolitan area, without actually being located in the city. D. L. Miller, businessman and influential leader in missions and publications, was the primary mover in making the change to Elgin. The modest denominational office developed within the purview of the publishing house, which came under church control in 1897.

Denominational editors greeted the decision of Zigler's selection. The *Missionary Visitor* noted, in an article written either by J. H. B. Williams or H. Spenser Minnich:

> We are pleased to announce that after a quest of almost a year, and over many States, a Home Mission Secretary has been elected by the General Mission Board. Bro. M. R. Zigler, Broadway, Va., has been chosen for this most important place. Bro. Zigler has been connected with the Army Welfare work in connection with the Y. M. C. A. Camp at Par[r]is Island, S. C., for the last two and one-half years, and comes to this new secretarial post splendidly fitted for his duties. He expects to be in the office sometime in December. It is hoped that through this appointment the General Mission Board will be in a position to serve the interests of home missions in a greatly enlarged degree.[19]

Editor Frantz of the *Gospel Messenger* reported on the selection in what was to be the first of innumerable mentions of Zigler in the periodical:

> Brother M. R. Zigler of Broadway, Virginia, has been secured by the General Mission Board for the important post of Home Mission Secretary. Brother Zigler reached Elgin Sunday evening, December 7th, and entered upon his work the next morning. After becoming familiar with the office routine, one of the first objects of his attention will be in the Southland.[20]

A more informal appraisal was given by church leader C. D. Bonsack to a group of faculty at Blue Ridge College in Maryland, just after returning from the board meeting at which Zigler was appointed. He reported, according to an account written years later by a former faculty member:

> We have a Home Missions Secretary. . . . The secretary is a young volunteer from Bridgewater [College] for the China Mission Field. His way is barred by unusual circumstances. During the War he served as Y. M. C. A. secretary and displayed absolute fearlessness and the ability to register his presence. We have hopes for the new office and its new occupant.[21]

Ordination

In connection with the appointment, Zigler was asked to receive ordination. Elder Early arranged for it to take place at Frederick, Maryland, with the local pastor, J. Kurtz Miller, assisting. Zigler always thought there might have been some irregularity about it, because of the haste of its arrangements and because that was not his home congregation; Early pointed out the precedents for special ordinations for missionaries at the request of the General Mission Board. Frederick was chosen so that Amy could participate.

It was an unusual service for other reasons. One was that M. R. Zigler showed up for the service wearing the only suit of clothes he possessed, his YMCA uniform complete with leg-wrappings (puttees). Although a landmark decision at the 1911 Annual Conference had made the wearing of the plain garb a matter for congregational decision (and thus broke with many years of enforcement of plain dress as a matter of discipline), it was still expected that all ministers would wear the special costume. Elder Early asked, "Don't you have another suit?" On hearing the negative reply, he huddled with the other officials, and soon the young couple was asked to take the vows of ordination. The charge laid upon him included these words:

> The church now authorizes you to appoint meetings for preaching, according to the general order of the Brethren, to administer the general ordinance of baptism, and, in the absence of an elder, to take the counsel of the church on the admission of an applicant for baptism, to serve the Communion in the absence of any elder, or at his or their request, if present; to solemnize the rite of marriage according to the laws of the State and the usages of the church.[22]

55

Zigler returned to South Carolina to finish out the last weeks of service, before moving to Elgin in December. One of his last projects was to organize a men's quartet from among the marines; its purpose was to provide music for a conference to be held in Cleveland in the fall of 1919 by the World and National YMCAs on the theme of their wartime experiences. Marines at Parris Island contributed money to pay the expenses of the quartet and of Zigler to appear on the program. They were enthusiastically received, securing standing ovations each time they performed. Members of the quartet told him privately that they were through with war; they had fought the good fight and expected that there would be no more wars (the slogan of President Woodrow Wilson in urging US participation had been the "war to end all wars").[23]

His final departure from South Carolina elicited warm expressions of appreciation from both the agency and military leadership. R. H. King, the executive of the YMCA War Work, wrote of his "deep appreciation for his very vital part" in the program, for which he was "genuinely grateful." The post commander of the Marine Barracks on Parris Island, Brig. Gen. Eli K. Cole, wrote to express his "appreciation of the work done by you while at this Post," and to extend his "wishes for your success in your future occupation."[24]

And so M. R. Zigler concluded his war-related service with the marines in the warmth of South Carolina and headed for Illinois and its winter weather. When he arrived on December 7, there were several feet of snow on the ground and the temperature was at zero. Years later, he dictated his attitude at that time in one breathless and ardent sentence:

> I came out of the war feeling that if the boys were willing to die for that cause that I ought to be willing to give my life to the church whole heartedly and as completely as the boys did and I promised some of them that went across and died that I should work for peace and good will the rest of my days that such a thing should never happen and I was keenly happy when the Board gave me the chance to work for the church. . . .[25]

He gave the agency most of the small amount of savings he had accumulated and took his wife to Elgin.

The New Home

The winter of 1919-1920 found the Ziglers in Elgin, establishing a modest home, adjusting to the Midwest, and gaining new friends. For the first several weeks, the Ziglers stayed at the home of J. H. B. William, his supervisor, before finding a small apartment (two rooms) furnished for light housekeeping. This had some urgency, because Amy Zigler was pregnant with their first child. They lived simply, not alone because of Brethren values but also because their budget was limited. M. R. Zigler's salary was $125 per month, of which $60 went for rent. H. C. Early had suggested that the salary would be adequate, but the young couple were severely stretched in the early years to make out on the income provided to them. They furnished the first apartment with grocery crates. Because of the limited accommodations on Parris Island, the Ziglers had spent most of their early married years in separate locations. Elgin was to be their first real home. Yet, the demands of the new position necessitated many absences from home as the energetic and determined Virginian made real his promise to H. C. Early to put "his whole soul and might" into succeeding in it.

Palm Sunday, March 28, 1920, brought with it a scare. Elgin was surprised by a thunderous tornado that caused $3,000,000 of property damage and killed seven persons, some of whom were trapped in devastated church buildings. Amy Zigler had not felt well that morning and remained at home, instead of accompanying her husband to the worship service at the Church of the Brethren, located on Highland Avenue. The tornado hit as M. R. was returning home by streetcar. With power off, the vehicle stalled. The concerned young husband leaped off the car and ran the blocks to the house where he had left his wife. Although the building was severely damaged and their apartment ruined, Amy and the unborn child were unscathed. She was in the only room not broken open by the storm. After it passed, she was given shelter by neighbors.[26]

The Ziglers found another, but more expensive, apartment and resumed their life. The tornado experience, however, was an event that they never forgot and often spoke of in later years. After some years, the Ziglers bought a house on Hamilton Avenue for $6,000. As he had no equity, it took him a long time to pay off this debt.

Robert Stanley Zigler was born in good health on April 16, 1920. Geraldine followed six years later, on April 26, 1926, shortly after the death of Zigler's father in Virginia. She later recalled that she knew as a child that her father was often away from home but that this was not particularly distressing to her. His return home was always a joyous occasion and he never forgot to bring a small gift for the children. He took time to play games with them, such as the card game Rook.

Zigler took the family along on some trips to attend a conference or other meeting. His daughter recalled one expedition in the Southwest when they attempted to hike up Pike's Peak. About four years old at the time, she became tired so her father placed her on his shoulders and kept walking. As they went onto a very narrow part of the trail, he passed out because of the exertion and the thin oxygen. Although both were frightened, there were no ill effects. On their travels they often stopped overnight at tourist homes, some of which had kerosene heaters. The odor often triggered attacks of the asthma that plagued Zigler for much of his life.[27]

Amy Arnold's brother, George Arnold, lived with the family for several years and in some ways took the role of the man of the house. He often read the comics to the children, for example. Amy's father also made his home with the Ziglers until his death. Zigler once said later that he merited entrance into heaven for that effort alone!

Given the gregarious nature of Bob Zigler and the kindly warmth of Amy Zigler, it was not long before they had a large number of friends among Brethren in Elgin. They participated actively in the life of the growing Brethren congregation. In 1928 he was asked to become the elder of the congregation and as such was responsible for the church program for two years; the congregation had, as yet, no pastor, relying on the older Brethren practice of plural, unpaid ministry. With the drive and energy of his leadership in the congregation, it was not long before the Elgin community became more aware of the Brethren. By the mid-1930s he was the chairman of the local ministerium and active in the local Kiwanis Club. (He later joined the Rotary.) Elgin had become their home.

NOTES

1. J. H. B. Williams to M. R. Zigler, July 11, 1918, and Oct. 28, 1918.
2. Zigler to Williams, Nov. 14, 1918; Williams to Zigler, Nov. 19, 1918.
3. Fred J. Wampler to M. Robert Zigler, April 25, 1919, and May 6, 1919.
4. Wampler to Zigler, May 6, 1919.
5. R. H. King to M. R. Zigler, May 22, 1919; Will W. Alexander to M. R. Zigler, May 24, 1919.
6. Vernon Miller interview with M. R. Zigler, 5/2-3.
7. H. C. Early to Robert [Zigler], June 14, 1919, and June 28, 1919.

8. Tom M. Jones to M. R. Zigler, July 10, 1919, and July 18, 1919; Edw. F. Goodridge to "Zig," July 21, 1919.
9. H. C. Early to Robert Zigler, Sept. 20, 1919; Zigler to H. C. Early, Sept. 23, 1919.
10. Early to Zigler, Sept. 20, 1919.
11. Zigler to Early, Sept. 23, 1919.
12. Early to Zigler, Sept. 26, 1919.
13. M. R. Zigler, "People I Met Along the Way," unpubl. essay.
14. John S. Flory to M. R. Zigler, Sept. 29, 1919; Roy Hoover to M. R. Zigler, Sept. 25, 1919.
15. *Missionary Visitor* (October, 1919): 276-277.
16. J. H. B. Williams to M. R. Zigler, Oct. 11, 1919.
17. Zigler to Early, Oct. 13, 1919; M. R. Zigler to R. H. King, Executive Secretary, Southeastern Dept., National War Work Council, YMCA, Oct. 13, 1919; Wampler to Zigler, Oct. 18, 1919, and Dec. 31, 1919.
18. Million transcript of M. R. Zigler, 2/2-3.
19. *Missionary Visitor* (December, 1919): 339.
20. *Gospel Messenger* (Dec. 13, 1919): 702.
21. F. E. Mallott to Marlin ?, Nov. 1962.
22. M. R. Zigler, "M. R. Zigler's Ordination," unpubl. essay; H. B. Brumbaugh, *The Brethren's Church Manual* . . . (Elgin, IL: Brethren Publishing House, 1916), 27-28.
23. Miller interview, 5a/3.
24. King to Zigler, Nov. 19, 1919; Brig. Gen. E. K. Cole to M. R. Zigler, Nov. 29, 1919.
25. M. R. Zigler to O. Winger, Dec. 31, 1929.
26. Janet Bowman, "50 Years Ago Today: It Was Palm Sunday, And A Killer Struck," *Elgin* [IL] *Daily Courier-News* (March 28, 1970): 5; M. R. Zigler, "Statement Concerning the Automobile Accident in Västervik, Sweden, August 16, 1958," unpubl. essay, Oct. 23, 1979.
27. D. F. Durnbaugh interview with Geraldine Zigler Glick, March 10, 1987.

6

THE CHALLENGE OF
THE NEW JOB

THE EXPECTATIONS facing M. R. Zigler as he began his work at Elgin were spelled out in the news item appearing in the February, 1919, issue of the *Missionary Visitor*; it read:

> Bro. M. R. Zigler, Broadway, Va., has been elected home mission secretary, with the General Mission Board, and is now located at Elgin and busy with his tasks. Bro. Zigler will endeavor to assist District Boards with their problems; his office will be intended for a "clearing house" for problems, suggestions, and new ideas relative to work on the home base; and he is eager to foster the interests of every local church. This is the first time that our church has had a home secretary, but the time is more than ripe for a careful cultivation of our missionary interests in America.[1]

The patriarch of Brethren missions, D. L. Miller of Illinois, gave the newcomer his blessing as he began his work. Zigler later recalled that he first met Miller personally (as over just reading his writings or hearing him speak) at the General Mission Board meeting in December, 1919. Although Miller had resigned from the board, he attended its sessions in an emeritus capacity. A rocking chair had been provided for the comfort of the aged leader, who had done more than any other person in bringing the mission concern to the church. "I can still feel his piercing eyes as he measured me for the task that I had assumed. I remember his outstanding advice to me was that I should adjust myself to the many situations I would have to meet as I learned to know the Brethren," hoping that the Brethren would respond to his "efforts to create a greater and stronger church in the United States in order to have a very meaningful program in Foreign

Missions." The aged church leader urged Zigler to secure financial resources "to undergird the total worldwide program of the church." He concluded his admonitions with a challenge for Zigler to consider giving his "total life to the building of the Brethren Church in the world."[2]

This interesting intersection between the domestic and overseas program of the church must be grasped to understand how the denomination was developing at this time. Long suspicious of any centralized authority and operated largely by committees authorized by Annual Conference, the church moved into an organizational pattern of established boards with employed staff in the first instance through its growing concern for missions. The General Mission Board was the only group with substantial funds at its disposal.

As Zigler began his work with Home Missions, it was with the intent of building up a strong domestic base in order to support the foreign program, just as the patriarch Miller advised. When Zigler first met H. Spenser Minnich, who had been given the task of raising mission funds, Minnich urged him: "Let's understand that we have to have a home mission program to establish a strong church to do a foreign mission program; therefore, let's raise our money for foreign missions and we'll subsidize home missions and other activities of the church." The main appeal was for support of the programs already underway and now being initiated abroad. The 1927 *Church of the Brethren Yearbook*, for example, urged the goal of "Church extension in the neglected places of America in order to save souls and to strengthen the home base for foreign endeavor." Zigler so internalized this admonition, according to his later recollection, by making so many addresses appealing for funds for foreign missions, that soon people were taking him aside. They began to tell him that if he were to be the Home Mission secretary, he should stay on that subject.[3]

Zigler thus began his work in the Elgin office. It was a small operation, with only one secretary for the three staff members—Williams (and later Bonsack), Minnich, and Zigler. He was used to a well-staffed and efficient YMCA office; three secretaries had been at his personal disposal. At Elgin he had to type his own letters on an old machine. "I was never able to spell very correctly and when I wrote a letter to the Home Missions Council. . . . I showed it to H. C. Early . . . to get his advice whether I should attend one of the meetings and seek advice as to how the Brethren should start home missions. When he looked at it, he said, 'You didn't send this, did you?' I said, 'I don't have a stenographer, [and] I don't know how to spell.'"[4]

Death of Williams

A tragic development changed his responsibilities. Within a year of his arrival at Elgin, J. H. B. Williams left for an extended trip around the world to visit Brethren mission fields and inspect possibilities for new openings, a trip from which he did not return. On the steamer from India to Eastern Africa, Williams became seriously ill with typhoid fever. He was mortally ill when he was taken off the ship at Mombasa, East Africa (Kenya), where he died on April 17, 1921. C. D. Bonsack, a respected church leader, who had been brought to Elgin to administer the General Mission Board in Williams' year-long absence, was asked to stay on as general secretary after Williams' death. The tragedy shocked the church but also gave impetus to the cause of missions. Over fifty years later, M. R. Zigler made a pilgrimage to the grave of his colleague at Mombasa; this occurred when he traveled to Kenya for the assembly of the World Council of Churches, convened at Nairobi in late 1975.[5]

Before he left, Williams had given Zigler some farewell advice, saying that he had learned to know and trust him and that Zigler should "take such steps . . . promoting Home Missions" as he felt wise to do; Williams would back him in them. However, if Zigler did not get along with the Brethren, he would have to take the consequences; he would "have to give up the position quickly" if he did not make good. One statement Zigler treasured was that Williams felt that he "understood both liberal and conservative positions in the Church regarding many of the debatable issues;" he should try to avoid taking sides and simply promote missions.[6]

While Williams was still in India, Zigler wrote to him reporting on his activities. The response was that "you're starting out a little fast" but Williams "guessed that it would be all right." He gave him also some interesting advice, that is, in Zigler's words, that he should "give special care to people who are developing wealth," in the hope that they would support the church in the future. Williams said that Brethren had "a habit that when a man became rich, they either made a preacher out of him or hit him with a brick." Zigler evidently took this counsel to heart, for he developed a group of supporters with means upon whom he could call.[7]

The Forward Movement

Zigler's call to work with an expanded mission staff was part of a larger denominational program of advance called the "Five Year Forward

Movement," launched on January 1, 1919. The *annual* goals of the movement, directed by C. D. Bonsack and later by J. W. Lear, included:

> Fifteen thousand members added to the Church of the Brethren by baptism. Three hundred aggressive spiritual young men called to the ministry. One hundred new Sunday schools started. Fifteen thousand new scholars enrolled and an average attendance of not less than 75% of the enrollment of the main school. Three thousand five hundred students enrolled in our colleges, at least 60% of whom are pursuing regular college courses. Three hundred thousand dollars raised for endowment. Ninety per cent of our students encouraged in some form of regular Bible study. Twenty per cent of our students looking toward a definite life of Christian service. Fifty per cent of our college graduates dedicating their lives to the ministry or mission work. Two hundred fifty thousand dollars given to missions under the General Mission Board. Fifteen new missionaries sent to foreign fields. Two hundred thousand dollars raised under district missions. One new missionary station under each district mission board.

Many observers believe that this program, although overly ambitious, was the impetus for the period of growth that marked the Brethren during the period before the Great Depression of the 1930s.[8]

Travels

In spite of J. H. B. Williams' assurance that "there would be no travel and no public speaking" in his "administrative" job, M. R. Zigler soon discovered that he had to travel extensively and speak often (as indeed, H. C. Early had warned him). Because of Zigler's feeling that he did not do well in public communication, the increasing necessity to preach and speak on his travels was nerve-wracking for him. Late in life he confessed that he had never been able to feel at ease at the lectern or pulpit: "I always felt unprepared, inadequate, and my knees trembled, and I found it very difficult to prepare [an] address and deliver it. . . . I never found the way."[9]

A difficulty that would have fazed a lesser man was his physical problem—asthma, which he had suffered from childhood. The attacks were triggered by dust and pollen. Many sleepless nights on trains, in hotels, or in private homes were spent sitting up or even standing, in order to breathe:

> I loved the job getting out among the Brethren churches. The style of the pastor's residence, which was always the place for the visitor—I should say,

the minister's, [for] they didn't always have a pastor, with free ministry—but the guest room had straw matting on it, and that always gave me asthma. But that was the style, every pastor had straw matting in the guest room. And the curtains hadn't been shaken for some time, and the pillows hadn't been moved. Small fragments of dust, but you couldn't see it. But I could tell. The next morning I'd wake up and I'd look tired. They thought I was overworked.[10]

Such a thing as the smell of peanuts could start him off and have him clogged within thirty minutes. At Dexter, Missouri, where the rooms had thin walls, his hosts heard his trouble and thought that he was dying; they wanted to call a doctor. But he convinced them that there was no point in doing so, that he would survive the attack as he had done all of those before. According to his recollection, this was the only place where his problem was noticed. This is not strictly accurate, for others did become aware of it. Henry C. Eller, in his autobiography, related that he traveled with Zigler on a tour of congregations in the Southeast. "We traveled first to the Spray Church [North Carolina]. In bed that night he had some difficulty with asmatic [sic] disturbance. The next night, following the N. C. Fraternity Church meeting, he was unable to stay in bed. (We had feather pillows.) After the Pleasant Valley (Floyd county) meeting and at the Sam P. Reed home, he decided not to go to bed. He sat up all night. We did not complete our tour."[11]

Zigler's first trips to investigate home mission possibilities were to the Northwest and to the South. This began a systematic plan of visiting all of the Brethren congregations. He thought that the only way in which he could succeed in his role was to become known and trusted. As a young man with no pastoral experience, and only one year of theological training, he needed to build a personal base. Visiting congregations, district meetings, and annual conferences became his strategy. By the end of his service at Elgin in 1948, he had visited all but twenty-five of the 1,100 Brethren congregations. He paid special attention to the approximately 800 churches with membership of 150 or less. Some of the twenty-five he never reached refused him admittance, for they thought him too liberal. He spoke of needing to take three different suits of clothes with him on trips, to meet the varying expectations of the churches: clerical vest, plain Brethren garb, and business suit and tie.[12]

The travel and other demands became so heavy that he thought, after some time, that he would need to resign his position. He took his problem to the Board, suggesting that someone without family responsibilities should do it. Board members discussed it in open session and with him privately, and asked the chairman, H. C. Early, to give Zigler their decision. "He gave me the verdict that the Board recognized the problem and they hoped that Amy and I could learn how to live in the spirit, even though we would be separated. I felt that this was good religion, a recognizable dedication, and though Amy raised many questions, she finally said, 'Let's do it' and she would take the responsibility for her share of our home life." Zigler mentioned that he knew that he was not living up to normal expectations as a husband and father, and that his dedication to the church's task caused his wife and family much sacrifice. He never lost a sense of guilt about this.[13]

Geraldine ("Jerry") and Robert ("Bobby" or later "Bob") recalled a happy childhood, with good times with their father when he was home. Robert went through a phase of resentment about his father's absence when, for example, he was participating in athletic events at high school. Both children wrote frequently to their father, Jerry more than Bob. Zigler was gratified that as an adult his son worked for relief agencies, including the Heifer Project, International Voluntary Service, and the US AID agency in countries such as Laos and South Vietnam.[14]

At this point, the Board did raise Zigler's salary from $1,500 to $1,800 per year, which helped but did not solve the financial problem. As he later put it, "It was not enough for me to catch up for a long time and I have always wondered if I had my life to live over if I would dare to go through that time like I did again." Later, during the Depression, the Ziglers were even more hard put to make ends meet. They were in debt for much of the time. Despite his economic straits, Zigler preserved his optimistic outlook. His longtime colleague, H. Spenser Minnich recalled during this time most people were apprehensive and were "pulling in their horns." Zigler, however, went out and bought a new car. Minnich wondered: "How can you afford this? Doing it on time?" The answer came, "Well, that is the trouble. Everybody has quit buying and so we have a depression. What I did helps the economy along."[15]

During one period in the early 1930s, in order to be with the family more, Zigler decided that they should move to Bridgewater, Virginia. They lived on the college campus while he visited all the Brethren congregations in the Southeastern area of the United States. He systematically visited a different church every evening, when his presence was not demanded elsewhere for administrative reasons.

Earlier, the Ziglers had lived for a time in an apartment at Bethany Biblical Seminary on the west side of Chicago. He wanted to learn to know the seminary community better and do some teaching. Seminary personnel encouraged him to take academic work there to complete a divinity degree, but he chose, instead, to take graduate work in sociology and church history at the Divinity School of the University of Chicago. This was in 1924-1925. He had also contemplated studying at Yale University for a year, but this never took place.

Home Mission Beginnings

At his first Annual Conference as Home Missions secretary, held at Sedalia, Missouri, in June, 1920, Zigler made a good impression. Edward Frantz, editor of *Gospel Messenger*, reported: "Brother M. R. Zigler, our Home Mission Secretary, gave an address, illustrated with stereopticon slides, which portrayed opportunities for Home Mission work in the homeland. It was an eyeopener, it is safe to say, to everyone who 'saw' it. The audience listened with the most rapt attention."[16]

He began there his intensive work with the district mission boards. He recognized that, if his work were to be successful, it would need to be as a result of ascertaining the needs and wishes of these boards and working for them, rather than developing an ambitious and centralized national program. These boards had been operating independently and had little feeling of unity. He called district representatives together in the early morning hours of the Annual Conference simply to talk about the current Home Mission program and how home missions could be advanced. The results were impressive. For the first time, district board members could discuss their own local problems in a larger context.

He had them decide how his office could help them to accomplish their tasks and how he could move into areas they were unable to tackle. "It was this act of comradeship between the General Office and the District Boards that really made my work easy for the rest of the time that I worked for Home Missions. . . ." The approach was typical of Zigler's developing administrative style—to enlist the support and enthusiasm of others by asking them how he could help them. The spirit was expressed in a note he placed in the *Missionary Visitor*: "The Home Mission Department of the General Board is in its infancy. It hopes to be your servant in every way possible. . . . The department will be of value in so far as it is used by the church at large."[17]

Zigler formed working committees and by December had secured some leading pastors to compose an advisory council for Home Missions.

They were: Edgar Rothrock (Nebraska); M. Clyde Horst, chairman (Pennsylvania); and D. J. Blickenstaff (Illinois, later replaced by E. E. Eshelman). These men met periodically with Zigler as secretary and C. D. Bonsack as board general secretary.[18] A Women's Work Committee was formed as well; its members were Mrs. M. C. Swigart, Mrs. L. Whisler, and Mrs. George L. Studebaker. The *Missionary Visitor* reported on the new wave on interest: "Various meetings were held at Conference to consider this subject, and with each additional meeting a new interest was shown in, and a new need felt for, more intensive work in the homeland. Not that this need has grown suddenly so much greater, but we have awakened rapidly to what has required attention all these years."[19]

An early inspection tour by Zigler of the states of Idaho, Oregon, and Washington in August/September, 1920, found some congregations "fully alive" to missions and others unaware of the aggressive goals of the Forward Movement. A special issue of the *Missionary Visitor* in late 1920, contained a long survey article "Opportunities in the Homeland," evidently written by Zigler. It was part of the developing plan he had promised the church for the work of his office. The carefully compiled statistics gave the number of unchurched to be about 58 million people, somewhat more than half of the population. The two general types of Home Missions work identified were urban and rural, with the population numbers shifting toward the former. "The task of the church is not to lessen our work in the country, in order that the city might be developed, but the country church must increase and not decline. The city will still look to the country for pastors and Christian leaders. It has always depended on the country for recruits."[20]

The author covered mission possibilities in Hawaii, the West Indies, and Alaska and analyzed the needs of immigrants, mountain people, Mexicans, Orientals, Indians, and Negroes. The rather general conclusion asserted: "It is evident that there lie at our door many opportunities untouched. It ought to call forth some good, hard thinking as to how we, as a church, can meet our share of the responsibility. Plans will have to be made, and hearts to soften to the needs before men and money shall be available to carry on service among those who require our service."[21]

Early in 1921 Zigler inaugurated a new department in the board's informational vehicle, the *Missionary Visitor*; this was called *Home Fields* and was devoted to reporting on all "vital things in the work of the kingdom." These included successful methods of church work both rural and urban, work of the district mission boards, targeted ethnic and vocational groups, church architecture, and the like. "It is desired that the Home Fields Department shall be a reflector of the needs in home mission territory, and from this reflector it is hoped that many may receive the inspiration to go out into the fields as laborers."[22]

By 1922 the work of Home Missions was well underway. It was given the featured role by the program committee of the Annual Conference at Winona Lake, Indiana. Zigler introduced there a special two-day preliminary conference for members of district mission boards, which met with good response; thirty-eight of the forty-eight boards were represented. An exhaustive survey of problems and solutions focused the attention of the church on the subject. The early morning Home Mission meetings, begun two years earlier in Missouri, were continued as well. The pattern here established of a special Home Missions conference before Annual Conference and other meetings during Annual Conference continued for many years and was a central pillar of Zigler's program.

Home Mission Projects

By 1922 as well, the Home Missions secretary had specific projects underway. The initiative for one early project came from a lay member, John Stump, in Falfurrias, Texas; it was directed at ministry to Mexicans. Zigler gave the project support and funding from the Elgin office. The first completely new Home Missions project that Zigler started was an industrial school in the Blue Ridge mountains of Greene County, Virginia. Since his budget was limited ($5,000 per year for all expenses, including his salary), he thought it important to concentrate the work on a few well-selected projects. Work in Appalachia seemed a promising beginning.

Zigler had visited the area in September, 1920, and heard of the vision of a few local Brethren for establishing a school to alleviate the poverty and neglect of the residents. He interested the General Mission Board in the project, which enabled the purchase of the first house in December, 1921; a 300-acre farm was acquired in 1922 and a large new school building was completed in December, 1922. Many local congregations and individuals picked up the project for support; the General Board itself invested $100,000 in the program. A dedicated teacher and social worker, Nelie Wampler, was the prime mover; she devoted her life to the school and area. Other early staff workers were Amsey and Florence Bollinger and Mabel and Orville Hersch. Zigler recruited H. C. Early himself to leave retirement in 1925 to become the superintendent of the school for a time until his health failed. The school, which brought great educational, social, and health improvements to the area, had to be closed in 1933 when the National Shenandoah Park was created, but related work continued.[23]

Summer Pastors

One of Zigler's most creative projects was recruiting college students to serve small rural congregations as pastors and evangelists for the three summer months. He often visited college campuses (going to non-Brethren institutions where Brethren were studying as well as to Brethren-sponsored schools) to select students for the program. Some men and women were selected from among those who had expressed interest in church vocations as a career. Sometimes he was known to ask the college janitor/custodian to identify "live-wire" collegians, not always noted for their piety. Often, he was able to challenge them by his offer (which included financial support) and in this way helped to develop some of the leading ministerial talent in the denomination. The only student to serve in the summer of 1921 was D. C. Gnagey, at Broadwater, Missouri.

Among others recruited for the summer program who went on to become pastors and church leaders were: Calvert N. Ellis, John D. Ellis, DeWitt L. Miller, S. Loren Bowman, Desmond W. Bittinger, Clement E. Bontrager, M. Guy West, Russell G. West, Rufus D. Bowman, William and Esther Beahm, X. L. Coppock, Arthur W. Shively, Ada Correll, Lois Sherrick, and Raymond R. Peters. They sent weekly reports to Zigler in Elgin and he wrote to them regularly. Many look back on the experience with great appreciation and remember vividly the encouragement and fatherly advice they received from M. R. Zigler. Calvert N. Ellis, who went to Piqua, Ohio, kept such a letter for years in his Bible after he went on to become a professor and then president at Juniata College.

The *Missionary Visitor* reported on the summer program in 1927: "This is one of the most promising pieces of work. To many students this is a leading step to definite, full-time Christian service. Successful work has been done by women. Last summer there were eleven men and eight women serving the churches."[24]

Home Missions Pastors and Evangelists

Some pastors were sponsored directly by the Elgin office in Home Missions projects and supported by denominational funds. By June, 1924, six pastors fell in this category, serving in Red Cloud, Nebraska; Fort Worth, Texas; Greene County, Virginia; Broadwater, Missouri; Fruitdale, Alabama; and Piney Flats, Tennessee. They worked in cooperation with the relevant District Mission Boards, which themselves were directly supporting workers. In the same year, twenty-seven of the forty-eight districts reported that they were sponsoring ninety-eight workers.[25]

In developing this program, Zigler was attempting to develop a new pattern of ministerial support. It was his idea that pastors of new congregations should receive salaries but that when these new churches became strong enough, they should revert to the "free ministry" or self-supported program traditional to the Brethren. This ran counter to the development of the time, which saw the shift from the unpaid plural ministry to the salaried professional minister. It was the latter trend which succeeded. Zigler's idea was not supported by the president of Bethany Biblical Seminary, Albert C. Wieand, whose vision was for two trained and supported ministers in each congregation—a pastor and a Christian education director—or by the increasingly influential college leaders. To the end of his life Zigler regretted that he had not been able to sway the course of development by continuing the free ministry system with local ministers spending time at Bethany in training and then returning to their homes to provide leadership.[26]

Zigler also sought to enlarge the often parochial thinking of the Brethren of the needs of other ethnic groups. A typical appeal appeared in 1926:

> The church in America must arise out of complacency. Satisfaction with present attainments must be displaced by a divine discontent.... The greatest task of the individual members of the Church of the Brethren is to be willing to submit their lives to the will of God. When this surrender is made, the Indians who have not heard will hear the Word of God; the Negroes will know that Christ is healing the nations; the unsaved will know that the heart of some one is beating in their interest. The borders of the kingdom will be enlarged. With this enlargement the poor will be helped, the hungry fed, the stranger taken in, and the sick healed. The great law of love will be encircling the broken hearts. Is this too much to expect?[27]

Besides pastoral placements, the Home Missions department also sent evangelists into the field. Chief among these were S. Z. Smith, I. D. Leatherman, I. N. H. Beahm, and E. S. Coffmann. Support from the Elgin office made it possible for them to visit smaller congregations whose contributions would otherwise not have been sufficient to cover the expenses of the evangelists. At one point he tried to enlist some of the strongest pastors in the church, men such as M. J. Brougher and J. O. Winger, for full-time evangelistic work but did not succeed.

Struggling congregations were aided by financial support. In 1930, for example, fifty such were recorded as receiving funds totaling over $35,000. This "strengthened many weak churches and helped many otherwise discouraged young ministers who toil in these difficult fields."[28]

The story of a congregation in Louisiana is a case in point. The Roanoke congregation reached out to a nearby community called Rosepine as a mission point. There was favorable response and the district agreed that a congregation should be organized there, which took place in June, 1924; the charter membership was twenty. The chief problem was to secure ministerial leadership. The congregation appealed to Zigler for help; he sent a summer pastor there and then found longer-term ministerial aid, which he supported with financial grants. Eventually he recruited R. K. Showalter whose labors resulted in the construction of a new church building and a significant impact on the poor community. Under the leadership of Showalter and his wife the Rosepine church "has been given a new conception of her duty to the community and in a marked way she is meeting the challenge," the Roanoke leaders reported. "Much of the success of the work at Rosepine has been due to the splendid interest and cooperation of our Home Mission Secretary, Bro. M. R. Zigler."[29]

The church was very concerned about growth and this was a period when growth took place. The membership of the church in 1920 was about 90,000; by 1940 it had virtually doubled, reaching about 177,000. During this period the rate of increase was the highest ever attained in Brethren history in America. Zigler thoroughly approved the emphasis on growth:

> We reported baptisms in the churches in the *Messenger* every week and gave the name of the evangelist, which in my judgment was the first item in the paper that most of the people read then they first received the *Messenger*. People liked to see and hear about growth. Churches like to be recognized when they do grow. It seems to me we used the great commission in those days, making disciples of the nations, baptizing men everywhere. "No baptisms, no church," was said again and again to inspire people just to double their membership by each individual finding one other person in a year's time.[30]

It was clear from all of this activity that M. R. Zigler had found a place where his leadership skills and great energies could be put to good use. He was increasingly being looked to for direction and for his vision of the church's future.

NOTES

1. *Missionary Visitor* (February, 1920): 34.
2. M. R. Zigler, "People I Met Along the Way," unpubl. essay; H. Spenser Minnich, "Farewell to a Friendly Old Building," *Gospel Messenger* (May 9, 1959): 18.
3. Million transcript of M. R. Zigler, 1/7; *Church of the Brethren Yearbook* (Elgin: Brethren Publishing House, 1927), 18.
4. Zigler, "Memoirs," 3/5-6.
5. Zigler, "People I Met;" Howard E. Royer, "The Saints Are True Liberators," *Messenger* (February, 1976): 40.
6. Zigler, "People I Met."
7. Zigler, "Memoirs," 3/10-11.
8. H. Spenser Minnich, "The Forward Movement," *Missionary Visitor*, Annual Report (June 1920): 10-11; J. H. B Williams, "A Movement of Great Significance," *Gospel Messenger* (Jan. 24, 1920): 51-52; H. K. Ober, "The Joint Board Meeting and Our Forward Movement Program," *Gospel Messenger* (Feb. 7, 1920). With the Feb. 21, 1920, issue of the *Gospel Messenger*, a "Forward Movement Department" was inaugurated, which brought articles every week about the program.
9. M. R. Zigler, "Statement Concerning the Automobile Accident at Västervik, Sweden, Aug. 16, 1958," Oct. 23, 1979, unpubl. essay.
10. Vernon Miller interview with M. R. Zigler, 5b/6.
11. Henry Cline Eller, *Time Flies!: Lest I Forget at 85. An Autobiography* (Harrisonburg, VA: author, 1987), 38.
12. C. Wayne Zunkel, "M. R. Zigler: Rebel With a Cause," *Bulletin of the* [Manchester College] *Peace Studies Institute*, 6 (August, 1976): 2.
13. Zigler, "Memoirs," 3/6; Miller interview, 2a/1.
14. D. F. Durnbaugh interview with Geraldine Zigler Glick, March 10, 1987.
15. Interview with M. R. Zigler, Sebring, Florida, June 9 [?], 4/3; Vernon Miller interview with H. Spenser Minnich, 16a/20. Although he was bold enough to buy a new car in 1930, he was cautious about the model. He reported in a letter to a church leader that he had been offered good deals on a Buick and a Graham-Paige but had been advised that driving one of these larger cars would make for negative public relations; he settled on Chevrolet: ". . . I know to drive up into the church yard of many of the churches I visit would make them

feel like I was a millionaire if I should travel in too fine a car . . ." (M. R. Zigler to Otho Winger, June 25, 1930).

16. *Gospel Messenger* (June 19, 1920), 356.
17. Sebring interview, 4/6; *Missionary Visitor* (November, 1920), 291.
18. "The Advisory Council," *Missionary Visitor* (February, 1921): 40; (March, 1921): 79; Annual Report, (June, 1921): 5.
19. "Women's Work Committee, *Missionary Visitor* (February, 1921): 40; (July 1920, 163.
20. *Missionary Visitor* (August, 1920): 194; (September, 1920): 227.
21. [M. R. Zigler], "Opportunities in the Homeland," *Missionary Visitor* (November, 1920): 299-308.
22. *Missionary Visitor* (February, 1921): 40.
23. Nelie Wampler, "A Dream Coming True" and other articles, *Missionary Visitor* (February, 1923): 44-49; H. C. Early, "The Outlook of the Work" and other articles, *Missionary Visitor* (November, 1926): 356-359; *Church of the Brethren Industrial School* [ca. 1926]; Nancy H. Morris, "Church of the Brethren Industrial School," *Brethren Encyclopedia* (1983-1984), 308; Roger E. Sappington, *The Brethren in Virginia* (Harrisonburg, VA: Committee for Brethren History in Virginia, 1973), 374.
24. *Missionary Visitor* (November, 1927): 361; see also "Our Summer Pastors and Sunday School Work," *Missionary Visitor* (August, 1922): 322-323; G. M. Garber, "The Summer Pastorate from a Student's Viewpoint," *Missionary Visitor* (November, 1925): 391-392, 402; "Summer Workers for Home Missions," *Missionary Visitor* (August, 1927): 257-258. Zigler stressed the value of the program as a recruiting device: Memoirs, 5/11-12.
25. "Annual Report," *Missionary Visitor* (June, 1924): 162-163.
26. Million transcript of M. R. Zigler, 1/9-10.
27. M. R. Zigler, "Is America on Your Heart?" *Missionary Visitor* (November, 1926): 353-354.
28. "Annual Report," *Missionary Visitor* (June, 1930): 162.
29. *Missionary Visitor* (November, 1927): 364-365, 378.
30. Million transcript of M. R. Zigler, 3/13.

7

GROWTH IN LEADERSHIP

BY 1930 IT WAS OBVIOUS to everyone that M. R. Zigler was gaining stature in the church. He was speaking widely in congregations, District Meetings, and Annual Conferences and writing often in the denominational journals. People were attracted by his hearty, good-humored manner and his great gift for friendship; he worked assiduously at the latter, not from any manipulative sense but because that is what he enjoyed doing.

It was not surprising, therefore, that in 1930 his responsibilities were strikingly increased. The Council of Boards added to his Home Mission task the administration of the General Ministerial Board, which had been in operation since 1921. As the Brethren moved increasingly to the pattern of the salaried professional pastors in their congregations, some machinery became necessary to place the right personnel in the right churches and to provide opportunities for growth and education for pastors. Zigler's tasks with Home Missions had already brought him into this field as he worked with students on summer pastorates and found ministerial leadership for new or struggling churches. It was, therefore, natural to ask him to add to his other assignments the specific responsibilities of working with ministers.

General Ministerial Board

The duties and objectives of the secretary of the General Ministerial Board had been spelled out in the minutes of Annual Conference for 1927. Duties included keeping records, making surveys, listing ministers, providing information, creating unity, and developing standards for ministers and congregations. The specific objectives are worth quoting:

> 1. Pastoral care of churches. It is the purpose of this Board to provide adequate pastoral care for the churches of the Brotherhood through such a system as is best adapted to the conditions of the local church.
>
> 2. Evangelistic program of the church. It is the purpose of this Board to develop an emphasis on evangelism throughout the church and to assist local churches in developing an efficient evangelistic program. The aim is a 10% increase in membership annually.
>
> 3. Efficient church management. It is the purpose of this Board to improve the executive and administrative machinery of the local church in relation to finances, records, reports, standards, and objectives.
>
> 4. The Ministerial force of the church. It is the purpose of this Board to recruit the ministry of the church wisely and to assist in the location and distribution of our present ministry so far as is practicable under our present system.[1]

An account of the General Ministerial Board's meeting of December 9, 1930, indicates how Zigler began the job: "A joint meeting of the General Missions and Ministerial Boards was held at which a report of the Home Missions and Ministerial Secretary, Bro. M. R. Zigler, was made. Bro. Zigler has been employed by these two Boards jointly and has been doing some field work which was badly needed. He has visited a large number of the Districts and held conferences with the District Mission and Ministerial Boards and is making surveys of the Brotherhood. Some valuable information is being secured."[2]

One of his first initiatives was to organize well-attended Pastoral Conferences for instruction, inspiration, and coordination. The themes and speakers at an early conference held at Bethany Bible School in Chicago on March 2-6, 1931, included: "The Message of the Ministry for Our Day," C. C. Ellis; "Messages from the Old Testament Prophets," Edward Frantz; "The Value of the Seminary to Our Church," J. Hugh Heckman; "The Pastor's Code of Ethics," Merlin C. Shull; "The Interpretation of the Peace Pact," C. Ernest Davis; "What to Read," J. E. Miller; "Building Church Attendance," J. Clyde Forney; "The Unemployment Problem," Dan West; "The Local Church Organization," J. W. Lear; and "Why Preach?" R. H. Miller. The presenters were among the top leadership of the church. The intent was to create a professional and informed ministerial force, loyal to the denomination and its program. Those attending developed and presented well-considered statements on "The Free Ministry" and "The Recruiting of the Ministry."[3]

Zigler reported on the December, 1931, meeting of the General Ministerial Board, emphasizing the "tremendous responsibility resting upon the shoulders of every member," claiming that the "future of the church rests largely in their hands." The issues under discussion were: developing a reading course for ministers, resolving continuing problems with placement of ministers; planning conferences for leadership training (to be carried out in conjunction with the Board of Religious Education), and updating statistics on the church.

According to Zigler's report, in 1931 there were 1,027 congregations meeting in 1,464 places. Of these 859 were rural, 278 were in small towns, and 215 were in cities. Total membership in North America was 143,425, with a net gain in that year of 5,252. Almost half of the congregations had less than a hundred members; the average size of the congregations was 139. Of the total congregations, 255 had full time ministers, 338 part time ministers, and 434 free ministers.[4]

Zigler had occasion to defend the need of pastors and churches to send in annual reports, which provided the basis for the statistics. Many protested that the questions asked were unimportant and answering them took too much time. His response was that the reports were necessary to track trends in the church, whether growth or decline. "When all the churches have reported this year it will make every member more deeply interested in the church to know how many men, women, young people and children are in touch with the church. A church throbbing with youth is not declining. A church that has many children coming to it for truth and light is destined to live and serve. . . . The report is a self-analysis."[5]

The impact of the Depression was felt deeply by ministers, when congregational members were hard put to raise funds to employ them because of their own financial straits. Some congregations resorted to scrip, or vouchers in lieu of cash payments. These were exchanged for food and merchandise. In some places actual groceries were pledged to assist in the support of the pastor's family. Writing in November, 1932, Zigler complimented the congregations because "most of our churches have entered this pastoral year without a change in pastors or the discontinuance of pastoral support. This was accomplished by heroic efforts in sacrifice both on the part of the ministers and the churches." He pointed out, nevertheless, that all pastors would need to have some cash payments to cover expenses such as insurance, taxes, education, clothes, and the like.

Therefore, "The members of every church should know the needs of their minister and do everything possible to help him meet his obligations."[6]

Beyond this was the problem of relieving the need of aged and unemployed ministers. The General Ministerial Board had to pass on all applications of needy ministers and recommend payments to the General Mission Board, which was the custodian of funds for ministerial relief. In the depth of the Depression, even minuscule payments were difficult to manage; recipients were asked to reduce their requests where possible, because the fund was overdrawn and money had to be borrowed to respond. The voluntary reduction amounted to nearly $1,000 in 1933.

In some cases yoked parishes were organized to meet the need. Zigler, for example, was credited with suggesting that one pastor serve the pastorates at Omaha, Nebraska, and Council Bluffs, Iowa, located ten miles apart. He wrestled with the problems of the isolated Brethren congregations in Canada, hard hit by the effects of the Depression. He formulated a plan to create a district superintendent and worked on financing and personnel.[7]

Pastoral Placement

Much of the work naturally involved placing ministers in individual congregations. Zigler released an elaborate and detailed statement of "Policy on Ministerial Placement" in September, 1933, which had been worked on by the Board for several years. It suggested the creation of a three-member local Ministerial Committee to arrange for pastors and act as an advisory board for them; the plan also called for the appointment of "at least three capable elders" to work as a District Ministerial Board to assist in placing pastors, to establish suggested salary standards, to reconcile problems, and generally to supervise the relations between ministers and congregations. Specific procedures were worked out for churches seeking pastors and pastors seeking places. The plan was revised in 1937 and 1942.[8]

In reflecting on his experiences in later years, Zigler ruefully summarized by stating that no congregation ever believed that it found the pastor it needed and no pastor felt that the congregation served was as good as it should be. As he put it, "You never got a man good enough for the church or a church good enough for the pastor." Despite this, the matches usually proved to be harmonious. At the same time he said that the recruiting at first was quite easy "for there was a large number of trusted free ministers

77

capable of giving fulltime [service] in many locations and the people were willing to support them because they had called them to the ministry and they trusted them." He identified the work of the colleges in this period as exemplary in preparing gifted leadership in the new system of trained pastors.[9]

It is a tribute to his judgment and tactfulness that scores of Brethren ministers remained grateful to him throughout their lives for his work. Many leading pastors gave him credit for launching their ministerial careers by finding the right assignments. At one time, Harper Will introduced Zigler to a gathering at an Ocean Grove conference by saying: "Who said the Brethren have no bishops? Meet Bishop M. R., who has been a bishop to me; [he] sent me to Twin Falls, Idaho; Wenatchee, Washington; [and] Chicago, Illinois." Other well-known ministers such as Merlin E. Garber, Warren D. Bowman, and McKinley Coffman, Sr., made similar statements. Doubtless one reason that they appreciated his efforts was that he did not simply place them and forget them. He followed up the placements with letters, calls, and personal visits. He was always available for encouragement and counsel in troubled moments. According to Merlin Garber, Zigler had a subtle method of changing pastors' policies, not by criticizing but by remaining silent when the person felt "he should be commended for an idea, a statement or some action." The silence prompted a reconsideration of the action or program.[10]

The type of delicate negotiation involved is illustrated by his involvement of the movement in 1937 of Rufus D. Bowman from his pastorate of the Washington, D. C., Church of the Brethren to the presidency of Bethany Biblical Seminary in Chicago. Dr. D. W. Kurtz, the previous president of the institution, had resigned because of health problems and moved to California. The seminary called Bowman, who had formerly been head of Christian Education at Elgin before going to the nation's capital as pastor. Through his strong leadership, he had built up the Washington congregation with increased membership, excellent financial giving, and positive attitude. He and his wife were beloved by the congregation. Therefore, when he announced his resignation on April 15, 1937, to accept the call to Bethany, the congregation and its leadership reacted very negatively. Bowman had made his acceptance contingent on the approval of the congregation.

Zigler was one of a delegation sent to the congregation to explain the call to them. Bowman wrote to Zigler soon after the latter's visit that the delegation had gotten off "pretty well" but that he now had to "face the music" in a "very trying experience." The congregational leaders were making them attractive financial offers in the effort to keep them. "The elder reminds us that the church here had planned to take care of us, to give us an opportunity to go to school, to travel, and to grow." He rehearsed the advances the congregation had made during his pastorate and how he had lifted their previously discouraged spirits by interpreting the possibilities of the future. "Things are going good now, crowds are large, finances good, spirit fine." And then came the resignation! An influential elder expressed bitterness toward the church for attempting to take their pastor.[11]

Letters flew back and forth as Zigler sought to work out the problem in a way satisfactory to the congregation, the seminary, and the Bowmans. To work it out, he had to contact board members, put off a long-scheduled speaking trip to Manchester College, arrange for a substitute, and travel to Washington prior to another responsibility in Florida on May 1. The resolution he worked out was to persuade Bowman's brother, Warren D. Bowman, at that time a professor at Juniata College, to accept a call to Washington. This eventually pacified the feelings of the congregation, for they knew of the brother's abilities. That freed the Bowmans to leave for Bethany.[12]

An epilogue became evident nearly thirty years later. While preparing a Thanksgiving sermon for his Virginia congregation, Warren D. Bowman was thinking of persons to whom he owed debts of gratitude. Zigler stood out in his mind and he therefore sent him a letter. "If if had not been for your interest in me, Bob, I might have remained an average, somewhat discontented college teacher. But you encouraged me to take the pastorate in Washington, which opened up new vistas and a new life for me. I shall never cease to be grateful to you for the part you played in getting me to make that move."

He then rehearsed other ways in which Zigler had helped him, including the following: "You got me on annual conference programs while I was at Juniata and afterwards. This enabled me to become better acquainted with our Brotherhood, after a number of years away from the center of Brethren life. For all these things and for many other touches you made on my life, from college days through the years, I wish now to express my profound gratefulness and appreciation. What you did for me, Bob, I am certain you did for scores of others over our Brotherhood. . . [13]

This episode is significant as an example of the impact Zigler had on the hundreds of people with whom his work brought him into contact. He had the gift of communicating his personal interest in others in ways that persuaded them that he did not simply see them as potential solutions to his problems or pawns to move across a chess board. Given the frustrations endemic to ministerial placement, this achievement is remarkable. It also highlights one of the secrets of M. R. Zigler's influence in the church—his expansive and genuine interest in others and his concern to see them grow and flourish. People sensed this quality and responded warmly to it. This created a large bloc of Brethren who developed keen loyalty to the man and his leadership.

Another way in which influence was felt was through counsel given to congregations. Paul M. Robinson recalled that when he was installed as a young pastor (twenty-four years old) at the large Hagerstown, Maryland, Church of the Brethren, Zigler preached the sermon. His blunt advice to the church was that they now had a young pastor and they had to help him grow. "He'll become pretty much what you let him become." A pastor had to have the opportunity to see more than his own bailiwick. He suggested that they could help provide nurture by making it possible for their pastor to travel outside the country. After several years of pastoral service by the Robinsons, the Hagerstown church gave a trip to Palestine to the couple, who attributed the action to the seeds planted by Zigler. According to Robinson, "it was Bob who really encouraged the church to see beyond the local congregation and see the world view."[14]

Christian Education

As if holding the two administrative positions with Home Missions and Ministries were not enough, on September 1, 1934, Zigler was also made the secretary for the Board of Christian (formerly Religious) Education. This was precipitated by the resignation of Rufus D. Bowman to take up the pastoral work at Washington, DC, mentioned above. The action to increase Zigler's already numerous duties was a tribute to his executive ability; more importantly, it reflected the financial crisis of the Church of the Brethren in the mid-1930s. Economic pressures had necessitated stringent budget restrictions across the line. Missionaries were brought back from their stations overseas, and those slated to leave remained in the USA. One way Elgin staff costs could be reduced was by failing to fill vacated positions. This was the case for Zigler's assumption of another post. His title became Secretary of Ministry, Christian Education, and Home Missions; alternatively he was called the Secretary for Home

Administration. The positive side of the action was that Elgin personnel had already been calling for a unified staff to serve the boards together. Financial exigencies now made that possible.

A brochure was issued in 1936 by the three Elgin boards describing "The United Program of the Church of the Brethren in Ministry and Education, Including Home Missions." Zigler was listed as *executive secretary*, evidently a recently acquired designation; the description stated that he:

> . . . serves as joint executive secretary of Ministry and Education, which includes Home Missions for the Home Department of the General Mission Board, the General Ministerial Board and the Board of Christian Education Gives special attention to the administrative work of the three Boards and to the development of a unified staff to serve the total church in America. Serves in the placement of ministers and the promotion of causes. Integrates the work of Home Missions. Seeks to integrate the work of the General and District Boards with the local church program.[15]

In addition, Zigler acted as chairman of the staff under the Council of Boards, the coordinating body that brought together representatives of the several church boards and the seminary. As such he acted virtually as a general secretary. He was clearly the major figure on the denominational staff level. His appearances at the Annual Conferences reflected this role. Articles summarizing the events of the conferences during the 1930s and 1940s featured his activities on every page.

The appointment to the Christian Education post especially pleased Zigler for one reason: this board had been assigned the church's respon- sibilities for peace concerns. His determination to strengthen the Brethren stance on peace had been a prime motivation for going to Elgin to take a staff position in the first place. Although not directly charged with peace activities in Home Missions and Ministries, he had nevertheless often written and spoken about peace. In his estimation, it represented the central contribution the Brethren could make to other Christian bodies and to the society. His significant involvements with peace action and educa- tion will be described in a later chapter.

The new position also brought Zigler into administrative alignment with the colleges affiliated with the Church of the Brethren. The General Education Board provided liaison between the church and the colleges related to it. It was composed of the presidents of the six colleges and the seminary.

Originally the educational committee had been made up of elders who were charged to inspect the colleges to see that they were run in harmony with the teachings and practices of the church. This proved to be too restrictive for the schools, who managed eventually to have the composition of the board limited to their own people.

Colleges as Research Centers

Zigler saw the colleges as key institutions in building a strong denomination. They provided a concentration of specialists in many fields, whose expertise should be called on by the church to help answer urgent problems as veritable think-tanks, to use a modern phrase. One of his most creative ideas of the mid-1930s was to ask the several college faculties to take on thematic areas, develop unified positions, and then publish the findings for the use of the church. He called it the *College Faculty Research Commission*. His vision was that the historians could provide the background on each theme, the psychologists and sociologists could contribute from their perspectives, and the theologians from theirs. Dramatists and musicians could produce artistic ways to interpret the findings to the people. College presidents had contacts with local congregations to facilitate the dissemination of the research data.

Somewhat arbitrarily, he asked Juniata to focus on family life ("Building the Ideal Home"), McPherson on economics ("Making a Christian Living"), Manchester on peace ("The New Patriotism"), Elizabethtown on rural life ("Rural Factor in Civilization"), Bridgewater on temperance ("The Efficient Life"), and La Verne on problems of individuals ("Creative Personalities"). He assigned Bethany the task of developing the "Message of the Church." The overall title was: "Frontiers of Faith." Several publications in fact emerged from the initiative, although the press of his other duties kept Zigler from following up as he planned with the colleges. The book, *Home Builders of Tomorrow*, by Warren D. Bowman of Juniata College was widely distributed and often reprinted, and it brought Bowman a reputation as an authority on the family.

One place the idea worked brilliantly was at Manchester College. This assignment stimulated C. Ray Keim and L. W. Shultz to mount an aggressive campaign of peace education and action. Keim was central in the cooperative work with other peace groups and Shultz compiled a useful collection of statements of the Brethren on war and peace. The same initiative encouraged Ira Frantz and others at Manchester to create strong anti-war plays, which were widely presented in churches and communities. Zigler credited the Manchester peace emphasis with providing the basis for a strong Brethren Service program later in the decade, with active support coming from Northern Indiana. A Manchester professor of history, Andrew W. Cordier, had already begun to specialize in foreign affairs. But this assignment, in Zigler's view, was instrumental in recruiting him for later work with the Brethren Service Committee and eventually for his contribution to the United Nations.[16]

In 1938 M. R. Zigler had to make a personal decision regarding the leadership of Brethren colleges. La Verne College in California called him in late April to succeed Dr. E. M. Studebaker in the presidency. After consulting with a number of trusted advisers, Zigler wired his refusal, terming it a "very difficult decision." In an explanatory letter he gave more detail for rejecting the attractive offer: pastors he talked to depended on his knowledge of their talents and interests to receive appropriate placements; Eastern Brethren would not understand the move, causing loss of confidence in the church; H. C. Early pointed out that "the church had invested a great deal" in preparing him for his present work and he should not think of changing. He explained in summary: "I must make my decision in the light of the total church program and I have secured the very best advice possible." He added in another letter to La Verne that he had also been unable to convince himself that he had the necessary preparation for the position of college president.[17]

A major focus on the work of Christian Education was naturally on children and young people. It was often expressed as "saving the children to the church." Much that was done had the motivation of preserving the offspring of Brethren families for the church, including the elaborate series of Sunday school quarterlies and periodicals, the camping program (which proliferated at this time), the youth work, and the colleges. In Zigler's later words:

> The church was perpetuated into the future by saving our children to the church. This "saving of the children to the church" was a slogan that was present when I was selected as Home Mission Secretary. As I remember, there were several queries that came to Annual Conference about that time from different parts of the Brotherhood, indicating a feeling that they were losing their children from the church, and, therefore, there was a strong emphasis on creating the colleges, having youth camps and conferences, and even developing a youth conference along with the Annual Conference, something that did not occur previously to any great extent. This was an understanding that

the children of our families would naturally go to our colleges for their training for life beyond the farm, entering professions, mainly teaching public schools.

He continued:

The seminary was coming on, training ministers for the churches, and the colleges for the laity. The General Board organization became the center of influence, unifying the church for action, and developing the objectives and goals for the future.[18]

In retrospect, for M. R. Zigler, the later 1930s were a fruitful period. The denomination survived the cruel Depression years, energetic new leadership was emerging, the colleges were attaining academic respectability, and the membership was increasing. The Church of the Brethren could look at itself and see a small but active Protestant body that had earned the right of recognition among the better established Christian communions. This had been one of his major objectives as he came to Elgin in 1919.

NOTES

1. *Gospel Messenger* (March 14, 1931): 2.
2. J. A. Robinson, "Meeting of the General Ministerial Board," *Gospel Messenger* (Jan. 3, 1931): 20.
3. "Pastoral Conference Program," *Gospel Messenger* (Feb. 21, 1931): 21; (Sept. 12, 1931): 18; (Sept. 19, 1931): 18.
4. M. R. Zigler, "Meeting of the General Ministerial Board," *Gospel Messenger* (January 2, 1932): 12, 20. The statistics for geographical location do not give an accurate total; possibly, some of the meeting places are included along with congregations.
5. M. R. Zigler, "The Statistical Report 1932-33," *Gospel Messenger* (October 14, 1933): 6.
6. M. R. Zigler, "The Present Ministerial Situation," *Gospel Messenger* (November 26, 1932): 14-15.
7. Fern Snethen, "Caskeys Accept Joint Pastorate of Two City Churches," *Gospel Messenger* (November 12, 1932): 12; E. C. Cawley, "Our Canadian Problem," *Gospel Messenger* (June 4, 1932): 6-7, 32.
8. M. R. Zigler, "Policy on Ministerial Placement," *Gospel Messenger* (September 9, 1933): 18-20; "Annual Conference Plan on Ministerial Placement and

Policy," *Gospel Messenger* (February 13, 1937): 19.
9. Vernon Miller interview with M. R. Zigler, 2/3; M. R. Zigler, "Biographical," 8-9.
10. Harper Will to D. F. Durnbaugh, April 22, 1987; Merlin Garber to D. F. Durnbaugh, May, 1987.
11. Rufus D. Bowman to M. R. Zigler, April 18, 1937 (Bowman Papers, Bethany Theological Library).
12. Zigler to Bowman, April 16, 1937; Bowman to Zigler, April 19, 1937; Zigler to Bowman, April 20, 1937; H. L. Hartsough [member of General Ministerial Board] to Zigler, April 22, 1937; Bowman to Zigler, April 25, 1937; Zigler to L. W. Shultz [at North Manchester, Indiana], April 26, 1937 (Bowman Papers).
13. Warren D. Bowman to M. R. Zigler, November 16, 1966.
14. Miller interview, 17a/1.
15. *The United Program of the Church of the Brethren in Ministry and Education* (Elgin, IL: The General Boards, n.d.). Staff members listed besides Zigler, were Ruth Shriver, Leland S. Brubaker, D. D. Funderburg, Dan West, and E. G. Hoff.
16. Interview with M. R. Zigler, Sebring, Florida, June 9, [?] 4/11-12. See also: M. R. Zigler to the College Faculty Research Commission, Sept. 10, 1935; Rufus D. Bowman to M. R. Zigler, Dec. 16, 1937; M. R. Zigler to Rufus D. Bowman, May 3, 1938 (Bowman Papers); L. W. Shultz, *People and Places, 1890-1970: An Autobiography* (Winona Lake, IN: Life and Light Press, 1971), 65.
17. Edgar Rothrock to M. R. Zigler, April 20, 1938; Zigler to Rothrock, April 25, 1938; Rothrock to Zigler, May 3, 1938; Zigler to Rothrock, May 9, 1938.
18. Miller interview, 6/2.

8

ECUMENICAL OUTREACH

ZIGLER WENT TO ELGIN to begin church work with an orientation toward cooperative work with other denominations. This pattern had already been set by his formative work with the YMCA. He found that the small Elgin staff was itself committed to this approach. The earliest official cooperation had developed in the late nineteenth century by Brethren working with the interdenominational committee producing Sunday school materials. Early Brethren activity in foreign lands conformed to the cooperative principle of comity. Also, just as he arrived in late 1919, the administrative leaders at Elgin were involving the Brethren in the most ambitious ecumenical effort yet launched in the USA.

The Interchurch World Movement

This was the Interchurch World Movement (IWM). Spurred by the cooperation of mainline churches during World War I and reflecting activist notions of the leading role now played by the USA in world affairs, IWM was generated in 1918 on a wave of optimism and idealism. It was a veritable crusade akin to Wilsonian dreams of ridding the world of war and making the world safe for democracy. And, like the president's dreams, the expansive ecumenical movement also foundered on the rocks of reality.

The intent was to organize Protestantism into a crusade of evangelism and world missions, using modern business and promotional techniques. Thorough research by skilled investigators would provide the data; coordination of otherwise scattered denominational energies would multiply efforts; millions of "friendly citizens"—business and professional people—would be reached to provide additional funding. The target was to raise no less than $336 million, an unprecedented and mind-boggling sum. Seasoned church administrators were swept up in the challenge and enthusiasm of the project. They reasoned that the United War Work Campaign of the YMCA had raised $230 million, and their cause was even better.

A huge staff (by May, 1920, numbering 2,612 employees!) was set in motion to realize the purpose of the IWM: "To present a unified program of Christian service and to unite the Protestant churches of North America in the performance of the common task, thus making available the values of spiritual power which come from unity and coordinated effort and meeting the unique opportunities of the new era." Immediate funds were secured by borrowing against denominational pledges; the plan was that program costs of an estimated $8 million would eventually be covered by the $40 million expected to come from the "friendly citizens." The movement organized itself on national, state, county, and township levels, intending to reach every local church; conventions were held on every level to develop interest and support.[1]

In September, 1919, the Joint Boards (the coordinating committee for the Church of the Brethren) endorsed the project and voted to cooperate with it "in so far as is consistent with the spirit of our people." Because of intense pressure from the IWM leaders, the Joint Boards agreed in January, 1920, to relate the denominational Forward Movement to the Interchurch World Movement, subject to approval by Annual Conference. Shortly thereafter a legal commitment was made to pledge five percent of the board's anticipated income for the next year. Persuaded by the IWM agents to make a generous estimate of this greatly increased expectation, the pledge amounted to $50,000.[2]

M. R. Zigler soon became involved with the activity. His first business trip was with J. H. B. Williams to New York City to attend an IWM meeting. He wrote an informal report to his mentor, H. C. Early, who was unable to be at the meeting. His assessment was both enthusiastic and cautious, and curiously prophetic:

> I have just returned from the offices of the I.C.W.M. and I want to tell that it is an immense proposition. The results of the movement is going to be great— either it will be a tremendous success or a great failure. ... It looks to me that if possible we ought to know pretty definitely where we are in the I.C.W.M. If we can go in and are [ready], then we ought to get busy. If we won't and are

not then I can rest easy. I know that down through the States many of our people are on Committees, so it looks that we are going into [it] and, if we are in the local congregations and districts our head office should sur[e]ly decide what to do.

Early expressed keen pleasure in receiving the letter: "I was more than glad for the very splendid letter you write. It makes a grey head feel good to have such a letter from one of his boys. I wish I could tell you how much I appreciate the spirit of the letter."[3]

The Annual Conference of 1920 censured the Elgin officials for committing the denomination to IWM and mandated withdrawal from the movement, after paying its obligation. Instead of paying a percentage of their actual receipts, the Brethren were held to a percentage of their *requests*, a much larger figure. As Zigler recalled the amount, it was for $100,000, almost a dollar per member. He stated that the treasurer of the General Mission Board, Clyde Culp, kept the framed check above his desk for many years. This happened shortly before the over-extended movement itself completely collapsed.

Chief among the reasons for failure was the shift from Wilsonian idealism to a mood of disillusion, cynicism, and reaction. There was insufficient attention given to denominational needs by the IWM staff, caught up in their own program. Fundamentalist voices attacked the "modernist" theology underlying the movement. A controversial IWM investigation of a steel strike at Gary, Indiana, alienated the support of business people. Instead of raising $40 million from this category, only $3 million were raised. (For their part, the denominations raised $176 million.) The rising tide of liberal Protestant thought that contended the kingdom of God could be realized with goodwill and united effort gave way to a chastened understanding of the increasing skepticism among the populace about the church.

This episode drastically set back the willingness of the Brethren to participate ecumenically, delaying full conciliar involvement for two decades. At the 1920 conference, when elections were held for the General Mission Board, there were a few votes against the reelection of H. C. Early, because of the Interchurch World Movement debacle. He had been used to unanimous support, and, taking the minor opposition as evidence of loss of confidence, he resigned from the board. Zigler called the failure a "disaster," stating that "it did not kill the desire to work together, but it was so disappointing that no one wanted to trust any movement of cooperation again."[4]

88

Home Missions Council

The unhappy outcome of the IWM venture, however, did not dampen Zigler's desire to work ecumenically. From the beginning, he understood his task in interdenominational relationships as two-fold: first, to coordinate Brethren activities with other churches, as he had learned to do in his YMCA work; second, to represent the Brethren in ecumenical circles so that the denomination would receive increased respect and attention. Generally, Brethren were little-known or considered to be a sect. His concern was to work in such a way that the Brethren would take their place alongside other communions: "I personally believed that the hour had come for the Brethren to seek the cooperation of other denominations and became very active in every movement possible, always representing the peace of the world in the name of Christ through this church. . . ."[5]

The record shows that from the first he sought to relate the Brethren program to the larger cause of Protestant activity. In 1920 he attended (initially in the role of an observer) a meeting of the Chicago-based Home Missions Council of America, founded in 1908 to replace the fierce competition between denominations by cooperative efforts. The Council specifically sought to allocate mission areas among the churches and foster other cooperative programs. Zigler soon became a member and in 1937-1938 was the chairman of the council.

He liked to repeat the advice given to him by Otho Winger, a leading churchman then chairman of the General Mission Board. Zigler asked him about attending ecumenical meetings and received this reply: "Don't ask us. If you ask us, we'll have to say no, so go. If you pull some kind of boner, we'll fire you and if you make good, we'll take the credit."[6]

The council gave him little encouragement about finding areas where the Brethren might develop their home missions work; a recent study of theirs showed that all areas along the Mexican border had been allocated by the rules of comity. Further, a survey of Indian reservations indicated that they had all been assigned, except one area assigned originally to a Lutheran body that was later rejected. Zigler said the Brethren were not interested in an area the Lutherans turned down. The geographical areas with black populations had also been occupied.

Then, because the Brethren were primarily a rural people, Zigler asked about the possibility of locating an area of unchurched farm population. The Council was at the point of beginning a survey of the state of North Dakota and invited him to participate in it. He spent several weeks traveling by car with representatives of the Congregationalist, Baptist, and Methodist churches. Their method was to drive to a church in the afternoon, ring the church bells, and there would be a full house at 7:00 P.M. despite no prior announcement. Even this method did not produce an area that seemed promising for the establishment of new Brethren congregations.[7]

The opinion of friendly home Missions Secretaries was that in view of the limited Brethren membership "it would be better to strengthen our congregations and center on few projects and give Foreign Missions our major thrust because our getting into the expansion movement was too late in the United States, considering the heavy competition."[8]

Federal Council of Churches

Besides working with the Home Missions Council, Zigler sought contact with a wide range of other ecumenical bodies. Although the Brethren were not yet a member of the Federal Council of Churches (FCC), he began to work with some of their agencies. Between World War I and World War II, the FCC developed a strong pacifist position; this made it easier for Brethren to relate to it. Brethren representatives consistently attended peace meetings called by the Federal Council.

M. R. Zigler often published FCC statements in the *Gospel Messenger*. A typical message was the Council's call to "Penitence and Prayer" for the week of October 2-8, 1932. Referring to the sufferings of the Depression era and the need for spiritual recovery, the statement confessed that Americans had worshipped at the altars of false gods—mammon, power, nationalism, pleasure, success, and magic. "The Church dares not stand aside and whisper peace either to itself or to the nation when there is no peace. . . . No social or political revival can come out of spiritual destitution, and no national awakening can arise out of religious indifference. The only adequate way is the way of Christ and the Cross."[9]

J. Quinter Miller, Zigler's close friend and a Brethren member, was an associate secretary of the Council and kept Zigler well-informed on its activities. They took counsel as to how the Church of the Brethren could be motivated to join formally in the FCC work, despite the continuing negative memories of the Interchurch World Movement. Finally, in 1941 the time seemed ripe to introduce a resolution to this effect at the Annual Conference scheduled to be held at La Verne, California. Zigler was a key player in the process.

He suggested that the church's Advisory Committee on Conscientious Objection bring a recommendation that the Brethren join the FCC on the grounds that the latter had been very helpful in the process of securing legislation to assure the rights of conscience. Other members of the committee agreed and a resolution, drafted by Zigler, was presented to the Council of Boards, who approved it and sent it to the Standing Committee of the conference. In Brethren polity, this body was authorized to prepare business items for the conference, accompanied by recommendations for conference action.[10]

J. Quinter Miller had also taken an initiative along the same line and was invited to interpret to Standing Committee what membership in the FCC entailed. In the process, a significant addition was made at the suggestion of M. R. Zigler; this was that language should be included that would authorize the Church of the Brethren to become a member in due time of the World Council of Churches, then in process of formation. As early as July 8, 1938, soon after the agreement was reached in principle to form such a world council, Zigler had written to the chief American churchman involved in the process, asking for copies of the proposed WCC constitution. He confided that he wanted "to do some careful planning to build up an interest in the World Council." That would take care because the Brethren still remembered their bad experience with the Interchurch World Movement of 1920. Zigler saw this method as a way of securing favorable action on the part of the denomination.[11]

After lengthy discussion, the Standing Committee accepted the resolution by a vote of fifty-three to eight and sent it to the floor of conference. It met with scattered resistance, primarily from the small Fundamentalist wing of the church, who claimed that the decision was sprung on the church, without going through the normal query process. The most suspicious supposed that the time and place had been calculated; conferences on the West Coast were not as well attended, because of the distance from the bulk of Brethren membership. That area was also thought to be more liberal in their views and thus more receptive to conciliar affiliation. After vigorous debate, a large majority of the delegates voted their approval.

The resolution adopted pointed out that the Brethren had shared unofficially for many years in the FCC program, and that the Council had actively supported peace movements in the nation and around the world. It explained that joining the FCC would not bind the church to any action and would not compromise its doctrinal position. Zigler, Miller, and their friends rejoiced in the action, so long in coming. Their victory marked the successful end of a long and patient campaign.

World Council of Churches

The birth of the World Council of Churches came through the union of two ecumenical movements—Faith and Order and Life and Work. They emerged in the early twentieth century as a result of many influences— growing cooperation in mission enterprises (highlighted by the landmark World Missionary Conference at Edinburgh in 1910), international student work, peace organizations, even revival movements. Faith and Order dealt with issues of belief and church practice, hoping that agreement on these basic points could smooth the way to eventual union of the divergent church bodies. Life and Work had as its motto —"Creeds divide; deeds unite." Its advocates stressed the urgent needs facing the world in the wake of the Great War and sought to move the churches to aggressive action to solve society's problems—war, economic privation, human rights, and the rest. The liberal social action agenda of Anglo-American church leaders was influential, although the outstanding personality involved was Archbishop Nathan Soederblom of Sweden.

In the 1930s it became increasingly clear to thoughtful ecumenists that the concerns of both movements had to be brought together. It was not realistic to focus solely on the issues of doctrinal and sacramental unity, given crying human need in the wake of the Depression. On the other side, Life and Work enthusiasts soon realized that they could not reach agreement on how to approach pressing social issues of the day if they could not find an agreed theological base on which to stand. The answer was to unite the two. The vehicle adopted was to plan the two separate international conventions slated for the summer of 1937 in such a way that those attending one could attend the other as well. Consequently, the carefully prepared Life and Work conference was scheduled for Oxford, England, on July 12-26 and the Faith and Order conference in Edinburgh on August 3-18. The idea of union was to be presented to both meetings, with the hope that a joint committee could then move forward expeditiously to create a new and united body, which was to be named the World Council of Churches.[12]

The Council of Boards, at Zigler's urging, considered the possibility of sending a representative to these meetings and decided to do so. The Men's Work of the church undertook the task of raising the necessary funds. An editorial in the *Gospel Messenger*, written by Harry A. Brandt, gave some of the rationale. After describing the purposes of the Oxford World Conference on Church, Community, and State—"to face the grave issues which confront the world today, and to consider the responsibility of the church to them"—the editor sought to dispel the reactions of Brethren who thought that the distant conference did not concern them:

> We do have an interest in the Oxford Conference and that because it is to face issues which we cannot wholly escape. But our stake in the Oxford Conference is something far more important than merely the gaining of advance information. It is rather that of sharing something on our part. There are ideals which have been the heart of our testimony for more than two centuries. We have a philosophy of life that is being appreciated more and more by others—if not by ourselves. We have something to contribute in the current crisis situation.[13]

The Council of Boards, with the approval of the Standing Committee meeting prior to the Annual Conference held in Nampa, Idaho, chose Zigler to go. At the conference, they called Zigler to the platform, announced that he had been chosen to represent the Brethren and was leaving that afternoon, accompanied by Amy Zigler (whose way was to be paid by contributions from the Women's Work). The assembled Brethren gave the Chautauqua salute with their handkerchiefs and sang "Speed Away," for the Ziglers an unforgettable and moving experience.

As it happened, immediately prior to this Zigler had just endured one of his most painful experiences. The General Board of the church met at Nampa to consider its business. He had gone out on a limb in the weeks before Annual Conference to raise funds for relief of victims of the Spanish Civil War. His method had been to send out postcards asking for contributions to every subscriber of the *Gospel Messenger*. Members of the boards of the Foreign Mission and Christian Education programs knew that he had not had clearance for the action and complained bitterly. The response had been quite good (more than $10,000 by conference time) which, if anything, increased his anxiety. Zigler genuinely feared that he would not be permitted to go to the United Kingdom for the conferences. His comment: "I think this experience made me more nervous than anything else in my lifetime;" it left him feeling "guilty and helpless, but at the same time successful."[14]

From the dock where the S. S. Bergengaria was moored, Zigler sent a message to the church for publication in the *Gospel Messenger*:

> We feel a keen sense of responsibility to serve as representatives of the Church
> of the Brethren at the Oxford Conference. . . . There is a possibility that we will
> attend part of the Edinburgh Conference. . . . At the request of the General
> Mission Board we will spend two weeks among the churches of Denmark and
> Sweden.
>   . . . It is our desire to represent worthily the faith of our church. We wish
> it would be possible to write a letter to everyone who has helped to make it
> possible for us to serve. Time will not allow us to do this; therefore we hope
> through this message to express our deepest and sincerest gratitude, and to ask
> an interest in your prayers that we may do the work assigned us in the Spirit
> of Christ. Robert and Amy Zigler.[15]

Zigler also planned to take the opportunity of being in Europe to meet
Dan West in Paris on his way to do relief work with the Friends in Spain
and to inspect for himself the relief needs in that country torn by a bitter
civil war.

Traveling to Oxford for the July conference was an awe-inspiring
event for Zigler, who later articulated his sense of inadequacy. A note to
a friend in Elgin confessed: "This town is so full of history that as an
awkward American I am in constant fear that I'll step on some sacred
spot." There were about twenty professed pacifists in attendance; the
conference management was cautious about the possibility of a passionate
message from them upsetting the conference, most of whose delegates
accepted the traditional *just war* doctrine. The conference met at a time of
great international tension; delegates from the Confessing Church in
Germany were not permitted to attend, and the two German representatives from the Free Churches did so only at the cost of making positive
statements about the condition of the churches in Nazi Germany.[16]

Pacifists were assigned to a small meeting place and were watched,
according to Zigler's later account, by no less than the Archbishop of
Canterbury, whose briefcase was being carried by a young theologian
named W. A. Visser 't Hooft. The latter, of course, became the executive
of the World Council of Churches "in process of formation" between 1938
and 1948 and then the longtime WCC general secretary.

Zigler presented the Brethren statement—and a Mennonite one as
well—and an American Quaker presented one from the Religious Society
of Friends. Despite the feeling of the pacifists that their contribution was
not fully appreciated, the final Oxford document made a significant
forward step in terms of official church pronouncements on war. It
recognized the position of conscientious objection as one of the three

legitimate positions available to Christians and urged that those holding divergent views meet together to find God's purpose. Zigler's attitude was that the Brethren would not accept every part of the final Oxford statement, but that the positive aspect was that people with such varied views could agree on a common statement.

For a formal worship service at Oxford, M. R. Zigler wore a robe for the first time. He reported on the sermon given at the conclusion of the Oxford Conference, at which members of the Faith and Order Conference also took part. The sermon, by the Archbishop of Canterbury, urged the uniting of all the world's churches. Zigler commented: "No doubt but this occasion will mark a point in church history that should be significant if the spirit of this meeting is carried around the world." He also noted the challenge in worshipping with Christians exiled for their faith from their own countries. "It is essential that the Church of the Brethren as well as all other Christian bodies in free countries give a helping hand to those who suffer."[17]

After several days at Edinburgh with Faith and Order, the Ziglers left to visit the mission churches in Scandinavia. They were kept to a busy timetable. Their schedule on Sunday, August 15, ran: 8:30 A.M., breakfast; 11:00, church; 12:30 P.M., refreshments; 2:00, dinner; 4:00, refreshments; 7:00, church services, meeting with young people; 8:30, refreshments; 9:00, closing services. They were hosted by J. F. and Alice Graybill, veteran Brethren missionaries in Denmark and Sweden.

At first Zigler found speaking through an interpreter a difficult task but soon got used to it. It was awkward for him not to be able to converse with worshipers following the service, but he found that smiles and handclasps spoke a universal language. He stayed in Sweden for a week, visiting all of the congregations and attending a meeting of the District Board. The Graybills then took the Ziglers by car and ferry to visit the Brethren in Denmark for four days. In an article describing his experiences, Zigler called on the church in America to continue their support for these friendly people.[18]

Following their visit to Danish Brethren, the Graybills and Ziglers together drove to Germany to visit Schwarzenau, a first for all of them. They met the cordial local pastor, Karl Pabst, who showed them the site at the "Valley of Huts" where the Brethren had erected temporary shelters. The visitors were shown an old Bible with marginal notes, in the possession of a Schwarzenau family, said to have been in use by the dissenters in the early eighteenth century. Some local people believed the annotations were in the hand of E. C. Hochmann von Hochenau, the man who "awakened" those who became the early Brethren. According to J. F. Graybill, the visitors felt that they were on "holy ground," for here the "first saints of the Church of the Brethren met to study the Word of God and find the more perfect way of the Lord."[19]

After leaving the Wittgenstein area, the party did some sightseeing, and traveled to Lutheran sites at Eisenach and Wittenberg before reaching Berlin. The Graybills then said goodbye to the Ziglers on August 29, 1937, and returned to Sweden. In later life, M. R. Zigler told of their experience in visiting the stadium in Berlin, the scene of the 1936 Olympic Games, where Jesse Owen, the black American track star, was snubbed by Hitler. The Ziglers' visit coincided with the celebration of the anniversary of Berlin's founding. Hitler and his entourage arrived with great drama. The brilliant lights had been extinguished and suddenly down a long corridor came the Führer, after which the lights were gradually turned on again. The assembled masses gave their frenzied "Heil Hitler" salutation. The Ziglers did not and received hostile looks from those around them. From this and other experiences, Zigler came back warning that a war was soon to come. He intensified his efforts at peacemaking.

Following Berlin the Ziglers went to Geneva where they visited the League of Nations; they also went to Rome where their passports (with visas) were stolen. Although the consulate provided new passports, the visas could not be replaced; this meant that Zigler could not follow his plan to accompany Dan West into Spain to inspect relief needs. He did meet with the Brethren relief worker in Paris and discussed the program with others in France. The Ziglers finally arrived home on October 8, where both were invited to speak to the Elgin congregation.[20]

Zigler's correspondence following his return demonstrates his commitment to align the denomination with the emerging ecumenical movement. He was alert to seize every opportunity to bring the Brethren on board. As we have seen, it was largely owing to his initiative that the Brethren in 1941 voted to join the WCC when it actually formed; for Zigler, this was the first time the Brethren were able to be on the ground floor of a cooperative endeavor.[21]

During the European trip, Zigler had sent on official messages from the conferences for publication in the *Gospel Messenger*. Unfortunately, a long article he had sent giving his own interpretations of these actions was lost in transit. And the burden of accumulated work made it impossible for him to spend time redrafting it.

In some ways, more important than these communications was the impact of the European travel on Zigler himself. It alerted him to the tremendous needs that war had already brought and to threat of wider conflict. The trip steeled his nerves to give leadership to the church in meeting those needs. There had been criticism of his selection as the Brethren representative to the ecumenical conferences, and he readily admitted that there were much better theologians around who could have gone. Yet, for many, it seemed providential that this formative experience came his way. It set the course for much of his future ministry and, through him, the course of the Church of the Brethren.

NOTES

1. Eldon G. Ernst, *Moment of Truth for Protestant America: Interchurch Campaigns Following World War I* (Missoula, MT: 1972); Robert T. Handy, *A Christian America: Protestant Hopes and Historical Reality* (New York: Oxford University Press, 1971), 186-197. Originally, the movement was known as the *InterChurch World Movement* and used the initials ICWM. The YMCA campaign is noted in Charles E. Harvey, "John D. Rockefeller, Jr., and the Interchurch World Movement of 1919-1920," *Church History*, 51 (1982): 198-209.
2. Roger E. Sappington, *Brethren Social Policy, 1908-1958* (Elgin, IL: Brethren Press, 1961), 53-55; Edward K. Ziegler, "Interchurch World Movement," *Brethren Encyclopedia* (1983-1984), 658..
3. M. R. Zigler to H. C. Early, Jan. 12, 1915; Early to Zigler, Jan. 15, 1920; Million transcript of M. R. Zigler, 4/1-6.
4. Vernon Miller interview with M. R. Zigler, 6a/1.
5. Miller interview, 6/3.
6. Miller interview, 3/6; C. Wayne Zunkel, "M. R. Zigler: Rebel with a Cause," *Bulletin of the* [Manchester College] *Peace Institute*, 6 (August, 1976): 1-4. Zigler repeated the story often, with somewhat different phrasing each time.
7. Million transcript of M. R. Zigler, 3/8-10.
8. M. R. Zigler, "To Work for Peace Through the Churches, *Messenger* (Nov. 21, 1968): 4.
9. "A Week of Penitence and Prayer To Be Observed Throughout America, Oct. 2-8," *Gospel Messenger* (Sept. 17, 1932): 18.
10. See the discussion in Sappington, *Social Policy* (1961), 70-72, 117-119; Zigler discussed his role in several interviews, for example, Million transcript of M. R. Zigler, 2/8-10, 7/18-23.

11. M. R. Zigler to Dr. Henry Smith Leiper, July 8, 1938.
12. Ruth Rouse and Stephen Charles Neill, eds., *A History of the Ecumenical Movement* (London: SPCK, 1954), 431-437, 587-592.
13. Harry A. Brandt, "Our Stake in the Oxford Conference," *Gospel Messenger* (June 12, 1937): 3-4.
14. M. R. Zigler, "People I Met Along the Way," unpubl. essay, 9.
15. *Gospel Messenger* (July 17, 1937): 16.
16. *Gospel Messenger* (Aug. 7, 1937): 16.
17. D. F. Durnbaugh, ed., *On Earth Peace: Discussions on War/Peace Issues Between Friends, Mennonites, Brethren, and European Churches, 1935-1975* (Elgin, IL: Brethren Press, 1978), 33-37; M. R. Zigler, "The Oxford Conference Closes and the Edinburgh Conference Begins," *Gospel Messenger* (Aug. 28, 1937: 15, 21. See also his articles, "Church, Community and State," *Gospel Messenger* (Sept. 11, 1937): 13-15; "The Church and the Economic Order," *Gospel Messenger* (Sept. 18, 1937): 6-7; "The Church and War and the World of Nations," *Gospel Messenger* (Sept. 25, 1937): 6-7; "The World Conference on Faith and Order," *Gospel Messenger* (Oct. 16, 1937): 6-8.
18. *Gospel Messenger* (Sept. 4, 1937): 4; M. R. Zigler, "Sweden and Denmark," *Gospel Messenger* (Oct. 9, 1937): 5-6.
19. J. F. Graybill, "Consolation for Those Who Wait," *Gospel Messenger* (Oct. 30, 1937): 15, 18-19; M. R. Zigler, "Schwarzenau Today," *Gospel Messenger* (Oct. 2, 1937): 5-6. Years later Zigler purchased the Schwarzenau Bible and donated it to the church library and archives.
20. Vernon Miller interview with M. R. Zigler, December, 1980, 19; *Gospel Messenger* (Oct. 16, 1937): 16.
21. After he gave his report on the conferences back in Elgin, the Council of Boards appointed a committee to study "the problems that have come out of the World Conferences, with a view of making practical suggestions for our church;" its members were V. F. Schwalm, Rufus D. Bowman, J. Quinter Miller, and F. E. Mallott. Zigler sent letters to these men on: Nov. 11, 1937; Jan. 14, 1938; and May 20, 1938. It was clear from them that Zigler was eager to move the Brethren into the ecumenical orbit.

9

MORE
ECUMENICAL OUTREACH

INVOLVEMENT IN VARIOUS levels of the conciliar movement did not exhaust M. R. Zigler's efforts with other denominations and agencies. In fact, some of his most effective work reached outside of organized religious circles. His entree was through the Brethren identity as a church predominantly based in rural areas.

Rural Church

Zigler's response to the evident lack of success in using the comity route to develop a Home Missions program in rural areas and to the counsel of the Home Missions Council "to stay with work within the Brethren orbit" was two-fold: he did concentrate on strengthening the large majority of Brethren congregations that were rural-based. But beyond that, he reached out to a wide variety of religious, secular, and government agencies to promote the welfare of Brethren and other rural dwellers. In some ways, this was his most ecumenical work—taking ecumenical in its broadest sense, not limiting it to cooperative work among the churches.

An early initiative was denominational schools for rural pastors, organized with the cooperation of Bethany Bible School. One of the first was held in Chicago early in 1924.[1] A photo of the gathering, which was well attended, shows Zigler in the top row wearing plain Dunker clothes. Also, he encouraged Brethren pastors to enroll in schools for rural church leaders held on university campuses; these were accredited by the Rural Life Committee of the Home Missions Council. He had special connection, as mentioned earlier, with the one sponsored by Vanderbilt University at Nashville, Tennessee.

The philosophy he followed is seen in a brief statement he wrote in 1941, asserting that any fellowship that hopes to exist for a long time must base itself in rural areas; he felt the story of the Brethren since their arrival in America proved the point:

> We bought excellent land or improved impoverished fields. Over several generations we constructed excellent farm buildings. The equipment of our homes and farms has been the best available. Family life and religion within these homes have been the secret of our integration. We have demonstrated that a family can live on a small acreage and possess the essentials of life. We know that local congregations can, by practicing the laws of mutual concern, build a strong and stable community that will survive. We have practiced in many areas the art of passing on land from one generation to another without loss to the church or to the family. Our land and homes in true faith are as sacred to the kingdom of God as the church building and grounds. We should not lose the art of building strong, Christian, rural communities capable of surviving through centuries.[2]

Zigler often pointed to the Waterloo, Iowa, Church of the Brethren as a case in point. It had been selected by a national survey as a model rural congregation for its attention to broad community concerns and to the welfare of all its members. It took particular pains to assist young farmers in finding land and getting started. This program was picked up by other congregations and then by the church at large.[3]

An editor of the *Christian Century* noted in 1943 a Brethren program to preserve farm families. This was a loan fund designed to aid young people in establishing themselves on farms. "The leadership of the Church of the Brethren has refused to accept the . . . drift to the cities as foreordained, inevitable or a move toward a larger life. [It] is wisely unresponsive to the superficial glamour of the cities and is helping its youth to push roots even more deeply into the American soil." The editorial concluded that by helping farmers buy land and begin Christian homes, Brethren were "undertaking the Christian mission to rural America on a level far more fundamental than that on which most home mission programs move."[4]

The comment captures the persistent goal that Zigler followed in his rural church emphasis. He was not only concerned with the spiritual life of farmers, he also wanted to work on the most basic issues of land use, economics, and survival. He wrestled with the problems of tenancy, of bankruptcy, of young people not returning to the farm after college training, of unfair taxation policies. To do this in a thoughtful, productive way, he sought help wherever he could find it.

One agency he worked with was the Farm Foundation, centered in Chicago. He had heard its president speak; this was Dr. Henry Taylor, formerly an adviser on agriculture to the US and Italian governments. Zigler secured an interview; he recounted his approach and the aftermath:

> I went to see him in his office in one of the high buildings overlooking Lake Michigan. . . . I told him that the Church of the Brethren was losing its land and I would like to find ways and means to be able to hold it for the Brethren communities, for the Brethren needed to continue community life and there was no better place to have community life than on the farm. He laughed at it a little bit and said, "The church wasn't worth much, why bother? Everything would be done by the government." Then he acted like he was asleep, and I didn't know whether he was awake or not, but I kept talking. Finally, I said, "I want a plan whereby a young man can buy a farm with a good wife, pay for it in his lifetime and have old-age security for him and his father and mother, if they still live." "Well," he said, "that was a good question." He would think it over.

Zigler returned to Elgin and after a few days Taylor called, asking him to go along with him to Dubuque, Iowa, to a meeting he had arranged and financed for specialists from all of the agricultural colleges of the Midwest. Taylor did not disclose that Zigler was from the church until he introduced him late in the evening session: "I think we can't agree among ourselves about the value of farms and the methods of farming and the methods of perpetuating community, but let the preacher say something."

Here follows Zigler's description of what he told the experts:

> The whole conference sounded like a church conference when different denominations get together and they had different ways of going to heaven. . . . I laid it on fairly heavy that the scientists and the educators had told the church to lay off of all fields that they belonged to and [told the church to be] responsible for and only preach the Gospel. But, I said, we are losing our farms, the economists are not winning the battle, and the sociologists can't explain exactly why we need to have farms and how to live on them and keep them. I thought the time had come when we ought to lay aside all these ideas of denominations and different theories of economics and get down to brass tacks and get something done for the sake of our youth. . . . [The] present trends at that time should change to help a young man and a wife start a farm as one of the basic principles of a future nation we hoped the United States would be.

An important representative from Iowa got up and said, "By God, that is the best preacher I've heard around talking about realistics." The Iowan continued: "He sure put us on the spot and those of us who think we're smart about all these things, we'd better get busy and get something done." The discussion became heated and serious, and a number of those attending talked late into the night with Zigler about solutions to the problem he identified.[5]

Out of this and another conference, Taylor mounted a major research effort involving members of his staff and those of the United States Department of Agriculture (USDA). Several books on the family farm were produced, giving credit to the Church of the Brethren for sparking the inquiry. Zigler became close friends with professional researchers Dr. Joseph Ackerman and Dr. Marshall Harris, although both were originally anti-church when they began their study. The Brethren leader worked closely with these men in Washington, D. C., and other places around the country.[6]

He found another ally through them in Dr. O. E. Baker, senior agricultural economist of the USDA. Baker pushed the value of the family farm, stating: "You place 10 families in a city and in 100 years their bloodstream would be finished, would not exist. But place the same number on the land and they would have 100 people to their credit." Zigler invited Dr. Baker several times to speak to Brethren gatherings. (Baker later bought land for retirement in Rockingham County, Virginia, among the Brethren and Mennonites.)[7]

Much of the cooperative work was done under the aegis of the Town and Country Committee of the Federal Council of Churches, which worked closely with the Home Missions Council. Zigler became a key worker in the committee and served as chairman in 1937 and 1938. During his two-year tenure he organized conferences across the nation focusing on the rural church. Black church leaders participated in these but had trouble finding accommodations. One national conference Zigler planned met in a black hotel in Washington, D. C., an unheard-of procedure at that time.

In the course of the conference, delegates had a meeting with Henry A. Wallace, secretary of agriculture in the Roosevelt administration and later vice president. To break the ice when the group met the secretary, a member said "You don't need to worry about us; there's Bob Zigler from a rural area, [from the] Church of the Brethren." Wallace smiled and said, "Well, I know the Church of the Brethren—the Dunkers, we call them in

Iowa." He continued wryly, "I worked for one of their elders one time and that is the hardest job I ever had in my life; those guys *work*."[8]

Zigler also developed a close working relationship with Monsignor Luigi G. Ligutti, the initiator and long-standing head of the National Catholic Rural Life Conference and the leading American expert on agriculture for the Roman Catholic Church in America. The story is told of Father Ligutti that he visited a rural parish suffering from the poverty of its soils as well as of its souls. As he spoke with the priest in his study, with its shelves burdened with theological books, Ligutti exploded: "What this parish needs is less theology and more manure!" The Brethren churchman and the Catholic leader enjoyed a hearty friendship that lasted over many decades; both jovial men, they enjoyed teasing each other. Once at a meeting of 10,000 Catholics at which he invited Zigler to speak, Ligutti confided: "I'm not going to tell them who you are, because I don't want them to know that I have a devil talking to them." Ligutti was influential later in getting the Heifer Project and the CROP programs established. Government officials were more willing to help if they could see that both Roman Catholics and Protestants were behind the programs.[9]

Father Ligutti went to Rome as the pope's permanent observer to the United Nations Food and Agriculture Organization; a biographer called him the "pope's county agent." It was he who arranged for M. R. Zigler to meet Pope Pius XII. Zigler told his friend that he didn't know how to behave at such an occasion; Ligutti replied that as a Catholic, he had to kneel and kiss the pope's ring but that Zigler should just shake his hand as he would with anyone else, which he did. Zigler used the occasion to ask the pontiff why he did not apply to war the same arguments about the sanctity of life he used to oppose abortion. Why did Catholics continue to kill other Catholics? The pope replied that Catholics were nationalistic before they were either Christian or Catholic.[10]

One of the most heartwarming episodes of Zigler's life came on July 7, 1977, in Des Moines, Iowa, when he attended the sixtieth anniversary mass of Ligutti's ordination to the priesthood. The only Protestant so honored, he was called to the platform, praised profusely by the honoree (who described the work of the Brethren in great detail), and asked to bring his greetings to the large assemblage. Ligutti's note of appreciation read:

My dear Brother Zigler:
   It was a real thrill and a treat to welcome you to Des Moines and to have you participate in the function at Saint Ambrose Cathedral. Your presence was inspiring and it was the pay off for whatever little work I did in the ecumenical

field and in the field of love of neighbour throughout the world.

You and your co-workers have inspired me all these years and I am proud of your example and of your friendship. On behalf of the people who were present, low and high, I thank you and your group for all your great work and for our friendship. May God's blessings be upon all of us in our work.

Fraternally yours in Christ,
L. G. Ligutti

It was probably because of this connection that Zigler received a special invitation from William Cardinal Baum to attend an ecumenical service of prayer and reception when Pope John Paul II visited Washington, D. C., in October, 1979. Zigler and Ligutti corresponded warmly and often over the years until the aged monsignor's death in 1983.

State Council of Churches

Linked with his wide-ranging work on behalf of members of rural churches was his election to the position of president of the Illinois State Council of Churches. He had become well-known around the state for his advocacy of better conditions for rural people.

At the time he took the office in 1939, the activity and reputation of the state body were at a low ebb. Its office facilities in Springfield were poor and its budget anemic. Zigler decided that if anything were to happen on his watch, he would have to stimulate action on the part of the two largest communions, the Methodists and the Presbyterians, who were at that time lax in their support and participation.

He made an appointment with the influential Methodist Bishop Waldorf of the Chicago area and made his pitch. He told him that he had little interest in holding an office with nothing to do and no action. He challenged him to lead the Methodists to greater involvement. The gruffly spoken bishop said that he could not personally attend state council meetings, but that he was willing to raise money. Zigler said that would be fine, although he should appoint someone as his deputy to attend meetings who had his trust, so the representative did not have to run back to the bishop for every decision. The bishop agreed.

When he approached the Presbyterians, they replied that they were soon to have a statewide meeting in Chicago and that he could have fifteen minutes on the program to speak to them. However, when Zigler arrived at the meeting, he was met by a committee who informed him that plans had been changed; he was not to have platform time but rather should meet with them. At this point, Zigler said: "Okay, if that's the way it is, I'm going back to Elgin. You asked me to speak to the assembly and I want the assembly to really join the Council of Churches as well as name some one person to be on the Board of Directors."

On hearing this ultimatum, the committee said that they would consult with the moderator; they did so and reported that the visitor could indeed speak but would only have five minutes. The following is Zigler's speech as he recalled it many years later; in its blunt, anecdotal, and effective way, it is a good example of the manner of his public speech. He began by chiding them for cutting down the time allotted to him; he had discovered the real reason for the change in time:

> When I found out that the reason for this is that you have been given free tickets to a baseball game, it made me wonder if it was worthwhile even to speak to you. What is more, when I was a child in my home community, I was told that I could attend other churches and Sunday Schools and I could invite other people to our church, but I shouldn't proselytize, just be friends, and we asked the churches not to proselytize our people. We had a Presbyterian church and Methodist, Southern Baptist, United Brethren [churches], in the village of Broadway, but the Mennonites were present in the congregation; we joined Mennonites and Brethren as farmers, as neighbors, but we didn't go to church together.
>
> When Mennonites would come to the Brethren church, they would sit way back like strangers. When the Brethren would go to the Mennonite church, we would sit back like strangers at the church service, even though by intermarriage a number of us were relatives across the lines. After church was out, we would talk in the yard of the church or, of it was raining, we would take time for it in the church.
>
> The Church of the Brethren had a salutation of a holy kiss and so did the Mennonites, but we never kissed each other. The line was drawn. We dressed nearly alike, except I could tell by their dress whether they were Mennonite or Brethren, both men and women. The Brethren men wore beards, the Mennonite men shaved.
>
> I think this is done specifically to identify, really, our presence in the community and with one another. I heard of a Lutheran church at some distance that I didn't get into; I knew there was a Catholic church in Harrisonburg, 12 miles away, and that was about it at the time.
>
> There were evangelistic meetings held in different places, in school houses, and people would then join the church they would want and it was understood that we joined churches by families. However, intermarriage changed this a bit now and then.

There was one event of a community where the Mennonites and Brethren sat together, and that was at funerals. The funeral of an individual related by marriage united and that was true with the other denominations, also, but not so directly and so specifically.

With this in my background when I was a boy growing up, the Mennonites and Brethren were called sectarians. We belonged to a sect and there were two sects, Mennonites and Brethren, and the rest of the churches were churches. I never could understand why I was called a sectarian. Nobody could explain it to me.

We didn't call ourselves a sect, as I remembered it, only we were a separate body. As I look back, the other churches behaved exactly like the Brethren church. They kept their children separated from [the others], like the Baptists and the Presbyterians kept themselves separated from the Methodists, and the Methodists were different from the Baptists, and of all of them, the Baptists were the most sectarian of all.

The Brethren believed in religious liberty, and granted it, and they asked for the freedom to be a church by itself, undisturbed. Of course, the Mennonites and the Brethren have a peace emphasis that had matured during the Civil War, where they suffered. Their barns were burned and they had suffered. Even one of our elders, probably the best-known minister in my church, a neighbor of the Zigler family, was killed by his neighbors deliberately, considering him a spy, and this is a problem to this day. But, on the other hand, I heard all these interdenominational organizations in the development of the Sunday School fight for the elimination of liquor and things like that.

I found that the other denominations preached for unity, and the Brethren, for some reason, did not take an active part in so many community affairs, that we were called sectarian because we didn't participate in the community. Of all the local people in my community, the Presbyterians preached working together as much as any of the groups.

When I got the assignment of being president of the State Council of Churches, I found that the Brethren were more cooperative than the Methodists, Baptists, and Presbyterians, and a whole host of others, and I come to you as a simple [member] of a 200,000 member church, [and as] president of the State Council of Churches, and ask for your cooperation.

Next week we are going to have a Board of Directors meeting. We want you to be present with a representative free to act for the Council and you will support him with $5,000.00 for the budget.

At this point the Presbyterians went into executive session and Zigler left. When he convened the meeting at Springfield the next week, a representative from the Presbyterians was indeed there with a check for $5,000, a significant amount at that time. The man became active in the

Council and succeeded Zigler as president.[11]

One of the achievements of his tenure on the State Council was to arrange for the visit to Illinois of the outstanding Japanese church leader, Dr. Toyohiko Kagawa. He had something of the stature in the 1930s that an Albert Schweitzer or Mother Theresa had in later decades, being known for his sacrificial service in the slums of Japan's cities. As Zigler traveled with him, the visitor quizzed him about the Brethren, being particularly appreciative as a pacifist of the Brethren peace position. He invited the Brethren to open work in Japan, but the Brethren declined because of their ongoing work in India, Africa, and China.[12]

Zigler undertook to reform the entire structure of the Council; he took as the framework the regional structure established by the state teacher's colleges, organizing the churches to meet in regions corresponding to the territory covered by their local college. Many new denominations joined the Council, its budget was greatly strengthened, a newsletter was started, the council's voice became respected in the governor's office and in the state legislature, and generally the council built up its strength in notable fashion. Both the Federal Council of Churches and the International Council of Religious Education wrote up its achievements. One well-known Illinois resident was so impressed by these accomplishment that he started a movement to draft Zigler to run for the United States Senate.[13]

It was during this same period that M. R. Zigler hit his all-time peak in ecumenical activity. At one point, while being responsible for the three denominational boards at Elgin of Ministry, Home Mission, and Christian Education, he held the following offices: member of the executive committees of the Federal Council of Churches and the Home Missions Council, observer at the Foreign Missions Conference, president of the State Council of Churches in Illinois, president of the Ministerial Association of Elgin, chairman of the District Board, and moderator of the local congregation.

Relations with Other Brethren Bodies

M. R. Zigler never believed in that definition of ecumenism which calls for adherents to love all other churches but their own. In spite of his dedication to reaching out to other churches, he wanted to make the Church of the Brethren the best church it could be. To do this, he thought its members should extend a hand of fellowship to members of the other Brethren groups. Throughout his life he preached that the division among the Brethren resulted at bottom from failure to practice the procedures of reconciliation spelled out in the classic text of Matthew 18:15ff., claimed by all Brethren as a basic scriptural guide.

He was particularly concerned for closer connections with the Brethren Church. Although in the 1880s division the Brethren Church was the "progressive element," by the 1930s the Church of the Brethren had changed so much that it was the more liberal in theology and practice. Because the Church of the Brethren now accepted all of the innovations which the smaller church had earlier championed, it seemed to many that there were no strong reasons for the separation to continue. Leading members of both groups worked through their respective Fraternal Relations committees to find ways of cooperation, looking forward to complete reunion.

At the Annual Conference of 1933 held at Hershey, Pennsylvania, a minister from the Brethren Church, C. H. Ashman, was invited to speak on denominational church life. Following him on the program, M. R. Zigler spoke on the topic of "Wholesome Denominational Cooperation." Citing the prayer of Jesus Christ for unity in John 17, he asserted that peace churches especially should emphasize those things that we hold in common rather than those on which we differ. He pointed out that there were at least seventy-two communities which had both Brethren Church and Church of the Brethren congregations, with resulting competition with each other. "It is interesting to figure out the cost of this competition—especially in the light of current mission deficits." [14]

Later that summer, Zigler wrote to Otho Winger, who had been invited as Church of the Brethren moderator to speak at the Brethren Church conference in August. "In your life is bound up so many things around which the Church of the Brethren organizes its life. You know our mission program thoroughly, our publishing interests and educational interests are at your finger tips. In you, I believe, as in no other person in the Brotherhood rests the greatest amount of confidence through the Brotherhood. I believe that the solution of this problem of merger in a large way rests in your hands. I don't know anything that will mean more to the missions of our church, to the publishing interests, etc., than a cooperative program between these two bodies." [15]

Winger's address, "A Message from the Church of the Brethren," was very well received. He used as the outline the three questions asked since the mid-nineteenth century of all applicants for Brethren baptism. He expressed his own enthusiasm for establishing closer relationships between the two sister churches. Shortly after this, members of the two Fraternal Relations Committee met. Zigler, who attended, reported to Winger that his address at the Brethren Church conference had been extremely helpful: "I do not remember of any address where the appreciation was greater than the one you gave at Winona last Saturday. You must have clarified the atmosphere tremendously, for everybody seemed to be so warm-hearted. . . . I want to express my sincere appreciation to you for the service you have rendered to both of our fraternities."[16]

Although neither side was ready to talk organic union, there was strong interest expressed in cooperation. Three areas were identified for possible common work: (1) locales where both denominations had overlapping work but weak congregations; (2) sites such as Columbus and Cleveland, Ohio, where neither had a sufficient nucleus of members to begin work but collectively could do so; and (3) cooperation in joint publications. During the next several years Zigler assiduously promoted the cause of Brethren cooperation; Charles A. Bame was the chief proponent from the side of the Brethren Church and often stayed in Zigler's home in Elgin.

The main discussions were carried on by the official Fraternal Relations Committees, but local initiatives were also taking place. In September, 1938, for example, the fourth annual "union services" of congregations affiliated with the Brethren Church and the Church of the Brethren was held in Northeastern Ohio. Twenty-two such congregations were represented. M. R. Zigler was one of the presenters, reporting on his recent visit to the Brethren birthplace of Schwarzenau. His message had the intriguing title: "Our Merging Highways."[17]

Unfortunately, there was an smashup on the ecclesiastical highway. In 1938-1939 tensions that had been building up in the Brethren Church erupted, leading to a split down through the middle of the denomination. The Fundamentalist wing, led by Louis S. Bauman of Long Beach, California, organized the Grace Brethren Church; one of their major grievances had been the interest on the part of Ashland Brethren leaders in closer ties with the Church of the Brethren. The latter's liberal theology and social activist posture were incompatible with the Grace faction's self-understanding. The willingness of Ashland leaders to discuss closer cooperation, let alone merger, with the Elgin-based body was tantamount to apostasy, in the view of Bauman and his colleagues.[18]

Once the dust had largely settled from the acrimonious schism, representatives of the Church of the Brethren and the Brethren Church (Ashland) again began meeting. A productive joint session in August,

1943, developed a long list of suggested joint activities, from combined mission efforts, to interchanges of speakers, to sharing articles in church periodicals, and on to consolidating small congregations. On the side of the Church of the Brethren, M. R. Zigler was assigned the task of bringing the plans to fruition; many of them were actually carried out.[19]

The coming of the conscription crisis of World War II was the catalyst which brought the Brethren bodies together again, seeking ways to react to the pressures of the draft on their young men. Here, M. R. Zigler was to play the central role. Later, in the 1970s, he used the friendships developed during the 1930s and 1940s as a foundation for a series of fraternal meetings with surprising results.

NOTES

1. M. R. Zigler, "A School for Rural Pastors," *Missionary Visitor* (January, 1924): 20, and "School for Rural Church Leaders," *Missionary Visitor* (March, 1924): 76, 80.
2. M. R. Zigler, "Our Brethren Colleges and Rural Heritage," *Gospel Messenger* (Nov. 1, 1941): 15.
3. For example, Million transcript of M. R. Zigler, 7/24.
4. "Church Acts to Keep Members on Land," *Christian Century* (Sept. 29, 1943): 1093.
5. Million transcript, 8/1-5.
6. Million transcript, 8/6-9.
7. Million transcript, 3/14; 8/9-11. 8. Million transcript, 8/13-16.
9. Million transcript, 3/15-17.
10. D. F. Durnbaugh interview of Hazel Peters, March 5, 1987. Raymond W. Miller, *Monsignor Ligutti: The Pope's County Agent* (Lanham, MD: University Press of America, 1981), 80-82; Miller reported that Zigler was influential in having an American pedigreed bull donated to the Vatican to upgrade the papal dairy herd. The pope accepted the gift with the remark: "This is a papal bull in reverse. We will use it."
11. Million transcript, 7/6-13.
12. Million transcript, 7/14-15; "Kagawa Visits Washington," *Gospel Messenger* (Feb. 15, 1936): 20.
13. Million transcript, 7/15-18.
14. *Gospel Messenger* (June 24, 1933): 4.
15. M. R. Zigler to Otho Winger, July 24, 1933 (Winger Papers, Manchester College).

16. Otho Winger, "Fraternal Relations," *Gospel Messenger* (Sept. 16, 1933): 5-7; Zigler to Winger, Aug. 29, 1933 (Winger Papers).
17. "Fourth Annual Union Services of the Brethren Church and the Church of the Brethren of Northeastern Ohio," *Gospel Messenger* (Oct. 8, 1938): 20-21.
18. The controversy is discussed from the Ashland point of view in Albert T. Ronk, *History of the Brethren Church: Its Life, Thought, Mission* (Ashland, OH: Brethren Publishing Co., 1968). 395-437; from the Grace point of view in Homer A. Kent, Sr., *Conquering Frontiers: A History of the Brethren Church*, rev. ed. (Winona Lake, IN: Brethren Missionary Herald, 1972), 129-170.
29. Rufus D. Bowman, "The General Conference of the Brethren Church," *Gospel Messenger* (Jan. 22, 1944): 5; see also Edward K. Ziegler, "Ecumenical Relations," in *Church of the Brethren: Yesterday and Today*, ed. D. F. Durnbaugh (Elgin, IL: Brethren Press, 1986), 190-191.

10

PEACE CONCERNS

THE LONG-RANGE GOAL of M. R. Zigler when he went to Elgin was to strengthen the peace message of the Church of the Brethren and, from that base, to make an impact on the larger society in the cause of peace. Although this formed the content of many of his messages, it was some time before this theme was part of his program responsibility. When the Board of Religious (later "Christian") Education was formed in 1928, it claimed the area of peace for itself. It was not until 1934 when Christian Education was added to his duties that peace education and action as such became a direct part of Zigler's staff work.

Naturally, with a passion for peace as large as his, it was impossible for him to suppress his convictions. Just as it was said of the old-time Dunker preachers that, no matter what the text or the title of the sermons, in due course they came to the topic of baptism by trine immersion, so did the peace cause always become a feature of M. R. Zigler's public presentations.

The first staff assignments with direct connection with peace came in the wake of refugee concerns. Brethren first became involved in international relief through the missions program, when missionaries in India and China responded creatively to crises of famine and epidemics. The first Brethren involvement with relief problems apart from the mission fields came in the immediate post-World War I era. They then responded generously to the plight of the Christian refugees from Armenia, victims of Turkish policies of deportation and extermination. Brethren gave over $267,000 to aid the Armenians and sent their first worker, A. J. Culler, to the Near East to help administer the program.[1]

This effort was originally thought of as strictly temporary, with a Relief and Reconstruction Committee organized to raise and expend the monies, but slated to be disbanded. However, this anticipated action did not take place at the Annual Conference of 1920 despite the committee's own recommendation. The committee was continued and M. R. Zigler (who had recently taken up his work as a staff member) was named to the group. He evidently had something to do with the continuation of the committee. Writing much later, H. Spenser Minnich, his colleague at Elgin and a member of the committee, reminisced: "We remember how you connived to see that our relief work was not closed down when the Armenian relief program was concluded back in the 20ties [*sic*]. You were prophetic of the days and programs ahead."[2]

At the 1921 Annual Conference, the committee again requested its discontinuation, suggesting that the work be assigned to an existing board with the machinery "to handle such funds whenever special need arises." By action of conference, the request was accepted and overseas relief assigned to the General Mission Board. In turn, the board asked J. E. Miller, M. R. Zigler, and H. Spenser Minnich to study the question of relief and report to the Board. This group recommended that the Board raise money and collect material aid for the relief of stricken Russian sufferers, with disbursement to be made through the American Friends Service Committee (AFSC) of Philadelphia. They suggested that two Brethren men be recruited to work with the Quaker distributing team in Russia but there is no record that this took place. The Board action was positive but restrained, concluding that monies should be solicited "but not to promote the campaign to the detriment of other existing work in the church."[3]

The committee continued its work throughout 1922 to collect funds and goods for both Russia and Armenia. In 1923 the appeal was expanded to collect money for relief of Germans suffering from postwar conditions, and over $6,000 was collected for that purpose. The funds were disbursed in the Erzgebirge Mountain area through German Mennonites, by a method of certificates that could be redeemed from the authorities for food. The certificates bore the label *Hilfswerk der Gemeinde der Brueder in Amerika* (Relief Work of the Church of the Brethren in America). Minnich at his own expense visited the targeted area to observe the distribution. Committee work continued on a relatively low key basis for several years. It was reactivated in the mid-1930s when wars broke out in China and Spain.[4]

Spanish Relief

The Spanish Civil War erupted in July, 1936, when rightist forces led by Gen. Francisco Franco rebelled against the socialist Second Republic. The bitterly-contested conflict, marked by atrocities committed by both sides, broadened its scope when military forces from Fascist Italy and Nazi Germany joined the rebel or Nationalist side and the Soviet Union and international volunteers joined the Loyalists. The Western democracies tried, ineffectually, to limit the carnage through the League of Nations. The war ended in late March, 1939, when the victorious Nationalist forces under Franco seized Madrid. The tremendous toll of life among the civilian population and material destruction were unprecedented in Spanish history and brought intense suffering to hundreds of thousands.

On Christmas Eve, 1936, the American Friends Service Committee, headquartered in Philadelphia, appealed to the Mennonites and Church of the Brethren as sister peace churches to join them in a concerted program of relief to civilians on both sides of the conflict. In the course of the 1930s leaders of the three denominations had developed a pattern of working closely together on issues related to peace. The Brethren were asked to contribute money and personnel to the combined program, to be administered by the AFSC.

Early in January, 1937, Zigler traveled to Philadelphia to discuss the proposed combined project with Clarence Pickett, AFSC executive. By correspondence, Zigler secured the tentative approval of the Brethren Board of Christian Education for going ahead. The board appointed Florence Fogelsanger Murphy, one of its members by virtue of her position as head of Women's Work, to represent them on a Committee on Spain working under AFSC auspices. Mrs. Murphy, the first woman of the church with an earned doctorate, lived in Philadelphia; this facilitated her work with the committee, which met virtually every week under the leadership of its executive secretary, John Reich.

Zigler, as administrator of the Board of Christian Education in Elgin, began with his staff a vigorous informational campaign to rally support for the cooperative effort. After February 20, 1937, almost every issue of the *Gospel Messenger* carried an appeal for funds or information about the Spanish aid program. He nominated Dan West, of the Elgin staff, to be the first Brethren worker in Spain, on a short-term assignment.[5]

One of the polled members of the Christian Education board reacted vigorously against the proposed project. This was the president of the

National Council of Men's Work, L. M. Davenport. He was critical of both sides of the conflict, thought that Brethren aid (though costly to secure and deliver) would be so limited as to be worthless, and contended that Brethren moneys should rather go to undergird the mission effort. "Our organization . . . in Elgin . . . is primarily for mission work or making our Christ known to those who do not yet know the saving power of our Lord. . . . There is so much to do in our own land as well as abroad and so little to do with." He continued: "I cannot bring myself to believe—and the Spirit does not seem to have any desire to lead me to believe [—] that to go to Spain is the proper thing to do. To try to feed the children and women folks would be like a wee small drop of water hanging on the bale of a bucket which is full and overflowing."[6]

Undeterred by this one flat disapproving voice, Zigler pushed ahead, suggesting that the board's next meeting, to be held at the Nampa, Idaho, Annual Conference, should decide final policy. He rather blithely wrote the board about Davenport's objections, remarking: "I am sure that if Brother Davenport had been with us through the last few years in planning for such occasions, he would be understanding and favorable of it." Another initiative on his part put him on thin ice. He unilaterally decided to send out postcards to *Gospel Messenger* subscribers asking for contributions, which action church leaders criticized severely. In the meantime, he borrowed church funds against the anticipation of contributions to begin sending money to the AFSC. In fact, at the Nampa meeting he was upheld in both actions and excused by the emergency nature of the cause. By the fall, he had forwarded $5,000 to Philadelphia for the work of the Committee on Spain. The first cadre of relief workers under the program left for Europe in early May, 1937.

Zigler used the expertise of the AFSC officials to arrange for a Spanish visa, expecting to visit the situation at the end of his travels in Europe in the summer and early fall of 1937. Before leaving the USA, he consulted with Pickett in the AFSC offices. Because Zigler's visa was lost when his passport was stolen in Rome, he was unable to cross the French border into Spain but did consult in Paris with Dan West who had just arrived in Europe on his way to four months service on the Nationalist side of the civil war. When Zigler returned to the United States, he took up again with vigor the prosecution of the effort to raise funds and recruit personnel for Spain.[7]

The second Brethren member sent to work with the Friends was David Blickenstaff, son of missionaries serving in India. Although much younger than West, he adapted quickly to the difficult situation in Spain and was soon highly praised by AFSC administrators. They pressed, successfully, for him to extend his service in Spain, which he agreed to do, finally returning in July, 1939; he was assisted by Paul Bowman, Jr., who continued the work after he left. Both worked in Southern France, after the end of the civil war, assisting Spanish refugees. The third young Brethren worker to serve in Spain was Martha Rupel, a nurse who served in Loyalist territory. All three of these Brethren workers, then in their twenties, were called on again during and immediately after World War II to establish Brethren relief programs in Europe. They were the first of scores who eventually volunteered with what came to be known as Brethren Service.[8]

This development meshed perfectly with the advanced thinking of West, who had been urging younger Brethren to participate in social service projects not only for their own sakes but as a kind of training. He argued that such service would stand members of the church in good stead in making their case for conscientious objection from military service in the war he saw on the horizon. This view was also interpreted to the congregations. An early statement on the Spanish relief project reasoned:

> The historic peace churches—the Friends, the Mennonites, and the Brethren—have been seeking closer bonds of fellowship in their common interests. We face the possibility of having to stand side by side some day as conscientious objectors to war. And the opportunity has now presented itself to join hands in a project of humanitarian service to a war-torn area. The Friends are willing to share with us their experience and the confidence they have won, if we wish to join them in a relief project in Spain.[9]

The note sounded in the last sentence was shared by Zigler, who in correspondence and conversation with the Friends expressed appreciation for their guidance of the unexperienced Brethren in the complexities of overseas relief. Zigler wrote, for example, in April, 1939:

> You have given us an opportunity to serve. You have led the way, and it was more than generous of you to let us have a part in the great work that you have set out to do in the world. We have gone a little this way in our church. You have emphasized another way of influencing life, and you are making a great contribution to us to allow our people to be a part of your people in serving the needs of Spain.[10]

For their part, the Friends expressed gratitude for the contribution of the Brethren: for funds and material aid, for the high caliber of the seconded personnel, and for the cooperative spirit. Without the pledge and actuality of Brethren support, they could hardly have undertaken the demands of the Spanish project on top of their other responsibilities.[11]

One result of the close working pattern was a move to cement the relationship organizationally. It was done by asking Mrs. Murphy to become a consulting member of the AFSC board and by asking a Midwest Quaker, Robert Balderston, to meet regularly with the Brethren counterpart in Elgin. This began in November, 1939.

The Spanish effort set the pattern for both cooperative and denominational relief work for the Brethren, which was to expand so greatly after 1945. Even-handed distribution to victims on both sides of the conflict without determination of right and wrong, solicitation and distribution of money and material aid, enlisting of younger and older volunteers for short-term assignments, redirection of staff time and energies at Elgin, and identification of relief with peacemaking—these were all harbingers of the future. Much change was to come in creating the appropriate organizational machinery for the long term, rather than in response to emergencies.

Brethren were sensitized to world needs by reports of people they knew and trusted. Indeed, it would have been hard not to have been moved by the graphic accounts of the misery encountered, nor to understand the frustration of being able to alleviate so little of the suffering. One passage of an eloquent communication from Dan West can represent many others sent back to the USA:

> Bread! Only now am I beginning to understand the meaning of "Give us this day our daily bread." . . . Perhaps our "daily bread" today is but 100 grams—3 1/4 ounces, but father and mother pool their grams, forget their hunger and give the extra pieces to the young ones. . . . We cannot bear to think that perhaps tomorrow there will be no bread. . . . Not long ago ten, long-looked for tons of wheat arrived. The men staggered in under the weight of the big sacks and dumped them in limp piles in our warehouse. The little puffs of dust that squirted out from between the sacks as they fell, seemed to hang still and golden on the air. Yesterday the bread from the wheat came in—good bread, brown bread, wheat bread, symbol of health and strength and work, of plenty and friendship and peace.[12]

Relief Work in China

As the Brethren entered fully into the work in Spain in the summer of 1937, war broke out on the other side of the globe. In July, 1937, the Japanese army occupied Peking, beginning the long-threatened Sino-Japanese War. This had immediate repercussions for the Brethren, as their mission fields were soon enmeshed in the hostilities; by November, 1937, three stations had been captured by the Japanese armies. Three missionaries disappeared in the midst of the fighting, having been ostensibly called from their compound to bring aid; they were never heard from again. One message from a missionary read: "We hope the church will soon send relief funds. We have 800 refugees in our compound." Many Chinese calculated that they would be safer from the brutal invaders under the protection of the foreign church workers. There was immediate interest in mounting an emergency campaign among the Brethren congregations to send funds to relieve the Chinese war-sufferers, using the staff in place to administer the relief. In addition, the son of missionaries to China, Howard Sollenberger, was sent specifically to administer relief aid in August, 1938, following an exploratory visit earlier by Leland S. Brubaker.[13]

The decision was made to link this project with the Spanish project, emphasizing the nonpartisan nature of both efforts. In November, 1937, the Council of Boards authorized the staff to create one relief fund; the moneys were to be distributed according to need between China and Spain. (Later a quota of $3,000 per month for China and $1,000 per month for Spain was determined.) Thus was born the China and Spain Neutral Relief Peace Work. By February, 1939, over $26,000 had been given for China and nearly $20,000 for Spain; clothing was also sent in some quantities to Spain. There was some effort to cooperate with the AFSC on the China relief program as well.

In an article in the denominational periodical appearing in January, 1938, M. R. Zigler attempted to define the deeper meaning of the crises and the Brethren response. Its theme was "Matching Sacrifice." Referring to the three missing missionaries (about whom he had inquired at the State Department in January), he recalled that missionaries have always faced physical danger and stand ready to give their lives as courageously as do soldiers. The workers in Spain had a somewhat different concept in seeking to make a witness for peace. "In fact, they are trying to place themselves between the two sides in Spain. They are willing to give their lives to try to force that wedge of love between the lines of hate personified by the two warring factions in Spain."[14]

Zigler's point was that the Brethren at home needed to match the sacrifices of their workers abroad by (1) being willing to rise above petty differences, (2) by working harder at their tasks, and (3) by dedicating the work of their hands "to the relief of the needy." He maintained that they were "called for an extraordinary sharing if we are to match in any significant way the sacrifices that are being made by our representatives in foreign fields."[15]

Peace Action

Brethren activity to respond to human need in other countries was placed within the framework of peacemaking. Other, more direct, pacifist efforts had been increasing since the 1920s. They were marked by a concerted effort to pursue peace in tandem with other churches, specifically with the Mennonites and with the Religious Society of Friends. After a late start, M. R. Zigler became actually the central figure in cooperation for peace action.

The exigencies of conscription during World War I had brought the peace churches together. One of the more satisfactory features of a generally unsatisfactory experience with the draft system was that sixty young Mennonites were permitted to serve alongside 475 young Quakers with Friends ambulance and Reconstruction Service units in France in lieu of military participation. Some young Brethren had also applied for this alternative but were not selected.[16]

The immediate postwar years saw the beginnings of a number of conferences designed to deepen the relationship initiated through common resistance to conscription. The most comprehensive was a series with the cumbersome title Conference of Religious Bodies (Who Hold That Peace Between Nations Can Be Maintained by Following the Teachings of Jesus). The first was held at Bluffton, Ohio, in August, 1922. Those participating came from Brethren, Friends, Mennonite, Moravian, and Schwenkfelder churches. The last of these annual meetings was held at Mount Morris, Illinois, in March, 1931, as the throes of the Depression hindered meetings for a time. Although proceedings published from the series contained useful information, the primary value was enhanced fellowship among the peace groups represented.[17]

A more significant meeting was convened at North Newton, Kansas, by Mennonite leader H. P. Krehbiel on October 31—November 2, 1935. This he called an Ecumenical Council of Historic Peace Churches in North America, marking the inception of the phrase, "Historic Peace Churches." One reason for the new coinage was that, for conservative Mennonites, the term *pacifist* bore an unwanted flavor of liberal theology. The largely

119

unstructured conference created a spirit of unity among the seventy-nine participants; they agreed on the urgency of cooperative work in the face of growing international turmoil and threat. They outlined quite specific plans calling for "unified action in case the United States is involved in war." To continue the spirit and work of the Newton meeting, a Continuation Committee was named: Robert Balderston (Friend), C. Ray Keim (Brethren), Orie O. Miller (Mennonite); they were asked to meet frequently, usually about four times per year.[18]

Curiously, M. R. Zigler did not attend. He was by this time in charge of peace concerns by virtue of his post as executive for the Board of Christian Education. His absence may well have been because the Newton meeting dates conflicted with a week of staff meetings, requiring his presence at Elgin. He asked Rufus D. Bowman, former secretary of the board and longtime peace activist, to represent the Brethren officially.

Those at Newton had agreed that the peace churches had an obligation to take their message to other Christian bodies. Therefore, teams made up of a Quaker, a Brethren, and a Mennonite went to several denominational meetings within the next year. The Newton meeting also decided to send a joint delegation to President Franklin D. Roosevelt to present their peace stance. Rufus D. Bowman and Paul H. Bowman, Sr., were the Brethren delegates who helped to interview the president on February 12, 1937. (Zigler had been part of a Brethren delegation to Washington, D. C., a year earlier to present the newly-adopted Brethren statement on war to the president's secretary and to Secretary of State Cordell Hull.) The intent of the delegation of 1937 was to go on record in a timely fashion with the government about their longstanding peace witness, the peacemaking contributions they were currently making, and their view of Christian citizenship. They concluded their brief statement with the plea: "We earnestly solicit your co-operation, Mr. President, now, and if, or when a war comes in discussing and dealing with the types of service in which those of us with deep religious convictions on peace may serve in the spirit of Christ with constructive benefit to humanity and without compromise of conscience."[19]

Following 1935 there was a heightened interchange of speakers between the Historic Peace Churches on local, regional, and national levels. Peace institutes became popular; these intensive educational workshops brought competent peace leaders to academic settings for short-term instruction. Peace literature was produced (see particularly the *Pacifist Handbook*, 1939), oratorical and essay contests for young people sponsored, work camps organized, and a host of other activities started. Conferences on the Newton pattern were held each year.[20]

As the members of the peace churches came to know each other better, there were invitations across denominational lines to work in each other's organizations. Quakers were instrumental in developing the Emergency Peace Campaign in 1936. With the approval of M. R. Zigler, Dan West was released from his assignment with Brethren youth to spend one year with this ecumenical program. His primary task was recruiting, training, and sending out ecumenical teams of young pacifists in peace caravans presenting programs across the country. This proved to be very successful. He also spoke extensively on college campuses. The Friends also asked to use the services of Andrew W. Cordier, professor of history at Manchester College, hoping the college would free him for a year but still pay his salary; in this they were unsuccessful. Following West's service with the Emergency Campaign, he was seconded to AFSC for the Spanish relief program, as described above.[21]

On April 11, 1936, M. R. Zigler announced to the Church of the Brethren a comprehensive Peace Action program prepared by the Board of Christian Education and authorized by the Council of Boards. Its general objectives ("for a short period of time") read:

1. To develop a vigorous Church of the Brethren Peace Program.
2. To co-operate closely with Friends, Mennonites, and other historic peace churches.
3. To maintain relationships with other churches and organizations designed to promote goodwill and peace as may be authorized by the Board of Christian Education.

Along with the detailed program, came a letter to church leaders from Zigler. It began: "Dear Friends: Work for peace NOW!" and continued with strong admonitions to respond to the threat of international conflict with an even stronger program of peace to avoid "drifting into war." He concluded with the following paragraphs, which quite well catch the spirit and the philosophy of the denominational peace position of the time; they mirror the liberal theological position of many Brethren peace activists of the 1930s:

I have faith that there are enough good people in the world that together we can promote a vigorous program of peace and goodwill that will make our cause felt in the world of affairs. However, this program will take much work

121

and diligent effort on the part of Christian people. Many of us will have to work harder and suffer more than we have ever done for the cause of peace.

Our program does not offer a solution nor a panacea to the war demon, but it does offer a highly constructive educational program in the fine art of Christian brotherhood. Energy as well as dollars spent now will help save the wasting of mind and soul as well as billions in another war catastrophe. We believe that by uniting the peace forces we can still prevent war.

May we together as members of the Church of the Brethren reach out to new frontiers of human understanding and establish a new pattern of patriotism as lived by the Prince of Peace.[22]

The progressive position represented by Zigler's letter was not shared by all Brethren. This was evidenced by reactions such as that of L. M. Davenport reported earlier. There was also a pointed interchange in the *Gospel Messenger*, when its editors featured part of an article by Andrew W. Cordier on the cover of the January 8, 1938, issue as a faith statement titled "I Believe in Peace." It drew a response from the brilliant but eccentric leader, I. N. H. Beahm, a near-Fundamentalist. Beahm attacked the "Cordier Creed" for not recognizing the "two-kingdom teaching of our Savior." Brethren will not succeed in bringing about a peaceful world, because "universal peace can come only through universal evangelization and universal regeneration." Again, "it is only the peace of Christ that can save the world from the carnage of bloodshed, and the atrocities of battle, and the hellish destructiveness of political and carnal devastations of war."[23]

Nevertheless, enough pastors and lay members of the Church of the Brethren supported Zigler and his colleagues in their peace orientation to allow their expanded program to continue. They were thus ready to respond when a major new challenge came their way—the outbreak of World War II.

NOTES

1. Roger E. Sappington, *Brethren Social Policy*, 1908-1958 (Elgin, IL: Brethren Press, 1961), 49-52.
2. H. Spenser Minnich to M. R. Zigler, Sept. 15, 1962.
3. "Russian Relief Situation," *Missionary Visitor* (May, 1922): 131; Sappington, *Social Policy* (1961), 51-52.
4. "Clothing for Russia: A Repeated Call," *Missionary Visitor* (December, 1922):

464; H. Spenser Minnich, "German Relief Work," *Missionary Visitor* (December, 1924): 432-433.

5. M. R. Zigler to Clarence Pickett, Jan. 29, 1937 (AFSC Archives). The Spanish relief program is discussed in D. F. Durnbaugh, ed., *To Serve the Present Age: The Brethren Service Story* (Elgin, IL: Brethren Press, 1975), 107-110, 144, 166; Sappington, *Social Policy* (1961), 75-80, and Glee Yoder, *Passing on the Gift: The Story of Dan West* (Elgin, IL: Brethren Press, 1978), 89-99.

6. L. M. Davenport to M. R. Zigler, Feb. 2, 1937; Davenport to Zigler, April 10, 1937.

7. Evidence of a close cooperation between Elgin and Philadelphia is found in the AFSC archives; see also Clarence Pickett's diary for many notations, beginning in January, 1937.

8. On these developments, see Sappington, Social Policy (1961) and Durnbaugh, *Present Age* (1975). The stories of Blickenstaff, Bowman, and Rupel are insufficiently recorded; they should be written up and published.

9. "Neutral Relief in Spain," *Gospel Messenger* (April 10, 1937): 13.

10. M. R. Zigler to John Reich, April 14, 1939 (AFSC Archives).

11. Reich to Zigler, March 1, 1938 (AFSC Archives).

12. Dan West, "Saving Lives in Spain and China," *Gospel Messenger* (Dec. 17, 1938): 12, 15.

13. "War's Harvest in China," *Gospel Messenger* (Nov. 20, 1937): 17; "A Word to Ministers," *Gospel Messenger* (Dec. 18, 1937): 17.

14. "Our Mission Missionaries," *Gospel Messenger* (Feb. 5, 1938): 2; H. Spenser Minnich, "China Relief," *Gospel Messenger* (Aug. 27, 1938): 10-11. See also the brochure, *Relief in—Spain and China* [1939] asking for donation of one cent per meal.

15. M. R. Zigler, "Matching Sacrifice," *Gospel Messenger* (Jan. 8, 1938): 5-6.

16. Albert N. Keim and Grant M. Stoltzfus, *The Politics of Conscience: The Historic Peace Churches and America at War, 1917-1955* (Scottdale, PA: Herald Press, 1988), 56-62.

17. This series has not been extensively studied, but there are general descriptions in Keim and Stoltzfus, *Politics of Conscience* (1988), 62-63, and Melvin Gingerich, *Service for Peace: A History of Mennonite Civilian Public Service* (Akron, PA: Mennonite Central Committee, 1949), 25-26.

18. "Secretary's Report of the Conference of Historic Peace Churches, October 31—November 2, 1935, Newtown, Kansas (Bowman Papers, Bethany Theological Seminary); Robert Kreider, "The Historic Peace Churches Meeting in 1935," *Mennonite Life*, 31 (June, 1976): 21-24; Bowman, *Brethren and War* (1944), 267-272; Keim and Stoltzfus, *Politics of Conscience* (1988), 64-65; Gingerich, *Service for Peace* (1949), 26-27.

19. "A Message by Peace Committee of Friends, Brethren, Mennonites," *Mennonite Weekly Review* (May 27, 1936); "Historic Peace Groups at Methodist Conference," *Friends Intelligencer* (June 6, 1936): 369; Rufus D. Bowman,

Church of the Brethren and War, 1708-1941 (Elgin, IL: Brethren Publishing House, 1944), 272-273.

20. Gingerich, *Service for Peace* (1949), 28-31.
21. Ray Newton (AFSC) to M. R. Zigler, Jan. 17, 1936; Dan West to M. R. Zigler, Feb. 21, 1936; Yoder, *Passing on the Gift* (1978), 53-56.
22. M. R. Zigler, "Peace Action Program for the Church of the Brethren, 1936-1937," *Gospel Messenger* (April 11, 1936): 21-23.
23. "I Believe in Peace," *Gospel Messenger* (Jan. 8, 1938): 1, from Andrew W. Cordier, "Peace on Earth," *Gospel Messenger* (Jan. 8, 1938): 6-7; I. N. H. Beahm, "The Cordier Creed," *Gospel Messenger* (March 19, 1938): 9-10.

11

CONSCRIPTION AND
ALTERNATIVE SERVICE

M UCH OF THE IMPETUS of the 1935 meeting of the Historic Peace Churches at Newton, Kansas, had come from the foreboding sense of impending world war. In fewer than four years after the meeting, these fears were realized: Hitler's invasion of Poland on September 1, 1939, precipitated the long-postponed European conflict, which soon became international. Although strong isolationist sentiment mobilized in the USA, hampering the eagerness of the Roosevelt administration to supply war materiel to the English and French forces, it soon became clear that at some point Americans would become involved.

Delegation to President Roosevelt

Leaders of the peace churches, who had been in close touch with each other since 1935 through the Continuation Committee and other vehicles, decided that another joint approach must be made to President Roosevelt. They initiated a process of consultation and drafting of their message; this lasted from September 17, 1939, to just before the interview itself, held on January 10, 1940. The Church of the Brethren was again represented by Paul H. Bowman, Sr., and Rufus D. Bowman; they had been assisted in the preparatory work by M. R. Zigler and other Brethren leaders.[1]

Actually two messages were prepared; the first was a general statement on peace, emphasizing the work that the churches had done in worldwide relief; the second was a confidential memorandum outlining suggested procedures for the government to use in dealing with conscientious objectors. The delegates pointed out the problems both sides had experienced during World War I and recommended discussions on the issue before any declaration of war. Important sections of the second message included: the creation of a civilian board to oversee conscientious objectors (COs), service projects organized and administered by the service committees and the need for respecting the consciences of those who could not accept any form of military or alternative service—a particular concern of the Quakers. According to those present, the chief executive expressed enthusiasm for the group's proposals; he approved their suggestion that the statement be laid before the Attorney General, which took place later that same day.[2]

Conscription

The intervention by the six peace church leaders was timely. As the war loomed larger in world affairs, voices grew insistent for greater American preparedness. By the summer of 1940 Congress was holding hearings on a conscription bill, called, following long custom by the names of its sponsors, the Burke-Wadsworth bill; the formal title referred to Compulsory Military Training and Service (S-4164). The Church of the Brethren Annual Conference, held in June, 1940, asked an already existing committee to direct its efforts to defeat the bill, or failing in that, to secure adequate provisions for COs. M. R. Zigler was a key member of this Advisory Committee for Conscientious Objectors.

The peace churches quickly mounted a campaign to improve the language of the bill as it affected conscientious objectors, a campaign unprecedented in its intensity and cooperation. M. R. Zigler was the key player for the Brethren. Amos Horst and Orie O. Miller came for the Mennonites. The Friends, led by Raymond Newton and E. Raymond Wilson, as the most experienced in lobbying in the nation's capital, guided the process. Some other churches, including the Disciples, Presbyterians, Episcopalians, also participated to some degree.[3]

Years later, Zigler commented about the experiences of his hero John Kline in the depths of the Civil War, writing to his congressman to secure exemption for his fellows. Zigler said that he could empathize with Kline because of his experience: "I went through this in 1941 [1940] so I kind of feel it, what it means to be alone, up against the United States Government all by yourself, writing letters to them," such as Kline did in 1861.[4]

A room at the Commodore Hotel became the nerve center of the effort; within a few weeks members of the task force had talked to 75 senators and some 250 representatives, military officials, and congressional committees. Zigler alone saw two dozen legislators. They had optimal and minimal objectives: ideally they sought absolute exemption for COs; practically, they wanted alternative service for a broad variety of objectors, whose sincerity would be determined by a civilian board. The language of the Senate bill, which passed on August 28, was improved, from the peace church point of view, over the original text but had serious limitations. It did call for a register of COs administered by the Justice Department; however, this was wiped out in the House version, despite careful legislative maneuvering.[5]

After the Senate and House versions were reconciled, the bill became law on September 13, 1940. Its most important provision for peace people was that those drafted men who by "religious training and belief" were opposed to participation in the military forces, if found sincere by a local draft board, were to be assigned to noncombatant military service or to "work of national importance under civilian direction." It did not grant exemption for those who objected in principle to the right of the government to conscript; these absolutists had no recourse under the law but refusal, leading to trial and imprisonment. The peace advocates were disappointed that their best efforts had not resulted in a better arrangement, but they were gratified that this law gave promise of better treatment for COs than that experienced in 1917-1918.[6]

Formation of NSBRO

The Friends were prepared to take the lead in organizing the CO program authorized by the legislation. Government representatives had indicated that they wanted one group to deal with, not a variety of individual groups. However, the Mennonites and Brethren indicated that they preferred a cooperative plan. A broadly representative meeting was called for October 5 in Chicago to decide the issue; M. R. Zigler was asked to chair the meeting. The upshot was the decision to organize a cooperative agency based in Washington to serve as liaison with the government. On October 11, 1940, the National Council for Religious Objectors was established; shortly thereafter the name was changed to National Service Board for Religious Objectors (NSBRO), which it maintained until 1969 when it became the National Interreligious Service Board for Conscientious Objectors (NISBCO).[7]

Prior to the general meeting in Chicago, representatives from the five largest Brethren groups met to discuss their reactions to the situation.

Rufus D. Bowman served as convener and began by asking someone from each body to express their opinions. J. W. Skiles of the Old German Baptist Brethren demurred, stating that the Old Orders were from the country and had no suggestions. Bowman encouraged him to speak anyway, saying that many around the table were also from the country. "But," said Skiles, "we came from the country this morning!"[8]

M. R. Zigler was named chair of the board of the NSBRO, serving from 1940 to 1948, a task which brought crushing demands on his time, energy, and emotions, particularly throughout the war years. Orie O. Miller of the Mennonite Central Committee was named vice-chairman of the board and Paul J. Furnas represented the Friends. The most active of the remaining board members were Charles Boss, Jr. (Methodist), James Crain (Disciples), and Walter W. Van Kirk (Federal Council of Churches). Membership on the board was limited to seven for the sake of efficient work but a broader consultative council eventually numbered twenty-seven. Despite the tensions and frustrations which went with this task, Zigler remained close to all of these men for the rest of their lives, especially so with Orie Miller. The two visited often over the years and corresponded regularly, often traveling great distances to meet each other.

Fortunately, a very knowledgeable and efficient executive was found in the person of Paul Comly French, a Quaker journalist with extensive Washington experience; he had helped with the lobbying effort of the summer before. Zigler, Miller, and Furnas, representing the Historic Peace Churches and thus responsible for the largest numbers of COs, played the dominant roles on the board, working along with French. The three bodies also bore the costs of the Washington office equally; later some other religious groups contributed to the costs as well.

Their counterparts on the government side were Dr. C. A. Dykstra, called from the presidency of the University of Wisconsin to become director of Selective Service and his aide, Colonel (later General) Lewis B. Hershey, who for many years had been responsible for military planning of wartime conscription. Afterwards, in contravention of the language of the law (which called for a civilian head), Hershey became the director of Selective Service, a post he retained until he retired at the age of seventy-nine in 1973, after heavy criticism during the period of the Vietnamese War. He served under six presidents. A bluff, genial type, he liked to talk of his Mennonite ancestors and was willing to sit on a fence and discuss the draft with Amish and Mennonite bishops in Lancaster County.[9]

Hershey and Zigler became good friends and enjoyed mutual respect. For Zigler's eightieth birthday, Hershey wrote a cordial note, remarking: "Our relationship began, technically, as adversaries. We proved that fundamental disagreement is no bar to mutual confidence, respect for each other and friendship." Zigler was instrumental in inviting General Hershey to speak to the Church of the Brethren Annual Conference in Huntingdon, Pennsylvania, in 1944. The general, dressed in his full military uniform, began his remarks by saying: "You're against war; who isn't?" (Members of the American Legion were laying odds that Hershey would not honor the commitment; Zigler reported that he had asked the church, in vain, to give him a large sum of money to cover the wager, as a way of raising funds for the CPS program.)

Much later, after Zigler attended the funeral for Hershey's wife, the widower wrote a warm letter of appreciation to him. When the two men met after the end of World War II, they enjoyed exchanging views on current affairs and reminiscing about the problems of Selective Service. Soon after the On Earth Peace Program was established at New Windsor, Maryland, in 1974, Zigler prevailed on the aged military leader to attend a meeting, which he did, bringing along a grandson.[10]

Civilian Public Service

Assurances had been made to government officials that the peace churches would cooperate with the government in establishing work projects for COs. The churches had in mind expanding on the work camp model, pioneered in North America by the AFSC after 1934. Many young Brethren and Mennonites had worked in them, serving in Appalachia or other needy areas. An article titled "Soldiers of Peace" appearing in a fall, 1940, issue of the *Christian Century* specifically related a Quaker work camp in the Westmoreland Homesteads of Pennsylvania to the impending projects under conscription.[11]

There followed a long process of negotiation with various government agencies to establish a unique project in church/state relations called *Civilian Public Service*. In late September and early October, Lewis B. Hershey of the Selective Service staff asked if the Historic Peace Churches would undertake to care for all those men who registered as COs. The Brethren suggested that three types of camps should be established: (1) those run solely by the government, with maintenance and wages provided by them; (2) those run cooperatively by a peace church and the government, with the church administering the camp and the government responsible for the work and for maintenance; and (3) those run solely by the church for COs who preferred this, with costs covered by the church. (Dan West drafted the memorandum outlining these plans.) Mennonites and Quakers made similar suggestions.

After several modifications of these suggestions, a governmental advisory committee recommended to Dr. Dykstra, Selective Service director, that three types of camps be established, much as the Brethren had originally requested: Type I, with COs working directly under governmental agencies, with costs carried by the agencies; Type II, with camps working directly with governmental agencies, but under the administration of either BSC, MCC, or AFSC, which would provide camp directors, nurses, and other staff, with the government providing tools, shelter, food, and compensation equivalent to that of a soldier; and Type III, with camps operated by recognized church groups and under their financial responsibility, with the government offering tools and equipments, and occasional inspection. The peace churches, through the NSBRO, adopted the proposal.

On November 29, 1940, Dr. Dykstra took the final proposal to President Roosevelt, who completely rejected the plan with "instant and aggressive opposition." Thus rebuffed, Dykstra called a meeting with the NSBRO leaders on December 5 and asked if they were willing to administer all projects for COs and bear all the costs except for transportation of the men to reach the camps; the only alternative, he told them, was to seek Congressional appropriation for the camps, which would be run solely by the government, with no opportunity for COs to serve under church auspices. There was no possibility, he said, for parallel programs—church-run and government-run, such as the peace churches had proposed.

This posed the churches with a major dilemma; if they accepted the task of running the camps, they would be undertaking a huge financial obligation; if they rejected the offer, their young men would have no chance of serving under the churches. After hurried consultation, on December 10 members of the NSBRO agreed among themselves that they would accept the assignment of administering and financing work for COs of "national importance" (as the law mandated) to the limit of their financial ability; they informed Dr. Dykstra of this decision. President Roosevelt approved the plan on December 19, and on December 20 the NSBRO and the director of Selective Service exchanged memos of agreement, specifying that the plan was to be evaluated in six months.[12]

This was the troubled background of a significant and hitherto untried experiment in church/state relations. A certain unclarity in the relationship was to bedevil the entire CPS program. The peace churches understood that they were engaged in a sacrificial exercise in cooperation between church and state; the government understood that the churches were acting as their agents. More than once, this led to sharp tensions but never to an absolute break. A vocal minority of COs came to feel that the churches had compromised their principles in making this agreement and criticized the church leadership in strong terms. M. R. Zigler, as one of these leaders, came in for much of the critique.

Writing in 1942, Paul Comly French reviewed the genesis of the CPS program, and explained the motivation of the Historic Peace Churches in taking on such a heavy load:

> Civilian Public Service was conceived as a way of giving the state-community the service which it asked of all its citizens and then going beyond that and paying for the privilege of serving. I think that most of the people who participated in the decision to accept the responsibility felt that it would give them an opportunity to prepare men for the tasks that would come with the ending of the war and the reconstruction period that would face us at home and abroad. All of the groups who agreed to the present church-financed program saw those values clearly when the suggestion was made to us that we might be willing to operate the program without Federal financial assistance on an experimental basis.[13]

Brethren Give Approval of CPS

As the decisions were made to enter this program, a special meeting of the Standing Committee of the Church of the Brethren was called at Zigler's urging, which met in Chicago on December 18-19, 1940. Members heard the latest information about government plans for the COs, and specifically faced the decision of accepting responsibility for CPS camps, understanding that this would be a major financial undertaking. The decision was to go ahead:

> Voted to assume financial responsibility for training our young men, with or without government aid (it not yet being clear what position the government will take as to financial aid) in projects of national importance under civilian control which are in harmony with our convictions regarding military training and service. This may run into large amounts.[14]

131

Zigler's daring to speak for his church was vindicated. They backed him basically because they trusted him. He went back repeatedly to the church as the program developed, always using the Annual Conferences as a way of building understanding and support. Several participants look back to a special prayer session at the Asheville, North Carolina, conference in 1942 as a milestone. "There in that crowded room, early that morning, plain garbed men, pastors, parents, young men from all over the Brotherhood got down on their knees and fervently prayed. I believe that meeting led by that Man of Peace [Zigler], had much to do with the success of our Civilian Public Service Program. . . ." Another voice: "The single most compelling memory I have is of a prayer M. R. gave at an Annual Conference. . . . The prayer was powerful, it poured out of M. R. with all that urgency and authenticity which characterized everything he did."[15]

Something of the way the arrangement came about can be seen in an intra-agency letter, sent by a member of the Camp Operations Section of the Selective Service office to the director of personnel of the Department of Agriculture:

> Though Congress approved the use of conscientious objectors in work of National importance, no specific appropriations for this purpose was made by them, and today an experimental solution is being worked out pending the time when Federal monies will become available, in whole or in part, for this purpose. A proposal was sent to the President by Mr. Dykstra, Director of Selective Service, after he had consulted with those concerned bureaus. The Departments of Agriculture and Interior agreed to provide technical supervision for projects together with necessary equipment to the extent of their ability. The Federal Security Agency and the War Department have agreed to furnish certain abandoned camp sites, cots, bedding and such equipment as might be available for this purpose. The Service Board for Conscientious Objectors, representing those church groups which include in their membership a large proportion of the conscientious objectors, have agreed to undertake the financing of the camps, which is to include clothing, feeding, recreation, and housing. This Agency will furnish general administrative and policy supervision, and inspection, and will pay the men's costs to the camps. . . . [It] is the present plan to use available abandoned CCC camps and available buildings which are now in the custody of federal agencies or religious groups. It is planned that such buildings will be transferred to this agency who will in turn issue certificates of occupancy to the involved church group.[16]

The original agreement of six months was extended several times. The intent was to have the term of service for COs to be commensurate with the period of enlistment for the military. Once the USA entered the war on December 8, 1941, the term of CO assignment was extended to the duration of the war; in fact, for public relations purposes, after the war ended final release of CPS men dragged far behind the schedule of release for those in the military. The last CPS men were discharged on March 29, 1947.

The long extension of time was detrimental to the morale of those in CPS; many had families and other dependents and there was no financial provision for them. As there was not even minimal wage paid, draftees could not help them from their own income. Participating churches developed modest dependency support, but it was woefully insufficient. On the one side, the government did not press Congress for compensation for CPS men, although the law would have permitted it, fearing that legislators would be critical. (In fact, at one hearing, when a Congressman heard of the situation, he exploded: "We're treating them worse than we are the Japs!" referring to arrangements made for prisoners of war). The church leadership portrayed the situation as an opportunity to show that the COs were good citizens, willing to sacrifice for their beliefs. The inequities here became part of the grievances of increasingly articulate groups of COs, who eventually came to the point of attacking the peace church leadership as stooges of Selective Service.[17]

Wartime Years

Zigler kept up a distressingly heavy pace during the war years, coping with the many problems of CPS and tending to the denominational tasks he still shouldered. Some insight into the pattern of his life during this period can be gleaned from a diary he kept in 1943. Portions of it read as follows:

> Sunday. January 31, 1943: Morris Keeton presented at the Elgin preaching hour his evaluation of Civilian Public Service.... After making some contacts regarding Youth's Year of Volunteer Service, staff work, etc., and lunch, there was the "family farewell" which during my life has been so frequent but which I have never learned to enjoy. Sometime I hope I may be home one month undisturbed. The train to Omaha proves beyond doubt that there is a war in progress and that we are the decline regarding proper behavior. Arrived too late to contact Milton Early, [Brethren] minister in Omaha. Therefore to bed in hotel.
>
> Monday morning. February 1, 1943: Seven o'clock by telephone Milton Early arranged to meet me at the station. We discussed the problem of living

in a city with increased cost. Also how to do pastoral work without automobiles [because of gas rationing], church attendance, and district activities. . . . W. H. Yoder [Brethren pastor] failed to arrive in time to go with me by train to attend a conference on farm ownership at Salt Lake City. The day and night was spent on the train. Rested and read and discussed many questions with citizens. Prophecy during the day summed up to the belief that we are facing a long and costly war, and that the church has the resources needed for this hour.

Tuesday. February 2, 1943: Arrived late at Salt Lake City. [Marshall] Harris of the Department of Agriculture and Joseph Ackerman joined me at breakfast. . . . Registered at the Temple Square Hotel, Latter Day Saint owned. Then we joined Paul Vogt, A. H. Rapking and others at the University to discuss problems of land tenure in Utah. Representatives of several denominations were present—Sherfy Randolph of the Presbyterian[s] and Wickhizer of the Disciples of Christ. . . . At seven in the evening we met at the Lion House, the home of the wives of Brigham Young, for dinner. About fifty people were present. At this meeting the story of land ownership and care of the poor was discussed.

Wednesday, February 3, 1943: We met in Temple Square Hotel. W. H. Yoder arrived at noon Tuesday to meet with us. The whole day was spent in hearing different individuals describe in detail the work of the Latter Day Saints. . . . At eleven o'clock we left Salt Lake City feeling that we had learned much from these strange pioneers of the West.

Thursday. February 4, 1943: On the train with Rapking, Vogt, Ackerman, and Harris. Arrived at Pocatello at seven in the morning. There was a delay to wait for the Chicago train coming from the East. I walked through the snow to the courthouse to talk with the farm agent. He agreed to come at eleven o'clock to talk with our group concerning the farm situation in Southern Idaho. . . . Interesting discussion on the train at night concluded on the note that the church holds the future.

Friday. February 5, 1943. George Brown met me at Portland and drove to Waldport C.P.S. camp. Excellent spirit there. Dick Mills and Kimmel are well liked. Mud and rain is very generous here at the Pacific Coast camp. There are 104 men in camp planting trees. Difficulty getting food but not pessimistic.

Saturday. February 5, 1943: Came to Cascade Locks. Mark Schrock is in charge and is doing a good piece of work. The camp is composed of a fine group of men. They are alert and anxious to do what they think should be done in regard to conscription. George Brown is serving as educational director. Meals and equipment are O. K. Library burned last week. Victor Olson of Selective Service is here. Had brief conversation with him. He seemed to be well pleased with the Brethren camps on the coast. Dick Mills came with us to the camp. . . . Saturday had a most excellent meeting with the men in camp. This is our most diversified camp from the standpoint of background and experience. . . . Brethren Church not so well understood. . . . Men are anxious to get detached service.[18]

The detached service to which Zigler referred was a later development in work assignment in the CPS program. Small units of men were transferred from the large base camps, where the typical work project was timbering or road construction, to various forms of public service. Many felt that this was more constructive and worthwhile, as people were being helped directly. Units worked in mental hospitals, general hospitals, in experiments, and in many other projects. A number of these were connected with agriculture.

The development of detached service did much to improve the morale of the CPS workers, who quickly saw that many of projects of the early mass camps were designed to remove the COs from public attention. The situation, the ebbing morale, and the role of M. R. Zigler are well caught in the recollection of Howard Schomer, a pacifist from the Congregational Church, who later became a colleague of Zigler's in postwar relief work in Europe:

> . . . It was in a very remote Civilian Public Service Camp, in Buck Creek Gap below the Blue Ridge Parkway of North Carolina that I next saw Bob Zigler, in the harsh mountain winter of 1942. Morale was sagging in many CPS camps assigned to trivial and untimely tasks under federal Agriculture and Interior Department staff who quite realistically saw their job as maintaining order in C. O. interment camps, with minimum contact with the local population, rather than to organize that "work of national importance under civilian direction" stipulated in the Selective Service Act. M. R. Zigler and Andrew Cordier spent a couple days in our Quaker-run camp, riding the trucks with us up the mountain, pounding rocks and chopping trees with us as we built—a picnic area!—as well as long evenings with us in our collective soul-searching. They could not promise us that more significant service lay ahead. They did communicate the certitude that we were not simply abandoned to ironic drudgery for the indefinite duration, that we had substantial friends who would continue to importune Washington to open the doors to our service where it would really matter, at home and overseas. Within six months the first CPS-men could volunteer to enter the terribly understaffed state hospitals for the mentally ill, helping care for some of the neediest of our brethren.[19]

It was in connection with CPS work on farms that one never-to-be-resolved problem developed. These men received going wages for their work; however, except for a modest amount retained to cover direct living costs, their wages went to a special fund set up in the US Treasury. This had amounted to well over a million dollars by 1945. The original understanding had been that the funds would be distributed to the church relief agencies for use in rehabilitation work at the end of the war. NSBRO also attempted to have some of it used to meet the pressing needs of CPS dependents. Because of a technicality, neither of these were permitted, and the Treasury insisted that it would take an act of Congress to disburse the funds. This was attempted repeatedly, with different charitable objects in mind and many times was at the point of success, before being blocked by a few hostile legislators. Finally, after a failure in 1958, the attempts ceased. The fund had been lost, most unfairly, in the maw of the federal machinery.[20]

Zigler was also at the heart of other issues. One of the strongest aims of the Historic Peace Churches was to use the CPS program as a way to train men for relief and rehabilitation work in war-torn areas. Special training units were set up on campuses related to the Brethren, Mennonites, and Quakers, involving 248 men by mid-summer, 1943. With Selective Service approval, the first trained contingent was sent via ship to China. However, when a right-wing columnist made the initiative public, an aroused Congress stopped the effort by attaching a rider onto an appropriation bill for the War Department that forbade CPS men to leave the USA. The men already underway, who had just passed the Cape of Good Hope, were forced to return.[21]

The best the peace churches could do was to continue to send some of the men to Puerto Rico, which as a US commonwealth, was not excluded by the language of the rider. A survey had found that the mountainous area around Castañer was the most needy section of the island. The Martin G. Brumbaugh CPS unit was established there in June, 1942, and soon developed a great variety of social service programs. The hospital was the most ambitious part of their efforts and flourished marvelously. After the end of the war, it was continued as a project under Brethren Service, and eventually was turned over to the local community in 1976. Some CPS men stayed on in Puerto Rico and made it their new home. Many Brethren have considered Castañer among the most successful of all Brethren Service projects in terms of impact on a large community over a long period of time in both spiritual and material ways.[22]

Significant influence from the CPS program was also observable in the mental health area. COs were assigned work as ward attendants to alleviate the pressing shortage of staff. They brought a new spirit of compassion and understanding to their demanding jobs. More than a few remained in the field after war's end and the closing of the CPS units. The Mennonite Church particularly remained heavily involved in this sector, eventually creating a string of clinics and hospitals across the nation. M. R. Zigler tried, but failed, to introduce a team of COs into the mental hospital at Elgin, Illinois; public pressure from veterans' organizations blocked the effort, even when high-ranking officers from the office of Selective Service assured them of its legality and desirability.[23]

Although CPS had its strong critics, particularly from within the ranks of drafted men of non-Historic Peace Church background, most who have studied its operations have concluded that it was the best compromise available at the time. Though certainly not perfect, and beset throughout with serious problems, it did make possible a better arrangement during the Korean War, when the government agreed to allow COs to do alternative service directly under the umbrella of the service agencies of the peace churches. M. R. Zigler never wavered in his commitment to the value of the CPS program to the church and to society. He also never ceased praising the government, working through Selective Service, as staunch defenders of religious liberty.[24]

NOTES

1. "Minutes of the Meeting of the Continuation Committee, and others, at Goshen [Indiana], Sept. 17, 1939" (E. L. Harshbarger Collection, Mennonite Historical Archives).
2. Rufus D. Bowman, *The Church of the Brethren and War, 1708-1941* (Elgin, IL: Brethren Publishing House, 1944), 274-282; Albert N. Keim and Grant M. Stoltzfus, *The Politics of Conscience: The Historic Peace Churches and America at War, 1917-1955* (Scottdale, PA: Herald Press, 1988), 71-77.
3. Keim and Stoltzfus, *Politics of Conscience* (1988), 84-93.
4. M. R. Zigler, "Dialogue Saved the Church from Division," *Gospel Messenger* (June 1, 1963): 8-10, 16.
5. Keim and Stoltzfus, *Politics of Conscience* (1988), 93-102.
6. Roger E. Sappington, *Brethren Social Policy* (Elgin, IL: Brethren Press, 1961), 88-91; Leslie Eisan, *Pathways of Peace: A History of the Civilian Public Service Program Administered by the Brethren Service Committee* (Elgin, IL: Brethren Publishing House, 1948), 39-43; Melvin Gingerich, *Service for Peace: A History of Mennonite Civilian Public Service* (Akron, PA: Mennon-

ite Central Committee, 1949), 47-50.

7. [Philip Jacob], *The Origins of Civilian Public Service* (Washington, D. C.: National Service Board for Religious Objectors, n.d.), 5-6.

8. H. Spenser Minnich, "Farewell to a Friendly Old Building," *Gospel Messenger* (May 9, 1953): 18.

9. George Q. Flynn, *Lewis B. Hershey, Mr. Selective Service* (Chapel Hill, NC: University of North Carolina Press, 1985), 126-134.

10. M. R. Zigler to Major Gen. Lewis B. Hershey, March 22, 1944; Hershey to Zigler, March 30, 1944; Zigler to Hershey, April 4, 1944; Hershey to Zigler, Oct. 13, 1971; Paul Kinsel to D. F. Durnbaugh, June 22, 1987; Million transcript of M. R. Zigler, 3/1-4; Ken Kreider interview of M. R. Zigler, May 27, 1977, 1/1-4;

11. Herman Keiter, "Soldiers of Peace," *Christian Century* (Oct. 2, 1940): 1202-1204.

12. [Jacob], *Origins of CPS* (n.d.), 4-8; Keim and Stoltzfus, *Politics of Conscience* (1988), 103-114.

13. Paul Comly French, "Civilian Public Service: An Organized Program of Tolerance for Religious Minorities," typescript, Sept. 15, 1942 (NSBRO Records, Swarthmore College Peace Collection).

14. M. R. Zigler, "Director of Brethren Civilian Service," *Gospel Messenger* (Jan. 18, 1941): 12; Sappington, *Social Policy* (1961), 93.

15. Bernard N. King to D. F. Durnbaugh, May 8, 1987; G. Wayne Glick to D. F. Durnbaugh, June 11, 1987.

16. A. S. Imirie to Roy F. Hendrickson, Feb. 13, 1941 (Selective Service Files, National Archives).

17. Keim and Stoltzfus, *Politics of Conscience* (1988), 117-126.

18. M. R. Zigler diary, mimeographed.

19. Howard Schomer to D. F. Durnbaugh, May 7, 1987.

20. There are many references to the "Frozen Fund" in literature on CPS; some selected references are: "Release the C.O. Fund for Children!" *Christian Century* (Feb. 26, 1947): 259-260; "'Frozen Fund' Bill Dies in House Committee," *[NSBRO] Reporter for Conscience' Sake*, 15 (May-June, 1958): 1-2; Ron Martin-Adkins, "The 'Frozen Fund' and the 'Freezing Out' of Religious Employers of Alternative Service Workers," *On Earth Peace* [Newsletter] (December, 1986): 1.

21. Gingerich, *Service for Peace* (1949), 305-308.

22. Eisan, *Pathways of Peace* (1948), 333-359; Everett R. Groff, "Castañer Hospital," *Brethren Encyclopedia* (1983-1984), 261-262.

23. Gingerich, *Service for Peace* (1949), 213-251; Eisan, *Pathways of Peace* (1948), 204-238.

24. A full discussion of these issues is found in the monograph, Mulford Q. Sibley and Philip Jacob, *Conscription of Conscience: The American State and the Conscientious Objector, 1940-1947* (Ithica, NY: Cornell University Press,

1952); the latest study, based on interviews of CPS men, is Cynthia Eller, "Moral and Religious Arguments in Support of Pacifism: Conscientious Objection and the Second World War," PhD thesis, University of Southern California (1988). See also Rufus D. Bowman, *Seventy Times Seven* (Elgin, IL: Brethren Publishing House, 1945), 48-60.

12

WARTIME STRESSES; LOOKING TO THE FUTURE

A LTHOUGH M. R. ZIGLER had always followed a busy schedule of travel, meetings, and administrative work, the pace of his life from 1940 to 1945 surpassed any previous experience. As newly created chairman of the Washington-based National Service Board for Religious Objectors, the agency responsible for the successful operation of the Civilian Public Service program, he found it virtually necessary to commute from his Elgin, Illinois, office to the District of Columbia, often making several trips a month. The path-breaking program was full of problems and headaches, as fervent pacifists clashed with ardent militarists, leaving the NSBRO staff in the middle.

Beyond that, he became the executive of the Brethren Service Committee, concerned to develop plans for far-reaching relief projects when the war ended. In this capacity also, there were innumerable meetings, usually in New York, demanding his attention. Brethren had gotten their feet wet in relief activities in the 1930s in Spain and in China, leaning primarily on the experienced leadership of the AFSC. Zigler was eager to develop Brethren-run initiatives, drawing on the experiences of personnel such as David Blickenstaff, Paul Bowman, Jr., and Martha Rupel. A small program of refugee resettlement of Jews immediately prior to the outbreak of World War II gave promise of developing into something much larger with the advent of peace. Although the CPS program demanded most attention and almost all of the resources of the church, throughout the war period there were smaller relief efforts of some significance.

As if these were not enough, there remained the substantial leadership tasks placed on Zigler by the church in the mid-1930s: ministerial affairs and Christian Education, along with his original job in Home Missions. He reported that he did not take a regular vacation from 1941 to 1948 and had very few Sundays off. This was an impossible load, even for someone as robust and energetic as Zigler. Something had to give and did.

Given all the stresses and problems, it is not surprising that Zigler had to take some time off to recover his energy and health. Little was said of it, but during the war M. R. and Amy Zigler went to Sebring, Florida, for several weeks of recuperation. Amy Zigler herself had gone through an operation in September, 1940, to relieve what was called a "critical and distressing ailment."[1]

Denominational Adjustments

The longer range solution was to find some able associates to take part of his impossible burden from his admittedly broad shoulders. Zigler was able to recruit Paul H. Bowman, Sr., president of Bridgewater College and a respected church leader, for the position of National Director of the Brethren CPS program. Bowman secured a leave from the trustees of the college to give what amounted to six months of volunteer labor from January to July, 1941. This was a key appointment because Bowman's stature in the denomination ensured that many Brethren would respond to the heavy demands in leadership and resources which Brethren entry into the CPS program demanded. His experienced administrative skills and ready pen were effective in organizing the Brethren response.[2]

But Bowman represented only the top appointment. If CPS were to work, it would demand tactful and firm leadership in the camps being established. Zigler reached out to seasoned pastors, most of whom responded favorably to the emergency situation. Many of them continued in denominational leadership posts after the demise of CPS, but not always in as favorable posts as they otherwise could have expected. One example was provided by Jefferson Mathis, who was serving in 1941 as district executive in Northern Iowa and Minnesota. In an autobiography he recalled his experiences:

> I was very happy with my work and might have continued there for the remainder of my working years had it not been for the second World War.
> . . . It came like a bolt from the blue: a call to take the Magnolia, Arkansas, camp for conscientious objectors. Our church representative from the General Board came to see me, not to offer the job of leadership of this camp but to tell me they were expecting me to take it. . . . For a while I put him off and told

141

him that I would have no place to go when the war was over. He countered with the promise that I could choose my job if I would take this one. . . . [Finally I] gave in and we prepared to leave in short order.

World War II was over and the boys were going home, so I began to look for a place to serve. To my surprise, those who had pressured me into giving up my place in district work and taking on the responsibility of the CPS Camps took no notice of what was to become of their directors. They were off on other projects and hardly knew us.

Others were more positive. Ora Huston, for example, who had been called by Zigler from pastoral work to direct CPS camps, wrote him in 1960 to thank him for both the inspiration and the vocational shift. Huston joined the Elgin staff with responsibilities for peace and volunteers: ". . . I am confident that the CPS program was the finest thing that happened in the Church of the Brethren in the '40 decade. To me it seems that the Volunteer Service has been the finest thing in the '50 decade. . . ."[3]

In July, 1941, Paul H. Bowman found it necessary to resign to turn again to pressing administrative duties at his college. In his resignation letter addressed to Zigler, Bowman stated:

In terminating my six months' period of voluntary service for the Brethren Service Committee . . ., I want to express my appreciation for the opportunity of working so closely with you. I have greatly appreciated your comradeship in this enterprise. . . . I leave this work with a profound respect for the public officials with whom we have worked and a deep appreciation for the earnest effort of our government to preserve the principle of religious freedom.[4]

With Bowman's resignation, the heavy responsibility for managing the burgeoning and complicated CPS camps fell back into Zigler's lap. He sought avidly for some relief in this demanding post and finally found it in March, 1942, in the person of W. Harold Row, a keen young pastor from West Virginia. Row, a graduate of Bridgewater College and Crozier Theological Seminary, joined the Elgin office as assistant executive director with special responsibility for the day-by-day administration of the CPS program.[5]

It had already become a substantial operation, with several hundred Brethren men enrolled in some six CPS camps, and it was to grow. By October, 1943, there were 1,780 men in Brethren CPS. The massive files of the NSBRO, now housed in the Swarthmore College Peace Collection, give mute testimony to the extent and complexities of the CPS program.

Problems with the Selective Service System and NSBRO

Given the intrinsic awkwardness of camps administered by the church agencies with work projects arranged by government agencies, operating during the strains of total war under a conscription system, it is not surprising that tensions grew in the CPS program. Zigler was at the storm center of this, but somehow managed to stay on good relations with the constituent church members of the NSBRO and also with military men, such as General Hershey and his aide and crony, Col. Lewis F. Kosch, of Selective Service. But this did not provide the only tension. In some ways more difficult were intra-religious concerns. Two will illustrate the many Zigler faced during this period as chairman of the NSBRO. The first involved the Quakers, the second the Methodists.

It will be recalled that the AFSC, under the executive leadership of Clarence Pickett, had originally sought to take over the administrative leadership of the CPS program but were rebuffed because of the wishes of the Brethren, Mennonites, and Methodists to work cooperatively. The churches had appointed Paul Comly French, a Quaker, to organize the NSBRO office in Washington, first sited in the Press Club. French did a tremendous job in building an efficient office setup to operate the complex alternative service system; he was also very skilled in representing the concerns of the churches to the several government agencies, particularly, of course, with attention to General Hershey and his Selective Service agency.[6]

In fact, he was too successful. It became apparent after several months of operation that the AFSC offices in Philadelphia were becoming uncomfortable with his smooth operation. Pickett had taken modest Quakerly pride in his ability to move in the top echelons of government circles, based primarily upon his close personal friendship with Eleanor Roosevelt. Increasingly, it became apparent to observers that French's success was hard to take for the AFSC leadership. Threatened withdrawal of support, while placed within the principle of unease with the church/state liaison, seemed equally aimed at French. At one point, he insisted that he had to resign, to resolve the inner-Quaker problem, and because of health problems resulting from fatigue and strain.

Zigler, as chairman of the board of the NSBRO, had to deal with the situation, which he approached both tactfully and skillfully. His letter of November 22, 1943, to French reveals his style:

143

My dear Paul:

Last week you had me worried for the first time about your future with the NSBRO. . . . Therefore, if everything you said about yourself physically is true, then you do have me worried. I did not let it get me down when you told me, and I have taken a long enough look at it to be sane today, I think.

You have done an excellent job. Your work has been far more significant than you will ever receive credit for. I can see how when one agency within our operation doesn't go along, it worries you. At that point I have given up hope doing anything to relieve the situation.

You asked me what we would do if you would resign. I did not answer. I can't answer for the group representing the NSBRO. I think I can answer for the Brethren. . . .

There is one way that we might move and that would be in the direction that you have discussed before with me, that is, that I might, as chairman of the Board, without any reference to the executive secretaryship, take over this work for a while and give you a rest. . . .

Finally and very definitely, I want you to know that I am not proposing a[ny] thing at this point except that which I think will be helpful to you if you feel you should take three to six months out, or even a month if that will be of help. . . .

We certainly have appreciated your work and I have not lost confidence in you in any way. I am quite sure that we need you now and in the future, maybe more in the future than in the immediate six months. . . . [7]

He was adroit enough to keep French on the team; the able leader continued to function effectively until 1946 when he moved to New York to become the chief executive of the mushrooming philanthropic agency, CARE. It is possible that his night-and-day work with NSBRO shortened his life, because he died at the age of fifty-seven.[8]

Zigler's involvement with the Methodists was more complicated. It began with the agreement of the Historic Peace Churches in setting up their CPS camps to accept men of other religious backgrounds. They followed a policy of allowing any pacifist drafted to be assigned to them, or, as Zigler expressed it, for "whosoever will, let him come." Nonpeace churches that counted COs among their membership often supported their men in CPS by reimbursing the sponsoring agency a fixed amount per month.

A rather large number of COs came from the Methodist Church; in fact, there were more Methodist COs than there were from the Friends. It became an embarrassment for the large and wealthy Methodist Church that inadequate funds were contributed to pay for the upkeep and expenses of their men in the CPS camps. This was a partial motivation for the influential leader Bishop G. Bromley Oxnam to start a campaign for the government to sponsor camps by itself at its own expense. Oxnam was also the head of the Federal Council of Church's committee for COs.

The peace groups feared that if a strong push came to press the government to establish camps at their own expense, it could jeopardize the delicate balance worked out so painfully with the CPS program. Zigler called a special meeting of the NSBRO board to defuse the issue. It was solved, in part, by the later establishment of a few government operated camps and the expansion of the detached units for COs, which ordinarily provided for their own financing from the sponsoring agencies or institutions.[9]

Other Adjustments

The major decision for Zigler and the church was to see how the diversion of some of his responsibilities should take place. It became clear to the leadership of the Church of the Brethren as well as to Zigler that he could not conceivably continue to carry the tremendous burdens of the Civilian Public Service program, the emerging work of the Brethren Service Committee, and his other denominational responsibilities—Christian Education, Ministries, and Home Missions. Denominational archives contain many letters exchanged between church leaders, seeking an answer to this dilemma.

Zigler himself was ambivalent. He was reluctant to give up any of the assignments because he had invested himself so deeply in all of them. He was also aware that he would lay himself open to criticism if he opted alone for the Brethren Service/CPS program. The demands for staff and resources were such that they could only be met, realistically, by curtailing personnel and funds for other programs.

Eventually, the church acted. In 1941 the portfolio of Christian Education was given to L. Avery Fleming. In 1943, Harvey L. Hartsough took over as Acting Secretary of Ministries and Home Missions, a particularly sensitive and difficult assignment; he was able to make a smooth transition because he had just previously served as chairman of the ministries board and thus knew many of the details of the position. As mentioned earlier, Zigler's tact in suggesting the right ministers for specific congregations had been instrumental in securing widespread support for his own initiatives. Many pastors were grateful to him for decisive intervention into their lives, as they saw it, and were ready to follow his lead in other areas of the work of the church. The understanding of the board members was that Zigler would return to his responsibilities with Ministry and Home Missions at war's end.

Creation of the Brethren Service Committee

Since 1918 Brethren had been sensitized to the needs of suffering humanity outside, as well as inside, the borders of the USA. Beginning with relief to the Armenians and continuing through aid to those suffering on both sides of the civil war in Spain in the 1930s, Brethren sent first their support and then volunteer social workers to alleviate in small but significant ways some of these needs.

With the threat of widespread war looming in the late 1930s, this concern became more articulate and demanding. At first, care for relief and rehabilitation was lodged with the Board of Christian Education; as its executive, M. R. Zigler was thus given direct administrative responsibility for Brethren involvement in these issues. It soon became apparent, however, that Brethren concern could not be entirely channeled in this way; Brethren missionaries became involved in meeting need, especially in China, but also in Scandinavia as refugees fleeing Hitler sought a haven there. That brought the General Mission Board onto the scene.[10]

From 1938 to 1939 a Special Neutral Relief Committee was active, at Annual Conference request. That functioned well but still reorganization was necessary to keep the burgeoning Brethren relief activities from becoming tangled and inefficient. The immediate answer was to achieve integration by unifying the two boards with major assignments for peace and relief, as a way of mastering the increasing tasks. Members of the General Mission Board and the Board of Christian Education together became in November, 1939, the Peace and Relief Commission of the Church of the Brethren.

As this was too cumbersome a body to handle detailed work, an executive committee was formed; each board named two representatives and these four selected a fifth member. L. W. Shultz and Paul Kinsel came from Christian Education and Leland S. Brubaker and Nora Rhoades from General Missions; Andrew W. Cordier was chosen as the member at large and named chairman. M. R. Zigler was the staff executive.

Paul Kinsel, as secretary, began using the term *Brethren Service Committee*, in imitation of the AFSC, as a shorter and more descriptive name than *Executive Committee of the Peace and Relief Commission of the Church of the Brethren.* The term caught on, but it was not regularized until the Annual Conference of 1941, meeting at La Verne, California, established it as a separate entity with seven members. It thus became one of the major boards of the denomination.[11]

A small but vocal element, grouped around the charismatic figure of Dan West, had pressed for the creation of a separate agency, along the lines of the American Friends Service Committee or the Mennonite Central Committee. Zigler opposed this, for he contended that such a move would take the concern away from the church. Most observers consider this attitude to have proved correct, for the rise of Brethren Service did occur solidly within the church's framework and, indeed, proved to be the most vital aspect of the life of the church for several decades. There was a potential loss in the decision, however. That was that placing the agency within the ecclesiastical framework of the Church of the Brethren prevented to a substantial degree the type of fraternal development experienced by the Mennonites with their aid agency. Although other Brethren bodies cooperated to some extent with the Brethren Service Committee, particularly with movements it sponsored such as the Heifer Project, the specific denominational ties discouraged wide and extended cooperation after the immediate wartime emergencies waned.

In 1941, then, the Brethren Service Committee was anchored yet more deeply in the life of the church by action of Annual Conference. Its charter was more clearly defined and its long-range ramifications identified. Despite the sweeping nature of its charter, the facts of the wartime situation, which prevented overseas activity beyond very limited areas, coupled with the pressing demands of the CPS program, meant that Brethren Service was largely a USA-oriented operation until 1945.

There were exceptions. Among these was the work of John Barwick, seconded by BSC to the World's YMCA for work with German and Italian prisoners of war in England. His work was recognized among voluntary agencies as very successful. This allowed and necessitated the Brethren to follow up his initiatives with further staff in the 1940s.[12]

The reorganized and enlarged Brethren Service Committee of 1941 also absorbed the duties of the Committee on Legal Counsel for Conscientious Objectors, created by the Annual Conference of 1935. This committee had been restructured in 1940 as the Advisory Committee for Conscientious Objectors, with three members, including M. R. Zigler. It was responsible to negotiate with the government concerning COs.

147

New Windsor

By common consent one of the most farsighted initiatives of Zigler during the dark years of World War II was the purchase of the former campus of Blue Ridge College in New Windsor, Maryland, as a relief center. Through a complicated series of financial reverses and shifts in ownership, the college campus, with its buildings and other property, was placed on public auction on March 1, 1944. Zigler had long had his eyes on the property (which stood vacant for several years). He attended the auction and succeeded in buying the property for the sum of $31,500. It was a typically aggressive move for Zigler and had its share of critics, not least among the administrators of Brethren colleges in the East, who sought the profits from the sale for their schools. The compromise solution was that Bridgewater College received the profits from the sale of the houses and farms connected with the campus and that Brethren Service received the twenty-three acres and the four large buildings. Zigler always regretted losing the houses and especially the farms, which he thought could have been well used for the Heifer Project. Some of his friends were men of means who encouraged the purchase.[13]

Using CPS men as staff, New Windsor soon emerged as the central depot for relief and rehabilitation programs, ranging from a collection and transshipping point for material aid, to a reception area for refugees pending relocation, to a training ground for Brethren volunteers. Very early, Zigler offered the facilities of New Windsor to other denominations and agencies; it soon became a center sponsored by the ecumenical Church World Service and other interdenominational bodies. It has retained that identification over the years and is known nationally and internationally as the Protestant center for relief and aid programs. M. R. Zigler was honored in May, 1968, with the dedication of a large hospitality building (costing $475,000) as *Zigler Hall*.[14]

Japanese Relocation

One of the sadder chapters in American history is the treatment of the Japanese-Americans after the entry of the USA into World War II. The tragedy inflicted on a loyal population, guilty only of an ethnic background now hated, has been recognized and partially atoned for by the act of the US Congress in 1988 authorizing monetary compensation to those citizens of Japanese ancestry who were removed from their homes on the

West Coast and interned in what can technically be called concentration camps.

President Franklin D. Roosevelt called the Japanese surprise attack on Pearl Harbor on December 8, 1941, a "day of infamy" which would never be forgotten. For others, February 19, 1942 will also live on as another day of infamy. That was the day on which the president signed Executive Order No. 9066 ordering the removal of all persons of Japanese ethnic origin from a large sector of the West Coast. Of the 120,000 persons affected by the order, fully two-thirds were US citizens. At very short notice, these persons were ordered to report to central locations to be resettled elsewhere. Very few were able to arrange for orderly disposition of their farms, businesses, homes, and property. Sad to say, there were those Americans who were quite willing to profit from their neighbors' misfortune.

Temporary dwellings for many were in such improvised shelters as abandoned racetracks and warehouses. Final resettlement was behind barbed wire in hastily erected camps in isolated locations in inhospitable regions. Heavily armed troops patrolled the camps. The tar-paper barracks provided only minimal protection from the elements.

Into this situation stepped several Brethren, most notably, Ralph E. Smeltzer and Mary Blocher Smeltzer from California. They intervened to assist bewildered evacuees as they were rounded up for transportation, providing meals and assistance in bringing their strictly limited possessions to the train stations. This intervention was welcomed by the military authorities but local officials harassed them and even threatened their lives. Later, the Smeltzers volunteered as teachers in one of the camps, Manzanar in California.

M. R. Zigler quickly placed the resources of the Brethren Service Committee behind the work of the Smeltzers and other concerned Brethren. It was the BSC that provided the framework for the creation of hostels, first in the Chicago area and later in the New York area, for the resettlement of younger Japanese-Americans from the camps. Staff workers at the hostels welcomed the incoming former internees, helped to find jobs, and assisted in locating accommodations. Over a thousand persons were helped in this resettlement process in Chicago alone from March, 1943, to April, 1944. In 1981 the General Board of the Church of the Brethren went on record to urge the US government to redress the wrongs committed upon the Japanese-American population.[15]

Relief Operations

It was clear to Zigler and his colleagues in the church that the end of the war would open the way in helping to meet the staggering needs of the world. He was clearly thinking and planning ahead to the time when the church would be facing the call of response to the desperate suffering of millions of people of many nationalities, refugees chief among them.

Consistent with his approach with other church programs, Zigler wished to tackle these assignments in cooperation with other churches. One of the channels he began working through was the American Council of Voluntary Agencies for Foreign Services, after it was founded in October, 1943. Dr. Joseph B. Chamberlain of Columbia University, active in many committees aiding refugees, was its guiding spirit. The ACVAFS served as a forum for coordination and consultation as well as a liaison to the US government; in effect it was a kind of accrediting agency, periodically gathering and distributing reports from member organizations. Zigler or someone he appointed as representative attended the required meetings in New York. It is significant that he was alert to the agency's importance and was active from the very beginning of its work. The veteran administrator of the agency, Elizabeth Clark Reiss, wrote an affectionate letter to Zigler when he retired from Brethren Service work in 1959:

> Retiring is sometimes a sad occasion but in this instance it gives us the opportunity for which we have long been waiting: to tell you (when you can't answer back!) what Bob Zigler has meant to us here at American Council headquarters over the years.
>
> Do you remember how you inspired us all in the early days of the Council, at those first policy-making, emergency-fraught and urgent meetings, not only with your bold thoughts (how many have seen realization!), but also with the sparkle in your eyes and the rebellious stirring of your hair? You led us to broader views when often we might have been satisfied merely to meet the emergency of the hour. You implanted some of your own great heart and soaring intellect into our minds and souls.
>
> And then you went to Geneva to work for your Church in a capacity that took you out of immediate proximity with the work of the Council in New York. But we want you to know this: there have been few occasions when, faced with problems needing the larger solution, weighted with the deeper significance, that we have not felt the presence of the man with the sparkling eyes and the rebellious hair at our table and sought our answers in what we believed he would counsel. . . .[16]

These contacts with the church agencies preparing to face the postwar challenge were of the utmost importance to M. R. Zigler as he made preparations for launching the Brethren into large-scale relief operations.

At the same time, a modest number of relief and peace projects were carried on in the USA, Mexico, South America, and elsewhere. They were hampered by wartime limitations and lack of funds but made their own contribution as well. Minutes of the meetings of the Brethren Service Committee in the first half of the 1940s bear testimony to the ambitious program pushed ahead by Zigler as its energetic executive secretary. The chairman of the board of BSC during this period was Andrew W. Cordier, whose international perspective and wide-ranging interests found their focus in the immediate postwar period with his staff relationship in the new United Nations.

Personal Arrangements

Keeping all of those programs going was a daunting task, before which less dedicated and vigorous people would have quailed. It was his practice to arrive at the office early, often by 3:00 A.M., to begin working through his correspondence. When the secretarial staff arrived at 8:00 A.M., they found several Ediphone cylinders ready for transcription. Zigler had the habit of pacing back and forth as he dictated, claiming that the movement helped him to think better.

About 1945 the Ziglers moved from their home on Hamilton Avenue and became house parents at the Brethren Fellowship House on State Street, a large residence used to house workers at the Elgin offices and other young Brethren singles. (The Zigler house on Hamilton was rented for a time and then sold in 1947.) The purchase of this house had also been a Zigler initiative, one which was resisted by the Elgin church administration for a time. A resident described the regular practice of leisurely Saturday morning breakfasts; Zigler's place was at the end of the table and the "center of attention." He led the sessions and "never seemed to run [out] of things" to relate—"happenings in his travels, answers to our questions, what the church ought to be doing, his dreams for world peace, and other subjects." He also could be an interested listener and was eager to hear the thoughts of others on these issues.[17]

So the war years passed in a stream of engagements, meetings, trips, and encounters. But the end of the war in 1945 did not diminish his work.

If anything, the pace escalated, as opportunities blocked during the war now came within the realm of possibility. It was to them that he turned.

NOTES

1. His colleagues were seriously worried about his health already in March, 1942; Ruth Shriver to Andrew W. Cordier, March 11, 1942 (Cordier Papers, Box 13, Columbia University Library).
2. M. R. Zigler, "Director of Brethren Civilian Service," *Gospel Messenger* (Jan. 18, 1941): 12; Paul H. Bowman, "An Open Letter to the Church," *Gospel Messenger* (Jan. 18, 1941): 12-13; Paul H. Bowman, "The Church of the Brethren Civilian Public Service," *Gospel Messenger* (Feb. 1, 1941): 8-9; Paul H. Bowman, "The Civilian Public Service Movement," *Gospel Messenger* (Feb. 1., 1941): 17-18; Paul H. Bowman, "Civilian Public Service—An Interpretation," *Gospel Messenger* (Feb. 15, 1941): 8-9; Paul H. Bowman, "Financing Civilian Public Service Camps," *Gospel Messenger* (Feb. 22, 1941): 8-9. Paul H. Bowman, "Our Combatant and Non-Combatant Brethren," *Gospel Messenger* (April 12, 1941): 12,
3. Jefferson Mathis, *Jeff's Stories: Raccoon Valley, Des Moines Valley, Hills and Valleys of Public Service, the Valley of the Shadow* [La Verne, CA: author, 1987], 68-71; Ora Huston to M. R. Zigler, Feb. 1, 1960.
4. "From the Retiring Director of Civilian Public Service," *Gospel Messenger* (Aug. 2, 1941): 17, the publication of a letter from Paul H. Bowman to M. R. Zigler, July 9, 1941.
5. "Peace News," *Gospel Messenger* (Aug. 16, 1941): 21; "W. Harold Row Chosen Assistant Executive Secretary of the Brethren Service Commission," *Gospel Messenger* (March 21, 1942): 21.
6. French kept a detailed diary through this entire period; unfortunately never published, it is a basic source for understanding the origin and evolution of the CPS program. The diary is part of the Swarthmore College Peace Collection. French also planned to write a history of CPS and began compiling materials, but left NSBRO employ before completing the task.
7. M. R. Zigler to Paul Comly French, Nov. 22, 1943; French to Zigler, Nov. 25, 1943 (NSBRO Records, Swarthmore College Peace Collection).
8. D. F. Durnbaugh, "Paul Comly French," *Brethren Encyclopedia* (1983-1984), 515.
9. Correspondence between Bishop G. Bromley Oxnam and Gen. Lewis B. Hershey, Dec. 1, 1941—July 26, 1942 (Selective Service Files, National Archives); Minutes, NSBRO Board of Directors, Oct. 9, 1942 (NSBRO Records, Swarthmore College Peace Collection).

10. The story is told most fully in Sappington, *Social Policy* (1961); see also David B. Eller, "Social Outreach," in *Church of the Brethren: Yesterday and Today*, ed. D. F. Durnbaugh (Elgin, IL: Brethren Press, 1986), 119-134; and Lorell Weiss, *Ten Years of Brethren Service* (Elgin, IL: Brethren Service Commission, [1951]).

11. Paul Kinsel to D. F. Durnbaugh, June 22, 1987.

12. Luther H. Harshbarger, "Work with Prisoners of War," in *To Serve the Present Age: The Brethren Service Story*, ed. D. F. Durnbaugh (Elgin, IL: Brethren Press, 1975), 131-143.

13. Harold E. Fey interview with M. R. Zigler, June 27, 1965 (FCC Papers, Presbyterian Historical Society); Ken Kreider interview with M. R. Zigler, May 7, 1977.

14. Kenneth I. Morse, *New Windsor Center* (Elgin, IL: Brethren Press, 1979); "Center to Dedicate M. R. Zigler Hall," *Messenger* (May 9, 1968): 15.

15. Mary Blocher Smeltzer, "Japanese-American Resettlement Work," in *Present Age*, ed. D. F. Durnbaugh (1975), 123-130; Ralph E. Smeltzer, "Report on the Japanese-American Relocation from Lindsay, California, 1942," ed. Craig Enberg, *Brethren Life and Thought*, 22 (Spring, 19770: 71-77.

16. Elizabeth Clark Reiss to Bob Zigler, May 6, 1959 (ACVAFS Papers, Rutgers University Library); Elizabeth Clark Reiss, *ACVAFS: Four Monographs* (New York: American Council of Voluntary Agencies for Foreign Service, 1985); J. Bruce Nicholson, *The Uneasy Alliance: Religion, Refugee Work, and U.S. Foreign Policy* (New York: Oxford University Press, 1988), 61-63.

17. Ruth Early to D. F. Durnbaugh, Aug. 30, 1987.

13

POSTWAR RELIEF
AND REHABILITATION

ONE OF THE FIRST American church leaders to travel in liberated Europe after the end of World War II was M. R. Zigler. His purpose was to inspect Brethren work already in place, largely through the World's YMCA and to gather information on areas of greatest need. He sought to learn how the Brethren could work together with other church bodies in a wide-scale relief effort. He also was preparing to launch a major campaign back in the USA to secure extensive material aid through the churches. It was a grim task. Europe lay devastated by the most destructive war in history. The pounding of heavy artillery as the war front surged back and forth had been massive. But worse by far was the impact of concentrated waves of bombing, designed not so much to pinpoint military targets as to level whole cities, especially through the dread effects of fire storms.

Gen. Dwight D. Eisenhower, commander-in-chief of the Allied forces, described in unequivocal terms what this meant for Germany, the focus of Allied battering in the drive to bring unconditional surrender:

> Germany is destroyed. At least the cities are destroyed beyond anything I have seen in this war: Frankfurt, Cologne, Kassel, Berlin are London at its worst multiplied by a hundred thousand. They are destroyed.
>
> In the dislocation of the transport system, breaking up of the agricultural system, mining—mining has almost ceased—they (the Germans) are facing a problem of real starvation.
>
> This is the first and emergency problem in Germany. What are we going to do just to prevent on our part having a Buchenwald of our own—not in this case from intent, but because we would not be able to help it?[1]

Eisenhower used the image of one of the Nazi concentration camps, sited ironically near Weimar, the famed center of German humanism and the home of Goethe. Newsreels taken of the emaciated survivors of these camps and the piles of the dead had shocked the world. Now, mass death faced the innocent civilian populations of Europe.

A history of American relief agencies in Germany began its description with a quotation from a report by M. R. Zigler of what he had found in Berlin in the fall of 1945 when he interviewed a widow with four children:

> The woman announced without apparent emotion that she must decide which of her children she would try to keep alive during the winter to come. She could not possibly find enough food for all four of her children, and so she had to choose which one or two had the best chance of surviving. The food she scrounged would go to them and she would have to watch the others waste away. This woman had seemingly gone beyond the point of grief and could make the statement calmly. It was reported from Berlin that during the winter most of the children under three failed to survive.[2]

During this trip, Zigler, as one of the first American churchmen in postwar Europe, made special efforts to visit European church leaders. In Germany, he met with Bishop Otto Dibelius in Berlin, Pastor Friedrich von Bodelschwingh in Bethel near Bielefeld, and Dr. Eugen Gerstenmaier. All of these men had been active in the Confessing Church, the minority of German Protestantism that had resisted the attempt of the German government to take over the church. (He missed meeting Pastor Martin Niemoeller on this trip, and just missed attending the historic meeting of ecumenical and German church leaders in Stuttgart in October 18-20, 1945, which was the first step in bringing the German churches back into the circle of the world church.)[3]

He also made a point of interviewing the American military leaders, at that time in effective charge of the occupied nations. According to Zigler, when he reached Berlin and found his way to the office of Gen. Lucius D. Clay, the general greeted him with: "Where in hell is the church?" Clay confided that he had on his desk a directive that he should not raise the starvation diet of the Germans above 1,300 calories per day until the French civilians were fed more. Zigler asked: "If we would come with food who would stop us?" Clay responded that he had orders not to feed the German civilian population, but no orders to stop others from feeding them. Zigler also interviewed General Mark Clark in Vienna. From each

155

he sought information on the plans of the occupying forces for relieving the misery of the populations over which they stood; to each he pledged the efforts of the Brethren, along with other American churches, to alleviate the staggering need.[4]

In announcing the trip, the Brethren Service Committee reported in the *Gospel Messenger*:

> . . . this European trip is not merely the journey of a man; it is the beginning of an effort on the part of our church to rise up in the hour of the world's need and say, "Lord, use us." And those of us who are staying here at home will want to keep Brother Zigler in our thoughts and prayers as he seeks to learn where we can be used best.[5]

Zigler had left the USA by air on August 30, 1945, to fly to England. He was met in London by John Barwick, the chief Brethren representative with the World's YMCA, who had gained a reputation for his imaginative and extensive work with Axis prisoners of war. Barwick had just returned from his own survey of need on the European continent. While in England, Zigler conferred with his close friend, Orie O. Miller, head of the Mennonite Central Committee, there on an administrative trip. Zigler also informed himself about the work of Martha Rupel at a children's home. From England he went to France, intending to meet Dr. Eldon Burke there, and then to Belgium, where Luther Harshbarger was in charge of the local Prisoners of War Aid work of the YMCA. Burke was the head of Brethren relief work in Europe and had himself made trips into France, Holland, and Germany to ascertain areas of greatest want.[6]

A highlight of Zigler's itinerary was his visit to Geneva, where the temporary offices of the World Council of Churches were located. Throughout the war, under the vigorous leadership of W. A. Visser 't Hooft, the WCC in neutral Switzerland had kept lines of communication open to churches behind the battle lines. Its assistance to refugees had strained all of its resources. It now sought to coordinate the activities of Protestant relief efforts.

The line followed by WCC leaders early on was to place primary effort on reestablishing the fabric and personnel of the church. They understood the huge tasks of feeding and sheltering the masses to be the task of the governments. Therefore, church contributions should be focused on restoring theological education, subsidizing pastoral support, rebuilding shattered church edifices, and the like. This ran athwart of the concept, held particularly by American church leaders, that the ecumenical move-

156

ment should respond to massive human suffering with its own aid program. This background difference on policy is reflected in a cable sent by Zigler to the American churches, cosigned by Elsie Culver, the representative of the Church Committee for Overseas Relief and Reconstruction. Stating that "Geneva is all out for material aid through the churches," the message first quoted J. Hutchinson Cockburn, who had been given the assignment of directing ecumenical aid for relief and reconstruction:

> Good Samaritan must come before evangelist. Have had to change our thinking regarding priority for material aid. Children must not die from hunger and cold this winter. American church help is imperative. There is no ceiling on European relief needs. Western civilization itself is at stake. Consider implications if pestilence strikes undernourished people in devastated areas. Hope and think material [aid] will not encroach on reconstruction funds. Even if it does for time being it will act as springboard and result in added spiritual gains.

Zigler and Culver added more information to the cable:

> Twelve million [refugees] displaced from Sudetenland, Silesia, Latvia are homeless. UNRRA [United Nations Relief and Rehabilitation Administration] assumes no responsibility for these. One million will die this winter. In some districts no child born in 1945 is alive. Needed are 100,000 shoes, million francs, gauze bandages, beds, blankets, hotel furnishings. Turning to churches as last hope. Geneva asking national churches establish committees to supervise distribution of warm clothing, bedding. Large quantities needed quickly.[7]

Years later Elsie Culver remembered the circumstances of meeting with Cockburn. The early meetings had actually taken place in the Brethren hostel in Paris. She recalled later discussions in Geneva, with Zigler "all wrapped up in a featherbed trying to keep warm." She further recalled that in the early discussions in the USA on foreign relief aid, it had often been the initiative of M. R. Zigler that had kept the churches active, against the continuing pull of domestic demands:

> Through this period the Brethren continued to speak in terms of human compassion and Christian commitment. I remember more than one occasion when your own statement of the Christian imperative that faced us changed the whole course of a meeting. This was particularly true because you could say

157

with assurance that the Church of the Brethren as a whole would back your commitments; sometimes you said that if the churches working together did not accept certain responsibilities the Brethren would have to go ahead and do what they could. Several times I know you made the first pledge of actual cash. More than once this precipitated cooperative action under conditions where time was of the essence, or where putting off a decision, would have meant, in effect, no action at all.[8]

Zigler and Culver joined as signatories in a widely-distributed appeal sent from the World Council of Churches asking for "physical relief in Europe." Emphasizing that its decision to gather and distribute material aid did not undercut its previously announced program to rebuild church life on the shattered Continent, the WCC called for the means to take emergency measures for the "winter that lies just ahead." In a private letter written to his wife from Geneva on October 8, Zigler reflected on this change of emphasis: "Well, I know that we have come to a turning point in the road of Protestantism. The World Council of Churches decided to do material aid. The whole organization is going to swing back of this movement. I can hardly believe that the shift has come. The need is so terrific that it can no longer be ignored. I hope the people in America will respond to the call of need." He continued, "I have fought for the church to do this work for four years and here it comes late but not too late. We will save some."[9]

In the first longer article reporting his findings to the Brethren, Zigler asked: "Europe Suffers: Will the Christian Church Respond?" In the article, which teemed with the tragic statistics of the war-torn continent, the author made a pointed comparison of the situation of the American and the European churches:

The church in America has not suffered like the church in England, France, Italy, Germany, Greece, Holland, Belgium, Norway, China, Japan, Russia, and other areas of warfare. True, our congregations have been greatly damaged by taking millions of men and women from our local communities, never to return. But our buildings still stand. Our homes are not laid low in city after city. We do not have hordes of people coming through our cities, villages and countryside seeking food, clothing, and a place to sleep and then moving on. For five years these people of Europe have been suffering destruction of homes and bodies. The letdown following a war has come. The power of the military recedes, and there seems to be no way to organize quickly for peacetime as we organize to administer a war. Suffering women pray to God for help as they bring into the world babies who will die within a few days.

Children pray to God for help in their search for parents who may be dead and for their homes which may have been destroyed. Millions of soldiers are returning to find their families totally or partially gone. What is the answer of the church? What is the answer of the Church of the Brethren?[10]

Traveling in former war zones required elaborate documents. Permits for travel had to be arranged through the military authorities. Zigler first obtained permits to travel in the British-occupied zone of Germany, the northern section, and also for Berlin, under four-power occupation. He stretched this permission to dip down (illegally) into the American zone to visit Schwarzenau. Later, from Paris, he was able to secure papers to visit the American zone, the first civilian under church auspices to do so. In all, Zigler visited Aachen, Hannover, Berlin, Schwarzenau, Marburg, Heidelberg, Karlsruhe, and Stuttgart. Added to his early inspections in England, France, Belgium, and Holland, these visits enabled him to get a balanced picture of the nearly incomprehensible immediate postwar situation. He found when he visited Geneva that he had seen more than any of the staff members of the WCC.

Zigler returned to the USA on November 12 just in time to report to the meeting of the Council of Boards of the Church of the Brethren. He gave a vivid picture of Europe's great need and reported that the first Brethren material aid supplies had arrived and were distributed.[11]

Zigler's initiatives galvanized the Brethren membership, and giving increased substantially. He also gave his attention to the broader religious scene, through interviews in the media, articles, and private communications. The *Chicago Tribune* headlined his report of European conditions: "Church Leader Tells Plight of Low Countries." The influential *Christian Century* took up the cause, with a series of flaming editorials. A typical one was entitled: "Are We Murderers?" It was directed at the American policy of accepting mass expulsion of German refugees from Eastern Europe agreed upon by the Allies at the Potsdam conference, and the reluctance of military authorities to provide food in occupied zones. The second source quoted in the editorial was "Dr. M. R. Zigler of the Brethren Service Committee," described as "a church leader respected for the sobriety of his judgment throughout American Protestantism."[12]

They quoted his report to the Federal Council of Churches in late November of seeing "15,000 orphan children without clothing huddled in one building with no windows and the cold winds howling through." A curious problem emerged with the interpretation. The prestigious American bishop, G. Bromley Oxnam of the Methodist Church, had also visited

Europe for two weeks and came home proclaiming that there would be no mass starvation, there was little need for urgency. At one point, Zigler refused to be quoted directly in a *Christian Century* article/editorial, for fear of offending Oxnam and creating the impression of a divided Protestantism. His message, nevertheless, was reported, attributed to a "Concerned Observer."[13]

One of the grimmest of his reports appeared in the 1945 Christmas edition of the *Gospel Messenger*, titled simply "The Angels Sang, 'Peace . . . Goodwill.'" After reciting conditions he saw in the fall in Europe, he predicted what would happen by February with the rigor of the winter conditions:

> By February women will have lost interest in life. They will no longer have mental or physical power to care for themselves or their children. . . . By February millions of strong men will be in the death struggle that comes to those who starve. Already their flesh is vanishing. . . . By February, the youth will be praying for food. It will not come. They will die too. . . . By February, if the present trend continues, there will be only a few babies alive under one year of age and they will starve. I felt the hand of a woman who said she had to let her baby die because she had food for only one. I saw the father weep, for he had no work and had been crippled during the war. . . . By February, the cold winter will be upon them. No warm clothing will be available; not enough blankets can be found for the people. Starvation and winter mean death, a slow death.

The article concluded with a strong appeal for Christians to give as they had never done before. He admonished: "I sincerely feel that unless the Christians who have materials to share really sacrifice and help now, the Christian church will not recover for many years the place she deserves in the life of the world."[14]

The Second European Trip

In the fall of 1946, M. R. Zigler went again to Europe on a longer tour to inspect the much larger Brethren presence and to assess continuing needs. He left on October 30 by plane for Berlin, then toured Germany, Austria, Italy, Switzerland (World Council of Churches), Belgium, Holland, France, Poland, Sweden, and England, returning in early February, 1947. He characterized his three-month journey as an attempt to develop a "long-time program of peace and goodwill" by (1) evaluating the present

160

relief program, (2) exploring possibilities for future relief efforts, and (3) helping to establish new projects.[15]

His first cable from Berlin read:

> Urgent need German civilian population. Reserve resources exhausted; conditions growing steadily worse. Harvest and imports fail to provide subsistence. Clothing need extreme and absence raw materials makes textile production impossible. Widespread sickness. Suffering inevitable owing to lack of fuel, housing, clothing, food. Desperate need for shoes and clothing aggravated by refugee population.[16]

In fact, the second winter after the end of the war was worse than the first. It was colder and the last reserves had been depleted.

Zigler participated in a meeting of Brethren Service workers held in Brussels on December 16-17. Those attending from Europe were: from Germany, Eldon Burke (chair), Ernest Lefever, John Bowman; from Sweden, Nils Esbensen; from the Netherlands, Cecile Burke, Lois Rupel, Martha Rupel, Isaac Earhart; from Italy, Walter Bowman, Bob Mays; from France, Ruth and Charles Webb; from Belgium, Helena Kruger, Grace and Roscoe Switzer, Opal and Dwight Horner, Marian and Luther Harshbarger, Virginia Bowman; from England, John Barwick; from Austria, Ralph Smeltzer; from Poland, Clara and Bruce Wood (and L. W. Shultz, as a visitor). Other personnel in Europe not able to attend were: in Poland, Thurl Metzger; in Sweden, Maren Esbensen; in Italy, Eloise and Eugene Lichty, Imogene and Merlin Frantz, Frances Bowman, Joyce Mays, and Mark Ebersole. Many of these early service workers were soon shifted to other locations, as needs were met and new programs opened.[17]

On Christmas Day, Zigler visited the Brethren birthplace in Schwarzenau, together with John Bowman and Ernest Lefever, making connections again with the local pastor. They reflected on the former days when Mack and his associates were refugees in the same place. The small village contained besides its usual residents 300 expellees from Eastern Europe and 250 bombed-out Germans. The old manor house was crowded with refugees; one family of eleven had but one room to live in. The father in the family had brought his family from Dresden in an ox cart. Zigler gave some gifts to the families living in the old house in the Huettental area, thought to have been Mack's residence; some thirty-four people were crowded in the structure.[18]

Pastor Karl Pabst of Schwarzenau wrote to "Mister R. Zigler":

> I am glad that you had visited us just at Christmas day and we had heard together the gospel: "Glory to God in the highest, and be on earth peace, goodwill toward men." We know that we are brethren for the sake of our Saviour Jesus Christ. Therefore I dare to beg that you, Mister R. Zigler, would take care of the distress of the community Schwarzenau. Our poor community had to receive 300 refugees. We have no clothes and shoes to give them. Please, say to the brethren in U.S.A. how great the distress is here. Now we ask you for the sake of our Saviour Jesus Christ to help us.

An immediate shipment of fifty bales of clothing was readied at the New Windsor processing plant for shipment to Schwarzenau and a new fund was set up to aid those in need in the village.[19]

Out of this and other encounters, Zigler concluded in a cable sent to the USA in February, 1947:

> If the church survives Europe must have extraordinary expression of Christian love. It must begin with food, clothing and end in spiritual brotherhood. Otherwise crisis upon crisis will result in dark despair. True Christian people will continue to respond to human suffering. I saw Brethren materials in Germany, Austria, Italy, Poland, Holland, and France. I urge all Brethren people continue identify with those in need by sharing generously money, materials undergirded with prayer.[20]

That this and other appeals were taken seriously by the Brethren is borne out by statistics. During the fiscal year ending on February 28, 1947, the value of material aid administered and distributed by Brethren Service was nearly $7.2 million; although the entire amount was not contributed directly by Brethren, observers concluded that the Brethren were the most generous donors in Protestantism. The official history of Church World Service states that "the small Church of the Brethren led the others in the amount of contributed commodities sent through ecumenical channels;" in 1946 the Brethren gave 884,000 pounds, while the Methodist Church donated 557,000 pounds and the Presbyterian Church (USA) some 388,000.[21]

In a long report written from Belgium on January 25, 1947, Zigler outlined the revised relief program that had been worked out in the earlier meeting of all Brethren Service workers and revised by a smaller committee. This called for continued and expanded programs in the countries already involved and the establishment of a central administrative office in Geneva. In the place of the current twenty-nine workers, the plan anticipated having sixty or more workers in place by September 1, 1947, with the following distribution: Germany (six), Austria (ten), Italy (twelve),

World's YMCA (ten), Netherlands (two), France (six), Poland (ten) and central office (five).[22]

After returning home (with some difficulty) in February, Zigler launched into a whirlwind drive of interpretation and communication. Each Sunday he averaged from three to five presentations with more during the week. He visited five of the six Brethren-related colleges and Bethany Seminary and the congregations in their areas. By March 13, he had spent only two days in the Elgin office. He broadcast messages over radio stations, including one from Chicago that brought responses from Wisconsin to Texas. In Johnstown, Pennsylvania, he spoke to an audience of some 1,500 people gathered in a high school auditorium, raising over $1,100 dollars in the process. He reported to the various interagency organizations with which BSC was affiliated, such as CRALOG and the American Council of Voluntary Agencies for Foreign Service, urging long-range planning and programs. He met with representatives of the US President to urge larger governmental responses to the needs.[23]

In a sequel to the Bishop Oxnam story, at about this time the venerated former President Herbert Hoover returned from Europe on a fact-finding mission for the government. His story tallied with that told by Zigler. In a letter to veteran relief worker and friend, John Barwick, Zigler confided:

> We have been receiving terrific news from abroad. Herbert Hoover followed me up in much better style than Bishop Oxnam did a year ago. Even Geneva, Switzerland, is beginning to call for help for the suffering people. In the *Christian Century* this week they admit that they did not anticipate the terrible misery that was abroad in Europe. When will Christian people of all types and organizations become sensitive enough to anticipate and be prophetic? I have almost lost my courage and faith in the Christian administration, and I don't mean just the church. I mean Christian men and women in Europe and in America.[24]

Visit to China

In 1947 M. R. Zigler was asked to visit China to evaluate the special Brethren Service project there. This was the "tractor unit," for which the Brethren recruited, trained, and administered fifty American men; the project ran under a contract with the United Nations Relief and Rehabilitation Administration (UNRRA) to work in China to train Chinese how to operate tractors made available by the international agency. The site of the project initially was to be the huge area (some two million acres) flooded

163

by the Yellow River. Under UNRRA auspices the Chinese had repaired the dikes but the ground was in no condition for agriculture. By February, 1947, all fifty members of the unit had reached China. Howard Sollenberger, the son of Brethren missionaries, was named as the head of the unit. By the middle of 1947 they had trained 1,000 Chinese operators and plowed nearly 67,000 acres. They worked primarily in the Honan and Shantung provinces, but also in Hopeh, Hunan, Anhwei, and Kwangsi provinces.[25]

Time magazine wrote up the project as a demonstration of applied Christianity. It quoted Zigler as pointing out the possibility of lay members to serve: "This is a new way for the layman to express himself; he can do so through his own skill. Ordinarily, churches send missionaries or ministers. This way the layman can serve."[26]

They were warmly praised by the American administrator of the China UNRRA program, Harlan Cleveland, grandson of President Grover Cleveland. He wrote to a meeting of the unit: "Some of you have achieved recognition by reason of your magnificent beards, but all of you earned something bordering on awed respect and admiration by the zeal and enthusiasm with which you have tackled some of the toughest jobs in China."

Pointing out that they had posed very few administrative problems for UNRRA, Cleveland praised the training given to them by BSC. He then noted some of the statistics of their achievements, concluding: "The figures are impressive enough in themselves but certainly do not tell the whole story. There is no statistical unit of measure for adding up the physical danger in which some of you have worked, the patience you have shown in connection with the training program, the ingenuity that was necessary on your part as a substitute for the supplies UNRRA was sometimes unable to bring soon enough. . . ." He praised them for their "painstaking and selfless efforts" as men who traveled thousands of miles "to bear witness to their convictions that all men are brothers."[27]

The danger referred to by Cleveland came from the fact that members of the Brethren unit served both in the Nationalist-held area of China and the Communist-held area, true to the principles of the Brethren to serve without distinction of political alignment.

Zigler's trip was at the cost of UNRRA. He left the USA from San Francisco on July 22 on Pan American Airways and flew to Shanghai by way of Hawaii, Midway, Wake, and Okinawa. He reported that it was an excellent trip but "a little long in the air for comfort." In China, extreme heat, poor transportation facilities, and exotic meals (fried sparrows—heads, bones, and all) were all in the experience.

He took part in seven different tours to visit as many of the sites as possible. The longer distances were mainly covered by air, but trains were also used. Some of the travel was by jeep to visit the projects where the tractors were stationed. "It rained very hard and therefore, we had much difficulty traveling through water and mud. I never saw anything like it before and never will again, I hope. But everyone was cheerful and we made the trip on scheduled time." Occasionally it was necessary to strip off all clothes and wade through deep water.[28]

Zigler also took counsel with Church of the Brethren missionaries stationed there. One of them, Wendell Flory, was detailed for full time relief work. At the end of the visit on September 20, Zigler recommended that the Brethren maintain a strong presence in China, even after the UNRRA tractor unit was completed. He also recommended extending work into Japan, where he spent one week on the return trip. The Brethren had shipped bulls to Japan under the aegis of LARA (Licensed Agencies for Relief in Asia); this had "placed BSC in the high regard of all the Japanese officials." A useful follow up program, he urged, would be to send shipments of goats, accompanied ideally by a trained agriculturist.[29]

For several reasons, the Brethren program was never fully implemented in Asia. The Communist takeover made it impossible to extend work in China and priorities for Europe took first call over personnel for Japan.

NOTES

1. Quoted in Eileen Egan and Elizabeth Clark Reiss, *Transfigured Night: The CRALOG Experience* (Philadelphia and New York: Livingston, 1964), 4.
2. Egan and Reiss, *Transfigured Night* (1964), 21.
3. Samuel McCrea Cavert, "The New Birth of the German Church," *Christian Century* (Dec. 12, 1945): 1380-1381.
4. Harold E. Fey interview with M. R. Zigler, June 27, 1965 (FCC Papers, Presbyterian Historical Society).
5. "M. R. Zigler Goes to Europe," *Gospel Messenger* (Sept. 29, 1945); 12.
6. *Gospel Messenger* (Sept. 29, 1945): 16; (Oct. 27, 1945): 21.
7. "M. R. Zigler and Elsie T. Culver, of the Church Committee for Overseas Relief

and Reconstruction, Cable American Churches," *Gospel Messenger* (Oct. 20, 1945): 9.

8. Elsie T. Culver to M. R. Zigler, Sept. 22, 1965; Culver to Zigler, Jan. 26, 1960.

9. "The World Council of Churches Appeals to the Churches for Physical Relief in Europe," Geneva, Oct. 9, 1945; M. R. Zigler to Amy Zigler, Oct. 8, 1945.

10. M. R. Zigler, "Europe Suffers: Will the Christian Church Respond?" *Gospel Messenger* (Nov. 10, 1945),7-9.

11. "Council of Boards Meeting," *Gospel Messenger* (Dec. 15, 1945): 10.

12. "Church Leader Tells Plight of Low Countries: Head of Brethren Says Food Needed Quickly," *Chicago Tribune* (Nov. 24, 1945): 12; "Are We Murderers?" *Christian Century* (Nov. 14, 1945): 1247-1249.

13. "Urges Immediate Aid for Europe," *Christian Century* (Dec. 5, 1945): 1366; "What Is Mass Starvation," *Christian Century* (Dec. 26, 1945): 1439-1441.

14. M. R. Zigler, "The Angels Sang, 'Peace . . . Goodwill," *Gospel Messenger* (Dec. 22, 1945): 6-7.

15. "European Mission," *Gospel Messenger* (Nov. 16, 1946): 21.

16. *Gospel Messenger* (Nov. 30, 1946): 17.

17. Minutes of the Meeting of Brethren Service Workers in Europe, Brussels, Belgium, December 16-17, 1946.

18. M. R. Zigler, "Visit to Schwarzenau and Sweden," *Gospel Messenger* (Feb. 8, 1947): 11; John Bowman, "This Was Christmas in Schwarzeanu," *Gospel Messenger* (March 29, 1947): 14-15.

19. [Karl Pabst], "The Pastor of the Schwarzenau Church Writes," *Gospel Messenger* (March 8, 1947): 20.

20. *Gospel Messenger* (Feb. 15, 1947): 17.

21. Harold E. Fey, *Cooperation in Compassion: The Story of Church World Service* (New York: Friendship Press, 1966), 36.

22. M. R. Zigler to Brethren Service Commission, "Report on Brethren Service," Brussels, Belgium, Jan. 25, 1947.

23. M. R. Zigler to all Relief Workers, March 13, 1947; *Gospel Messenger* (March 29, 1947, 21; *Gospel Messenger* (May 17, 1947): 18.

24. M. R. Zigler to John Barwick, March 17, 1947.

25. "Brethren Service Primer: Lesson 13," *Gospel Messenger* (Oct. 4, 1947): 21; Howard E. Sollenger, "The UNRRA Brethren Service Unit," in *To Serve the Present Age: The Brethren Service Story*, ed. D. F. Durnbaugh (Elgin, IL: Brethren Press, 1975), 155-163.

26. "Tractors for China," *Time* (Sept. 2, 1946): 69-70.

27. *Gospel Messenger* (Oct, 4, 1947): 21.

28. "A Letter from M. R. Zigler," *Gospel Messenger* (Sept. 20, 1947): 11-12; "Letter from M. R. Zigler, received August 21 [1947], from Shanghai, China—," mimeographed.

29. "Report on China: Report of Survey in China, July 22 to September 20, by M. R. Zigler."

━━━━━━━━━━━━━━━14

COOPERATIVE CHRISTIANITY

T HROUGHOUT THE STORY thus far, one thing has become quite clear: M. R. Zigler, for all of his undeniable loyalty to the Church of the Brethren, was firmly dedicated to the principle of ecumenical cooperation. Soon after taking up his first Elgin assignment in 1919, he ventured his first steps of conciliar activity. In his successive appointments, he pursued the same trend. He was a leader in persuading the reluctant Brethren to take full membership in the Federal Council of Churches in 1941. Perhaps his greatest success along this line was his leadership in the National Service Board of Religious Objectors, which he chaired through perilous times. It is revealing to look closely at several endeavors that took much of his time and emotional energy in the 1940s. These all have to do with the leadership he gave to the role of the churches in addressing worldwide problems of relief and rehabilitation.

The Creation of Church World Service

In April, 1945, M. R. Zigler wrote to Rufus D. Bowman, president of Bethany Biblical Seminary in Chicago, about his recent activities:

> During the past three weeks I have been working diligently to try to get Protestantism to unite in a common action program to do relief. I would never have thought that the Christian church would say what it has been saying concerning errands of mercy. I am convinced that the Church of the Brethren must lead in Protestantism. . . . The time has come for somebody to lead in the integration of united Protestantism so that the Church of Christ in America might give to the Church of Christ in other lands materials that might be distributed without regard to race, creed or color.[1]

The story of this united approach, however, begins much earlier. In 1939 a Committee on Foreign Relief Appeals in the Churches was organized in New York by the Federal Council of Churches of Christ in America and the Foreign Missions Conference of North America. As the staggering needs of refugees and other war-sufferers became evident, concerned Christians began a number of initiatives. There was danger of cross-purpose and unnecessary duplication of effort. The committee was designed to secure information on existing programs and coordinate their efforts.

Leslie B. Moss, the committee's executive director, asked the Brethren Service Committee for a report of its activities. L. W. Shultz, chairman of the committee, replied on September 16, 1940, that the Brethren had sent more than a thousand dollars for stranded European missionaries. Beyond that, the BSC had sent moneys through its own agents in China, England, and the Friends' Committee in France. The denominational goal was $3,000 a month. That goal was surpassed in July ($4,000) and August ($6,000). The Brethren received an appeal in April, 1941, from the committee addressed to American churches, urging even greater efforts at meeting the crisis.[2]

Alongside this coordinating committee were formed action committees, such as the Church Committee for Overseas Relief and Reconstruction and the Church Committee for Relief in Asia. Working with them were other groups, such as the YMCA and YWCA, the World Student Christian Federation, and the American Bible Society.

At the same time that American churches were seeking to work together on relief needs, the World Council of Churches in Process of Formation, at its Geneva headquarters, was active as well. It originally worked through the Central Bureau of Inter-Church Aid, an ecumenical body developed in 1922 and led for much of its life by the Swiss professor Adolph Keller. The office gave particular attention to pastors and other church workers who could be reached from neutral Switzerland. The work of the Keller office was later incorporated into WCC's Department of Reconstruction and Inter-Church Aid.[3]

As committees and agencies proliferated, there were calls for unification and integration. An eleven-member committee was organized in New York, headed by Wynn C. Fairfield, an executive of the Congregational Christian Church (later to join with other bodies to form the United Church of Christ). The initiative was called by the Federal Council of Churches, the Foreign Missions Conference, and the American Committee of the

World Council of Churches. From the work of the committee came the new agency, Church World Service, on May 4, 1946. Seventeen denominations pledged their cooperation in the new effort, among them the Church of the Brethren; M. R. Zigler signed for the Brethren.

Church World Service was not expected to pool all of the individual efforts of the member churches, but "it was assumed that the coordinating organization would provide a conference center around which decisions regarding a world program could be discussed, agreed to, and carried out." CWS would also provide an instrumentality to do what the churches wanted to accomplish together.[4]

But the path to this agreement was not a smooth one. There were several problems. One was the natural resistance of functioning denominational bodies to new forms of cooperation. Another was the reluctance of existing relief agencies to give up their share of the work. Still another was the ambivalent attitude of many mission agencies. And overall was the philosophical debate whether churches as *churches* should be doing relief work at all. Was not this the role of the governments (who alone were thought to have the resources to meet such tremendous needs on a world basis) or of secular agencies? The UNRRA, had been established for example, for just such a purpose. Should not churches stick to their proper job of preaching, teaching, and worship?

A key meeting had been held on May 19, 1945. The Commission for World Council Service (the American branch of the WCC) called a meeting to hear three distinguished European church leaders, fresh from the war zone. (The armistice ending World War II was ratified in Berlin on May 8.) The guests included Dr. Marc Boegner, head of the French Federation of Protestant Churches; Dr. George K. A. Bell, Bishop of Chichester; and Dr. W. A. Visser 't Hooft, secretary of the World Council of Churches. The guests emphasized the need for material aid for the churches, but stressed that the World Council had "primary responsibility for spiritual aid"; they should not let a "material aid program interfere with that which is our particular task" that would not be addressed by secular agencies or governments. Much aid should go to theological books to assist deprived pastors.

The minutes of the meeting record that "Dr. Zigler spoke of the eagerness of the people to provide material aid through the churches rather than through UNRRA and the necessity for setting up some effective cooperative scheme." He later looked back at that intervention as his special contribution to the genesis of the Church World Service program.

It was in fact, Dr. Ralph E. Diffendorfer, who pointed out the proliferation of effort of several agencies and called for the appointment of a committee to study ways in which integration could take place.[5]

In Zigler's own version, he had patiently waited through the week of meetings to get a chance to ask about material aid. Finally on the last day, he was able to ask three questions:

1. Is material aid needed in Europe?
2. What do they need?
3. Is anybody else willing to help the Brethren [meet these needs]?

The visitors, characterized by Zigler as "very weak and very pale," responded with a firm "yes" to the question of need. They asked for food, clothing, bicycles for pastors, and the like. Zigler announced that Brethren Service had just purchased the New Windsor campus for relief purposes and was about to send out an appeal to Brethren churches to forward material aid there for packing and transportation overseas. He offered to use the New Windsor facility for similar processing for other church groups. The chair suggested that any of those present who wished to help should talk to Zigler over the meal break. At first no one came forward, but then a woman, head of the interdenominational church women's work, volunteered, after which others came. This was the beginning of New Windsor as the center for Protestant relief work.[6]

The meeting was publicized in a well-written article by Dr. Robbins W. Barstow, the newly-appointed director of the Commission for World Council Service, who then became the first director of Church World Service. He explained that the commission worked with American churches, channeling designated and undesignated funds to Geneva to meet the needs in Europe. In consultation with the distinguished visitors from Europe, the commission had established a four year budget of $8,840,000, with most funds allocated for the first year to meet immediate emergencies, tapering off then in successive years.[7]

These askings were part of a larger sum of $19 million requested for world needs. Church officials in New York estimated that in addition, another $30 million would be raised and disbursed directly by the churches. The standing problem that Zigler had with CWS officials was that he could not get them to accept the Brethren program in total as part of their program. He pointed out that the published accounts of Brethren contributions did not reflect the total Brethren contribution. An impassioned letter to CWS director, Barstow, in December, 1947, listed all of the ways in which he personally and the Brethren generally had worked for CWS. This included intensive interpretation work, which had resulted in thousands of dollars of gifts, the preparation of the New Windsor facilities for joint processing for CWS and much more.[8]

His constant appeal was for the American churches to send more personnel, not just dollars and material aid. He was convinced that the personal touch was needed. Typical of this vision was his letter to an executive vice-president of CWS:

> The only way to send the spiritual side of our church life in America is by men and women; and I think they should go by the thousand. Let them walk the streets filled with hungry people. Let them help rebuild churches and homes. Send mechanics; send bricklayers; send farmers; then the people here in America will begin to send materials in a spiritual sense. I think it just as impossible to clothe people over there without sending clothes as it is to talk about sending a spiritual ministry without sending men who have the spirit to give.[9]

Heifer Project

No relief project became so identified with the Brethren as did the Heifer Project—which flourishes today as Heifer Project Incorporated. Its story has often been told: Dan West, Brethren farmer and peace leader, agonized as he worked as a relief agent in Spain in 1937. He had too little food to disperse to the starving children and adults. What he would not give for some of the productive milk cows in his native Northern Indiana. He then thought of the possibility of asking American farmers to donate bred heifers to be shipped to those in need. The one condition he would impose was that the recipient would promise to give the first healthy female calf to some other needy person; in this way the gift would be extended. Of equal importance, in so doing, recipients could preserve their self respect. Not simply helpless objects of charity, they would stand taller by sharing their good fortune and taking responsibility for helping others.[10]

The idea lay in abeyance until the impact of World War II. West then presented it to the Brethren Service Committee, which formally approved it in January, 1943. Belgium was chosen in 1943 as the first country to receive the cows, but conditions did not allow the program to begin there until the war ended. Three other governments asked for the program— Spain, Holland, and Yugoslavia. The Brethren worked closely with US government agencies in planning the project. Conscious of the practical and logistical difficulties involved, the committee developed detailed plans for receiving donated heifers, holding them, and preparing them for shipment. In fact, it was not at first possible to send animals abroad. In July, 1944, the first shipment was directed to Puerto Rico, an American dependency, where CPS men were active.

At one point good fortune helped the program along. In the fall of 1943 Zigler was traveling by train to Washington, D. C., and joined a man at breakfast in the dining car. He did not know him but had once heard him speak. He was Raymond W. Miller, a Methodist layman and public relations consultant. Zigler told him that he was on his way to the capital to speak with officials controlling freight allocations, to see if he could gain clearances for the Heifer Project, which he proceeded to describe to the interested Miller. According to Miller's later account, the Brethren had run into stone walls in getting requisite authorization in the present wartime situation. "He said that there was just one man who could really decide the issue for him and that was Donald Nelson of the War Production Board."

When they parted at the station, Miller invited Zigler to join him the next morning for breakfast with a "few friends." It so happened that Miller had organized a series of informal breakfast conferences of fifty to sixty leading men from government and private organizations. Donald Nelson would be attending such a meeting the next day. When Zigler showed up at the appointed place, a rooftop dining room at a large Washington hotel, he was astonished to see the large assemblage. Miller sat his guest next to Nelson and asked Zigler to describe the Heifer Project idea: "As the breakfast progressed, Mr. Nelson rose to his feet and . . . told us how interested he was in a new program of which he'd just learned from his table neighbor, Mr. Zigler. He explained it briefly and said he felt the proposal had such merit that he, personally, was going to see to an experimental shipment or two of heifers at the earliest possible date."[11]

The real breakthrough for overseas operations finally came in connection with the organization of the UNRRA program. This agency collected thousands of head of livestock to replace the depleted herds of Europe (and later of Asia). But they had no attendants. It was M. R. Zigler who negotiated an arrangement whereby UNRRA would provide transport if BSC would come up with attendants. The Brethren went on to recruit hundreds of attendants—soon dubbed *Seagoing Cowboys*—in return for UNRRA's provision of ocean freight for the animals collected for the

Heifer Project. By August, 1944, some 1,000 donated animals were awaiting shipment. In this manner the ambitious program got underway. The editors of *Time* magazine called it "A Down-to-Earth Project" and its practicality did appeal to many Americans. It broke through the skepticism many had about giving money or even goods, fearful that those most needy might never see the gifts. The living aspect of the Heifer Project gift was also appealing.

Time editors also followed the story with the UNRRA link. Referring to the shortage of livestock handlers and the resultant inability to send the animals, *Time* wrote:

> Into the breach stepped brisk, friendly Benjamin G. Bushong, dairy farmer . . ., chief red-tape cutter of the . . . pacifist Church of the Brethren. . . . For months Dunker Bushong had been pushing his own church's overseas relief program . . ., only to strike a snag. City Dunkers had raised money for calves and feed. Country Dunkers had fed and fattened the animal into fine bulls and heifers. The Dunkers had the cattle but they had no ships. Dunker Bushong made a suggestion: if UNRRA would provide shipping space for Dunker cows and bulls, the Brethren would rustle up seagoing hustlers to herd the UNRRA animals.[12]

The program not only drew wide attention, it drew public praise. Fiery New York mayor, F. H. Laguardia, director general of the UNRRA, praised the Brethren in a letter of November 26, 1946:

> The fine spirit of practical Christianity and the faith that your group has shown, are examples to us all in these days when, without faith, we cannot progress. Your movement, beginning modestly as it did, has spread its spirit and its work. Transcending barriers of nationality and religious conviction, it has drawn to itself members of many denominations, and illustrated what can be accomplished when conviction and efficient enterprise and fine Christian generosity are combined.[13]

Animals even reached the Soviet Union in 1957; others went to many other countries. By 1969, on the twenty-fifth anniversary of the program's beginnings, more than 40,000 heifers and goats and 1.5 million chicks had been distributed in eighty-five nations.[14]

M. R. Zigler had been closely related to the project from the beginning. He had originally gone to the United Nations agency to seek support for the sending of the heifers. At that point, they said that they were not shipping live gifts. At a later date, when the international agency offered the breakthrough agreement to provide shipping in return for attendants, it was actually Zigler who recruited the first team. He recalled that he had traveled immediately to Washington, D. C., when the call came to sign the papers. He then went to Bridgewater College, only to find that the students had gone home for the summer. He contacted several farmers who had just changed jobs, with W. B. Wilson, the first man to agree to serve.[15]

He alerted the Brethren regional representatives and BSC personnel of the emerging program. This took place just before the Brethren Annual Conference held at North Manchester, Indiana in June, 1945. At a meeting of the Brethren Service Committee, he stated that someone was needed to run the program. That man, he said, was Ben Bushong, who should "return to Washington, clear the arrangements with the United Nations and then go to New Windsor to operate. He recalled: "I still remember him putting on his hat, pulling it down over the right eye, leaving the Committee Room and instead of going to the Annual Conference, he went to Washington. From that hour, Ben Bushong was responsible for the Heifer Project."[16]

It was also Zigler who worked with the sometimes idiosyncratic Dan West, not always an easy task for an administrator. Zigler was asked to speak at the latter's memorial service and alluded to the problem. Referring to West's manner of working, he said: "We never knew where he was going to come up or what he was going to say or what he was going to propose. But when it's all said and done, that's a good man to work with. It's hard on you, but you're always alive." He spoke of the message of brotherhood which West articulated—brotherhood within the church, brotherhood among the churches, and brotherhood in the world. "I know he suffered because a lot of us didn't go along with him. I couldn't go along a lot of times. I knew where he was going; I knew I couldn't get there yet quite. I wasn't quite ready to go, the Brethren weren't quite ready to go. Some were going in opposite directions and along with you."[17]

No doubt it took the qualities of all three leaders to make the Heifer Project what it became—the visionary Dan West, the promoter M. R. Zigler, and the tireless administrator Ben Bushong. Added to their talents, of course, were the contributions of countless thousands of donors, seagoing attendants, fund raisers, and the rest.

Christian Rural Overseas Program

Another very successful relief program with substantial Brethren formative input was what came to be called CROP—the Christian Rural

Overseas Program. The focus of the project was the securing of bulk donations of actual farm commodities—wheat, rice, corn, soybeans—for shipment to those in need the world over.

Some precursors of the program were collections of grain across the USA as part of material aid drives. The first boxcar of wheat shipped through CWS came from Navarre, Kansas, in September, 1945; it was designated for Holland. Church of the Brethren congregations together with those from the Evangelical and Reformed cooperated on this. At about the same time, Mennonites in Kansas began sending carloads of flour to Holland through the Mennonite Central Committee. Later, early in 1946, a Wheat for Holland committee in Pampa, Texas, chaired by Brethren pastor Russell G. West, collected several carloads of wheat. Also in 1946 the regional office of the Church of the Brethren in McPherson, Kansas, launched an appeal for bulk goods by purchasing ten carloads of wheat. Many Congregational churches joined the effort.

In April, 1947, a Wheat for Relief Project was initiated by CWS in the plains states, with statewide committees established in Oklahoma, Kansas, Colorado, Nebraska, and the Dakotas. Organization took place on a community-wide and county-wide basis. The idea of working cooperatively was appealing to farmers, county agents, and others who understood the importance of united effort to achieve substantial goals.

The genesis of CROP as an organization was something as follows: in late 1946 the American Council of Voluntary Agencies for Foreign Service called a meeting in Westchester, New York, to discuss a cooperative national solicitation. M. R. Zigler attended on behalf of the Brethren. The meeting selected ten major cities as the focal points for the solicitation. Then Zigler spoke up to say that the Brethren could hardly enter into the program because they had so few members in those cities. Would the meeting accept the proposition that the Mennonites and the Brethren would take the rest of the country, concentrating on rural areas? The Catholic and Jewish representatives favored the idea, moved, and seconded it.

Zigler immediately phoned Paul H. Bowman, Sr. (chairman of the Brethren Service Committee) and Orie O. Miller (executive of the Mennonite Central Committee), both close personal friends and longtime colleagues. They both approved. Zigler returned to the meeting to say that he was organized. He proceeded to seek incorporation of a program called Rural Overseas Relief (ROR).

He sought out Clifford R. Hope, a Congressman from Kansas and

175

chairman of the House Agricultural Committee, to present the idea. Initially granted five minutes, he wound up spending ninety minutes on the idea, during which time the Congressman called other members of his committee. The upshot was that the legislator told him that if he could get Catholics and Protestants working together, they would go along. Zigler recalled: "The Catholic representative said that if they could have John Metzler as director, they would be satisfied. The Brethren Service Committee met and appointed John Metzler . . . and Ben Bushong to take responsibility at New Windsor. Ben Bushong had already started Heifer Project administration at New Windsor."[18]

John D. Metzler, Sr., had been a regional executive for the Church of the Brethren in the 1930s and became active in the work of the Brethren Service Committee in the 1940s. After the Blue Ridge College campus at New Windsor, Maryland, had been secured as a relief center in 1944, he directed that emerging program with great effectiveness. Zigler hated to see Metzler leave that post, but because of his ecumenical commitment was willing to make the sacrifice. Church World Service approved the plan, and eventually became the sponsoring organization, although the beginnings were independent.

Because the heart of the program was anticipated to be the rural areas of the Midwest, it was decided to start the process in Chicago. On August 1, 1947, John Metzler, Sr., went to that city and found a temporary site on the west side at Bethany Biblical Seminary, the Church of the Brethren school of theology. The early name of the program, *Rural Overseas Relief*, was then renamed *Concerted Rural Overseas Program* before the final name was established.

In late August, 1947, Metzler wrote Zigler, at that time in China, about the organizational problems still slowing the work. Although the office was already established and work begun, the sponsoring agencies were still not united. The Catholics, represented through the Catholic Rural Life Conference, wanted involvement beyond the religious component, but the Lutherans (Lutheran World Relief) and CWS, under A. L. Warnshuis, feared that the nonreligious organizations might take control. Metzler concluded: "This business of trying to work out cooperation between groups that don't want to cooperate very badly is certainly a difficult one. I can understand more now why peace treaties and conferences have difficulty at arriving at conclusions. The major thing there is national sovereignty. Seemingly the major thing here is denominational or organizational sovereignty."[19]

About that time the national columnist Drew Pearson had sponsored a *Friendship Train*. The plan was to start a train on the west coast and run it to New York city, collecting relief goods along the way. The Association of American Railroads agreed to pay the expenses. It was intended as a gesture of goodwill from the people of the USA to the people of Europe. CROP welcomed the initiative and soon became by far the largest participant in the scheme, organizing the gift of more than 100 carloads. The attendant publicity was extremely beneficial in promoting the CROP plan.

The Friendship Train idea spawned a successor, the Southwest Friendship Train, which moved through Texas, Oklahoma, and Kansas. This surpassed the original venture in size. CROP co-sponsored this affair. A third project, totally organized by CROP, originated in Lincoln, Nebraska, on February 12, 1948. This was called the *Abraham Lincoln Friendship Train*. At each stop along the way, as more cars were added, Catholic, Jewish, and Protestant leaders led informal services of blessing. Each car carried the name of the participating groups. Civic and governmental leaders added their encouragement to the enterprise.[20]

The program blossomed, aided by its earthy practicality. A descriptive CWS report explained part of the genius of the program:

> The beginnings of CROP resulted from grass-roots pressure toward commodity giving. Commodities represent a value far more real and significant than mere cash. When a local community sees and dedicates its carload of wheat or of soya or of rice, it represents part of the life of that commodity in a far more real sense than a check for the value of the car would do.... Second: leadership and activity in these cooperative programs of meeting human need comes more frequently from the non-professional Christian people of the community than from the professional Christian workers, the clergy.... Too often nothing challengingly big and satisfyingly significant comes to the laity to satisfy their desire to use their abilities in Christian causes. CROP helps to provide such a use for abilities and uses those abilities in the same framework that business life is lived, the community.[21]

By late 1951 the CROP program had shipped 5,400 freight carloads of foodstuffs to thirty-two different countries. Of this amount some 45 carloads had been donated directly by Brethren. Many of the CROP staff were Brethren, a proportion which remained constant over the years. By 1957 the value of the gifts distributed through CROP had risen to over $15 million.[22] In 1954, John D. Metzler, Sr., was called to Geneva to work on material aid projects through the World Council of Church's Division of Inter-Church Aid. He took with him the ecumenical spirit that had guided his work and that of his mentor, M. R. Zigler, throughout the various aspects of the material aid program.

NOTES

1. M. R. Zigler to Rufus D. Bowman, April 23, 1945 (Bowman Papers, Bethany Theological Seminary).
2. L. W. Shultz to Leslie B. Moss, Sept. 16, 1940; John R. Mott and Lewis B. Mudge to Denominations having Relief Work, April 4, 1941 (FCC Papers, Presbyterian Historical Society).
3. Ruth Rouse and Stephen C. Neill, *A History of the Ecumenical Movement, 1517-1948* (London: SPCK, 1954), 558, 712.
4. Harold E. Fey, *Cooperation in Compassion: The Story of Church World Service* (New York: Friendship Press, 1966), 29-42.
5. Minutes, Commission for World Council Service, May 19, 1945, 7pp. (FCC Papers).
6. Ken Kreider interview with M. R. Zigler, May 27, 1977, 2/1.
7. Robbins W. Barstow, "Help for Europe's Christians," *Christian Century* (June 20, 1945): 731-732.
8. M. R. Zigler to Robbins W. Barstow, Dec. 9, 1947 (FCC Papers).
9. M. R. Zigler to A. L. Warnshuis, Jan. 14, 1948 (FCC Papers).
10. See Glee Yoder, *Passing on the Gift: The Story of Dan West* (Elgin, IL: Brethren Press, 1978), 100-114.
11. Raymond W. Miller, *Monsignor Ligutti: The Pope's County Agent* (Lanham, MD: University Press of America, 1981), 79-82.
12. *Time* (July 24, 1944); *Time* (July 23, 1945), reprinted in *Gospel Messenger* (Sept. 1, 1945): 10.
13. Reprinted in *Gospel Messenger* (Jan 11, 1947): 21.
14. "25 Years of Giving Life," *Messenger* (Aug. 28, 1969): 20-22.
15. M. R. Zigler to Virginia Wilson Miller, Jan. 31, 1980.
16. M. R. Zigler, "Biographical, Ben Bushong," unpubl. essay.
17. Transcript of M. R. Zigler's statement at the Dan West Memorial Services, North Manchester, IN, January 10, 1971, 3-4.
18. M. R. Zigler, "Origin of CROP: Conversation with M. R. Zigler, July 28, 1984," unpubl. essay; M. R. Zigler, "Before CROP," in *Community Compassion: The Story of CROP* (Elkhart, IN: CROP, 1967).
19. John Metzler, Sr., to M. R. Zigler, Aug. 27, 1947.

20. John Metzler, Sr., "How It All Began," in *Community Compassion* (1967).
21. "CROP," [1949] (Warnshuis Papers, Union Theological Seminary).
22. "In the Field with CROP," *Messenger* (Sept. 29, 1966): 14-15.

15

THE SHIFT TO EUROPE

I N 1946-1947 THE CHURCH OF THE BRETHREN completed a
major shift in denominational organization. At that time a number of
separate and basically independent boards were replaced by one General
Brotherhood Board, divided into five commissions. Several of the commissions continued the work of the former independent boards: these
included the Foreign Mission Commission and the Brethren Service
Commission. One of the largely unstated but operative reasons for the shift
was the feeling that the Brethren Service operation had become overly
dominant in the life of the church. The drama of the desperate needs of war
sufferers, the excitement of such programs as the Heifer Project and
CROP, the charismatic leadership of M. R. Zigler—these had so swept the
church that other, older programs felt that they had been upstaged, that
their outreach had been limited. By organizing one total board with control
of the budget, the freewheeling fundraising of BSC could be contained.
Deserving, but less dramatic, programs of the church could be allocated
their necessary funds by logical and rational planning.

A call for such unification had already been heard as early as 1944 but
had been put off because it had seemed too disruptive. In 1945 a blue-
ribbon Committee of Fifteen was asked to study the whole problem and
bring back a report to the Annual Conference. This took place, with the
report first approved by the Standing Committee and then by the entire
conference. In 1946 a General Brotherhood Board of twenty-five members was created, with specific assignments; it was to: "consider the total
brotherhood program, evaluate all phases of the program, and determine
the general policies and budget needs in each area of its work." Further, it

was to "correlate and unify the work of all commissions." In practice, the allocation of budget set the parameters of the work of the commissions. Funds were to be donated to the total program, rather than having each group raise its own finances.[1]

The effect on the work of the Brethren Service program was, on the one hand, to blend its work more closely into the life of the church; on the other hand, it had the effect of clamping tight administrative controls on its operations. It soon became clear that the freewheeling and expansive days of the immediate postwar era were now limited. At the first general meeting of the board in March, 1947, the new manner of working became clear. And in the November, 1947, meeting of the board, a more decisive action was taken involving Zigler, as director of the BSC program.

A central feature of the reorganization was the creation of the executive position of *general secretary*, as the top administrator of the program. Zigler had formerly played a similar role, as coordinator of the several boards and longtime holder of several executive positions concurrently. It was a reasonable anticipation that he would be asked to take on the new position. But it became clear that another, less charismatic and more efficient personality would be given the nod. Zigler was in fact passed over. Raymond R. Peters, a younger colleague who had been brought onto the Elgin staff by M. R. Zigler, was named to the post. In later years, Peters reflected that Zigler had been the "logical person to become the first General Secretary"; however, "his aggressive style caused many of his colleagues and Board members to feel a different type of leadership was needed for the new Board."[2]

European Representative

Shortly thereafter, there was a move to create a new position in Europe and appoint Zigler to it. This would entail the direction of the expanded European program of Brethren Service, tied to representation of the Brethren with the emerging final organization of the World Council of Churches. This entity had been active during the war years in a provisional way, under the phrase "in process of formation." The end of the war opened the way to full unfolding. The grand assembly of delegates was slated to meet at Amsterdam on August 23, 1948, to effect the actual creation of the World Council.[3]

The crucial meeting of the new General Brotherhood Board was in November, 1947. Zigler's recollection of the meeting ran as follows:

> When the chance came to appoint someone to go to Europe, it was being discussed who should do it. I had already been appointed by the church to be representative to the World Council of Churches First Assembly in 1948. Dr. Paul Bowman was sitting beside me and he whispered to me "Who should it be?" I told him this was something I would like to do. I do not know anything about the conversations among Board members. However, by the next day their proposal came into the open and I accepted the call to go.[4]

One of the motivations of his acceptance was the consideration that the post would allow him to have more time together with his wife. For much of their married life, he had been on the road for extensive periods, never more so than during the harried years of World War II and the exciting days of postwar relief endeavors. Both of their children had reached the age of independence, so that the couple was free to leave.

There were other considerations; these he voiced in a later interview. They concerned more the shift in the emphasis in the church and the conclusion of the wartime services of BSC. As he recalled it:

> But that was a time when it was getting very clear that either Harold Row or I should kind of give up, because of the decline of the CPS program. We were moving over into the relief game, and you didn't need two executives there. And I knew the time was coming, and I couldn't see anybody that I thought could go, would go to the World Council. But I was dead set to make it [Brethren Service] a church affair . . . whatever the cost, rather than going independent. I wanted to go in the World Council—[to] influence the World Council. . . . I said to myself, the Brethren aren't strong enough to do the peace game, and we've got to get more than the Historic Peace Churches working on this thing.[5]

Beyond this, there is a rather clear picture that major church leaders felt that M. R. Zigler was too powerful and weighty to work well within the new structure. His tendency was to move ahead and ask for permission later. They saw the younger BSC executive, W. Harold Row, as someone who would fit in better. So they needed a graceful way in which to remove Zigler from the Elgin scene. The challenge of the combined Brethren Service and ecumenical post seemed ideal, in terms of Zigler's interests and experience. And it succeeded. The canny church worker was not ignorant of some of these currents. He later expressed his feelings in these words: "It was one of these quick moves, about me changing. And when I looked at it a day or two after, I wondered whether they weren't trying to get rid of me . . . and exile me to Europe." Ever after, he had a kind of ambivalence about the shift, and often fretted at being so far from the place where the crucial decisions were made. He had been at the center of so much of the pivotal movements of the church for so long that a position overseas, out of immediate touch with events, felt in some ways like a banning. But true to his nature, he took on the assignment with vigor and was soon as creative there as in all of his other jobs.[6]

Further corroboration of this view of church affairs was later given in a letter to Zigler from an associate, Jefferson Mathis. He wrote: "When did the church turn the corner? It began when you selected your successor. The tide in administrative circles was turning against you when you took the overseas assignment. You knew it for you said to me: 'I know what they are doing—getting rid of me.'" This is also the judgment of Charles E. Zunkel, at that time a member of the General Brotherhood Board: "Bob was so consumed with Brethren Service and peace that he was causing the Brotherhood Board problems organizationally and financially."[7]

The formal announcement of the appointment is worth quoting. It was written by the board chairman and seminary president, Rufus D. Bowman:

> The General Brotherhood Board at its November meeting called Bro. M. R. Zigler to become the Church of the Brethren representative in Europe. Brother and Sister Zigler will live in Geneva and Bro. Zigler will begin his work as soon after March 1, 1948, as suitable arrangements can be made. . . .
>
> Bro. Zigler will supervise and unify the service of our church there. He will be a voice from our Brotherhood to the European churches helping to bring new life to them. He will lead our workers in relief, rehabilitation, and in dealing with agencies like the YMCA and CRALOG. He will bring fellowship to our workers, including our scattered members in Scandinavia. He will carry out the Orlando Conference assignment to serve as the representative of the Church of the Brethren to the World Council of Churches.
>
> The age of pioneering is not dead. Bro. Zigler gave to our Brotherhood devoted leadership during the war period and since for the cause of Christ in the fields of peace and relief. Now Europe is a field white unto harvest for the message of Christ, for the touch of friendship and for a Christian voice that understands.[8]

Send-Off from Elgin

As it developed, it was not until late spring that the Ziglers were able to leave; they sailed for Genoa, Italy, on May 18 and arrived in Geneva on May 29.[9] Before that was the flurry of winding up affairs in the States and handing over the reins of BSC to the new director, W. Harold Row. A highlight of this busy period was a Civic Recognition dinner given in Zigler's honor on April 9, sponsored by the local YMCA and other Elgin organizations. A close friend, Andrew W. Cordier, by that time a leading official of the United Nations, agreed to come to speak at the occasion. Some 250 guests came to honor the life and work of M. R. Zigler.[10]

Besides Dr. Cordier, local ministers and educators spoke, as did Calvert N. Ellis, moderator of the Church of the Brethren, and Raymond R. Peters, general secretary of the General Brotherhood Board. M. R. Zigler, deeply moved by the tributes, made an eloquent response, saying that the honor paid was "not so much to me but to the cause which I uphold—peace." For this occasion, friends and colleagues to write letters of appreciation; these were bound into a volume and presented to Zigler.

Some typical comments follow:

—from Dr. Ernest Fremont Tittle, nationally prominent pastor of the First Methodist Church in Evanston, Illinois:

> Dr. M. R. Zigler is one of the outstanding church leaders of our time. He is regarded by leaders in other denominations as a tower of strength and the possessor of extraordinary capacity for long-range vision and effective organization. I am but one among thousands in The Methodist Church who thank God for him and rejoice that he is to be associated with the World Council of Churches in Geneva, Switzerland.[11]

—from Dr. Andrew W. Cordier:

> When I first thought of writing this letter, I rather quickly came to the conclusion that I had already written it, for our happy and congenial years together speak much louder than anything I can say now in appreciation of you and your work. . . . I was always impressed over the years with your deep devotion to the causes which you championed. You gave your energies to the church and to the cause of peace most unselfishly. In fact, I have always been amazed that your health was not seriously impaired by your over-exertion. I can only explain by saying that you always loved and enjoyed the work that you were doing. It was close to your heart and you put all of your energy into it.[12]

—from Gen. Lewis B. Hershey:

> The circumstances of our association have been most unusual. We have met as representatives of viewpoints impossible to reconcile. In spite of our

viewpoints we have jointly carried out a program during most difficult times. From these associations I have gained a respect and an affection, the stronger because of circumstances overcome. As you go to your new field of endeavor I want you to know that you have my deepest appreciation for your consideration of the viewpoint which I represent. The memory of our association will always remain one of my prized possessions.[13]

European Assignment

The terms of the initial five-year appointment to Europe provided Zigler with a salary of $4,500 per year, plus "$4.00 per week for high cost of living." Any amount over $60.00 per month for housing would be carried by the board; six cents per mile reimbursement was allowed for church use of his personal car. The salary and expenses were to come out of a $12,000 allotment for the Geneva office.[14]

Administratively, Zigler was responsible to Peters for matters of general policy, employment arrangements, and regular furlough visits to America. It was anticipated that three return trips to the USA would be made during the time of the appointment. On matters of Brethren Service program, Zigler was now responsible administratively to W. Harold Row, his former assistant. The potential for stress in this situation was obvious, and it did come. Zigler was a volatile leader who believed that sometimes it was necessary to take actions and seek approval later; he often reacted spontaneously. He depended on his ability to secure financial support and administrative acquiescence by demonstrating the urgency of the cause. In this he had notable success through the years of the relief emergency during and after the war. Row, a more analytical, less visceral personality, believed that the church needed to develop carefully-thought-out policies for longtime service, rather than responding so much to individual emergencies. He believed in a tight administrative approach and was committed to the new denominational reorganization. Two very different leadership styles were here brought into play.

Choice of Geneva

Brethren Service had already established a central office in Geneva. John Bowman and Wilbur Mullen moved there in February, 1947, to administer the extensive work across the Continent. They rented office space in the city at 20, rue du Cendrier. When Zigler arrived, he received varied opinions about the best place to locate permanently. A longtime friend and

185

former classmate at college, Paul Garber, had become bishop of the Methodist Church in Europe. He advised against close connection with the World Council. A representative of the Baptists suggested that Paris would make a better center of operations. Some Brethren Service personnel favored Germany as a good central location and less expensive in living costs than the Swiss city. Dr. Tracy Strong, executive of the World's YMCA, with whom Zigler had worked for years, heard of Zigler's arrival in Geneva and immediately offered him office space in the YMCA headquarters in Geneva at negligible cost.

But M. R. Zigler went his own way. He was determined to work closely with the World Council of Churches, at that point readying itself for complete organization later that year, as earlier mentioned. So, Zigler sought out Dr. Visser 't Hooft and asked him about the possibility of securing an office in one of the temporary barracks pressed into service as office space on the WCC grounds. This was located on the estate of a small chalet at 17 route de Malagnou, which the small WCC staff used as its headquarters. Also influential in the choice was the financial head of the WCC operation, Frank Northam, who offered logistical support. Northam became a close personal friend.

Visser 't Hooft seemed gratified by Zigler's offer and quickly agreed that the Brethren could rent an office there. After some negotiations, the inner city office was closed down and work was transferred to the barracks. There were three connected rooms, one for the secretaries, one for Zigler, and one for an associate. Zigler reported that he began meeting with the staff of the World Council almost like a "paid secretary" of one of its programs. This proximity obviously facilitated that part of the appointment which called on Zigler to represent Brethren interests in the ecumenical movement.[15]

There was another consideration. Zigler had developed a close working relationship and a warm personal friendship with Monsignor Luigi Ligutti, head of the Catholic Rural Life Conference. By this time Ligutti had become well recognized by the Vatican as an expert on world agriculture. He became, in fact, the Pope's representatives at the Food and Agriculture Organization, with headquarters in Rome. Zigler expressed his reasoning in these words: "I felt if somehow I could work with the Catholics in Rome, it would be a natural for a Protestant body to locate in Geneva . . . only several hours to the Vatican."[16]

After a short time John Bowman returned to the USA, Wilbur Mullen returned to Germany, and Zigler was left alone in the Geneva office with the secretary. Originally this was the Swiss national Jacqueline Mueller (Richez), who stayed with the Brethren for many years; she was later joined by Alice Kachkachian, of Armenian background. The Ziglers, who originally had a small apartment near the railroad station, moved to the apartment the Bowmans had used, at 37, route de Malagnou, a few blocks from the WCC center. The Ziglers used the small apartment extensively for entertaining, a skill in which Amy Zigler excelled. It served also as a kind of hostel, putting up the surprisingly large number of visitors who came through Geneva. Brethren Service personnel thought it natural to descend on the Zigler apartment for several nights. Zigler commented: "It was amazing how many visitors we could put into this one-bedroom apartment. Especially was this true as people began to come to Europe as volunteers and men assigned to do certain jobs but, also, travelers."[17]

Eventually, shortly before he returned home, Zigler arranged for quarters in a new and commodious apartment building overlooking Lake Geneva; the initiative was not favored by stateside officials and considerable tension followed. Executives in Elgin did not understand the pattern of hospitality that the Ziglers followed, which included numerous invitations of members of the WCC staff to their apartment, a gesture long remembered and appreciated by these mostly foreign personnel. Much later, Philip Potter, as general secretary of the World Council, recalled with warmth and gratitude, that the Ziglers had been among the first to invite his wife and him to their home.[18]

In 1979, when Pope John Paul II visited the USA, Zigler was invited to a reception for the pontiff in Washington, D. C. While there, he observed that seated on the right side of the pope was Archbishop Iakovos, representing the Orthodox Church. Many years earlier, the orthodox prelate had served on the WCC staff. When Zigler greeted him after the formalities were over, he met this response: the archbishop saluted him with the holy kiss and said: "When I came to Geneva as a young man, you and Amy took me in as a stranger and the fact that you are here today makes this day a wonderful experience for me to thank you for your kindness."[19]

Relationship with the World Council

Although placing the Brethren Service office in the World Council headquarters provided access, it was not all that easy for Zigler to work his way into the heart of the WCC organization. For one thing, he was not a theologian, as almost all of the WCC staff were. For years, European church leaders had looked down upon the Americans as theologically naive: they were good at raising money and at promotion but they were hopeless in serious theological matters. In his own way, M. R. Zigler fit this stereotype perfectly. He was bluff, cordial, and energetic, but often seemed unaware of the excellent theological and ecclesiastical reasons why certain things could not be done. "Why not?" he would ask, and proceed to try to do them.

When Zigler waxed eloquent about the Heifer Project, the superior Europeans smiled inwardly and often enough openly. What did talk of pregnant cows have to do with serious ecumenical endeavors? Once Zigler suggested having a conference on rural life in the WCC academic study center in the chateau at nearby Bossey, purchased with Rockefeller money. "They laughed at me and they didn't think it was relevant." But Zigler persisted. He got in touch with his former colleagues in the USA and many agreed to come to the meeting if he would arrange the program. This he proceeded to do. The Bossey staff decided "to take a vacation when they talked about rural life" and gave the twenty-five American rural church experts the entire center for their program.

In what became standard procedure for visitors, Zigler also arranged for them to tour through Europe to see the current problems and what the churches were doing about them. He took them "to the places where the heifers had been located, and this was amazing to these rural men. We also were able to take them to a few homes where we had exchange students that had been in America [in rural homes]." The effect was that the visitors became enthusiastic supporters of projects such as CROP, Heifer Project, and Church World Service.[20] Eventually the staid and sober WCC executives caught the vision of the importance of the rural life for the churches and became advocates of the programs. The crowning success of this initiative came with the ecumenical project in Greece, which will be described later.

Zigler developed very warm relationships with other denominational representatives who had offices in conjunction with the World Council; an example was Charles Arbuthnot who represented American Presbyterians. Zigler also hobnobbed with WCC staff. Some of his closest relationships were with the communications team, made up of author John Garrett and photographer John Taylor. They became fascinated by the dramatic potential of such programs as the Heifer Project and developed striking audio-visual representations of its practical outreach. Photos of refugee families embracing their "gift of life" were featured in the displays they mounted to portray the Inter-Church Aid side of the ecumenical movement.

Zigler once recounted that the communications team had been intrigued with the intensity that Brethren displayed for service work. They studied the Brethren to try to understand how this had developed. Their conclusion, reached only after much deliberation, was that it was the feet washing service that was the key. Brethren were used to washing each other's feet; it was just a logical step from there to "wash the feet of the world." They asked Zigler to arrange for the home offices of the Brethren to send over visual material demonstrating the Brethren practice of the feet washing; they wanted to feature this in an exhibit at a major ecumenical gathering. Zigler sadly reported that the home offices saw little point in cooperating with the project, which therefore was never carried out. Typically, Zigler stayed in close touch with Garrett and Taylor long after he, and later they, left Geneva. Their affectionate letters remain in the correspondence files left behind by the Brethren church leader.

The Amsterdam Assembly

To participate in the organizing session of the World Council of Churches in Amsterdam, August 22–September 4, 1948, was a thrilling experience for M. R. Zigler. The grand old man of the ecumenical movement, John R. Mott, presided. Zigler could remember the days of World War I when he heard Mott speak at YMCA conferences. Now he himself was taking part as a leader in the historic new beginning of the world conciliar movement.[21]

Other Brethren came from the United States for the Amsterdam conclave. Raymond R. Peters, general secretary, joined Zigler to represent the denomination as official delegates. Calvert N. Ellis, chairman of the General Brotherhood Board, and J. Quinter Miller, executive on the FCC staff, came as alternate delegates. Carl Myers attended as the youth representative, and Doreen Myers and Floyd E. Mallott were observers.[22]

Peters and Ellis were appointed by the General Brotherhood Board to act as a deputation to review the Brethren Service projects in Europe in conjunction with M. R. Zigler. Their evaluation would have significant impact on the amount of budget allocated to the European program, so Zigler gave extremely careful attention to their itinerary. He was always very alert to the necessity to "sell" the Brethren program on the Continent to visiting Brethren, conscious that even casual observations of those

189

returning to the USA could affect the church's willingness to support the program.[23]

Work at Geneva

After the ceremony and grandeur of the Amsterdam assembly, marked by elaborate liturgies held in the three major languages (English, French, and German) of the gathering and the processions of church dignitaries from many countries in their colorful vestments, for Zigler it was back to the day-by-day labor at the ecumenical headquarters. Here he made his way in the informal gatherings at tea, the innumerable committee meetings, and the routine and complicated necessities of running an office in a world setting. He was very conscious of the responsibilities resting on him as a representative of a small church body quite new to the conciliar movement. In some ways, it was a replay of the circumstances he faced in the 1920s and 1930s as the Brethren began their cautious involvement with other church communions in the United States.

One of the ways he worked was to be present at as many meetings and conferences held by the WCC as possible. He went, for example, to the fifth meeting of the Central Committee of the World Council, held in Lucknow, India, beginning on December 31, 1952. All members of the WCC had the privilege of sending observers to these meetings, even though they had no specific representation in the committee itself. In his report about the sessions, he expressed concern at the trend towards pessimism evidenced at the gathering: "Here is where I am convinced that the influence of evil takes hold like a cancer on the human body." The antidote, he said, was that "men and women who dare to meet, representing their constituencies, to plan for the ongoing of the Christian enterprise must set the target of the kingdom of God clearly and attempt to reach it whatever the cost." He called for courage on the part of the churches to face into the question of war, acknowledging that such discussion might well "break asunder the cohesion that now exists in the fellowship of churches." In connection with this trip, Zigler also visited the Brethren missions in India.[24]

Appointment to the Central Committee

The long patient work by Zigler eventually paid off. This was demonstrated at the Second Assembly of the World Council of Churches, held in

Evanston, Illinois, in August, 1954. At the end of the gathering, which Zigler attended, his name was announced as a member of the powerful Central Committee. In the WCC structure, the Central Committee is the hundred-member body which meets regularly in the intervening years between Assemblies (ordinarily held every six to seven years). It functions as the chief policy committee, with responsibility for appointing and replacing staff personnel, developing programs, and making statements on behalf of the Council.

Zigler well knew what the honor represented. The Brethren were one of the smaller participants in the WCC in membership. With over 200 member bodies in the council, most smaller denominations could expect to wait years before one of their representatives was chosen. Zigler himself expected that it would not be until the year A.D. 2000 that the Brethren might have their turn. Dr. Visser 't Hooft later confided to Zigler that the reason for the appointment was recognition of the strong world-wide program the Brethren sponsored in relief and rehabilitation "in the interests of peace." At the same time came his appointment as a full member of the Committee on Inter-Church Aid and Service to Refugees. Zigler was one of the two representatives from the Central Committee named to this important body. He stayed on this committee even after he retired from Brethren Service work, concluding his appointment in 1961. He made it a point to communicate the work of the Central Committee to the Brethren at home through letters and articles.[25]

Zigler became known as the patient and persistent gadfly at such ecumenical gatherings who kept raising the question: "When will Christians stop killing each other?" Other participants might personally be pacifists, but as representatives of nonpacifist churches they could not commit their denominations officially to a peace position. Privately, they encouraged Zigler to keep up the pressure.

A typical interchange took place at the meeting of the WCC Central Committee in Rolle, Switzerland, in August, 1951. A sub-committee brought in a draft resolution favoring the rights of conscientious objection to war. Orthodox and Lutheran members stated that it was all well and good to support conscience, but the statement overlooked the demands of the community in emergency situation over the individual. Zigler commented, according to the minutes, that "this is the first meeting, to his knowledge, of the Christian churches where C.O.'s could feel at home. It would be helpful if there could some day be a discussion long enough so that C.O.'s and others could understand each other and thus bridge the gap

191

between them, which so frequently makes the Christian C.O. lonely within the Christian fellowship."[26]

At the last session of the Central Committee he attended, which met in Scotland, he took the opportunity of a debate on religious liberty to introduce his standing concern for peace. He sketched the Brethren background and concluded by stating: "Then I would like to make a motion that we eliminate war among us as Christians." But, he went on, "There's nobody that can second my motion." The Mennonites and Quakers were not represented on the Central Committee. He spoke on this vein for eighteen minutes, although there was ordinarily a strict rule that no speaker should exceed eight minutes. The Archbishop of Canterbury praised Zigler's talk but said that he could not second the motion because the Anglican Church held another view. A Baptist theologian said he could second the motion as a person but not as a representative of his church. The motion died for lack of a second but the witness had been made.[27]

NOTES

1. The shift in polity is discussed in Roger E. Sappington, *Brethren Social Policy, 1908-1958* (Elgin, IL: Brethren Press, 1961), 144-146.
2. Raymond R. Peters to D. F. Durnbaugh, April 19, 1987.
3. W. A. Visser 't Hooft, "The Genesis of the World Council of Churches," in *A History of the Ecumenical Movement, 1517-1948*. eds. Ruth Rouse and Stephen C. Neill (London: SPCK, 1954), 697-724.
4. M. R. Zigler memoir, 3/4.
5. Ken Kreider interview with M. R. Zigler, May 27, 1977, 2/7.
6. Kreider interview, 2/7.
7. Jefferson Mathis to M. R. Zigler, undated [1966]; Charles E. Zunkel to D. F. Durnbaugh, April 13, 1987.
8. Rufus D. Bowman, "Called to Serve Christ in Europe," *Gospel Messenger* (Dec. 6, 1947): 17.
9. *Gospel Messenger* (May 8, 1948): 17; (June 19, 1948): 16; "The Church Roll," *Christian Century* (Aug. 11, 1948): 815; "Zigler Goes to World Council," [Harrisonburg, VA] *Daily News-Herald* (June 4, 1948).
10. The event was given front-page coverage with photograph in the local paper: "Honor Dr. M. R. Zigler at Farewell Dinner; Leaves May 18 for Europe," *Elgin* [IL] *Daily Courier-News* (April 10, 1948), 1, 3; program, M. R. Zigler Recognition Dinner, Friday Evening, April 9, 1948, 6:30 o'clock, YMCA Banquet Room.

11. Ernest Fremont Tittle to Harry K. Zeller, Jr., March 19, 1948, Letters of Greeting to M. R. Zigler.
12. Andrew W. Cordier to M. R. Zigler, March 24, 1948, Letters of Greeting to M. R. Zigler.
13. Lewis B. Hershey to M. R. Zigler, March 11, 1948, Letters of Greeting to M. R. Zigler.
14. Raymond R. Peters to M. R. Zigler, June 1, 1948.
15. Million transcript of M. R. Zigler, 10/14.
16. Million transcript, 10/9.
17. Million transcript, 10/18.
18. Philip Potter to M. R. Zigler, Aug. 29, 1972.
19. *On Earth Peace Newsletter* (Oct. 23, 1979).
20. Million transcript of M. R. Zigler, 10/12, 10/20-21.
21. Marlin J. VanElderen, "And So Set Up Signs . . . The World Council of Churches' first 40 years," *One World* (August-September, 1988), special issue; "Commemorating Amsterdam 1948: 40 Years of the World Council of Churches," *The Ecumenical Review*, 40 (July-October, 1988) special issue.
22. Raymond R. Peters, "The Amsterdam Assembly," *Gospel Messenger* (August 21, 1948): 10-11.
23. *Gospel Messenger* (July 24, 1948): 8.
24. *Brethren Service Commission European Program—News Briefs* (Feb. 6, 1953): 2; M. R. Zigler, "Central Committee of the World Council," *Gospel Messenger* (May 8, 1953: 12-14; M. R. Zigler, "Finding Footprints in India," *Gospel Messenger* (May 16, 1953): 8-10.
25. *Gospel Messenger* (Sept. 11, 1954): 16; "World Council Assembly," *Gospel Messenger* (Sept. 25, 1954): 18-19; "World Council Officers," *Christian Century* (Sept. 22, 1954): 1166-1167; interview with M. R. Zigler, Florida, 5/13-16; M. R. Zigler, "The Report of the Central Committee," *Gospel Messenger* (Sept. 24, 1955): 12-13; M. R. Zigler, "World Council Central Committee Meets," *Gospel Messenger* (Oct. 5, 1957): 18-19; M. R. Zigler, "World Council Meetings," *Gospel Messenger* (Oct. 10, 1959): 10-12. Zigler mentioned to an interviewer that W. A. Visser 't Hooft told him at the Nairobi Assembly that Zigler would have been made one of the WCC presidents if the Brethren had allowed him to continue on the Central Committee, instead of being replaced by Norman J. Baugher in 1961—Vernon Miller interview with M. R. Zigler, 1a/3.
26. Minutes, WCC Central Committee, Rolle, Switzerland, August 4-11, 1951.
27. Ken Kreider interview of M. R. Zigler, May 27, 1977, 1/27-19.

16

BRETHREN SERVICE ACTIVITIES

ONE OF THE FIRST actions of M. R. Zigler as he took up his new position in Europe was to visit as many of the Brethren Service projects he was to administer as possible. His earlier fact finding tours in 1945 and 1946-1947 had given him an introduction to the work; moreover, as the BSC executive until spring, 1948, he had received reports and sent instructions. Still, it was a challenging experience to visit sites and talk with the personnel who were now his colleagues.[1]

The basic program featured work in France, the Netherlands, Germany, Austria, Italy, and Poland. Much of the activity still involved the distribution of material aid—food, clothing, soap, medicines, blankets, and seeds. Some Brethren personnel in Germany still worked for the World's YMCA with prisoners of war. Dr. Eldon Burke, on leave from his teaching position in Indiana, had become the senior staff member in the CRALOG office in Bremen, Germany; this office handled the transportation of all material aid brought into West Germany, whether directed to indigenous relief organizations such as the Protestant *Hilfswerk* or the Roman Catholic *Caritas*. For his efficient work, Burke was later to receive the highest civilian award from the West German government.

The Italian program had developed an active community outreach in Carrarra, with special attention devoted to children and youth; the project in Dunkerque, France, was rather similar. In Poland, some Brethren workers taught courses at universities. Under the aggressive leadership of Ralph E. Smeltzer in Austria, a large number of innovative programs were started. The inimitable Helena Kruger ranged over the four-power occupation lines in blithe disregard of regulations in her determination to help the helpless. Just beginning was the student exchange program that sent several outstanding young Europeans for study in Brethren-related colleges. A new kind of project was underway in Germany—Byron and Ruth Royer were assigned to a youth home for endangered adolescents, housed in an abandoned castle near Vaihingen/Enz.

It was thus an active and multifaceted program that Zigler was called on to direct. But change was very much evident. By the summer of 1949, the work in the Netherlands, Poland, and Italy had ceased. In the first case, the Dutch agreed that the wartime needs had largely been met; others deserved help more. In Poland, an increasingly suspicious Communist government closed down the American-based program; BSC workers there were assigned to other countries. In Italy, a flourishing work was discontinued as one of the casualties of the diminished overall BSC budget from the United States. One of the chief objectives of the new administrative arrangement under the integrated board was to rein in the very large Brethren Service budget; as priorities shifted to more emphasis on BSC programs in the United States, the European program was given a definite and smaller budget, within which parameters it had to live. Thus, painful choices had to be made.

Zigler had seen the shift in priorities coming. Just before the crucial board meeting in November, 1947, he had written a general letter to all of the BSC workers in Europe: "I am quite sure this time that they will really dig in on Brethren Service. Several reasons for this will be the budget, integration, etc. . . . As long as the Brethren Service Commission budget is as large as it is—larger than the Brotherhood fund or the Conference budget—we will have difficulty. . . . The Mission Commission had that criticism ever since I came to Elgin in 1919 and I think it will continue to be necessary to criticize any agency that receives the most funds."[2]

The shifting currents were also discerned by Ralph E. Smeltzer, who returned to the USA to complete his seminary training. In a perceptive letter written in mid-November, 1949, he observed that the church was different. "I have received the feeling that the Elgin program is more centralized, more rigid, and more hierarchical. Channels are increasingly emphasized." He further observed that there was a much greater emphasis upon local program, with new buildings and a more professional (and better compensated) clergy. The resulting concern was that the Elgin "overhead" would need to be reduced and staff cutbacks instituted. As a result, the strongest pressure then felt was to reduce program to fit the smaller budget. In an earlier day, an "M. R. Zigler or John Metzler could stump the country for B. S. C.;" now the possibilities for promotion and fund raising were more limited. Those involved in the regional structure (recently introduced with the church reorganization) also showed greater interest in pushing their programs rather than the outreach of the church nationally or internationally.

Beyond this Smeltzer noted that with the change in Brethren Service executive came a change in policy. More emphasis was now given to long range social action and peace education concerns and less to emergency and crisis appeals. The role of BSC was to assist the local church in becoming more active and aggressive in peace matters. The base of the pyramid was to be at home, not abroad. Relatively little staff time was given to the European program. Smeltzer believed that this change in emphasis had not been adequately communicated to Brethren Service workers in Europe.[3]

Despite these limitations, which he felt keenly, M. R. Zigler was not discouraged. He reported, primarily to the BSC workers in Europe, that on a trip to Schwarzenau on July 4, 1948, his fourth visit there, he had received great inspiration:

> I left the church on Sunday morning with a new dedication. It seemed to be a new starting point in my life. There have been a number of such times, but nothing has ever struck me quite so hard spiritually as to walk through the streets of Schwarzenau and up in the hills toward the valley of small huts where the founder of our early church lived and worked. I left Schwarzenau with a burning passion to be worthy of the traditions that have come to since 1708. ... I would like to appeal to each one, that ... we all join in the delivering of the message of Christ and continue in the emphasis of peace that our church has held from the beginning, with the hope that we may have a part in making peace come to all the world.[4]

Indeed, it was not long before Zigler's innate energy and drive resulted in a blossoming program within the countries in which BSC was still active in Europe. He revitalized programs and eventually received many more personnel because of the introduction of the Brethren Volunteer Service plan to Europe in 1949. He took several completely new initiatives. By the end of his first five-year term (1953), he had built a dynamic program. He was not the person to perform a caretaking function. Analogous to Winston Churchill, he had no interest in presiding over the decline and fall of the Brethren Service empire.

Administrative Style

His spirit is reflected in his communications to his staff. He lost no occasion to spur them on, encourage them, and challenge them with the unique possibilities of their positions. Several administrative letters he wrote in 1949 reveal his style. Such an exhortation to Wilbur Mullen early in the year also inadvertently paints something of a self-portrait. He wrote: "Do not let anything worry you. Do a good day's job, plan next day's work, do that which you are able to do and then be sure to get a good night's sleep. There are too many blue people in Germany for relief people to add to the procession; therefore, I am very anxious that you keep enough reserve so that you may be an inspiration to everyone you meet. All the government officials that I meet need the fellowship of an optimist and one who has faith in others and that the goodwill will win."[5]

In July, 1949, he needed to tell BSC staff in Germany about several persons who wanted to visit the work in Kassel. It took a page and a half of enthusiastic challenge before he got to the "reason to write this letter." Among other things he stated:

> As I view the activities of the Church of the Brethren for the year 1949, I an convinced beyond any reasonable doubt that you are on the most significant mission of the Church. There has never been anything like it and there can never be a repetition. . . . I am hoping that quickly you will get a vision that will challenge you and the Church of the Brethren for the next 25 years and one that I can transmit to the churches next winter, climaxing at Annual Conference 1950. . . . I am hoping that there will be much seriousness and at the same time a good mixture of joyous experience. I hope that our work will be so good that crowds will come like the 5,000 that came to Christ and that [we] will be able to minister to them.[6]

Several months later he wrote to Kurtis Naylor, director in Germany, and to Ira W. Gibbel, director in Austria, following a staff meeting to plan the work of BSC in Europe:

> Both of you have the best opportunity of any in Europe to use your capacities and latent potential resources. Your opportunity will either make you a greater asset for the church or it will keep you just an ordinary man or less. I have seen great growth in both of you. There is nothing I enjoy more than to see young men put on their "long pants." There is no surer foundation for the future of the Church than men like you with faith, courage, and an experience that transcends the masses with humility and patience and "off the rostrum"

leadership. . . . I promise all I have to make you two of the finest leaders our Church will produce in this next five years. You will have to dig for the best I can give you, for in my desire to work here in Geneva, I may forget you. You must not let me do that. Youth must make the old man alive.[7]

Similarly, in 1955 he wrote to the directors of the German and Austrian programs, Wilbur Mullen and Don Durnbaugh:

In very bold letters I would like to write my very best wishes for both of you that out of this experience you shall become great and outstanding administrators who maintain vision, cut red tape, deal with small things quickly, set long-time goals and patiently strive to attain the impossible.[8]

These quotations reveal Zigler's basic administrative philosophy. This was to select younger people and throw them into challenging situations, making them aware of the massive responsibilities facing them but imbuing them with confidence that they could succeed. He believed that most often this would produce good results, that most people have more potential than they ever recognized, and that they should be given the chance to succeed. He believed very strongly that the gifts of material aid would mean much more, and, especially, be a stronger contribution toward peace, if they were accompanied by a human being. Perhaps such Brethren representatives did not have complete professional skills, perhaps there was some immaturity; still, they could communicate caring and concern in ways that would penetrate the suspicion and cynicism of the refugee and war-shattered survivors. It might be called an incarnational philosophy of relief management.

He tried manfully but largely unsuccessfully to convince the ecumenical leadership of Geneva that the Brethren program, including personnel, should be considered part of the larger program of Inter-Church Aid centered in Geneva. This ran afoul, however, of their preferred plan of American denominations providing funds and materials for distribution through the indigenous reconstruction agencies. The plan in Austria came the closest to meeting the WCC approval.[9]

Brethren Volunteer Service

The formal inauguration of the Brethren Volunteer Service program took place at the Colorado Springs Annual Conference in June, 1948, shortly after Zigler left for his European assignment. Yet he had actually been instrumental in starting this important breakthrough. He had persuaded many people to give volunteer service to the church, beginning in the mid-1930s. In 1942, at the Asheville, North Carolina, Annual Conference, he presented a formal challenge to Brethren youth to volunteer for service with the church to match the draft-necessitated Civilian Public Service. Young people who responded worked as attendants in mental hospitals, assisted with material aid collection, and aided local congregations. Many, however, were channeled through the organization of the Brethren Service Committee (later Commission).

The immediate origin of BVS was Zigler's powerful address to the assembled Brethren youth at the Orlando, Florida, Annual Conference, in 1947. His first-hand accounts of the suffering he had seen in Europe shook his hearers: "His message was electrifying. It shocked the youth into a state of horror; dismay and soul-searching followed, then the question, 'What can we do?'" The decision was to begin praying and wait for an answer. A twenty-four-hour prayer vigil was spontaneously organized, lasting throughout the conference. In modified form, it was perpetuated through the following year.[10]

During that time, some of these young people worked with peace caravans; that initiative had emerged from a powerful work camp experience in Salina, Kansas, in 1947. This involved volunteers touring Brethren congregations; a carload of young people would visit for several days to a week, presenting programs and working extensively with the young people. Others at the work camp pledged to give sacrificially from their wages to support the caravans.

As these young people came to the 1948 conference, they decided to hold prayer vigils before each business meeting. Their primary concern was that the church provide a structure that would allow young members of the church to do something positive for peace and not simply say "no" to war. With the behind-the-scenes advice of Dan West and some others, the young people prepared a query to present to the delegates at the conference. Breaking with polity procedures, the question was accepted as a new item of business and then adopted by the voting body, which then delegated the new program to a surprised Brethren Service Commission for implementation.

Action followed quickly, so that the first training unit for the first Brethren Volunteer Service unit began in September, using the facilities of the New Windsor, Maryland, service center and Camp Harmony, Pennsylvania. Following a two-month training period, the first projects began in such areas as migrant labor, peace caravans, and work with Hispanics at Falfurrias, Texas. By summer, 1949, the question arose: could some BVSers be assigned to Europe?[11]

There was some initial reluctance in Europe, even from M. R. Zigler, always a promoter and encourager of young people. The declining budget item for the European program might be impacted adversely, if expenses for young people were added. Searching questions were posed: would they be mature enough to handle the social pressures, job requirements, and complexities of postwar Europe?

Eventually, clearances were secured and the first band of six, all college graduates, headed for Europe in the fall of 1949; they were selected from the third training unit, which had begun in the summer of 1949. Edson Sower of the German BSC staff was detailed to guide the new program of volunteers. They arrived in Europe in time for the last part of the European Annual Conference of BSC workers and friends, held near Schwarzenau.

After several group projects, the volunteers went out in teams or as individuals in several places in Austria and Germany. Before long, they were asked to assist in regular BSC programs, such as material aid distribution, refugee resettlement, student exchange, international work camps, and the like. Zigler quickly saw how these young people could develop his long-standing position that material gifts can best contribute to a peaceful world if they are presented by living representatives of the church in America. He became the foremost champion of the program.

Brethren volunteers responded devotedly to his leadership, struck by his vitality and optimism, and warmed by his encouragement and appreciation. He had an unusual ability to reach across the generational gap; he could speak frankly to them without their taking offense. They glowed with admiration as he dared them to think years ahead, to set goals for themselves and for the church. He recruited many for lifelong service to the church. For decades afterwards, they remained loyal to him and to the vision he represented.

Every three months, more volunteers followed the first six; the program continues in 1989. The personnel structure of Brethren Service in Europe featured a handful of administrators, who directed the larger numbers of BVSers in an expanded program. (This, Zigler quickly saw, was one way to cut through the budget cuts and limitations.) Many volunteers were also seconded to other agencies and soon made fine records there. The program was a definite success.

Inter-Church Service to Greek Villages

A personal triumph came to M. R. Zigler when he succeeded in developing a fully ecumenical team to bring renewal and rehabilitation to needy
villages of Greece. This achievement was well-regarded in Geneva and
was, indeed, taken as a pattern for other ecumenical work teams. The
background was a visit that Zigler paid to the Greek Orthodox Church in
October, 1949. He made a general survey of needs (which were great) and
reported back to the World Council of Churches and the Brethren Service
Commission in the USA. Among his contacts was an interview with
Spyridon, archbishop of Athens and All Greece. As it happened, the
Brethren had a good reputation in Greece because of an earlier action. In
1945 the Heifer Project had donated six pure-bred bulls to establish an
artificial insemination program. The hierarchy was convinced of the
necessity of agricultural reform as the basis for rebuilding the country,
which was not only devastated by World War II but also by four years of
bitter civil war following liberation from Nazi occupation. The country
was trying to absorb 1.5 million Greeks fleeing Asia Minor. In a follow up
letter the archbishop summarized Greece's most pressing needs.[12]

He then gave an open invitation to Zigler to begin a program of aid,
with particular attention to the plight of the desperately poor northern
region bordering on Albania. Greek government leaders also gave their
blessing to a program, as did American consular officials. Zigler recruited
BSC worker Edson Sower and BVSer Dean Neher and sent them to the
area of Ioannina in the autumn of 1950. Because the Brethren did not have
the resources to begin to meet the bitter need, Zigler launched a campaign
to find additional team members from other churches, asking each for a
qualified person and $5,000 in support per year. The first breakthrough
came with the Lutheran World Federation. The LWF chairman, Franklin
Fry, responded to the overture after some deliberation with a personal,
handwritten note: "The Lutheran World Federation at its meeting today
approved $5,000 and the appointment of a man for the Greek team,
without a murmur. Yours for peace, Franklin Fry."

Thus encouraged, Zigler approached other bodies, and secured similar
promises from the Disciples of Christ, Presbyterians, Evangelical United
Brethren, and American Baptist Convention. Later, the Mennonites,
Episcopalians, Evangelical and Reformed, and Methodists added their
support. Zigler then broadened the search to include European churches.
He succeeded with the Swedish Lutheran Church, British Council of

Churches, Danish Council of Churches, and the Council of Churches of Holland. Church World Service funds supported special projects.

An administrative committee was formed in Geneva to oversee the project, then called the *Inter-Church Service to Greek Villages*. By 1952 the team was fully staffed and making an impact on the area it chose for its operations. The manner of working was for small teams or individuals to spread out to the villages in the mountains at the beginning of the week, working there until the weekend, at which time they would return to the home base in Ioannina for rest and regrouping. The focus was on improving agriculture and family life. Introduction of hybrid grain slowly won adherents among the conservative farmers. Team members demonstrated soil conservation and improvement measures. Home economists showed how food could be conserved by canning.

A dramatic venture was the opening of a long-unused drainage tunnel, at Pontikates-Delo, which succeeded in making 200 acres of ground available for cultivation after two centuries of neglect. It took three grueling and dangerous years of work on the part of the team and interested villagers to complete.

The longest lasting, if less dramatic, project, however, was the introduction of poultry raising, through the importation of fertilized eggs and incubators. After a slow start, this innovation succeeded so well that the Ioannina area has become the source of poultry for the whole country and brought great prosperity to the region. In the 1960s, with church aid, a farmers' cooperative installed an automated plant, costing $1 million, to process 500 broiler chickens per hour. Church World Service provided technical aid for the project.

Zigler had the pleasure of going back many years later to visit friends and to see firsthand what a revolution had been started with the ecumenical team. With little direct Brethren funding, the program to assist villages had succeeded beyond anyone's expectations. Beyond that, the pattern established at Ioannina was picked up for other areas in Greece and used beyond that in Southern Italy, Morocco, Tunisia, and elsewhere. By 1968 the WCC Inter-Church Aid committee had a teams committee supervising such teams in several different locations from Cyprus to Lesotho.[13]

Eirene: International Christian Service for Peace

Another new program, partly stimulated by the success of the Greek teams, was *Eirene*. Using the word for peace in the Greek language, the program was instituted jointly by the three Historic Peace Churches, in large part to provide a vehicle for alternate service for European conscientious objectors. The possibility of aiding young pacifists after arriving in Geneva in 1948 had always been close to M. R. Zigler's heart. It was a continual matter of concern at the meetings of the peace churches.

In 1952 Zigler pushed hard for the creation of the European equivalent of the NSBRO, wishing to develop some organizational structure to facilitate placement of COs from those (few) nations in Europe that allowed an alternative to military obligations. Representatives of the Mennonite Central Committee, like Orie O. Miller in the USA and Henry Fast in Basel, were supportive of the idea but the resistance of W. Harold Row killed the possibility. Row did not see how this would be workable in the European setting and was unwilling to see any new funding made available.[14]

The creation of a project in which COs could serve, however, was not dropped. The ardent French pacifist, André Trocmé, was a forceful advocate. Finally, late in 1957, following prior approval by MCC and BSC in the USA, a long period of planning and negotiating paid off with the formal organization of the program. As it developed, the Friends dropped out as sponsors, and the International Fellowship of Reconciliation (IFOR) was on the margins. W. Harold Row, in meetings both in Europe and America, became a strong supporter of the concept, which also enjoyed the approval of Dr. Visser 't Hooft of the WCC. Milton Harder of the Mennonite Central Committee became the first executive secretary and Zigler was chairman. The project was established in Morocco, with a Dutch volunteer as project director. Volunteers from Germany, France, and the USA were the first members of the team. The purpose was "to provide a channel through which young people of various countries can render a voluntary service as Christian pacifists, particularly in places of tension, where Christian love can contribute to reconciliation."[15]

The initial work project at Oulmes, Morocco, was the construction of a shelter for cows on a government experimental farm. This was followed by further agricultural development measures, such as fence building, well digging, and advising sheepherders. The plan for future work included development of pasture land; introduction of a high-grade cattle population; organization of a farmers' cooperative, and creation of garden clubs for young people.[16]

By 1965 the team in Morocco numbered seventeen members from the USA, Germany, France, Holland, Belgium, and France, working in

203

several locations from Larache in the far north to Agadir in the deep south. Agadir had been hit hard by an earthquake, and the Eirene team was the channel for ecumenical aid through the World Council of Churches. Branching out from the earlier agricultural work, the Eirene teams later sponsored vocational schools, reeducation for delinquents, social work among children, school feeding programs, infant care, instruction in hygiene and sanitation, and poultry farming. In 1988 the program still continues, although it has largely lost its original religious orientation.[17]

Relationships with the Historic Peace Churches

The Eirene program was not all that brought the peace churches together. In the United States, Zigler had played a key role in bringing the Historic Peace Churches together to make common cause. After he arrived in Europe, he set out to do something similar. Early in 1949 he contacted the American representative of the Mennonite Central Committee, Robert Kreider, at MCC headquarters in Basel, and Algie I. Newlin, of the Religious Society of Friends, in Geneva. In addition, Zigler also reached out to the leadership of the International Fellowship of Reconciliation. Some outstanding peace activists, such as Hans de Graaf (Netherlands), André Trocmé (France), Jean Lassere (France), Heinz Kloppenburg (West Germany), and Kaspar Mayr (Austria) worked actively with the IFOR.

He succeeded in bringing together a small planning group in a Swiss retreat center, the Abbaye at Presinge, in May 5-7, 1949. It had taken all of Zigler's energy and persistence to bring this about. A findings committee recommended that a Continuation Committee be established to plan subsequent meetings and to keep information flowing between the Historic Peace Churches. It also called on them to prepare a plan for an approach to the World Council of Churches in the interests of peace. The May meeting was the first of a long series of meetings, usually two or three each year, with significant outcomes. Probably the most important fruit of these meetings was a combined document on the peace positions of the three churches and the IFOR; its title was the important phrase from the Amsterdam conference: *War Is Contrary to the Will of God* (1951).[18]

The impetus for the drafting of the document came from the appeal in the Amsterdam statement for theologians and church leaders in the cooperating church bodies to break the logjam in ecumenical thinking about war. The peace churches wanted to seize this opportunity to bring their message to the world denominations no later than the next assembly

(1954). This concern was in fact welcomed by the WCC staff in direct communications from Dr. Visser 't Hooft, general secretary. A long process of meeting and drafting produced the statement. This was duly presented to WCC officials. But there was a problem; the booklet consisted of semi-official and independent statements from four different bodies: Quaker, Mennonite, Brethren, and IFOR. Visser 't Hooft's comment was pointed and pungent: How could the peace churches expect several hundred churches under the WCC banner to unite in a statement on peace when they themselves brought in a disunited document? They saw the logic of the criticism and went back to the drafting board.

The subsequent statement, *Peace Is the Will of God* (1953), represented the combined effort of the peace church Continuation Committee in Europe. The predominant labor of theological drafting was done by Mennonite relief workers and graduate students in Europe, Paul Peachey and John Howard Yoder, in conversation with British theologians from the Society of Friends and the IFOR. The final editing committee was composed of John Howard Yoder (Mennonite), Colin Fawcett (English Quaker), and Zigler (Brethren). They met in a hotel room in Paris to complete their task. Yoder recalled that he and Fawcett worked carefully over the manuscript: "Bob was on the hotel bed and as we worked carefully at matters of phrasing, sometimes to respect Colin's taste in English and sometimes to respect Quaker theology, Bob said: 'You guys write it and I'll sign it.'" Yoder acknowledged, however, that without Zigler's intercession and collaborative cues, no joint statement could have emerged.[19]

A follow-up meeting in the summer of 1955 developed into something quite dramatic. The meeting at the retreat center at Crêt Bérard, Puidoux, was designed as a time when the peace groups could pool their thinking on war/peace issues with the critical help of several leading European theologians, chosen from the ranks of the continental state churches, primarily from Germany. What happened at the meeting was something quite different. It became a true dialogue and colloquium between representatives of the Radical Reformation (the Historic Peace Churches) and the Magisterial Reformation (Lutheran and Reformed theologians). Observers said that this was the first time representatives of these groups had talked seriously since the sixteenth century disputations.

So significant were the deliberations that all participants agreed that the conference must be continued. Thus it was that the so-called Puidoux conferences came about; their formal title was "The Lordship of Christ over Church and State." Four in number, with some regional meetings in addition, they were to have historic consequences for the cause of conscientious objection in Europe. In part because of their stimulation, the West Germany government provided a liberal policy for alternative service for COs.

After the last Puidoux conference, held in July, 1962, in Oud Poelgeest, Netherlands, another smaller, more academic series was launched under the general sponsorship of the Evangelical Study Institute of Heidelberg (FEST). Eventually, the initiative was continued by the Church and Peace movement, spearheaded by the Lutheran pastor, Wilfried Warneck. This merging of peace interests, motivated by Zigler's initiatives, proved to have long lasting results. The cooperative spirit he developed brought a fresh wind into the European fields of peace dialogue and had far more significant repercussions than generally recognized.

Brethren Service in Europe

Some informed observers of developments within the Church of the Brethren suggested that if Zigler had not gone to Geneva in 1948, the entire European program would have been phased down, with interest shifting to the Near and Far East. In fact, the program became more vital and active, if less extensive, than it ever had been. Strong programs continued in Austria and Germany; the volunteer program flourished; the highly-successful Greek team concept was born and blossomed; and a cooperative program with European pacifists was established. The latter, combined with the theological and academic orientation of the Puidoux conferences, contributed strongly to the development of a pacifist minority within European churches. This is recognized among peace circles in Europe but little known, even among Brethren, in the United States.

As the end of his second five-year appointment neared in the summer of 1958, M. R. Zigler could look back on a string of varied and exciting developments, owing in great part to his own determination and drive. There were, however, serious crises yet to come.

NOTES

1. Zigler's own account of the Brethren Service work in Europe was included as the first five chapters of the book, *To Serve the Present Age: The Brethren Service Story*, ed. D. F. Durnbaugh (Elgin, IL: Brethren Press, 1975), 17-75;

a succinct survey was drawn up by Margaret Glick, "In His Name—Brethren Serve: A Report of Brethren Service Commission Activities in Europe," (1952), mimeographed.

2. M. R. Zigler to "all the workers in Europe," Nov. 19, 1947.
3. Ralph E. Smeltzer to Kurtis Naylor, Ira Gibbel, and M. R. Zigler, Nov. 18, 1949.
4. M. R. Zigler, Report No. I, July 7, 1948; see also M. R. Zigler, "Thoughts at Schwarzenau," *Gospel Messenger* (Oct. 2, 1948): 7-8.
5. M. R. Zigler to Wilbur Mullen, Jan. 15, 1949.
6. M. R. Zigler to Kurtis Naylor and Edson Sower, July 26, 1949.
7. M. R. Zigler to Kurtis F. Naylor and Ira W. Gibbel, Oct. 6, 1949.
8. M. R. Zigler to Wilbur Mullen and Don Durnbaugh, Jan. 7, 1955.
9. The Austrian BSC story is related in Ralph E. Smeltzer, "The History of Brethren Service in Austria: From its Beginning (November, 1946) to July, 1949," research paper in Brethren history, Bethany Biblical Seminary (Nov. 28, 1949); Merlin G. Shull, "History of the Brethren Service Commission in Austria," research paper in Brethren history, Bethany Biblical Seminary (November, 1953); Eleanor Williamson, comp., "Brethren Service in Austria, 1947-1958," unpubl. paper (June, 1958).
10. Gerry Pence to D. F. Durnbaugh, July 13, 1987.
11. On BVS, see Charles L. Boyer, "Brethren Volunteer Service," *Brethren Encyclopedia* (1983-1984), 202-203; see also the special issues of *Brethren Life and Thought*, 3 (Summer 1958), 13 (Autumn 1968), and 18 (Autumn 1973).
12. Zigler told the story in "Interchurch Service to Greek Villages," *Present Age* (1975), 188-195; see also, for example, "Our Project in Greece," *Gospel Messenger* (March 24, 1951): 18-19; "Lost: A Tunnel in Greece," *Gospel Messenger* (Sept. 29, 1951): 18-19; Million transcript of M. R. Zigler, 11/1-18.
13. "Special Teams Number," *Newsletter, Division of Inter-Church Aid, Refugee and World Service, World Council of Churches* (March, 1968); unpubl. report by Anita and Walter Kilpatrick (ca. 1970); *On Earth Peace Newsletter* (Oct. 23, 1979); Edgar H. S. Chandler, *The High Tower of Refuge* (New York: Frederick A. Prager, 1959), 79-84.
14. M. R. Zigler to Orie O. Miller, Sept. 27, 1952; Miller to Zigler, Oct. 2, 1952; Zigler to Miller, Oct. 21, 1952; Miller to Zigler, Oct. 28, 1952; W. Harold Row to Zigler, Nov. 7, 1952 (MCC Records, Mennonite Historical Archives).
15. Milton Harder, "Memorandum. The Development, Purpose, and Organizational Structure of EIRENE: International Christian Service for Peace," Feb. 1, 1958; *Newbriefs from Europe* (Jan. 20, 1958): 3.
16. "Morocco," *Gospel Messenger* (Aug. 2, 1958): 22-23.
17. Geoffrey Murray, "Eirene Brings a Message of Peace," *Messenger* (July 22, 1965): 9-11.
18. See the introduction in D. F. Durnbaugh, ed., *On Earth Peace: Discussions on*

War/Peace Issues Between Friends, Mennonites, and Brethren and European Churches, 1935-1975 (Elgin, IL: Brethren Press, 1978), 17-29.
19. John Howard Yoder to D. F. Durnbaugh, May 6, 1987.

17

FURLOUGHS AND
PLANS FOR RETIREMENT

P ART OF THE ARRANGEMENT under which M. R. Zigler went to
represent the Brethren in Europe was the promise of regular home
leaves or furloughs. This was for several reasons. In the first place, Zigler
was eager to stay in touch with American plans and developments. Then,
church leaders understood that regular reporting on and interpretation of
European conditions and opportunities were imperative if Brethren members
and congregations were to maintain their extraordinary efforts in funding.
It was natural that, unless otherwise instructed, Americans distant from the
war-ravaged areas would let down in their commitment to aid, assuming
that with the course of time, recovery and rebuilding would occur without
their assistance. Denominational publications throughout this period were
at pains to bring before their readership the massive needs yet remaining,
although several years had passed since the end of hostilities in Europe.

Typical of this approach was a column in the Brethren Service section
(which ran regularly in the *Gospel Messenger*) of March 11, 1950. It was
titled: "Can We Quit Now?" The answer was formulated in the statement
by M. R. Zigler: "It will take twenty-five years of good giving to finish the
job and to restore love." The column indicated that "many people have the
idea that it is time to quit our job of service and to divert all our efforts and
income to other fields." The writer insisted that the premise of this thought
was not true, that desperate need still existed, and that it was imperative
that the Brethren continue their generous response. "Do not Christ's
teachings reveal to us that every time we feed the hungry, clothe the naked,
take the stranger in, visit the prisoner, that we are ministering unto him"—
referring to the classic passage in Matthew 25 about the judgment scene.
If that is the case, asked the columnist, then will our job ever be finished?[1]

M. R. Zigler underscored the same message in articles published about the same time during his first furlough. His article "Peace Through Acts of Charity," is typical:

> Every dollar given for relief and reconstruction and every package for relief express love and friendship and immediately fear begins to vanish. A personal contact of a church representative with a gift rapidly eliminates suspicion. I have spent two years in Europe since the war witnessing the struggle back from the horrors of war. The people treading the streets and highways still pass by the rubble of their homes, churches, schools, business houses and hospitals. ... They are seeking work but there is so much unemployment. Pay is unequal to the cost of living. ... The delivering of gifts gives people hope and patience to wait a little longer for the peacemakers of the earth.[2]

Zigler was concerned to stay in touch with the home base; he had always worked conscientiously and systematically to remain in close contact with both leaders and ordinary members in the church. His sense of what they were thinking and feeling was one of the bases of his unusual influence and leadership. He recognized that once he was out of sight across the Atlantic, he could also be out of mind. Periodic trips "stateside" would permit him to keep these contacts fresh.

Beyond this, in fact, he made a concerted effort to maintain correspondence with a wide range of friends. He urged them to write regularly to him, relaying their perceptions of trends in the mood of the church membership. Many of these letters he typed himself, despite his miserable lack of typing skill; his handwriting was even worse. Recipients of the letters and notes were generally flattered and encouraged that such a busy man would take time to communicate with them. Their return letters expressed their pleasure that he was thinking of them.

The First Furlough

The first return to the United States after the 1948 departure lasted nearly six months. The Ziglers arrived in New York on December 21, 1949, and returned to Europe in mid-summer of 1950. The Annual Conference at Grand Rapids, Michigan (June 27-July 2) was the last stop on a busy itinerary. In a general letter written to the BSC workers back in Europe (he wrote of his experiences in diary style every week or so), Zigler mentioned his surprise that "the arrangement of my itinerary is filled practically every day from January 1 to Conference time."

After conferences in Elgin, he returned to the East Coast to begin his interpretation tour: "My first public appearance was in Washington, two sermons in the morning, well robed. Response excellent. Laymen very much interested. Women, excitedly so. Youth seemed to be in a department and have to be approached differently."

From the District of Columbia, the Ziglers traveled to Manassas, Virginia; Bridgewater, Virginia; and Winston-Salem, North Carolina. Then the tour brought the Ziglers back into Virginia, concluding at his home congregation, Linville Creek, at Broadway: "Some people I haven't seen for forty years were there. Most excellent spirit. Offering good. People stayed for an hour after the service. Received the greatest inspiration of my life since I joined the Church there. . . . Something happened there that gives me greater faith in God and man."

In this and other congregations, Zigler's message went over well. He was, nevertheless, concerned that he was "putting it on too hard;" in one congregation a man walked out. Zigler was gratified that the man returned somewhat later in the service: "My sin is to preach too long. It just seems impossible to pack the stuff into a ball and keep within reason. If I try to say something about each one of you and about each project, then I can't say anything about fear and love, democracy and the abundant life, the need for the Christian church. Gradually my message is maturing."

The busy schedule took its toll on the energetic Zigler. Referring to a discussion with lay leaders after one session that lasted until midnight, he wrote: "These after conferences plus some eats kill you off more than the public address." He reported having what he called the "heaves"—asthma attacks—three times since he had arrived, curiously coming about 6:00 P.M. instead of the "usual midnight stunt."[3]

The tour continued on to Indiana before returning to Middle Pennsylvania after February 11. In the Stone Church of the Brethren at Huntingdon, Pennsylvania, he found the choral music and worship superb, wishing "that choir could go up and down the streets of Kassel and other cities singing." Yet, he found that the beautiful worship services did not produce action. "The response to my speech reveals that people like to be challenged to rigorous living and helpfulness if they are assured that it is really building the Kingdom."[4]

Items from the *Gospel Messenger* track some of his activities in the USA, following early appearances at Elgin headquarters and Bethany Biblical Seminary in Chicago:

The annual mission rallies of Southern Ohio will be held in the Brookville and Covington churches on Sunday, Feb. 5. Speakers will be William Beahm, Wendell Flory, C. Ernest Davis, and M. R. Zigler. M. R. Zigler, our European representative, will speak in the Windber church, Pa., Feb. 12, 7:30 P.M. He is being sponsored by the young adults of Western Pennsylvania. [Some 300 attended][5]

From the Johnstown, Pennsylvania area, the Ziglers went back into Middle Pennsylvania, and then on to the Lancaster vicinity, arriving at 1:00 A.M., needing to meet the next appointment at 8:45 A.M. and the second at 10:30 A.M. In this area the attendance was large and the interest high. He found that there was great readiness to help in the congregations using the free ministry. Some churches were "hungry to have people come to talk to them."[6]

The announcements of his travels and speeches continued in the church periodical:

M. R. Zigler, European representative, will be in the Chicago and California areas during this week: Feb. 26, Chicago and York Center; March 1-3, Pacific Coast regional conference; March 4, Bakersfield and Lindsay; March 5, Fresno and Modesto.[7]

M. R. Zigler, European representative, will continue his tour in the Pacific Coast Region during the week March 6-12. He will be in the following churches: March 6, San Francisco or Oakland, Calif.; March 7, Sacramento, Calif. . . .; March 9, Portland, Oregon . . .; March 10, Olympic View, Seattle, Wash. . . .; March 12, Wenatchee and Yakima, Wash.[8]

M. R. Zigler, European representative, will complete his tour of the Pacific Coast churches with the meeting at Nampa, Idaho, on March 13. Then he will visit Western Region churches as follows: March 14, Denver, Colo.; March 15, Lincoln, Nebraska; March 16, 17, and 19, McPherson and McPherson College, Kansas; March 18, Eden Valley, Kansas; March 19, P.M., Wichita, Kansas.[9]

After the first major part of his interpretative swing, Zigler's conclusion was that there was "tremendous interest in Brethren Service among old and young, rich and poor, for practically everything we are doing. . . ." However, his visit to the General Board meeting held at Elgin, Illinois, in March 20-22, caused a rude reawakening. The Goals and Budget Committee report, which provided the basis for the budget allocation, barely mentioned the work of Brethren Service. He compared the situation to a fog as dense "as when, with Mrs. Zigler, Mrs. Naylor, and John Eberly, we dodged a bus along the Rhine River to save our lives. . . ."

His gloom continued as the board divided into commissions to react to the reduced budget. "For the first time since 1940, heart trouble set in—coronary thrombosis. How many attacks like this I can stand, I do not know, and I confess that I was unable to help Harold [Row] like I wanted to do. I feel clearly on the outside of the policy-making of the total Brotherhood activities; being away for two years is almost like a strange man coming from Mars."

With his customary resilience, he rallied at the end of his disappointing recital:

> I have gone through many days like this at Elgin. I feel blue many times, but to me the Church of the Brethren was never more significant because of the message which we possess and the kind of a world in which we live, and I pray if we let the light go out that somebody else will carry on. I want to report truly what my observations have been and, [as] heretofore, I am sure affairs will work out to the glory of Christ and His Coming. I know that I will be able to write to you more optimistically, and I pray that whatever the cuts must be that we will take them with contagious enthusiasm.[10]

After the meeting of the General Brotherhood Board, Zigler began again to itinerate at much the same breathless pace as before; he traveled among the Ohio churches in late March and early April, before moving on to Pennsylvania and Virginia by mid-month. He reported that while in Kansas, he was so tired that he had slept between sessions on a hard church bench and woke refreshed and "ready to preach" when the people returned. He was back in Pennsylvania at the end of April, and journeying to West Virginia in May, speaking in the Sandy Creek, Eglon, Petersburg, Beaver Run, and Keyser congregations—all within three days.[11]

Later in May he attended an important peace conference in Detroit, Michigan, which brought together several hundred pacifists from across the nation. As he readied himself for a major address at the Annual Conference at Grand Rapids, he asked each worker with Brethren Service in Europe to send him "the most evidence you can find for the promotion of material aid in the interest of peace in your experience." He needed it because he felt that he was "getting ready to throw the last ball" with "three men on base and two strikes" on the batter. He reported that former BSC workers were homesick for Europe. Therefore, he counselled, "it pays to

[do] the best you can while you are over there." He continued: "It will probably be the best part of your life and the most you can do effectively will make your future life the most attractive for it will be something you will have which cannot be taken away from you. This something you are getting is a something you can always give away and yet always have a constant supply, that never wears away as long as memory lasts." Zigler admonished: "But remember you will have to stand on the street corner to take your place in the world for people are not making much room for the inspired men in behalf of others. You will have to blaze your own trail."[12]

Many people have stated that Zigler's address at the Grand Rapids conference was the most effective he ever made. At the conclusion he asked for the audience to bow their heads in prayer. As they did so, he had a long line of German exchange students, staying that year in Brethren families, arrange themselves behind a similar line of young American Brethren. When the worshipers raised their eyes, at a signal the two lines became one as Germans and Americans joined hands.

He was otherwise much in evidence at the conference. The report on Brethren Service in the *Gospel Messenger* noted:

> M. R. Zigler's presence added decidedly to the effectiveness of Brethren Service emphases at Grand Rapids. A Conference without him has been a rare thing in the past generation. . . . This year he was on hand again. Most sections of the Brotherhood had already seen him during the past six months, but people were eager to see him again, to talk to him, and to hear his addresses. He spoke at the Brethren Service luncheon, the young people's "Mother Hubbard dinner," and the general session Saturday evening. Two of the important emphases in his messages, delivered in his usual informal style, were (a) Europe's spiritual need for the gospel of peace, and (b) the opportunity for the Brethren to demonstrate that gospel through service projects. The Ziglers left immediately after the conference for Europe. The *Gospel Messenger* reported that he "had been waiting rather impatiently for that time during the past two months."[13]

The Second Furlough

The second home leave also lasted about six months. This time the leave began in June, 1954, and extended to December 24, 1954. The Brethren Service Center at New Windsor, Maryland, was his home base for the leave, which also featured extensive traveling and speaking. It was not as exhaustingly full, however, as the 1950 experience. An early, and somewhat unusual assignment, came already on June 13, when he spoke at the dedication of a plaque honoring John Naas, the Brethren leader in colonial New Jersey. This just preceded the annual conference at Ocean Grove, New Jersey (June 15-20).[14]

He was an active participant in the Historic Peace Churches consultation held at Bluffton, Ohio, on July 15-18. This was a natural involvement for him, given his earlier work with the Continuation Committees of the peace groups both in North America and Europe.

The highlight of the leave was his participation in the Second Assembly of the World Council of Churches, held at Evanston, Illinois, on August 15-31. He and Norman J. Baugher, general secretary, were the representatives of the Church of the Brethren. It was at Evanston that he received the signal honor of appointment to the powerful WCC Central Committee, as mentioned earlier. He worked hard at the assembly to push forward the agenda of the Historic Peace Churches, using the combined statement developed by their Continuation Committee in Europe. The Brethren petitioned the World Council to hold a top-level conference on peace, a "full dress theological conference," as it was expressed by John Howard Yoder, a young Mennonite theologian. According to Zigler, the suggestion was making its way through the ecumenical machinery and had a good chance of approval at the next meeting of the Central Committee, scheduled for the summer of 1955.[15]

He spoke at the Central Regional conference, held at Manchester College, Indiana, on October 18-21. Later that month, he was a featured speaker at the National Convention on the Church in Town and Country, Salina, Kansas (October 26-28). This invitation brought him back to one of his great loves, the role of the rural church. His topic was "The Christian Mission to the Rural Billion."[16]

A personal high point for Zigler was his visit on November 1 to his close Mennonite friend, Orie O. Miller, at the Akron, Pennsylvania, offices of the Mennonite Central Committee. The visit had been set up after Zigler's appearance on October 14 at a meeting of the National Service Board for Religious Objectors, held in Washington, D. C. Miller responded in writing that he "was thrilled" to learn of the prospective visit. He said that Zigler must come to his home for a meal, to allow "some return for the wonderful breakfasts you folks gave us in Geneva."[17]

Not long before Amy and M. R. Zigler sailed on the Dutch-American liner S.S. Vesterdam from New York on December 24, Zigler was a leader for a conference of former Brethren Service Volunteers in Chicago.[18]

215

The Third Furlough

The third and last furlough from the work in Europe was briefer; it lasted from spring to mid-summer, 1956. The Ziglers sailed aboard the S. S. United States from Bremerhaven on February 24 and arrived on March 1. One of his first engagements was to speak at his alma mater, Bridgewater College, on March 19. He challenged the student body to "follow the way of peace" and to consider joining the Brethren Volunteer Service program. About a month later, he spoke to the students at Juniata College. Zigler continued his college tour with a baccalaureate sermon at La Verne College, California, on May 27.[19]

A major appearance, and his last, came with his address at a peace convocation attracting 800 Brethren from the Eastern and Southeastern regions, held on July 1 at the Brethren Service Center at New Windsor, Maryland. He focused his address on the peace message of the church and on the contribution that young people were making and could make for peace.[20] M. R. Zigler returned alone to Geneva, leaving the USA on July 3, as his wife wished to stay longer in the USA for family reasons. She was scheduled to return later with family friends.

As was true with earlier visits, he had spent much time persuading church members of the necessity of continuing to back the Brethren Service projects of reconstruction, relief, and peace education. He summed up his appeal in these words:

> How long must the Church of the Brethren sacrifice for peace? The answer is very simple and easy. As long as your love lasts. The way to implement the answer is within the temple of each and everyone committed to "peace-making." Two world wars have created so much ill-will. It is amazing how much love is created when one of your representatives in a land where we killed people by the millions steps forward to shake hands and give a gift of reconciliation. Through your living workers in Austria, Germany, Greece and elsewhere you can give your testimony in a personal way. Fill our hands abroad with your testimony and peace will really come.[21]

Return to Europe

After returning to Geneva in early July, Zigler took up again the accumulated burdens of the European directorship. It was obvious that he missed his wife, because he wrote her every day. He had much to report, because they had sublet their apartment on the rue de Malagnou in anticipation of moving into the new apartment near the lake. He stayed temporarily in the apartment of his friend Frank Northam, WCC executive. Zigler reported a few days later that it had become clear that the new apartment would not be available until December, so they gave notice to their sub-tenant in the old apartment that they would need to move back in at the end of August.

He had an important checkup in mid-July with a Swiss physician, to see if his diabetic condition was stabilized. This medical problem had been discovered before he left the USA and a course of treatment was initiated; however, he had to return to Europe before the treatments could be concluded. The Swiss doctor was experimenting with a new drug which could be taken in tablet form instead of by shots. Zigler was also ordered to reduce weight. He ended his report on his medical condition with this statement: "Up to this date, 'I have been living to fight;' from now on I shall 'fight to live.'" His future travel schedule would be determined by the results of the examination. Fortunately, the results were positive, and he was given a green light for leaving Geneva.

The positive report raised his spirits tremendously. This was revealed in a buoyant letter to his Amy, written on the same day he received the good news:

> Yesterday and today have been very extraordinary days and you will never know how life releasing this experience has been. Am sure you will join me in enthusiasm to live in the future to continue the purpose of our lives, long established, from which it would be most difficult to curve away to retirement or convalescence. I see the future so full of opportunities and challenge so that I don't see how one could stop this side of death. I want to work right up to the last. . . . I hope you shall live with me until we finish our life work that seems to have been cut out for us to do. Our work will never be done. This most hopeful aspect of our life and work is working with Young People who will carry on in the future. I would not trade with anyone the job we have to do. . . . Let[']s set our stakes for the future.

Sadly, this brave and bright statement of life purpose was not to be fulfilled. M. R. Zigler himself went on for nearly thirty more years. But it was not with Amy Zigler at his side.[22]

Retirement Plans

M. R. Zigler was sixty-five years old on November 9, 1956. He had originally expected to retire at that time, but was delighted when the

217

General Brotherhood Board invited him to complete his second five-year appointment. This would enable him to finish out his tour of duty after the 250th Anniversary celebration. It would also round out ten years of foreign service for the church as its representative in Geneva. Health-wise, he had felt very well in Europe, free at last from the exhausting bouts of asthma that had so longed plagued him. He had been concerned about the diabetic condition that developed during his furlough in 1956, but now that was also under control.

For a man of his temperament and experience, the thought of a peaceful and relaxing retirement in a warm place held little attraction. Many friends had, indeed, urged him to plan a retirement in Sebring, Florida, which had developed over the years as a center for aging Brethren. He did engage in some correspondence with friends there late in 1956. One serious reservation about the area presented itself: on an earlier visit, he had suffered during the first night there a severe asthmatic attack. He wrote to a correspondent in Sebring: "It is a thing that I don't want to live with the rest of my life. I've had enough of that and I hope I'll never have to fight for the chance to live like I used to." He speculated about the possibilities of a donated lot near the Sebring Church of the Brethren and a work camp of volunteer laborers to put up a house. Other friends at St. Petersburg also urged retirement there.[23]

He also thought a great deal of moving back to his childhood home at Broadway, Virginia. One possibility was using the Zigler homestead, then owned by his good friend Charles Lantz, as a summer home. After considerable deliberation, he asked for his letter of membership in the Highland Avenue Church of the Brethren in Elgin, Illinois, to be transferred to the Linville Creek Church of the Brethren at Broadway. All through his stay in Europe he had kept up his financial commitment to the Highland Avenue congregation, at the rate of two dollars per week.[24]

Although much uncertainty marked his reflections about his post-European plans, he did develop a plan in some detail for presentation to the General Brotherhood Board. This included a proposal to spend time over several years to sketch "observations of [the] life and work of the Brethren from 1900 to 1958." The purpose would be to document and preserve in writing the development of the church, largely involving his own leadership, in the areas of social outreach.

Concurrently with this, he proposed that he establish himself in New York city as a liaison for the Church of the Brethren with the National Council of Churches and the United Nations. His particular concern would be the cause of religious liberty and conscientious objection around the world. In his language: "If feasible, give much time to help create a world movement in behalf of religious liberty with special reference to conscientious objection to work for peace and eliminate war as a method of settling disputes." He thought that finances would be forthcoming for such a ministry and was personally prepared to defray much of the expenses from his own retirement income.[25]

Zigler's attitude toward his personal finances was remarkably trusting. He took the Geneva assignment at the age of fifty-six without a clear commitment from the church as to his financial position upon retirement. It was only late in the day that the church had developed a retirement plan for its staff members. As one of the senior members, Zigler had little time left in which to build up equity in the plan. He recalled a private conversation that the chair of the Board had with him in 1948. Rufus D. Bowman assured him at that time that the Board would care for his retirement on the same basis as other veteran and senior employees.

In 1958, when retirement loomed large, Zigler wrote the general secretary to establish what his status would be. After some research, Norman J. Baugher clarified the situation. In 1943 the General Mission Board had established an annuity for Zigler and his colleague H. Spenser Minnich, which would ensure them a retirement pension of thirty dollars per month. This was increased to forty dollars per month by a subsequent action of the Board, with the proviso that any Social Security income would be deducted from the amount. This arrangement was modified under the General Brotherhood Board in more generous manner: upon retirement, the Ziglers could expect (assuming their income was less than $1,200 per year) a monthly Social Security payment of $162.80 per month; in addition to this the annuity payment would add $48.17, for a total of $210.97.[26]

On June 7, 1958, Ralph E. Smeltzer, director of social education for the Brethren Service Commission, wrote to Zigler inviting him to spend three months (November, December, and January) after his return traveling among the churches to interpret the BSC program. Collections taken in the church meetings were expected to cover travel expenses and a fifty dollar per week salary. Zigler's reaction was cool. He replied that the invitation had come quite late, that in his experience, very careful preparation needed to be made if such visits were to be fruitful, and that many people were telling him that he should take time after returning simply for resting. He concluded: "I regret to write this kind of letter, but when plans are

219

pretty well in mind you can't forget all plans and do what you have suggested."[27]

He was very conscious that it would be a difficult matter for a man of his temperament to leave a mobile and varied task in Europe and withdraw to a quiet and withdrawn site in the USA. He thought that the shift might create a feeling of bitterness on his part and was determined to avoid it. His attitude at this time is revealed in a letter he wrote to a former BSC worker in April, 1958:

> There is one thing I decided a long time ago that I was not going to be bitter about criticism, disappointment and I was going to try to live as if everything was alright. Not because it was alright, but because we had a chance to make things right not only for ourselves, but for all those wherein we have an influence now and in the future. Believe me, the supreme test of my decisions will be coming in the future when I cut loose from the old fellowships that I have had in the working days of my life. I'm looking toward September 1st with unusual interest and I'm trying to prepare for it and I'm trying to be an old man that will not be bitter. . . . I know so few men who have grown old with magnificence. I do not mean to be an example of unusual ability in this field, but I would like to come through spiritually alive, alert, happy that one lived.[28]

The reference to bitterness came from a background of several months of administrative tension in 1957. The top Brethren administrators in Elgin, Norman J. Baugher and W. Harold Row, had been sharply critical of Zigler's administration of the BSC program in Europe. For his part, he felt that they had not provided sufficient funds for the program, yet had forbidden him to secure extra-budgetary resources from his network of friends. During several weeks in the autumn of 1957, he was on the point of resigning and returning to the USA. Eventually, the three men agreed for the sake of the program and the church to "let bygones be bygones" and hold matters together until Zigler's anticipated retirement in the fall of 1958. The strain, however, was not completely forgotten on either side.[29]

NOTES

1. "Can We Quit Now?" *Gospel Messenger* (March 11, 1950): 19.
2. M. R. Zigler, "Peace Through Acts of Charity," *Gospel Messenger* (March 4, 1950): 10-11; see also his article, "A Challenge to the Church," *Gospel Messenger* (June 10, 1950): 8-9.

3. M. R. Zigler to BSC Workers and Volunteers, Report # 2, Jan. 13, 1950.
4. M. R. Zigler to BSC Workers and Volunteers, Report # 5, Feb. 27, 1950.
5. *Gospel Messenger* (Feb. 11, 1950): 17; (Jan. 28, 1950): 16.
6. M. R. Zigler to BSC Workers and Volunteers, Report # 5, Feb. 27, 1950.
7. *Gospel Messenger* (Feb. 25, 1950): 16.
8. *Gospel Messenger* (March 4, 1950): 17.
9. *Gospel Messenger* (March 11, 1950): 17.
10. M. R. Zigler to BSC Workers and Volunteers, Report # 8, March 27, 1950.
11. M. R. Zigler to BSC Workers and Volunteers, Report # 13, April 25, 1950.
12. M. R. Zigler to BSC Workers and Volunteers, May 20, 1950.
13. "Service Echoes from Grand Rapids," *Gospel Messenger* (Aug. 19, 1950): 18-19.
14. C. Ernest Davis, "John Naas Memorial Plaque Dedicated," *Gospel Messenger* (Oct. 23, 1954): 13.
15. M. R. Zigler to John Howard Yoder, Eric Tucker, and Percy Bartlett, Oct. 15, 1954 (MCC Records, Mennonite Historical Archives).
16. *Gospel Messenger* (Oct. 9, 1954): 16; (Oct. 16, 1954): 16.
17. Orie O. Miller to M. R. Zigler, Oct. 20, 1954 (MCC Records, Mennonite Historical Archives).
18. *Gospel Messenger* (Dec. 11, 1954): 16; (Jan. 22, 1955): 21.
19. *Gospel Messenger* (Jan. 28, 1956): 17; (April 14, 1956): 17; (April 28, 1956): 17; (May 12, 1956): 17.
20. Howard E. Royer, "An Explosion for Peace," *Gospel Messenger* (June 9, 1956): 7; (Aug. 25, 1956): 23.
21. "Our Brotherhood Giving," *Gospel Messenger* (Sept. 1, 1956): 16.
22. M. R. Zigler to Amy Zigler, July 12, 1956; July 13, 1956; July 14, 1956; July 16, 1956.
23. M. R. Zigler to Katherine Rinehart, Oct. 11, 1958; Oct. 26, 1958; April 23, 1957.
24. M. R. Zigler to J. C. Myers, elder of the Linville Creek Church, Jan. 7, 1957; M. R. Zigler to A. Stauffer Curry, moderator of the Highland Avenue Church, Elgin, Jan. 8, 1957.
25. "Tentative Retirement Plan for M. R. and Amy Zigler after Sept. 1, 1958."
26. Norman J. Baugher to M. R. Zigler, March 10, 1958.
27. M. R. Zigler to Ralph E. Smeltzer, June 12, 1958.
28. M. R. Zigler to Don Durnbaugh, April 22, 1958.
29. See especially, M. R. Zigler to Norman J. Baugher, Sept. 6, 1957; Zigler to Baugher and W. Harold Row, Oct. 9, 1957; Zigler to Baugher, Oct. 24, 1957; Zigler to Baugher, Nov. 1, 1957; Zigler to Row, Nov. 15, 1957; Zigler to Baugher and Row, Nov. 19, 1957.

18

THE 250TH ANNIVERSARY
CELEBRATION

T HE YEAR 1958 MARKED the projected end of M. R. Zigler's tour
of service in Europe. It also marked the 250th anniversary of the
founding of the Brethren movement in the little village of Schwarzenau on
the Eder River in west-central Germany. Schwarzenau had meant much to
Zigler, ever since his first visit there following the Oxford and Edinburgh
ecumenical conferences in 1937. He went there as often as possible. When
summarizing the reasons for choosing Kassel as the center of the work in
Germany, he put among the highest its proximity to Schwarzenau. When
Brethren visitors came to Europe, he always made a point of taking them
there. In his articles written for the *Gospel Messenger* dealing with his
European experience, an unusual number were written following visits to
Schwarzenau and explaining their significance.

He had picked up quickly on the suggestion of Brethren tour leader and
longtime friend L. W. Shultz that the Brethren in the USA should help the
village secure an adequate school facility. This became a reality on
September 7, 1956, with the dedication of the Alexander Mack School,
made possible by the gift of DM 60,000 from Brethren in America.[1]

This was some of the background for the elaborate 250th anniversary
observance in Germany from August 2 to 7, 1958. Initiative for the event
went back to Zigler's foresightedness. At the time of his appointment in
1948 as director of Brethren Service in Europe, he had called attention to
the anticipated anniversary and proposed the appointment of a committee
to begin planning for a worthy celebration. Subsequently, however, little
was done, as he discovered on one furlough leave. When he reminded the
General Brotherhood Board of its former commitment, the board chose a

high-level committee, chaired by the distinguished church leader Paul H. Bowman, Sr., to make plans. They agreed that the total program of the church should be keyed to the anniversary celebration, from the creation of new churches to increased giving. Special publications and audio-visual materials were projected to renew interest in the Brethren heritage. The climax would be anniversary observances, centering in the USA at Germantown, Pennsylvania, and the Annual Conference in Des Moines, Iowa, and in Europe at Kassel and Schwarzenau.[2]

M. R. Zigler and his European staff entered enthusiastically into the spirit of the anniversary year. They saw it as an excellent chance to tell the story of their work to influential visiting church leaders. Of particular importance in this regard was the planning for the reception of an official delegation of Brethren from the USA and other countries. Zigler's attitude to the planned celebration can be gleaned from an open letter which he sent to all Brethren Service workers in Europe early in 1958:

> My dear Friends;
>
> This is the Anniversary year of the Church of the Brethren and I am sure that those of you among us who are not members of our church will rejoice with us that God has granted this church the right to exist over 250 years. It is a wonderful thing to study how a small group of people can exist through 250 years and still have a message to deliver. . . .
>
> You will observe also that we have bet our lives on using young people in the promotion of the great message of peace and using our service program as a demonstration of sincerity and concern for the abundant life for all people. . . .
>
> This year let us work with renewed vigor and courage in the interest of peace and goodwill. By our example let us show others the grace and truth of love. When the next year is born perhaps we can look behind and see a world made better by our efforts.

He was, as an administrator, also concerned that visitors receive a good impression of the Brethren Service work and asked BSC staff members to do all they could to develop an excellent program, worthy of favorable recognition.[3]

M. R. Zigler's approach with visitors had been highly honed by his practice of personally shepherding as many as he could around Europe, helping them to have an enjoyable time but making sure that they got the Brethren Service message. He persisted in his campaign even under difficult circumstances. Marie Brubaker, wife of Elgin executive Leland

S. Brubaker, told of an incident when Zigler was escorting the Brubakers and the Rufus Bowmans through Europe. The crankcase of Zigler's car was shattered on a mountain road in Italy at night. The group was stranded:

> In the face of all of this, Bob, whose car it was, got in the back seat and with a cheery word of "Call me if anyone comes," was fast asleep in less than five minutes. . . . The motor patrol came along and took one of our group down to the village to phone. We got a garage man from Bologna, Italy, to come out and tow us back to the city. Fortunately he was able to fix the car the next day. While the man worked on the car Bob enthusiastically sold the cause of Brethren Service in Europe. There were enough of the crew who spoke English so that the word got around.
>
> He had them all believing that another war would be impossible if we would but be willing to help our friends and our enemies whenever they were in need and refuse to kill one another. A letter from the owner to the garage to Bob . . . expressed the desire to be able to learn more of his philosophy.[4]

Visit of the Official Delegation

Among the official delegates were: Norman J. Baugher, general secretary of the Church of the Brethren; Desmond W. Bittinger, moderator of the 1958 Annual Conference; S. Loren Bowman, chair of the General Brotherhood Board; Paul H. Bowman, Sr., chair of the 250th Anniversary Committee; Kenneth I. Morse, editor of the *Gospel Messenger*; Mark Roller and Rufus King, representatives of Men's Work; Sarah Halladay and Anna Warstler, Women's Work; E. Stanley Davis, youth. From other countries were Anggaya Mahelbwala, Nigeria; Juan Benalcazar, Ecuador; William R. Bhagat, India. M. R. Zigler himself was named a member of the delegation. In addition, small delegations from the Brethren Church (Ashland, Ohio) and from the Christ's Assembly in Denmark also came.

When the delegation arrived, Zigler acted as host on an extensive survey of Brethren work in Europe, which included interviews with leaders of church and state and visits to sites relating to early Brethren history. Superintendent Georg Traar of the Lutheran Church in Austria, paid glowing tribute to the spirit in which the Brethren had entered into cooperative work with his small Protestant Church, a minority in that overwhelmingly Catholic land. Leaders of his church had at first feared that the Brethren would use the opportunity of bringing relief goods to proselytize. They were relieved when experience showed them that the Brethren were truly interested only in supporting the ecumenical work in

Austria and acting in a genuinely fraternal spirit. He spoke of the warm friendships which had developed over the years between members of the church in Austria and the Brethren Service workers:

> An essential service of the Church of the Brethren was and is that she has made a personal friendship so easy. . . . This warm brotherly fellowship was accompanied also, of course, with another fact. The Church of the Brethren has renounced the beginning of churches in our country, and as far as I know, in all Europe. The temptation to do it has certainly existed. . . . By this fact your witness of deeds has come with greater weight. Christian love cannot be practiced alone, but above all, must be practiced with the deed. The Church of the Brethren has at no time and in place sought nor advocated her own interests. Her witness is thereby so genuine and convincing.[5]

In Schriesheim, north of Heidelberg, Germany, local historian Dr. Hermann Brunn told the delegation about the early life of Alexander Mack, Sr., first minister among the Brethren and a member of a prominent Schriesheim family. "You have seen this morning the mill, in which he spent his youth. You have gone through the streets which are still the same as in his time, and you have been in the church, where he listened to the sermon of the Reformed pastor. You know also, that he was a young miller of 27 years when he made his first steps to a new way of understanding and interpreting the Bible."[6]

Outstanding German church leader Dr. Martin Niemoeller regretted that he would be in Berlin when the delegation came through his area. He wrote Zigler: "If otherwise I can be of any assistance to you and to your delegation I should be only to[o] glad to do so." Zigler later commented that one omission in the anniversary planning was the failure to work out the presence in Schwarzenau of Martin Niemoeller, who in fact expressed interest in coming. Because of a rule of the German churches that the invitation had to be approved by the presiding officer of the territorial church (*Landeskirche*), which was not secured in time, this did not happen. As it turned out, he phoned his greetings to Schwarzenau on the day of the celebration.[7]

Members of the delegation were much impressed, even overwhelmed, by the scope of the BSC program (as Zigler intended). But they were more impressed by the genuine appreciation expressed by the Europeans they encountered, who found this official visit an opportunity to respond to the help given to them over a period of years. The delegation met with high-level ecumenical leaders in the Zigler apartment in Geneva, and saw how their simple and homey style of hospitality had its effect on the high dignitaries of the world churches.[8]

The Kassel Conference

A team of planners at Kassel, led by Wilbur Mullen, developed the details of the events scheduled for August 2-7. It was to be an extended and expanded European Annual Conference, based on the yearly gathering of service workers some place in Europe. The first meetings were to be held in Kassel, featuring interchange with the local churches. The scene would then shift to Schwarzenau and Berleburg as historic sites.

And so it happened, beginning with registration at the Kassel House. The German church hosted a reception prior to the conference for visiting Brethren leaders at its Evangelical Academy located at Hof Geismar; in the course of the affair, Bishop Wuestemann, head of the Lutheran Church in North Hesse, gave the delegation a mosaic. On Sunday, August 3, twenty-three Brethren pastors occupied the pulpits of Lutheran and Free Church parishes in Kassel; a few spoke in German, though most used translators. This was followed by an open house at the Kassel center, to which representatives of churches, governmental bodies, and voluntary agencies were invited. In typical German fashion, many greetings were exchanged at this time, using the simultaneous translation equipment earlier installed in the house. A reporter noted: "M. R. Zigler expressed the feeling of many when he said, 'It is amazing that only a few years ago we were taught to hate each other but now we meet in a spirit of love.'"

Later in the day an ecumenical service in the rebuilt Martinskirche brought together nearly 1,000 worshipers, German and foreign. Representatives of the Lutheran and Free Churches spoke. Bishop Wuestemann preached on the call of God to Abraham that necessitated his leaving his home and family to be faithful to the call. The bishop applied this text both to the leaving of Brethren from Germany in the eighteenth century and in their return to it following 1945, stating, "The practice of love is of greater value than theoretical formulations." Norman J. Baugher responded for the Brethren, using the passage from Luke 4 on concern for the poor and distressed.

Monday and Tuesday focused on the activities of Brethren Service, with reports and addresses from Brethren staff, volunteers, and European guests. Those attending the conference were taken to a distribution of heifers on Monday afternoon and to the Friedland reception center for refugees from Eastern Europe near the border with the German Democratic Republic on Tuesday afternoon.[9]

The Schwarzenau and Berleburg Meetings

On Wednesday, August 6, the scene shifted to Schwarzenau where the local authorities had been feverishly preparing for the festivities. A large tent had been erected in the schoolyard, in front of the Alexander Mack School. M. R. Zigler presided at the service in the forenoon, which featured addresses from Dr. W. A. Visser 't Hooft, general secretary of the World Council of Churches, and Dr. Desmond W. Bittinger, moderator of the Church of the Brethren.

The ecumenical leader's address pointed out that the Brethren had begun as a small band of Pietists who separated from the church establishment but were now full participants in the ecumenical process. He explained the change as deriving from two developments. In the first place, the Brethren movement had changed. It had lost its sectarian characteristics and was now much more like other churches. At the same time, the churches in Europe had changed. No longer were the churches tied tightly to the state; the recent totalitarian era had shown the dangers of such alliances. Visser 't Hooft credited Pietism for bringing much of the change in the former state churches, "the unfreezing of a frozen church situation." While Pietism bore the brunt of many theological attacks, it had made positive contributions, including helping to form the ecumenical movement. The speaker listed three areas of importance for today's churches. They must be mission-minded, seeking to extend the gospel to all people. They must recognize the sovereignty of God in all areas; in this connection he commended the peace churches for their witness to the broader church. They must, finally, heed the call to unity.

Desmond Bittinger based his remarks on the love chapter of 1 Corinthians, proposing that Brethren rededicate themselves to the high ideals there delineated. He urged his audience to recommit themselves to the principles of love, of open minds, and of unity with God.

In the afternoon session, Ernst Wilms, church president of Westphalia, spoke as the representative of Bishop Dibelius, who was out of the country. Wilms spoke on how he learned the truths of ecumenism in a concentration camp, where doctrinal and practical differences were dissolved in the face of paganism and terror. "There," he said, "we found each other as brothers." He stressed the urgency of reconciliation between churches and

227

nations after the tragedy of war. "Don't build bulwarks, build bridges." He applied the image to the tensions between East and West, reminding his hearers of the thousands of Christians on the other side of the Iron Curtain. In this context, he commended the Brethren for their witness of peace across political and ideological barriers.

The second address of the afternoon was made by Dr. Paul H. Bowman, Sr., chairman of the committee that had planned the anniversary year. He used the occasion to put forth seven principles that Brethren had traditionally held: (1) an emphasis upon the open mind in the search for truth; (2) the appeal to religious freedom; (3) the universality of life, the principle upon which rests the Brethren emphasis upon service, peace, and reconciliation; (4) the recognition of certain civic duties but more importantly the prior allegiance to God; (5) the conviction that faith must issue in works; (6) the simple life; and (7) the fundamental recognition of the lordship of Jesus Christ. "If we are true to our heritage, Christ will be Lord or our personal lives, Lord of the Church, and Lord of history."

A concluding worship service on the banks of the Eder River, led by Desmond Bittinger, included Brethren from several countries and Germans alike. "Out in the open air of the evening, the representatives and friends of the church felt in close touch with the pioneers whose memory they honored and also intimately aware of the living Lord whom they promised now to serve more devotedly than ever before."

Dr. Eugen Gerstenmaier, president of the West German parliament and formerly head of *Hilfswerk*, the Protestant relief agency, sent a telegram to the gathering:

> In bonds of gratitude I send my best greetings to the Church of the Brethren on the occasion of the 250th anniversary of its foundation. I am extending my special thanks and wishes to the Brethren Service Commission for its unforgettable, unselfish service which it has rendered also to the people of Germany in the days of utmost distress. May God's blessing guide the Church of the Brethren also in the future and may He make it a pioneer in His service for a peaceful life among individuals and nations.

Local Schwarzenau residents arranged overnight hospitality for the visitors in their homes.

On the final day of the celebration, the foreign visitors travelled to nearby Berleburg, in the midst of a celebration of its 700th anniversary. The visitors attended a well-planned church service and then toured the Berleburg castle where the resident prince welcomed them. The program was concluded with an exchange of gifts; the Brethren presented a 1776 edition of the Christopher Sauer Bible from Germantown and a copy of the recently published source book on Brethren history. In return the Berleburg dignitaries gave the Brethren a manuscript describing a meeting of Pietists in the Berleburg area.

Total attendance at the conference sessions in Kassel and Schwarzenau amounted to about 750. Of this number, about 400 were from the United States (including several tour groups) and the remaining 350 came largely from Germany.[10]

Reaction to the Celebration in Europe

German newspapers did not miss the newsworthiness of the event. There was rather extensive coverage, with the local journals naturally giving the most space to the celebration. Most emphasized was the ecumenical angle, allowing former separatists and established church representatives, Americans and Germans as recent enemies in war, to meet amicably and in a spirit of tolerance. Journalists repeatedly mentioned the peace emphasis of the Brethren; they picked up on a phrase of Church President Wilm, likening the Brethren visit to an "invasion of peace."[11]

One of the most knowledgeable articles came from the pen of Dr. Reinhold Freudenstein, son of the director of the Protestant Inner Mission, Erich Freudenstein. The younger man had taught previously at Manchester College in Indiana. The title of his article, written to introduce the Brethren before the actual anniversary observance, was "Building, Serving, Loving;" it included a concise history of the Brethren background and a recapitulation of the work of Brethren Service. "American people have a special talent in recognizing problems and, more than that, in working out practical advice for their solution. The members of the Church of the Brethren are always, through the church and the New Testament, informed and instructed regarding peace, military service, race problems, and many other questions of the simple daily life."[12]

A national newspaper, *Die Zeit*, published a well-informed article headlined ". . . but love is the greatest of these—Church of the Brethren, Church of Brotherhood; the Brethren celebrate an anniversary in the Eder Valley." The reporter featured the friendship of a young German with an American school teacher; they had met in a Brethren international work camp in 1949. The article mentioned the work done by Brethren Service in Germany after the war, pointing out the spirit of practical love for the neighbor they manifested. It concluded with a quotation from M. R. Zigler, who pointed at a map of Germany full of pins representing food deliveries, heifer recipients, work camps, and exchange students, remarking: "No matter where I point my finger to this German map, I am certain that in a circumference of 25 miles there will be a family who would give us a warm meal and take us in overnight."[13]

Naturally, there was full reporting back in the United States. A special issue of the *Gospel Messenger* on September 20, 1958, featured articles and many photos, primarily the work of the editor, Kenneth I. Morse, who had been part of the delegation.[14] In the midst of all of the jubilation and good feeling occasioned by the many kind words received in Europe, a thoughtful disclaimer came from Warren S. Kissinger, a Brethren pastor who had participated in the European events. He was disquieted by the facile reference to love as the answer to problems. "Is love an easy possibility or does it also bring with it judgment and a conviction of our inability to love as we ought to love.... At times I felt that love had become our God, that we had forgotten that while the Bible says God is love, it does not say that love is God." In essence, Kissinger articulated an informed theological criticism of the simple liberal stance of M. R. Zigler and many of his colleagues in Brethren Service.[15]

Summary Report on the 250th Anniversary

Reporting continued at the 1959 Annual Conference, when a final summary of the anniversary year was presented by Paul H. Bowman, Sr., on behalf of the planning committee. He began by comparing the scene in 1708 with the scene in 1958: "In contrast to the disfavor which confronted our fathers in Germany two hundred fifty years ago, the Brethren of today hold a position of high respect in Europe, especially in Germany, Austria, and Greece. Officials of both church and state were warm in their expression of appreciation of our work in Europe and insisted that we still have an important ministry to perform in that part of the world." He concluded his thorough report with an analysis of the place of the Church of the Brethren in world Christianity:

> On the basis of our observations in Europe, we urge the Church of the Brethren to accept her place in the world church as a minority communion, but as a vital and living force in the world dedicated to peace and goodwill, to brotherly love, and practical Christianity, to the dominance of Christ in personal life and in the affairs of the world, and to a devout and prayerful sensitivity to the will

and the purpose of God. This we can do within the framework of the ecumenical movement and still maintain the respect and helpfulness of our identity as the Church of the Brethren.[16]

This summed up perfectly the line which M. R. Zigler had followed and had long urged the Church of the Brethren to follow. He was well pleased with the results of the anniversary year and the picture of the work he had guided in Europe that was taken back to the home church. It seemed to him and to many others an apt note on which to conclude his ten years of service in Europe.

NOTES

1. *Gospel Messenger* (June 7, 1958): 11.
2. Kenneth I. Morse, "Two-hundred Fiftieth Anniversary," *Brethren Encyclopedia* (1983-1984), 1282-1283.
3. European News Briefs (Feb. 3, 1958): 3-4.
4. Marie Brubaker, "An Advocate of Peace," Feb. 4, 1953.
5. "Message of the Evangelical Church of Austria to the Church of the Brethren," July 23, 1958.
6. Dr. Hermann Brunn, [undated address to the delegation].
7. Martin Niemoeller to M. R. Zigler, May 3, 1958.
8. Kenneth I. Morse to D. F. Durnbaugh, June 10, 1987.
9. [Kenneth I. Morse], "European Annual Conference," *Gospel Messenger* (Sept. 20, 1958): 8-13; see also Paul H. Bowman, ed., *The Adventurous Future: An Anniversary Volume* (Elgin, IL: Brethren Press, 1959), 231-273, for the official record of the European observances.
10. [Kenneth I. Morse], "After 250 Years," *Gospel Messenger* (Sept. 20, 1958): 14-19.
11. One of the most extensive of the local reports was: "Hoffung—Glaube—Liebe: Froelich in die Zukunft! 250 Jahre Church of the Brethren: Ein grosser Tag fuer Schwarzenau," *Westfalenpost* (Aug. 8, 1958); a long article stimulated by the anniversary appeared in the Netherlands, prominently mentioning M. R. Zigler: "Church of [the] Brethren 250 jaar: Vredeskerk vond rust in Surhuisterveen," *Drachtster Courant* (Feb. 6, 1959).
12. R[einhold] F[reudenstein], "Aubauen, dienen, liehen," *Evangelischen Sonntagsbote* (August 3, 1958).
13. ". . . aber die Liebe ist die groesste. Kirche der Brueder: Kirche der bruederlichkeit—Die 'Brethren' feierten Jubilaeum in Edertal," *Die Zeit* (August 15, 1958).

231

14. See also Kenneth I. Morse, "Love Feast at Kassel," *Gospel Messenger* (Nov. 22, 1958): 5.
15. Warren S. Kissinger, "Impressions of European Conferences," *Gospel Messenger* (Sept. 27, 1958): 2, 22.
16. "After 250 years: New Respect, New Challenges, New Opportunities," *Gospel Messenger* (Sept. 19, 1959): 12-15.

19
THE VÄSTERVIK TRAGEDY

ONE OF THE HIGHLIGHTS of the Kassel events planned for the 250th anniversary was a ceremony honoring the Ziglers and recognizing their approaching retirement. This was a very moving time for the Ziglers and their friends, especially for the young people serving in Europe with the Brethren Volunteer Service program. At the ceremony, the Ziglers received a bound volume of letters from former and current Brethren Service staff and volunteers. The testimonials glowed with memories, plaudits, and deeply felt emotions. Some examples will convey the flavor of the letters:

—from Jake and Leona Dick, former BSC staff workers in Germany:

> Both of you have served as a team, and each of you had your own way of inspiring us as workers. As our World Council of Churches representative you carried the concern of our church to high levels and you did it with dignity and enthusiasm. Your being promoted to high offices in the Council speaks eloquently of the high esteem with which they held you.
>
> You are a hero for peace. Your plans for peace in our world were not so much theory as practice. You had your theory, but you had an unusual way of getting that theory carved out into practice. The vast network of Brethren Service work in Europe is a living witness as to your dream made flesh. You both kept the church at the heart of your witness. I know there were many temptations to take your witness outside of the church but always you kept the church central . . .
>
> You have both been "given to hospitality." Your warm concern for others was always felt. No mid-night call was too much trouble; no home-sick, love-sick volunteer too adolescent to take into the warmth of your hospitality. You

were always out there on the cutting edge of a spiritual ministry. You lived on new ideas. You saw relationships; when Christians across national lines killed each other in wars you wondered why, for they were all brothers in Christ. . . .[1]

—from Paul Grubb, former BVS worker in Germany:

The first time I heard you speak, M. R., was at the Peace Conference held at New Windsor in July of 1956 while I was in unit training. You spoke of needing volunteers, a thousand of them, to shake hands and show love and concern for the people of Europe. When I saw you at work in Europe and some of the results of your efforts and the seeds you had sown I realized how much Amy and you are living that sermon. Like every other volunteer I always looked forward eagerly to the hours you would spend with us—the hours when we would receive new insights, challenge and inspiration. A visit with the Ziglers in Geneva was always a never-to-be-forgotten experience for each volunteer. I was fortunate to be with you on two occasions and both times I came away with a new urge to be a better Christian and peacemaker.[2]

—from Nancy Hoff, BVS worker:

It was sometime during March, 1957, and M. R. was sitting in the lounge with four green volunteers, when suddenly the words ". . . you kids just aren't worth your salt the first year you're over here . . ." jumped out at us. It wasn't until later that we noticed the twinkle that danced in his eyes when he said such things. And this was but the first of "M. R. sayings" that we remember when we think of him. I always marveled at the way he found time to talk to each volunteer during his short visits to Kassel, and the hundreds of encouraging letters that were written from his desk. A person always felt a little bit bigger and inspired to "keep on keeping on" by the type of letters that came from him.[3]

—from Vera and Harley Kline, BSC staff workers in Greece:

The great quality which we all admire in you, M. R., is your faith in the ability of inexperienced persons young and old, to grab onto a worth-while cause regardless of circumstances and carrying that cause to the point of realizing amazing results. What most people don't understand is that to have faith in the ability of a human personality to face problems, arrive at a solution, and act accordingly, actually gives that person a big push in the direction of success from the start. You, in our judgment, are a master of having faith in persons as to spur them on to do things they never dreamed they could do.[4]

—from Eleanor Williamson, former BVS worker:

Don't think that there will be an end of what you have done when you leave
Europe. In a sense there will, because things won't be quite the same without
you. But the effects you have had on people are only just *beginning* something!
Count the number of people who have come and gone in the past ten years; look
at their ages; and see where they are now. And you have planted in all of us
ideas that will never die! These are Christian ideas and inspire us to live the
ideal Christian life; but it was you who taught us to hold fast to our visions and
carry out our dreams—and showed us that it could be done, by your own life.
And so this is just the beginning of your influence, as we return to our homes
and our churches and try to spread to others what we have come to believe. You
know the others who used to be here—how many of them are appearing now
as church leaders in various fields! All this wouldn't have been possible if it
weren't for the people who saw that it is good for young men and women to
learn how to serve.[5]

The Västervik Tragedy

The last scheduled official act for M. R. Zigler was to attend the WCC
Central Committee meeting, slated for Nyborg, Denmark, in late August,
1958. Following the conclusion of the elaborate 250th anniversary observance in Kassel and Schwarzenau, the Ziglers decided to take a few days
of rare personal vacation in Sweden before the Nyborg meeting. On
August 10 they celebrated their fortieth wedding anniversary.

The Ziglers drove to Sweden in a 1956 Chevrolet belonging to the
German BSC program. They arrived late in Stockholm and had difficulty
finding lodgings. The next day they drove leisurely southward along the
east coast of Sweden, observing the rule of the road that mandated driving
on the left side of the road, as in Great Britain. They passed the city of
Västervik (population of 30,000) and were proceeding along the highway
in rainy and foggy weather, with M. R. feeling rather tired. The motor of
their car began to misfire and the Ziglers discussed whether they should
turn back and seek help. He then started to look for a place to turn, thinking
(in momentary confusion) that he would need to have the car on the right
side of the road in order to be able to swing around on the left side of the
road to return. Just then he noticed a car coming toward them at a rather
high rate of speed. He attempted to move back to the left side of the road
to avoid the oncoming vehicle. He failed to complete the maneuver. Amy
Zigler cried out "Oh no!" and the two cars met in head-on collision. The

Ziglers were thrown against the windshield as were the two occupants in the other car.[6]

When M. R. Zigler came to, he was again at the wheel. Amy was slumped over and he realized that she had died instantly. After a time, help came; he was urged to move to the ambulance for removal to the hospital, but he refused to go without Amy. Then the occupants of the other car were taken away. Both died shortly afterwards, one on the elevator in the hospital, the other in the operating room. When Zigler emerged from the car he realized that his hip was broken but felt no pain. It was not until he was brought to the hospital that pain began. After that he recalled nothing.[7]

Hospital authorities found the Geneva address in his passport and notified the Brethren Service office. Immediately friends came. Norman J. Baugher and S. Loren Bowman, in Europe for the 250th anniversary, flew to Sweden. An attending physician marveled that after the notification was made, there was a stream of people coming to be with him: "They poured in and we couldn't understand that—what a remarkable man that was that could draw that attention—that public. Around his bedside within 24-48 hours were sitting 8-10 people." Longtime friends Margaret and John Metzler, Sr., arrived from Geneva as did Wilbur Mullen, director in Germany. These three were the first visitors Zigler saw when he regained consciousness. Later others came, including Mary Mummert and her mother from Austria. Frances and Wendell Rolston, older volunteers, stayed for many weeks. His dear Mennonite friend, Orie O. Miller, interrupted his travel schedule to visit, as did several from the World Council staff. Pastor Hansen, a minister of the Christi Menigheid church of Denmark, with Brethren connections, made a special visit. As soon as it could be arranged, Zigler's son Robert, also made the long trip to visit his father. Because of family responsibilities (a newly born infant), it was not possible for his daughter Geraldine to make the trip.

In all, Zigler stayed 102 days in the hospital. He was massively injured. He suffered severe concussion of the brain, multiple fractures of his ribs, fractured shoulder, and a compound fracture of one hip. Involved physicians at first did not expect him to live. The surgeon commented: "He must have been on very, very good terms with his God, because we didn't give him a chance." For that matter, at first, as Zigler later described it, he had little will to live, when the realization sank in that Amy was gone. But his inherent courage and optimistic spirit took over. Visitors were struck by his determination to recover. Several operations were necessary to repair the damage, and they were hampered by his previous condition of gout.[8]

236

Communications of Concern

Hospital staff were amazed at the reaction to the accident that happened to this unknown foreigner. In addition to the many visitors, cables, letters, and cards came to their patient from all over the world. On a single day forty-two communications arrived!

Expressions of concern came from Brethren in Europe and the USA and from a remarkable number of ecumenical friends. Lutherans, Waldensians, Presbyterians, Dutch Reformed, Mennonites, Disciples, and many more expressed their shock and assured him of their prayers. The messages bear eloquent testimony to the love and respect people had for the Ziglers. Church World Service made a gracious gesture in contributing $10,000 to the World Council of Churches in the name of the Brethren. This took place at the Central Committee meeting in Nyborg, Zigler's intended destination after Sweden. Conference moderator Desmond W. Bittinger wrote to Zigler about the event:

> Today I had the privilege of presenting the statement by the Brethren to the Central Committee and the WCC staff members and the visitors. It was preceded by a statement concerning you and your contribution to the Central Committee and the WCC. They spoke also of your accident and the loss of Amy. I then spoke also of your work among us and for peace. After I had read the paper Pres. Fry asked that I remain at the podium. Visser 't Hooft then read the paper concerning a gift of $10,000 by Church World Service for the new WCC headquarters which would memorialize the Brethren, particularly Amy and the others who were lost en route to America. I tried to respond to this but I was deeply moved. Tears were shed by many.

Bittinger reported that after the session was dismissed, scores of people came to the Brethren delegates to express their sympathies and emphasize what a contribution the Ziglers had made in Geneva. "All of us were busy all the time telling of your condition to the many who inquired."[9]

The chairman of the WCC Central Committee, Lutheran leader Franklin L. Fry, wrote these words in his own hand: "You will never know how constantly you have been on our hearts during these days of the Central Committee meeting. Many of us wept inside when we heard of your tragic bereavement and injury and day by day we have followed your recovery with affectionate and prayerful concern." Knowing of Zigler's passion for peace, the eminent churchman noted: "Earnest thought was given to the prevention of war in our atomic age, more than to any other subject," adding, "The address from the Church of the Brethren was cordially received."[10]

Zigler's close friend Paul H. Bowman, Sr., wrote just before embarking on the return trip to the USA:

> There are times in life when human resources are wholly inadequate for life's burdens and frustrations. This is one of those times for you. I want you to know how tenderly and prayerfully we think of you and yours. May the sustaining power of God undergird and uphold you.
>
> Flora and I leave here [London] today for home. We scarce knew whether to go or stay, so great is our sorrow. We have checked here and there seems nothing more we can do. You know how ready we stand to be helpful when possible.[11]

Gen. Lewis B. Hershey, director of Selective Service, cabled that he had "just learned through Mr. [Ora] Huston of [the] tragic accident involving Mrs. Zigler and you." He added: "Realize no words can soften [the] sorrow of your loss but I do want to express my deepest sympathy and hope for your speedy recovery."[12]

An executive of the National Council of Churches, Robbins W. Barstow, wrote:

> You were one of my earliest collaborators in the first days of Church World Service, and in these later years it has always been a pleasure to see you and your wife in Geneva or elsewhere. Words cannot express my admiration for the quality of Christian service you have given so unstintedly, and through you, I have come to have new and most respectful understanding of and admiration for the Church of the Brethren. We all have been the gainers in our cooperation with you in our generous program of practical ministry along many lines.[13]

One of the most appreciated letters came from his associate of many years, Andrew W. Cordier, of the United Nations. It read, in part:

> The news of the accident came as a tremendous shock to your tens of thousands of friends in this country. Ever since that moment you have had the constant prayers and expressions of concerns of all of your many friends. I can fully understand how you felt at that time, indeed how you continue to feel about it all. Amy was a wonderful companion. She was so helpful to you in every respect and shared with you the friendship of so very many people. Her life was very well lived as she was always on the wholesome and constructive side of every question and thus gave encouragement to a great many people who came

under the blessing of her influence. As time passes the poignancy and grief of her passing will diminish, while the precious memories of her will continue forever in their full warmth and glow.[14]

Howard Schomer, an ecumenical colleague in Geneva, who knew M. R. since CPS days, wrote an encouraging letter on Columbus Day; he pictured M. R. on the edge of his chair . . .

> . . . eager to dare and to launch still other actions for the Lord. But this is one of the "hightimes," if I guess right, in your life—a time when it is given you to see clearly that all your deeds and all your hopes are safely in His hand. . . . Bob, I will not try to say anything about your great loss, and ours, in Amy's death. Nor will I try to console you for your own physical and inner suffering. Others far abler, who themselves have suffered as I have not, doubtless have said all that can be said by fellow mortals. I just want to assure you, though no assurance is needed, of my firm friendship and, indeed, our family's undying affection.[15]

The outstanding Quaker author and professor, Douglas Steere, who had worked with M. R. Zigler on issues of conscientious objection, wrote:

> Bob, you will never know how many people have counted on you two to do something in Europe to keep the flickering hope of reconciliation alive by a tangible outside witness. Without you and your staunch helper, so many things there simply would not exist today. Now you must mend and go on alone. . . . We need another decade of your wisdom, initiative and guidance in the peace movement.[16]

Zigler's Response to the Communications

On the afternoon of August 30, after he had undergone four hours of major surgery on his leg in the forenoon, Zigler began to dictate to a volunteer secretary answers to the twenty-three letters that had arrived that day. He was concerned to answer all of the correspondence and resume his active life, even though he was confined to a bed. The spirit in which he answered the letters can be gleaned from some excerpts:

—to Amy's brother and sister-in-law.

> Many people have written. It scares me when I know so many prayers are offered for my healing. I don't known how to be worthy. And I have not yet

239

learned yet how to feel that I'm putting as much effort into the healing as I would feel capable if I knew how.

. . . If I continued to live I know there must be a purpose. This thing occurring simultaneously with my retirement time in a way makes it easy to think through what to do. On the other hand, it is difficult to try to map out your own trail when for such a long time the road was clear and the objective fixed. Anyway, I shall try to go through it with good faith, and in a little way worthy of the prayers of so many people. I'm still trying to live by my life formula—to be thankful when a new day begins and work vigorously at your life purpose and then to be tired enough to want to sleep and rest so that you'll be ready for the next morning. After all there isn't much else to life.[17]

—to the wife of Robert Bilheimer of the WCC staff, thanking her for flowers:

It seems to me that in my lifetime I had never really prepared myself for the thoughts of death and eternal life. The two months I'll have to spend in the hospital I hope will pull me through physically. The next stage will perhaps be harder, meeting friends, going home, determining next steps. Amy and I have always had a life when we had to learn to live together spiritually because we were gone so much from each other. It seems she is waiting for me somewhere and she has an interest in the decisions I will have to make and that she shall always be present to help me. I know that I must face the situation bravely. This I will endeavor to do and I pray that I shall be worthy of all the prayers for my recovery.[18]

—to Paul H. Bowman, Sr., longtime associate:

While waiting for the ambulance for a long time the dream of my whole life came to me and I seemed to feel satisfied even though I picked out many situations where I had such wonderful opportunities to do greater things for God and for Christ in the name of the Church. I was so thankful for the hosts of people I could remember with whom we had worked. They seemed to pass by from my youth until the Anniversary and our final communion service. I am so glad that I was able to go through this whole thing conscious. It seemed so much like the end that I can't remember much what I thought about the future except that I was sure beyond doubt that the world waits for a vigorous deliverance of the peace message of the Church of the Brethren and I had no doubt but what that will be done. Then came the terrific shock of waking up and trying to live again. And I'm so thankful that my mind was so clear soon after the first shocks had receded. I couldn't hardly help but promise that if I live it must be for a purpose, worthy of the chance to live and something that

240

would seem to make all the prayers uttered in our behalf a real achievement for everybody.[19]

—to Norman J. Baugher, general secretary of the Church of the Brethren:

Of course I want to go home and be with my loved ones but that's going to be a hard experience. As pain gradually leaves me and gives me a freedom of mind some of these things begin to stare me in the face. I knew they would come but I had not really thought through. . . . I must close expressing what I think if I have the health is to find something to do that will take all my thinking and my time. I wish it could be something new. I wish it could be in the implementation of the [Brethren] message to the World Council. I'm sure this message must be followed up by somebody's actions. Somebody must do it who believes in it and has had some experience concerning it. I'm convinced that now is the ripest time to work on it. . . . But I think I'd like to dedicate my life to it unless somebody else takes it up who has the time and money and will to do it. Most people are afraid to talk about it both inside and outside the church. But personally I've never had fears. It seems that every time I've tried sincerely and persistently a little advance was made. . . .[20]

—to Dr. Leslie E. Cooke, director of Inter-Church Aid in Geneva:

I have not yet found words to express my grief. It is too deep. I have not found words of appreciation with the quality of meaning I feel for the many expressions of love and promises of prayer. . . . Now the question that concerns me is—what in the world can I do in the future that can be worthy of all this love and concern. The purpose to live seems different than what I had been anticipating. However, the sense of direction has not changed. I have a great faith in God and the power of Christ over all creation. I have a more profound conviction that man must do more for himself than he has ever done before in order to have the abundant life. I'm convinced that the World Council of Churches has the potential opportunity and resources to bring peace and good will to this earth and the abundant life for all people. I think we must not be afraid to attempt great things for I believe if we only try, God will help us. But if we fail to make an effort, God cannot cooperate with us.[21]

M. R. Zigler welcomed the task of answering his correspondence because he had always thrived on communication with others; his precarious health and loneliness made only more urgent his need for contact with others. In the process of dictating letters, he was able to work through at least some of the agony of separation from his deceased wife and to think through his next steps.

241

Impact on Hospital Personnel

When M. R. Zigler was admitted to the Västervik hospital in the early evening of August 16, the doctors and nurses had no idea who he was. But they soon found out this was no ordinary patient. As already mentioned, the first clue was the number of friends who rushed to be at his side. The flow of visitors continued during his stay. Then came the avalanche of communications of all forms—cables, cards, letters, and telephone calls.

The greatest impact, however, came through the personality of their patient. He was eager to learn to know personally all of the staff with whom he came into contact; as most of them knew at least some English, the language barrier was no great hindrance.

Through long hours of conversation with his surgeon, Dr. Kit Colfach, Zigler came to know him intimately and to become a close friend. He learned the dramatic story of Colfach's dangerous activities as a spy in wartime Denmark, his capture by the Gestapo, and his dramatic escape from prison. After Zigler regained consciousness and made some recovery, Dr. Colfach told him about the tragedy of the downed KLM flight, which took the lives of a score of Brethren returning to the USA from the 250th anniversary observance. Zigler wanted to pray and asked Colfach if he would pray with him. The surgeon said: "It's a long time since I prayed. The last time I prayed was when I was in prison, but I'll try." After that they spoke often about religious matters; Colfach was much impressed with Zigler's message of peace, reconciliation, and service to others. In later years they stayed in close contact through visits to each other and continued correspondence.[22]

Zigler had a member of the hospital staff draw up a list of all of the nurses and aides who had helped him. He wrote each one a letter of appreciation after he left Västervik and received many responses. One, by Sister Ulla, is typical; it gives simple testimony to how they perceived him: "Dear M. R. Zigler. Many thanks for the letter and the good words. We find a big empty place after you. We are thinking of you very often because we appriciated [sic] our patient very much. Kindly regards and our admiration from [Ward] 3. . . ."[23]

Despite the painful memories, which he never forgot, M. R. Zigler returned many times to Västervik to visit the friends he made during his hospital stay. He also felt close to Amy there. Tragic though the experience had been, his reaction to it and the impact he had on others despite his pain and loss, provide clear testimony about the man he was.

The Legal Complications

Because Zigler had caused an accident that resulted in the death of three people, he had to stand trial. This was of real concern to him, because of the possibility that he would be sentenced to prison. The uncertainty also made it difficult to plan his return to the USA. On October 2, after allowing time for recuperation, the police interviewed him for three hours about the accident. Trial was postponed until he could walk with the aid of crutches. His friends sought the assistance of the US consulate in Stockholm, which cooperated fully.

Finally, the trial date was set for November 25. He was represented by a Swedish lawyer. In his defense, the lawyer recounted the achievements and accomplishments of M. R. Zigler's work for others and offered testimonials from many authorities. The final verdict was a sentence of six months in prison, with three years probation. The incarceration was waived in view of his previous record of outstanding social contribution and his physical condition. But Zigler made a private vow, which he kept, that he would never drive a car again.[24]

Amy Zigler's body had been sent back to the USA with the assistance of the American consular service and a memorial service held for her at the Harrisonburg church on August 24. A cable message was read at the service from the widower. Geraldine Zigler Glick, their daughter, made a tape recording of two songs, which were played at the service; it was led by I. S. Long, Warren D. Bowman, and Merlin E. Garber. Another service was held at the Linville Creek cemetery on August 27 for a smaller number of relatives and friends.

Although September 15 had been given as the termination date for board employment, under the circumstances, Zigler was continued on a salaried basis until September 1, 1959. The salary was put under the Social Security maximum of $1,200 dollars per year. It remained for him to pull his life together again after the cataclysm in Västervik.

NOTES

1. Jake and Leona Dick to Dr. and Mrs. M. R. Zigler, June 30, 1958.
2. Paul Grubb to Dr. and Mrs. M. R. Zigler, July 9, 1958.
3. Nancy Hoff to Amy and M. R. [Zigler], n.d.
4. Vera and Harley Kline to M. R. and Mrs. Amy [Zigler], June, 1958.

5. Eleanor Williamson to M. R. [Zigler], n.d.

6. M. R. Zigler recounted the events leading up to the accident and its aftermath many times in letters, taped interviews, and his own writing. See, for example, M. R. Zigler to Geraldine Glick, Oct. 3, 1958; "A Statement to Advocate Jaernestroem Concerning Dr. M. R. Zigler," Nov. 10, 1958; M. R. Zigler, "Statement Concerning the Automobile Accident at Västervik, Sweden, August 16, 1958," Oct. 23, 1979, unpubl. essay; Ken Kreider interview with M. R. Zigler, May 27, 1977, 2/30-33. There are slight inconsistencies in the description of the events immediately prior to the accident.

7. "Mrs. M. R. Zigler Is Killed in Swedish Crash: Husband Hurt," Elgin (Ill.) Daily Courier-News (Aug. 18, 1958); "Brethren Lost in Accidents," *Gospel Messenger* (Aug. 30, 1958): 17; *Gospel Messenger* (Sept. 27, 1958): 16; W. Harold Row and Hazel Peters, "To those who have served in the Brethren Service Program in Europe or who have been related to that program," Aug. 17, 1958; "About People," *Christian Century* (Oct. 2, 1958): 1166.

8. Dr. Kit Colfach, address given at New Windsor, Maryland, [Oct. 21, 1979].

9. Desmond W. Bittinger to M. R. [Zigler], Aug. 22, 1958; "In Memory," *Gospel Messenger* (Sept. 20, 1958): 5.

10. Frank Fry to Bob Zigler, August 29, 1958.

11. Paul H. Bowman to Bob [Zigler], Aug. 19, 1958.

12. Lt. General USA Lewis B. Hershey to Dr. M. R. Zigler, Aug. 26, 1958.

13. Robbins W. Barstow to M. R. Zigler, Aug. 26, 1958.

14. Andrew W. Cordier to Dr. M. R. Zigler, Sept. 27, 1958, following up a cable sent earlier.

15. Howard Schomer to Bob [Zigler], Oct. 12, 1958.

16. Douglas Steere to Bob [Zigler], Sept. 14, 1958.

17. M. R. Zigler to George and Ada Arnold, Sept. 7, 1958.

18. M. R. Zigler to Dorothy (Mrs. Robert) Billheimer, Sept. 16, 1958.

19. M. R. Zigler to Paul H. Bowman, Sr., Sept. 11, 1958.

20. M. R. Zigler to Norman J. Baugher, Sept. 23, 1958.

21. M. R. Zigler to Leslie E. Cooke, Sept. 11, 1958.

22. Colfach address, [Oct. 21, 1979]; "A Visitor from Sweden," *Gospel Messenger* (May 30, 1959): 5.

23. Sister Ulla to M. R. Zigler, Dec. 3, 1958.

24. Sentence of Director Robert Zigler, Nov. 27, 1958.

20

RETURN TO THE USA

THE DREADED TRIAL was over, his battered body was largely
repaired, and the indomitable spirit restored. M. R. Zigler was free to
return to the United States. Yet, it was with unsteady body and subdued
spirit that the trip took place. The idea of retirement itself was daunting;
the prospect of taking up this new stage in his life without Amy was nearly
unthinkable. She had always been there in the background, encouraging,
patient, supportive. She had been an important balance for him. This was
recognized by friends, but it was Merlin Garber who articulated what
many thought in a letter. The family had called on him to draft the tribute
to Amy at the memorial service in Harrisonburg, Virginia, in late August.
The Roanoke pastor was unusually frank:

> With all I have said about the physical and mental adjustments you need to
> make to accomplish this future greatness, I believe I know you well enough
> and I know I love you well enough to talk about the area where I believe your
> greatest conflict will come—the emotions. . . . As humans we run through
> cycles of depression and exhilaration. But we all keep them in balance and
> control. This is the thing you must face with all open mindedness and
> objectivity. . . . It would appear that here is where Amy made her greatest
> contribution to you as a wife, in helping you to adjust to your emotional
> feelings. . . . Now of course you will have to do for yourself what Amy always
> assisted you in doing.

Garber had written of future greatness. He challenged M. R. Zigler to
press ahead regardless of society's expectations of what older men should
do. "Just as our culture is wrong about the matter of war so it is wrong about
the matter of age. If one realizes this and is willing to buck the culture he

245

can go ahead and do great things." For Garber it was clear that Zigler should not shrink back into idle retirement. "Frankly and sincerely I believe that you have a good twenty years of active and fruitful service left for you in the years ahead." Mentioning Adenauer and Churchill, he prodded: "Why shouldn't you be God's statesman, working just as hard, putting in just as many hours, making just as many speeches, etc. as they do?" Garber saw an activist denomination needing someone to give direction and provide the vision, someone to "interpret, counsel, reconcile, forgive, and make the church realize its destiny." The tragic occurrence could become a time to rethink, regroup, and reset directions and goals.[1]

And so it was, after a rather brief time of convalescence, that Zigler set out to reshape his life. As it happened, Garber's optimistic prediction of twenty years of active life yet to go was not optimistic enough. It turned out, in fact, to be almost thirty. Some of M. R. Zigler's most creative and significant projects came after his retirement from regular church employment.

Travel to the USA

Zigler was released from the *Lasarett*—the hospital—in early December after a stay of more than three months. Many of the hospital staff gave him a great early morning send off from the local train station.

Zigler chose to return to the USA by ship, leaving from Bremerhaven on the S. S. America on December 8. It was clear from several statements in his correspondence that he did not wish just then to travel by air. The reason is not hard to find. The tragic accident that he had caused had taken three lives. Much worse was a disaster that took twenty Brethren lives; this was the crash on August 14 of a KLM plane off the coast of Ireland. Among the ninety-one aboard were a contingent of Brethren returning from a Brethren Heritage Tour built around the 250th anniversary. None of the passengers or the eight crew members survived the plunge into the sea, caused—it was speculated—by a defective propeller.[2]

Many friends had anticipated that he would return to his European home in Geneva, where the World Council of Churches staff wished to bid him farewell and Godspeed. But Zigler decided against it, presumably because of the pain it would have caused to have once again been where he and Amy had lived. Instead, he traveled first by train to Kassel, Germany, discovering in the process that he was not as strong as he had imagined. He still was on crutches as a result of the massive injuries. A volunteer working in the Geneva office did the necessary packing and shipping of personal effects from Switzerland, aided by Margaret Metzler.

He was met in New York city on December 16 by John Bowman, former Brethren Service worker in Europe, and his son Robert Zigler, at that time working with the Heifer Project Committee. Then came the sad but yet heartwarming reunion with his daughter Geraldine, his son-in-law John Glick, and their family, and the many relatives and friends in Virginia.[3]

The Glicks had converted a garage into a large room for him, insisting that he make his home with them, at least for a time. They had corresponded about this with M. R., who was both appreciative of the gesture and also cautious, lest it disrupt their family life. He pointed out that he would be traveling a great deal anyway, which would alleviate the possibility of becoming a hindrance. And travel he did.[4]

Evidently the first public appearance he made in the USA was in answer to the invitation from the Mennonite Central Committee to address their staff at Akron, Pennsylvania. He spoke in their chapel service on January 20, 1959, and then conferred with the administrators about cooperative peace work in Europe, with special attention to the Eirene program for European conscientious objectors.[5]

New Activities

It had been agreed that despite his retirement Zigler would remain the Brethren representative to the World Council of Churches. He was also asked by the WCC to retain his active role in the Division of Inter-Church Aid and Service to Refugees. This was a welcome assignment, because in this way he could feel that he was not entirely outside of the flow of events and actions. So it was, that already in February, 1959, Zigler traveled back to Europe to attend an administrative committee meeting of the WCC agency. He was made welcome at the new apartment in Geneva, now occupied by the family of Wilbur Mullen, acting director of the European Brethren Service program. He returned to the USA in mid-March, to take up the tasks to which the church now called him.

The tasks were two-fold. The first was to participate in a program of interpretation of the work of the church, particularly of the Brethren Service program. This was a continuation of the Anniversary Call, a major evangelistic and fund raising effort initiated at the time of the 250th

247

anniversary. During the months of April and May, he spoke at thirty area rallies in Illinois, Indiana, Ohio, Pennsylvania, Maryland, Virginia, California, Oregon, Washington, Idaho, Colorado, Kansas, Missouri, and Iowa. The theme was "Advance Peace." Reports were enthusiastic:

• *Illinois:* "Excellent response, especially in view of the fact that a bad storm struck just before the service."
• *Colorado:* "Bob Zigler has come and gone, but his being here lifted us to new visions and has left an unforgettable challenge with us."
• *Iowa:* "The people attending the M. R. Zigler meeting . . . were thrilled with the challenge and testimony for Peace which Bob brought. He was very worn and tired from such a strenuous schedule, but his message was powerful and should bear lasting fruit."
• *Oregon:* "Bro. Zigler was very well received."
• *Indiana:* "Excellent, even better than was expected. . . . Many persons stayed for a long time for questions and answers."
• *California:* "The response was very good. Bro. Zigler spoke some over an hour and the audience gave him rapt attention, and people flocked to the front of the church afterward to greet him. They seemed to recognize that here was a man with a message growing out of first hand vital experience."
• *Virginia:* "Brother M. R. was at his best at the Bridgewater College Chapel service."
• *Ohio:* "Bob gave a truly moving presentation. His statement on the work of the Brethren in Europe was vivid and clear. The people hung on his words. He presented the peace message in a way that even the military men came up afterwards . . . and showed their appreciation."
• *Maryland:* "Bob really did a bang up job here. He was the best I have ever heard him. He spoke to the Sunday School and had everyone in tears.
• *Pennsylvania:* "Very good and meaningful. Excellent witness. His emotional presentation was well disciplined—thus tremendously effective."

Many who had known him well commented that this was a different Zigler. The "old Bob Zigler" just did not exist any more. "M. R. redeemed his reputation in this area," one pastor wrote, referring to an overlong presentation at an earlier Annual Conference that had turned off many in the auditorium, with some leaving early. Wrote another: "The masses of people were not interested in his talks five years ago. . . . His manner of putting the message across, his appeal and his attitude was so different." Some felt that he was driving himself too hard and feared for his health. "It seems that he feels obligated to the dead, for one thing, to give himself without stint."[6]

A close younger friend, Inez Long, teacher and writer, caught some of Zigler's spirit and spark during this period. She came to a meeting where he was to speak, dreading to see what she anticipated would be a broken shell. As she entered the vestibule of the church, some one said "He's a broken man; he's going to try to speak, but he's a broken man." She focused her attention on the speaker:

> The size of the man caught my attention at first. I was struck by his sheer gallantry—a man standing on his own feet, erect and unaided, his posture pushed resolutely into place. He might have played the role of a cripple by speaking from a chair. He might have elicited sympathy by directing a few self-pitying remarks to a host of friends in the audience. He might have indulged in his personal crisis to be a broken hero. But he chose to do none of these. He kept his pace and his pose as it had always been: a man in a hurry in an age when killing comes quickly. . . . If the recent deathblows to which he had been an unwitting partner brought delays, Robert Zigler saw no reason for halt or retreat. "My job as I have understood it since World War I," he stated, "is to stop the race of humans—many of them Christians—who are poised to kill each other as a solution to their problems." If he had been wounded by the idealism of that message, he returned to embrace it with a loyalty that made his personal sufferings endurable.[7]

Zigler Memoirs

Besides the speaking and interpreting, Zigler had been given another major task. This was to write a narrative of Brethren Service work, with particular attention to the European program. The assignment was described as writing his "memoirs," as the Board felt that this would provide "more latitude in including your observations, impressions, and evaluations" than a straight history.[8]

He was henceforth to spend considerable time in both the USA and Europe pulling together the threads of the complicated story. Although those urging him to do this were correct in their insistence that no one else knew the details of this often poorly-documented development, it was not a task that suited his temperament. He had never enjoyed writing, although his church positions had often called for interpretative articles and messages. He could, and did, write moving appeals for assistance and communicated well the urgency of the moment. What came harder were reflective, analytical pieces. He was accustomed to a discursive and anecdotal approach, almost a free-association mentality, which made meticulous, detailed analytical jobs unpleasant to him.

He had always depended on secretaries or aides to put his dictation and speech into more coherent and organized form. His own prose tended to be sprawling and disjointed. He was not naturally a gifted prose stylist. There was a further practical difficulty. Digging into dusty files triggered his asthmatic tendency and caused physical problems.

In September and October he worked on the BSC manuscript in Kassel, Germany; Linz, Austria; and Geneva, Switzerland. He was aided in his work by Frances Clemens (Nyce) and Suzanne Windisch in Kassel, who went through the files and made many notes for him; Frances Clemens also traveled to Geneva to assist there. The Brethren administration had anticipated that at the most two months would be spent in Europe on gathering materials. They saw little necessity to support the costs of secretarial assistance. However, Zigler, always conscious of his limitations in writing and research, felt very dependent on skilled help. As he often did, if blocked by administrative channels, he went directly to a personal friend and supporter, in this case Horace Raffensperger of Elizabethtown, Pennsylvania, for financial support.[9]

In fact, the writing of the memoirs was extraordinarily delayed in its completion. This caused strain with the Brethren administrators, who had understood it as a graceful bridging employment and as a way to extend some limited compensation to the retired church leader. They expected it to be completed no later than the end of 1959, even if the final product was more an archival compilation for future historians than a finished manuscript. When the project was not completed, it was seen henceforth as a personal project. Zigler solicited support for assistance by Edith Barnes in Elgin, again turning to Horace Raffensperger in Elizabethtown. The Elgin staff was at that time, 1962, not willing to give church credit for the donation, because it was no longer considered to be a church project.[10]

A manuscript was eventually finished but Zigler did not push for its publication. He seemed to be sensitive about its imperfections, fearing that it would not be received well. He arranged that one person was to make it known after his death. However, when the Brethren Service memoirs, *To Serve the Present Age*, was under way, the editor found the manuscript in the Brethren archives and used five of its chapters, with Zigler's permission, as the framework for the book. It thus received partial publication in this form.[11]

While at Kassel collecting material for his memoirs, he was delighted to host his old friend from CPS days, Gen. Lewis B. Hershey, who was traveling in his private capacity. Zigler reported to Elgin that the Hershey's visit had been very fruitful. "He left a very fine impression on the part of the BSC workers, and I am sure that it has helped the relationship of our group with the military administration of this area." Before returning to the USA on November 8, Zigler went back to Västervik, to see his Swedish friends, particularly Dr. Colfach.[12]

Other Activities

On June 1, 1959, M. R. Zigler was honored by a doctorate of laws at Manchester College (one of four he received over his lifetime). He had spoken to the student body at a chapel service earlier that spring and greatly moved his audience. Gladdys E. Muir, professor of peace studies there, reflected that he was "a living example of the truth the writers of Greek tragedy so constantly expressed—that suffering is often the road to deeper insight."[13]

This followed an earlier honor, in which he was given an award for forty years of service to the church at a ceremony at Elgin during the spring board meetings. On April 7, he addressed the board, stressing the place of the denomination in ecumenical circles. "When I represent my church, I am unafraid and I am welcome," for the Brethren are known as a peace church, he stated. "Our task is not to maintain a comity of geography but to support the comity of message. No one in the leadership of the World Council wants us to give up our peace message."[14]

The awards continued for him. At the Ocean Grove, New Jersey, conference, a special service of recognition was held on June 13, 1959, again for his forty years of service and marking his official retirement from church employment. This included the presentation of a book of letters "from his many friends and associates," repeating many of the over-whelmingly laudatory words expressed in the similar compilation of the summer of 1958. Many came from ecumenical leaders in the USA and abroad, often recounting memories of their first or outstanding encounters with him. It was in this collection that the oft-repeated quip was found, produced by Charles P. Taft, leading American layman. "I am certainly sorry that you are retiring from the official relationship to the Church of the Brethren. Nevertheless, I am not fooled by any such procedure. I fully expect to see you riding heifers up to the moment when one escorts you to heaven." This is usually retold as Zigler riding the heifer into heaven.[15]

By mid-summer, the restless Zigler was again traveling back to Europe on ecumenical business. On July 4, on the ship leaving the USA, he wrote a message for the churches, to be used on church bulletins; it distills in a few sentences the burden of his appeals to the Brethren and other denominations in America:

> Only a SUPREME EFFORT can avert the world crisis mankind is facing today. Nations are threatening to use the absolute evil, WAR, to cure secular tensions. . . . One nation must courageously lead [in finding a new way] and thus challenge others. The first nation to act must be supported by people who believe in making a supreme sacrifice in a different way than is made in war.
>
> I believe the churches in the United States can furnish the necessary spiritual dynamic. . . . They have life and resources which, if not dedicated to peacemaking, will be called by the state to do that which the church was organized to avoid, and that which the World Council of Churches has called "Sin."
>
> During nearly two decades the Church of the Brethren has been sending persons and resources to many nations in a purely reconciling mission. The reward is trust on the part of those served. . . . The witness of Brethren volunteers has been enormous, and this witness should be increased quickly before it is too late. This movement has been tested. I firmly believe PEACE awaits our expansion.[16]

During this extensive European visit he sought out the Greek team in Epirus, and then went to Thessalonica in late July for a WCC study conference on rapid social change. From there he traveled to Austria for another WCC committee meeting, before going on to Rhodes for the WCC Central Committee (August 19-28). Following these events, he traveled about Europe collecting materials and speaking to former associates.

Church Visitation

Zigler was back in Broadway, Virginia, on November 15, 1959, shortly after his sixty-eighth birthday observance. He plunged again into a heavy schedule of church visitation. It really seemed as if he felt obliged to deplete his energies in conveying the message of peace and goodwill, as if his survival of the accident made it mandatory to wear himself out. Also, it was difficult for a man of his temperament, who had always been at the center of the work of the church, to accept relegation to the sidelines. He *needed* to be in the midst of things, to count for something. It was also a way of dealing with the intense loss he felt in his wife's absence.

Hence, the next months were spent in an almost hectic burst of traveling. In December, 1959, he itinerated in Pennsylvania churches. He was back in Germany, in January, 1960, returning to the USA in February. He spoke in Brethren congregations in Virginia, Pennsylvania, and Kansas in February and March, 1960. He was back in Europe for WCC meetings in April, 1960, then traveled on to Austria. In May and June he was in Västervik, Sweden; visited Kassel, Germany, in July; attended a WCC consultation in Berlin in late July; attended the Central Committee meeting of the WCC in Scotland, in August; and returned to the USA in September. Expenses of the Central Committee attendance were covered by the Brethren and travel to the other WCC work by the World Council. He was given hospitality by the Brethren Service program when he visited their units in Austria, Germany, and Switzerland.

Back in the United States, he attended a meeting of the Inter-Church Aid and Service to Refugees in New Windsor, Maryland, in October, 1960. The next month found him in Washington, D. C., where he was honored at a twentieth anniversary meeting of the National Service Board for Religious Objectors, which he had helped to found and had served as first chairman. And then his restless pace was crowned with an around-the-world trip lasting more than a year.

World Trip

The stimulus for the lengthy trip was the planned assembly of the World Council of Churches in New Delhi, India, in late 1961. In planning for this trip, he sought the advice of his good friend Orie O. Miller, a world traveler in the interests of the Mennonite Church. Zigler began his trip in Geneva in January by attending a meeting of the committee on Inter-Church Aid and Service to Refugees. A member of the administrative committee which met four times a year, he was determined to keep up with its work and to attend all meetings. In between he visited the HELP program on Sardinia, initiated by his young protégé, actor Don Murray.

He went on to visit Brethren missions in Nigeria for several months in the spring of 1961, before returning to Geneva for a WCC meeting in June. He then went to Morocco to be with the workers in the Eirene project there. November, 1961, found him in India, visiting the Brethren missions prior to the world assembly, which began on November 18 Following that important gathering, which saw many Eastern Orthodox churches joining the ecumenical fold, he traveled on via Calcutta, to Thailand, Laos, Hong Kong, Indonesia, Japan, and Korea, before arriving back on the western coast of the USA in early March. He had a close call in Indonesia, arriving in the capital Djakarta in the midst of civil strife. With the aid of American consular officials he was able to leave the country without being harmed. Despite this, according to the report of Brethren missionaries serving in that country, he made a vivid impression on the church workers there he was able to meet.[17]

Once back in the USA, after March 1 he began touring churches on the West Coast. In April he was in Oregon, in May in Idaho, before arriving in Elgin to spend two weeks on speaking engagements in Illinois and Indiana.

A typical schedule would be like the one he experienced in Decatur, Illinois, in April. He was the main speaker at a Spiritual Life Institute held at the local Church of the Brethren congregation. On a Friday evening he addressed deacons and wives of the Southern Illinois Brethren churches on the needs of the world and how they could help meet them. On Saturday evening he spoke on "Let's Prepare for Tomorrow;" he spoke twice on Sunday morning: the sermon was entitled "The Church Reconciling Through Service" and the Sunday school session was "The World As I See It." Following a luncheon, he answered questions at 1:00 P.M., which was followed by a meeting with youth of the district at 5:00 P.M. on the topic "The Church in Forty Years." On Sunday evening he spoke at a large ecumenical gathering on the topic "The Secular Curtain." On Monday morning he spoke to pastors and wives on "What Shall We Discuss," followed by a meal and discussion. In the evening he spoke on "How Can a Local Church Break Through the Secular Wall?" A special meeting for church women on Tuesday morning focused on "Living on the Edge of the Future." Zigler's last presentations on Tuesday evening featured an address to church leaders on world reconciliation and the concluding sermon: "The Rock of Lives." Wide publicity was given to these occasions.[18]

The Brooklyn Church

During this time Zigler entertained several ideas about different forms of activity. One of the most intriguing was the possibility of taking the pastorate at the First Church of the Brethren in Brooklyn, New York. This came about during the course of the year 1959. He learned at the Annual Conference in Ocean Grove that the congregation was without leadership, was discouraged, and might be disbanded. He mentioned to a group there "that some one should go to Brooklyn and not sell the place and that I did not know a place I would rather serve a church in some new type of a Brethren church." It greatly intrigued Zigler for several reasons. One was that he had dreamed already in Geneva about a post in New York where he could be related to the work of the United Nations. Some of his friends, such as Orie Miller, had suggested that he should become a kind of elder statesman, lobbying there for the interests of world peace. A base at Brooklyn would make that possible.

He was also concerned that the Brooklyn congregation stay in close contact with the denomination. In its isolated position, begun as it was as an urban mission, it was rather distant from the center of Brethren denominational activity. Its largely Italian ethnic character also made it somewhat unusual in Brethren circles.

He was encouraged in this idea by the Eastern regional executive, Harold Z. Bomberger, and the moderator of the North Atlantic District, Donald H. Shank, in the summer of 1959. Conscious of the weightiness of a decision, Zigler queried a large number of church leaders: these included Norman J. Baugher, Dan West, and Galen Young. He also wrote to the presidents of the Brethren institutions of higher learning, suggesting that a number of their alumni living in the metropolitan area could be gathered into a Brethren fellowship. There was, however little response. Correspondence sent to him in Europe in the late summer of 1959 from the North Atlantic leadership seemed, nevertheless, very positive.

At the same time Zigler indicated that he would need to have an arrangement that would allow him time to travel in the interests of peace; he also wished to keep up his connections with the World Council, necessitating four trips a year overseas. He suggested that the best arrangement would be to have as an assistant a young pastor interested in studying in New York; such a man could take Sunday responsibilities in Zigler's absence. His wife might also function as a secretary.

He showed real ambivalence about his intentions—strongly inclined to do it but hesitant about tying himself down to a pastorate. He had never been a pastor, although for many years he had placed pastors in congregations in his Home Missions office. He therefore suggested that a year's trial would be useful. He also thought of a new kind of parish, one which would involve much visitation of Brethren with no formal tie to a local congregation.

After returning to New York, Zigler met with the local congregation on November 16, in the presence of representatives from the District Board.

Evidently the wishes of the local church for full time pastoral leadership did not fit with Zigler's vision of the congregation as the base for a larger effort for reaching Brethren in the metropolitan area and also as a base for peace work. A brief note from the executive board of the congregation in February informed Zigler: "After discussing the possibility of your coming to us as a pastor, it was decided that we would not recommend your name as a candidate to the church council." And so this venture, which at some points seemed to provide an ideal base for his future work, proved to be unsuitable. Given his restless nature at this time, it was probably a good thing that the congregation turned him down. It would not have been a good fit for either side.[19]

The Peace Corps

It was also during this period that he was offered a leading administrative job with the US Peace Corps. One of his friends was Raymond W. Miller, a public relations executive and active Methodist layman. He had known Zigler well in the days of the rural life emphasis, working closely with him and with Monsignor Luigi Ligutti. (He had brought the two together.) Miller pursued the idea by looking Zigler up at an Annual Conference in Ocean Grove, New Jersey (probably in 1962). This is how Zigler remembered the overture, expressed in his typically rambling manner:

> He worked on me Friday and Saturday and I'd seen the Peace Corps and government people and I knew what they do to entertain everybody and all this stuff you got to do, and it didn't appeal to me at all. But finally they offered me a pretty good salary to come. But in his portfolio of recommendations, and he showed me what they had on me, my relationship to Civilian Public Service was the outstanding one. Governmental, you see. The work with the United Nations, with the [China] tractor unit, and the Heifer Project was in there a little bit, but not too much. . . . [H]e said that I had the best experience of anybody they could find in the United States for the Peace Corps. He claimed that if I got in there, they'd put the priority high up in the organization. . . . Should I go government or church? And I decided to stay with the church. . . . I told him I think the Brethren [would] give me more credit for going in with the Peace Corps than they would to stay with the Brethren, but I still think I'll stay with the Brethren.[20]

He devoted much of 1962 and 1963 in Elgin working on his memoirs. But during the same period, he was thinking also of final retirement plans.

Although his daughter and son-in-law had kept their special room for him, he was scarcely ever there. He had moved his church membership to the nearby Linville Creek congregation, which named him as one of its delegates to the Annual Conference of 1963. For years his friends had urged him to settle in Florida. At one point it looked as if he would chose St. Petersburg, but the growing Brethren community in the inland town of Sebring proved more attractive. Therefore, he arranged for the purchase of an apartment in a renovated hotel and proceeded to "retire" in the sun-blessed state.

NOTES

1. Merlin Garber to M. R. Zigler, Sept. 20, 1958.
2. "Brethren Lost in Accidents," *Gospel Messenger* (Aug. 30, 1958): 17; "Riders to the Sea," *Time* (Aug. 25, 1958): 21-22; Paul H. Bowman, ed., *The Adventurous Future: An Anniversary Volume* (Elgin, IL: Brethren Press, 1959), 282-282, 289-290. A Brethren tour group led by L. W. Shultz donated 23 trees, which were planted on the lawn of the Brethren House at Kassel, Germany, to commemorate the victims of the KLM disaster and the Vastervik accident—*Gospel Messenger* (Jan. 3, 1959): 22.
3. *Gospel Messenger* (Dec. 20, 1958): 16.
4. Geraldine Glick to M. R. Zigler, Sept. 4, 1958; M. R. to Geraldine, Sept. 9, 1958; Geraldine to M. R., Sept. 14, 1958; M. R. to Geraldine, Sept. 16, 1958.
5. William T. Snyder to M. R. Zigler, Dec. 30, 1958; Snyder to Peter J. Dyck, Jan. 23, 1959 (MCC Records, Mennonite Historical Archives).
6. "Area Peace Meetings," *Gospel Messenger* (April 18, 1959): 17; M. R. Zigler Tour, mimeographed itinerary; "General Response on the M. R. Zigler Tour," undated typescript (Brethren Historical Library and Archives).
7. Inez Long, "Unbroken Soldier for Peace," *Christian Living* (October, 1960): 16-17, 39. Zigler appreciated the article so much that he ordered 25 reprints—Daniel Hertzler, editor, to M. R. Zigler, Nov. 18, 1960.
8. Norman J. Baugher to M. R. Zigler, Nov. 19, 1958.
9. Norman J. Baugher to M. R. Zigler, May 8, 1959.
10. Norman J. Baugher to M. R. Zigler, Jan. 29, 1960; Baugher to Zigler, Sept. 21, 1962.
11. D. F. Durnbaugh, ed., *To Serve the Present Age: The Brethren Service Story* (Elgin, IL: Brethren Press, 1975), 17-75; M. R. Zigler to Emma K. Ziegler, Nov. 10, 1982..
12. M. R. Zigler to W. Harold Row, Oct. 9, 1959.

13. Gladdys E. Muir in "Newsletter to Students of Peace Studies," June 11, 1959.
14. *Gospel Messenger* (April 25, 1959): 16; "20 Employees Are Honored At Brethren Headquarters," *Elgin* [IL] *Daily Courier-News* (April 10, 1959): 20.
15. Charles P. Taft to M. R. Zigler, April 15, 1959.
16. M. R. Zigler, "Supreme," bulletin message, [n.d.].
17. Joel Thompson to M. R. Zigler, April 28, 1962, from Indonesia.
18. "Brethren Leader For Institute, Service Sunday," *Decatur* [IL] *Review* (March 7, 1962).
19. Donald H. Shank to M. R. Zigler, July 28, 1959; Shank to Zigler, Aug. 29, 1959; Harold Z. Bomberger to M. R. Zigler, Aug. 30, 1959; M. R. Zigler to Galen S. Young, Sept. 8, 1959; Norman J. Baugher to M. R. Zigler, Sept. 8, 1959; M. R. Zigler to Warren D. Bowman, A. C. Baugher, Calvert N. Ellis, Harold D. Fasnacht, A. Blair Helman, D. W. Bittinger, and Paul M. Robinson, Sept. 8, 1959; Zigler to Shank, Oct. 8, 1959; Elizabeth Maxwell for the executive board to M. R. Zigler, Feb. 9, 1960.
20. Ken Kreider interview with M. R. Zigler, May 27, 1977, 2/12-13.

FLORIDA, MISSOURI, ILLINOIS, AND MARYLAND

W HILE STILL IN GENEVA, the Ziglers had contemplated where they might spend their retirement years, and Florida was in the picture. They thought of buying a trailer and stationing it somewhere. Friends at St. Petersburg had been eager to invite them to that location. Sebring also seemed attractive because of the growing number of Brethren settling there. But in vintage Zigler manner, he decided on checking out the locality before making a decision. "When I decided to consider Sebring, I went up and down the streets asking people who these Brethren were, like I did when I went to Elgin in 1919 to consider accepting the call there to become Home Missions Secretary. At Sebring I found the same type of reflection on the part of the city people concerning the Brethren. . . . Conservatism and separatism still abounded." He found that the Sebring community respected the Brethren and sent their children to its Sunday schools. Sebring had been originally promoted by J. H. Moore, veteran *Gospel Messenger* editor. Later J. H. Garst, a bank president, became active.[1]

What triggered the decision was the earlier action in 1951 by Brethren living in Sebring to buy a hotel, the Manor, for a retirement home. Zigler arranged for them to reserve the northwest corner room on the top floor— on the cool side and high enough to escape flying insects. Finally, in September, 1964, he made the move to Sebring and began living there.

He enjoyed showing people through the apartment, which he decorated in an unusual manner. The predominant color in his room was red; in it he placed many of the objects he had collected in his travels. Everywhere he lived he had heaps of books and papers, usually poorly ordered. His generous and expansive manner made it difficult to keep things neat. Maid service saw to it that his surroundings did not become too untidy. He enjoyed having photographs and pictures about, again from his many travels. Some were enlargements of photos he had himself taken, although he was not what could be called an expert photographer. The apartment had its own distinctive character. It was a point of pride with him to entertain graciously.

It appears that in Sebring, as well as in Geneva, there were women who felt that, after Amy's death, he needed a companion to care for him. He was wary of any romantic entanglements. He told one visiting couple, whom he entertained most graciously, that he would not allow a woman to assist him in serving: "He was not being trapped by one of these women in Florida!" While said jocularly, there was evidently some seriousness in the message. He told two close friends, John and Margaret Metzler, that the real reason he would not remarry was that many thought of him as someone exceptional. "He knew that he had feet of clay and that after marriage the spouse would soon find that he was entirely human, and her semi-idealized picture of him would fade." The marriage would not survive that disillusionment. He also never forgot the closeness of his attachment to Amy. In letters written late in life to other widowers, he confessed that he had never completely gotten over the loss.[2]

Zigler subscribed to a host of magazines and journals because it was important for him to keep up with both world and religious affairs. He read the *Gospel Messenger*, of course, the periodical of the Church of the Brethren, but he also subscribed to the official publications of the other Brethren bodies. He took and read *Christian Century, Christianity Today, Mennonite Weekly Review, US News and World Report*, and other current news magazines. A typical touch for him was his subscription to *Ebony* magazine, a black publication that he presented to the maids at the Manor. Later he subscribed to *Sojourners, The Other Side*, and similar publications with a radical Christian perspective.

Sebring Church of the Brethren

He became active in the local church, which is a story in itself. The Sebring Church of the Brethren was known throughout the denomination as a very conservative church. Its pastor at the time of Zigler's arrival was a noted conservative and in this reflected the majority position of the congregation. The contrasts with the newcomer were many.

Sebring believed in saving souls; Zigler believed in humanitarian action. There was never any doubt about his theological orientation; he was an unreconstructed liberal. The very programs into which Zigler had thrown his life were questioned in Florida. This is well illustrated by the characterization that some there were making—as he soon picked up—that support for his beloved Heifer Project was tantamount to worshiping the "golden calf." Much of his life had been spent in the church's headquarters at Elgin; Sebring distrusted Elgin. Worst of all, Zigler had been associated with the World Council of Churches, that "superchurch" associated with "Christians" from Communist Russia. Zigler was just too liberal for Sebring's conservative leadership. Although the presiding elder was very friendly as a person, he had deep suspicion of Zigler's churchmanship.

The elder let it be known that M. R. Zigler was not fit to lead in prayer, teach a Sunday school lesson, or preach. Zigler's comment was: "I never got mad about it. I had learned through the years to adjust myself to the different varieties of Brethren traditions and actions, and commitment. . . . I knew I was a member of the church at large, and I had my membership paper from Elgin and from my home church in my pocket. [When] I finally put my membership in, they had to accept it." But strange to say, given this situation, before much time had passed, he was made elder of the congregation![3]

It happened in this way: the pastor of the church had resigned and the elder had arranged for another man, a pastor in Philadelphia, to be the replacement. Also, the elder had to move from the area for family reasons. The plan was for the new pastor to preach on a Sunday morning, meet the congregation, and be voted in at a business meeting the following Monday evening. Everything was set for a smooth transition.

Then on the day before he was to preach, the Philadelphia pastor called to say that he had to decline the call. In that emergency, the elder came to Zigler and said *he* had to become the elder, saying "I know that you're not the right man to be elder of this church, but you've got to be that, because I promised to be with my mother and here we are without a pastor, and the man that we thought would come turned me down on Saturday before the business meeting on Monday." Zigler's comment was: "This was a shock to me and to the membership of the church."

But he entered into the work with a will, actually giving full time to the responsibilities, and the people responded. Attendance and membership increased. Zigler pushed a successful remodeling project to make the church more accessible for older people. This resulted in the J. M. Blough

Memorial Education Building, honoring a beloved missionary; it was dedicated on February, 4, 1968. The Sunday school class he taught attracted 170 members, the largest attendance ever for that class.

He was also put in charge of the task of securing a new pastor. Many asked him to become the minister but he demurred, never having had experience as a pastor. He also knew that Sebring posed several problems for a pastor: people came there from different parts of the Church of the Brethren, from the plain congregations in Pennsylvania and the more liberal congregations in the Midwest. He recruited a strong pastor from Ohio, Fred Hollingshead. Long term residents of Sebring enjoy recalling that when the new pastor arrived, some members of the congregation helped him unload the moving truck. M. R. saw a box marked "Sermon Notes" and told Hollingshead: "Burn them up; we don't want any old stale sermons!"[4]

At a luncheon honoring the new minister, held on September 23, 1965, Zigler moved the Brethren into an unaccustomed ecumenical posture by inviting all of the local clergy to participate in the program, both Protestant and Catholic. He also was instrumental in arranging the beginning of an annual "inter-faith fellowship dinner," to bring together the spiritual leaders of the Sebring community.[5]

Hollingshead was a good choice as pastor, because, as Zigler stated, he was "very strong in public relations and everywhere he would go he would make friends." Under his leadership the congregation became much better known in the area. More and more Brethren began coming there, especially in the winter, so that it became one of the largest congregations in the denomination.

Community Involvement

Another project that needed Zigler's promotion was a new nursing home. It was to be one of the first built in Florida in connection with a retirement home; later, of course, this became the standard arrangement. Plans had been developed already before his arrival but a major fund raising effort was required. He got behind this with his usual vigor and the project succeeded. It was called the Cottrell Memorial Nursing Home to honor A. Raymond and Laura Cottrell, both of whom had been Brethren medical missionaries in India for thirty-six years before retiring in Florida; they taught a large Sunday school class in the Sebring congregation. Zigler wrote an extensive article for the *Gospel Messenger* promoting the cause.

He also presided at the dedication ceremonies for the nursing home, which occurred on January 3, 1965. A government grant of $97,000 aided in the completion of the project, built on one level and later expanded to two levels.[6]

As part of his involvement, he became active in the local chamber of commerce. One of his suggestions was to invite the chamber to hold a meeting at the Manor and then visit the new Cottrell center; this occurred and built good will for the developments. He also became the Brethren representative to the Florida Council of Churches.

M. R. Zigler spoke at the meeting of the Bridgewater College alumni, on February 6, 1965. It is one of the few of his speeches for which a text has been preserved because of his habit of impromptu address. Part of the speech was written out; the other is covered by a lengthy outline. The theme was that for the church to survive, it must have a college. He likened the flow of college graduates into the life of the church to a blood transfusion for the human body. "Without this refreshing mass of young men and women the church will die both in body and in spirit." He criticized the use of the term "church-related: because of its "coldness;" it did not display the warmth and dedication of the college to the church he felt was required for both institutions.[7]

For much of this time he served as public relations representative for the Brethren homes in Florida. Besides the Manor and the nursing home, Florida Brethren Homes, Inc., also developed the Lorida estates nearby for those wishing to build a house or locate a trailer in a more rural setting. Friends advised him not to get into the administrative side of the business, because that would tie him down too much. He would be unable to travel and speak, which he so enjoyed doing.[8]

By 1969, Zigler's interests had moved on and he submitted his resignation as elder to the church board. The board was shocked at the news, but accepted it "with deep regret and appreciation." They were deeply indebted for his tenure of more than three years. His "spirit, statesmanship," and "wide Christian experience" and dedication had "helped to move us forward to develop the kind of church that we want to belong to." They paid tribute to the "worthwhileness of his dreams, tireless energies, and Christian enthusiasm" spent for Christ and his church. "We know your contributions here will never be forgotten in the Sebring Church because many have been influenced by the greatness of your spirit and leadership."[9]

Break from Sebring

Despite the obvious success and accomplishment that Zigler enjoyed through his church work in Florida, it was not completely satisfying to him. Somehow, he felt that retirement, even such an active retirement, was not worthy. He still longed for a more active role in the church. A letter written about ten years later reveals some of his attitude about Florida. A well-wisher had written inquiring why he had "retired so early in life." This was part of his response:

> When Amy, my wife, did not return with me and I lived with sad memories, I came to the conclusion that I was not worth much and I did not want to see people and I had lost my creative spirit. That came partly through the physical effects of an automobile accident, plus a fairly severe threat coming through diabetes that nearly killed me twice. While a number of opportunities came to me to do certain things, I had a kind of disease, I felt, that prevented me from taking on a worthwhile project, so I chose to go to Sebring, where Amy and I had agreed we would try when we retired if we did not go to Puerto Rico or some place like that. So between the age of 70 and 80 I did a lot of work in the Retirement Home and with the local Sebring Church of the Brethren.[10]

The attitude expressed here reveals that Florida for M. R. Zigler was seen as a place to lick his wounds and "loaf" rather than as a normal place for an aging person to spend the later decades of his life.

Thus it was that he seized upon an invitation to break from the retired, but still very active, life he was experiencing at Sebring. He received an invitation to make a swing through the Great Plains in late 1968, visiting Brethren congregations from North Dakota to Falfurrias, Texas. He had made just such an investigative trip at the beginning of his Home Missions assignment in 1919. He accepted the task and enjoyed it. It seemed to him as if he were back in harness. In the course of this trip, he was invited to become an interim pastor at the Messiah congregation of the Church of the Brethren in Kansas City, Missouri. This began in the spring of 1969. It was a new challenge for him, to stay with a local church week after week, instead of delivering a stirring message and moving on to the next speaking assignment.[11]

He assisted the congregation to secure a permanent replacement, and was then called by the District of Illinois and Wisconsin to take another interim pastorate, this time at Naperville, Illinois. He had been pleased with the experiment at Kansas City and had his name put on a list for prospective placement through denominational channels. The Illinois assignment began in mid-October, 1969, and lasted until early January, 1970, when he had to leave abruptly because of a serious illness of the prostate. He flew to Virginia and was immediately placed in the Rocking-ham Memorial Hospital, Harrisonburg, Virginia. His term at Naperville had made possible a happy reunion with many former volunteers and Brethren Service workers then living in the Northern Illinois area.

Although his style was unorthodox as a pastor, it was effective. One of the innovations he introduced was to highlight a member family of the congregation each Sunday. He introduced them and told of their lives and ministry. It was his way of praising the "ordinary" church members and giving a sense of accomplishment. It often came as a surprise to other members to learn of all of the things that their fellows had in fact done over the years. There had simply never before been a format for them to have an opportunity to discover these facts.

Although he had to leave abruptly, with the district executive only learning about the move after the fact, he left many warm memories behind. Nine months after his departure, a congregational leader wrote to him, apologizing that Zigler had written him before he got around to writing Zigler: "Oh well, that's Bob Zigler for you. Always one step ahead of the rest. . . ." His impact was still fresh. "Your spirit and warm heart were and still are an inspiration for many of us;" they will be long remembered. "You left us with something that no man can sell or buy."[12]

Next Steps

Because of his medical problems, Zigler stayed with his daughter and son-in-law in Broadway, Virginia, for some time. He was well enough to travel to New Windsor, Maryland, on May 6, 1970, for the dedication of an oil portrait of him which was placed in the newest building in the Service Center complex. This was Zigler Hall, dedicated in his honor already on May 26, 1968. This facility was made possible, in large part, by funds derived from the sale of the Kassel House in Germany. This was ironic, because Zigler had bitterly opposed the sale of the house, which he was instrumental in building. Other funds were donated by the member churches of the National Council who used the center for the processing of material aid goods through the Church World Service program. In fact, Zigler himself donated $500 to its construction, upon the solicitation of W. Harold Row.[13]

Before long M. R. returned to Florida but was still looking for something to do. Learning that W. Harold Row, at that time head of the Washington office, had contracted cancer, Zigler informally offered to help in the Washington office if that would be of assistance. The Elgin administrators appreciated the gesture but had nothing concrete to suggest. Row believed that he could carry the responsibility despite his health problems. When the executive of the World Ministries Commission reported this to Zigler, the response was revealing. Zigler said, among other things:

> I can return to Sebring and work the limit. I can go to a number of local churches. I can loaf. I have enough invitations to come to speak in churches to keep busy and all this would pay dividends except loafing. My old body is promised by doctors [to last] another ten years. I [have] just been to New Windsor where I felt [an] older man with some wisdom and vision could meet the people and go out to the Churches to interpret, not only [for] Brethren, and promote new types of Conferences for the new day, in the Brethren manner. . . . Several years ago the staff at New Windsor asked me to come to New Windsor on the staff. I did not feel good at that time and was afraid to try it. Now since I have lived so long I wish I had tried.[14]

New Windsor

In late 1971 this dream became a reality, as so many of M. R. Zigler's dreams tended to do. During that period, he corresponded with his young friend H. McKinley "Mac" Coffman, then director of the work at New Windsor. As Zigler liked to describe the development, Coffman came to Florida and found him at rest; he challenged him: "You're down here paying your room and board, loafing and going to hell; why don't you come to New Windsor and pay your room and board, work and go to heaven?"[15]

The reality was more complicated. As noted above, he had proposed such an assignment to Joel Thompson already a year earlier. Thompson later reflected that some of the Elgin staff believed that it would be a strategic move to have Zigler on the inside, where he would be put in a position of understanding and defending the church program, rather than stay on the outside, where he was vocally critical of the Elgin administration. He had, therefore, suggested to Coffman that something be worked out at New Windsor.[16] Evidently while still in Broadway, Virginia, in the fall of 1971, the idea had been discussed between the aging church leader and the young New Windsor executive, one of his former protégés in Europe. Zigler's response to Coffman of October 15 shows his longing but also his hesitation:

> Just received the doctor's report that I am better physically than I was when tested three months ago and that was better than when I got out of the hospital. I do think I should do something worthwhile but don't know anything better than to return to Sebring about November 9. I don't want to embarrass you but I don't hesitate to take a chance. You have teased me about being at New Windsor. I never thought I should follow up too closely what you meant I could do except to retire there.
>
> It is my firm belief you have a fine set up of staff and I believe you have a vision to carry you through at least a quarter of a century. If I were forty years or less young I would beg you to let me slave with you into the future. But if at eighty there is something you think will add to your vision and strength I would be silly not to offer what I have left. . . . You do not need even to answer this letter. As I will soon start my eightieth year and I just want to say here am I. You know me better than myself. You know New Windsor. Therefore. . . . [ellipsis in the original][17]

Zigler's longing for a participatory role was clear. Coffman decided to invite him to come on a volunteer basis, to see what could develop:

> I received your letter about the time that you were off to Argentina. I called to invite you to join us here at the Staff and to talk over the arrangements but you were off gallivanting around the world. When you get back, I would be glad to have you give me a call as I think there are several ways we could work out a period of time when you could spend some time here at the Center and we could be mutually supportive.[18]

The reference to the South American trip needs some explanation. Never content to sit quietly, Zigler had found other things to do. In November/December, 1971, he traveled to Argentina, a part of the world still foreign to him. Little is known about the trip, except that he met with Mennonites there. He did have correspondence about this with his long-time friend Orie O. Miller, of the Mennonite Central Committee. Miller's reference is to a "surprise trip" to Argentina. It may have an impulsive undertaking, much as many other Zigler ventures.

In the invitational letter from Coffman, there is tentative language, indicating that the idea was still not fully worked out. The language doubtless faithfully reflected the tentative assignment Coffman had in mind. Zigler was to be at the center, at first, for a period of three months on a self-supporting volunteer basis. Coffman contemplated using him in interpretation but also just having him present "to do his thing." He was to interact with the volunteers at the center "to raise their level of commitment," to be on the grounds to "visit with the older set that comes through," and to just "let goodness rub off wherever it can." A secretary was to be provided to encourage him to communicate with old friends about the current work of the center. Some friends of M. R. Zigler quietly helped to underwrite the modest costs of his presence at the center.

In a later letter extending a more formal invitation, Coffman had more definite assignments. Zigler would be expected to carry on correspondence with his wide circle of friends to interpret the work of the service center. As a resident of the center, he would be able to associate with the personnel, especially with the younger volunteers, and work informally to raise their commitment and motivation. He would be available to do interpretative work, by speaking to groups in the area. Future possibilities would include developing seminars or adult work camps using the New Windsor facilities. The center would provide secretarial help and office space, but Zigler would be expected to pay a nominal cost for lodging and meals. The aging leader accepted.[19]

The time frame envisaged was an initial three-month period, probably to be stretched on through Annual Conference time (late June). Zigler anticipated a two-month trip to Europe in the spring in any case. The arrangement went well for both sides. Zigler appreciated the opportunity to live at the center (which he was instrumental in developing), having secretarial help for his large correspondence, and feeling again in the midst of the life of the church. The center profited by its relationship with him, given his wide circle of supporters in and outside of the church, and the intangible plus of his inimitable presence.

The relationship continued beyond the suggested initial period. In late 1972 Zigler donated $500 to the center program and was thanked profusely for this by its leadership. The arrangement allowed him freedom to travel, accept speaking engagements, and develop his own pursuits. It seemed ideally suited to his situation. He could, for example, travel in Europe in April/May, 1972, travel among the congregations in Middle and Western Pennsylvania in October, 1972, and take two months in January and February, 1973, to itinerate among the churches in the Pacific District.

In a letter written to the center executives on September 1, 1972, Zigler crystallized some of his thoughts about interpretative work that needed to be done and how he related to it. He found that the Brethren congregations, even in nearby Baltimore, did not really know what the center program was. He concluded that the center should be present at the district meetings nearby to interpret the meaning of New Windsor. Executives of other districts should be informed by mail of its activities. He believed that each issue of *Messenger* should carry a column, or at the least, a half column about New Windsor. A newsletter (which was later introduced) should be distributed widely, among Brethren and other supporting denominations.

He reported that he was scheduled for every Sunday until December, which month he was keeping open. A typical comment was:

> I am convinced that the General Board members are not very well informed about the operation of New Windsor and I have some fear that there is a tendency for the Board and the staff to separate themselves from the responsibilities where I think they should be vigorously alive. I will not mention other projects that I think it will be easy for the Elgin administration to neglect.[20]

From the Elgin side, his contribution was appreciated. A cheerful note came from Joel Thompson in late 1972: "It seems as if was only a few months ago that Ken McDowell, Mac Coffman, and I discussed the possibility of attempting to twist your arm to get you from the luxury of Florida into the hard, day-by-day work of New Windsor and I'm very grateful that you have been able to give of yourself so fully over the past months. I'm sure the contribution you've made will not be forgotten and the impact of you and New Windsor upon the life of the church will be much greater because of the volunteer service you've given.[21]

The experiment thus seemed to be of mutual benefit for both sides. Zigler was in the midst of the life of the church; the denomination was profiting from his standing with many people to promote the program of the church. But something more dramatic, and more laden with tension, was yet to emerge. This was his vision of New Windsor as the center of a movement to revitalize the peace concerns of the Brethren. It was what he came to call *On Earth Peace*.

Eightieth Birthday

M. R. Zigler's family arranged for a special birthday party for him as the eightieth anniversary of his birth approached on November 9, 1971. They sent out a large number of invitations to a gathering at the Linville Creek Church of the Brethren in Broadway for October 31. This brought forth, besides the number actually attending, a landslide of congratulatory cards, cables, and letters. A few excerpts will give the celebrative flavor of the whole-hearted gratitude for the gift of friendship over the years and for the contribution that Zigler had made to the church and to the world:

—from Desmond and Irene Bittinger, writing from Mozambique:

> They tell us that you have now been under the smiles and blessings of God for eighty years or a little more. . . . During these eighty years you have done just about everything that the Church of the Brethren allows its people and some things which it does not. You have pried the church loose from some stuck places and moved it up many stairsteps to higher visions and loftier plateaus. You have touched many lives and made them richer. You have moved churches and churchmen ahead. You have served God well.[22]

—from Harold D. Fasnacht, president emeritus, La Verne College:

> How satisfying it must be to look back over those years with the knowledge that you were a pioneer, a champion, a great churchman. You came into the Kingdom for an important era of pioneering. You saw the need and you tackled the issues. Indeed, the Church of the Brethren, and all of Christendom will always cherish what you accomplished. Few men have had that "far reach" that you have.[23]

—from Friedl Garber, Vienna, Austria:

> In my mind you belong to the few people where I would say you are such an outstanding Christian and have the gift of teaching, preaching, and counseling with result because Christ looks out from your eyes, since the eyes are the mirror of the soul. . . . With you it is like in the Revelation 3: 8: ". . . you have followed my teaching and have been faithful to me. I have opened a door before you, which no one can close." That is why people who have met and talked to you will remember you as a person to look up to and want to be alike.[24]

—from G. Wayne Glick, president, Keuka College:

> As the *Christian Century* so beautifully said of Harold Row, so it can be said of you that your hallmarks are brotherhood and service. In a world that daily becomes more perplexing, these qualities mark you as one of God's noblemen, as one who has seen truly and acted on that vision with a complete fidelity.[25]

—from Glenn and Ethel Harris, Jennings, Louisiana:

We count it a privilege to greet you on your eightieth birthday anniversary. To have lived so long speaks of a strong constitution given by God, and a disciplined life on your part. You have lived so purposefully, so dedicated to the cause of peace and goodwill in a war torn world. Undoubtedly you have changed lives and even the course of history to a large degree. The Church of the Brethren witness in the years following World War II, especially in relief and service activities, has had untold influence on Western Christendom. It is good you have had the satisfaction of living to see some of the results of your dreams and labors.[26]

—from Margaret Glick Hunkins, former BVSer in Europe:

The reasons I remember you and indeed, love you, go beyond your contributions. . . . The reasons are simply that your enthusiasm for living and your mastering the art of life have always impressed me greatly. I saw this first in a Chinese restaurant in Geneva, Switzerland on a New Year's evening around 1952. It continued when we all left the restaurant and went to a huge Catholic church for the Midnight Mass and we nearly froze, and it went on after the Mass when we joined the festivities in the square and you were as joyous as all those Swiss (and sober, too, which they weren't). . . . It was the first time I really realized that life didn't have to be a sober ritual, even if it is a serious business! Thank you for being a good, joyful man, and for your genius in imparting that kind of spirit to everyone around you.[27]

—from J. Robert Nelson, Boston University School of Theology:

We always enjoyed hearing the stories of your work in Greece or elsewhere, and several of them have stayed with me. I was impressed also by the fact that you never allowed yourself to be overcome by the excitement and glamour of international living. In meeting the cosmopolites of Geneva, you took everything in stride and remained yourself. Especially I recall your friendly arguments with Visser 't Hooft (whom you pronounced Veezer Tooft), and your resolute resistance against any threats of Barthian theology.[28]

—from Robbins Strong, WCC executive:

It hardly seems any time at all that you were buzzing around the Geneva scene in your charismatic style, cutting red-tape and short-circuiting many of our committee bureaucracies. But you got things done. And many of these things

271

still exist. I think of some of the teams to which you gave an impetus—and some of which could use the kind of shot-in-the-arm that you could administer with a smile.[29]

—from W. A. Visser 't Hooft, general secretary of the WCC:

Since I have just returned from a journey in the Middle East, this congratulation comes after your eightieth birthday. But it brings very warm wishes. I have not forgotten the happy collaboration we had in the post-war period and your very great contribution to bridge building and peace making among the European peoples in their hour of need.[30]

—from R. Norris Wilson, conciliar executive:

I think the singular contribution which you made to the Ecumene over the years was to give it heart. I suppose we all know how necessary bureaucracy is. Certainly we know how wasteful it is when it has no pulse and when it gets tangled up in itself. You had the wonderful and gentle knack of always putting us on notice that beyond the organizational and administrative essentials, there was a human need that had to be met and nothing should stand in the way of meeting it in the most direct, agile and loving way possible.[31]

Most octogenarians rest content with what they have managed to achieve by that time. Not so M. R. Zigler. The decade of his eighties was one of the most active and fruitful of his entire life.

NOTES

1. Million transcript of M. R. Zigler, 8/23-32, 9/1-3.
2. John D. Metzler, Sr., to D. F. Durnbaugh, June 12, 1987; Lorton G. Heusel to M. R. Zigler, June 14, 1978.
3. Vernon Miller interview with M. R. Zigler, 8/27ff.
4. Earl Seese to D F. Durnbaugh, June 8, 1987.
5. "New Brethren Minister Honored at Dinner," [Sebring, FL] *Highland Herald* (n.d.).
6. M. R. Zigler, "Cottrell Memorial Nursing Home," *Gospel Messenger* (Sept. 19, 1964): 24-25; "New Nursing Home to Have Open House Jan. 3," [Sebring, FL] *Highland Herald* (Dec. 28, 1964): 1.
7. M. R. Zigler, "To Survive the Church Must Have a College," typescript.
8. Donovan R. Beachley, Sr., to M. R. Zigler, July 24, 1964.

9. Church Board of the Sebring Church of the Brethren to M. R. Zigler, Jan. 22, 1969.

10. M. R. Zigler to Maude Diehm, Aug. 9, 1978.

11. M. R. Zigler to the Churches of the Brethren [in] Iowa, Minnesota, North Dakota, and Montana, Dec. 6, 1968; *Messenger* (March 13, 1969).

12. Ralph Wagoner to M. R. Zigler, Sept. 23, 1970.

13. W. Harold Row to M. R. Zigler, Jan. 18, 1968; Row to Zigler, April 19, 1968; "The Tentacles of New Windsor," *Messenger* (Aug. 1, 1968); "Portrait of Zigler Given to Brethren Center," [Frederick, MD] *Carroll County Times* (Mary 14, 1970); "Zigler Portrait Presented," *Messenger* (July 16, 1970): 15.

14. M. R. Zigler to Joel K. Thompson, Broadway, Sept. 11, 1970.

15. Transcript of M. R. Zigler address, Bethany Theological Seminary, May 15, 1976, 4-5.

16. Vernon Miller interview with M. R. Zigler, 17b/8.

17. M. R. Zigler to J. McKinley Coffman, Oct. 15, 1971.

18. Coffman to Zigler, Nov. 30, 1971.

19. Coffman to Zigler, Jan. 7, 1972.

20. M. R. Zigler to Mac Coffman and Miller Davis, Sept. 1, 1972.

21. Joel K. Thompson to M. R. Zigler, Dec. 18, 1972.

22. Desmond and Irene Bittinger to M. R. Zigler, Nov. 15, 1971.

23. Harold D. Fasnacht to M. R. Zigler, Oct. 20, 1971.

24. Friedl Garber to M. R. Zigler, Oct. 20, 1971.

25. G. Wayne Glick to M. R. [Zigler], Oct. 18, 1971.

26. Glenn and Ethel Harris, Oct. 24, 1971.

27. Margaret Glick Hunkins to M. R. [Zigler], October, 1971.

28. J. Robert Nelson to M. R. Zigler, Oct. 25, 1971.

29. Robbins Strong to M. R. Zigler, Oct. 25, 1971.

30. W. A. Visser 't Hooft to M. R. Zigler, Oct. 29, 1971.

31. R. Norris Wilson to M. R. Zigler, Oct. 14, 1971.

22

ON EARTH PEACE

THE LAST YEARS of M. R. Zigler's life were devoted to his drive to revitalize the peace witness of the Church of the Brethren, an effort that showed both the best and the problematic sides of his character. As he often related, he came out of the World War I experience as a YMCA secretary determined to work through the church to bring an end to war. The form his efforts took in his last decade was the On Earth Peace movement, organized in late 1974. Paradoxically, this peace thrust was to cause major conflict with the leadership of the church, strain with some of his most devoted followers, and much mental anguish for him.

The story of the origin and evolution of the On Earth Peace movement is quite complicated. It is likely that these events are too recent to allow a dispassionate and accurate accounting of its history. All those involved have their own understanding and will probably not find the following interpretation completely satisfactory. Yet, it is imperative to attempt the task, because so much of the M. R. Zigler story is to be found in it.

There should be agreement on several statements. One is that the movement displayed the creative nature of Zigler's personality. Although the outer form of the movement seemed like a replay of his past involvements, the movement also well displayed his unusual creativity and freshness of ideas late in his life. Another is that the movement showed his unbreakable commitment to the process of working through the church to carry on and strengthen the peace witness. Yet another is his dedication to the young people of the church, his hope for a better future. And, finally, it demonstrated how hard it was for M. R. Zigler to relinquish direction of any of his brain-children.

The On Earth Peace movement was an experiment—Zigler often said—to see whether a minority could be allowed to flourish within a larger church structure. He understood the genius of the On Earth Peace concept as operating in the church but yet on its own terms. This basic posture explains much about the continual conflict that the movement generated. Many advisers urged him to keep it completely separate, but he insisted that it be worked through the church. The problem was that while he wanted the movement to be linked to the denominational program, he was basically unwilling to subordinate his ideas and directions to accepted and established church procedures.

Also, just at this time the church bureaucracy was completely committed to a management-by-objectives philosophy. This dictated that programs were to be developed by a planning process with coherent goals and objectives, that resources and staffing were to be allocated on a minutely worked out plan, that staff were to be held strictly accountable for meeting the stated objectives, and, especially, that fund raising was to be centrally administered.

All of this ran directly athwart Zigler's style of leadership, which was charismatic, impulsive, direct, and centered very much around the personal loyalty to him that had built up over decades. While he gave lip service to working through the structures, he really insisted on doing things his way. This trait had been observable over the years. He had often acted and then asked for permission. This developed in part because of the exposed role he had played in bringing an essentially conservative church into twentieth century ecumenical relationships. Probably real movement was only possible by a leader willing to take risks, to get out ahead of his church, but not so far ahead as to be disavowed.

The assignment of M. R. Zigler to the Geneva post in 1948—as has been seen—was largely the result of dissatisfaction with his freewheeling administrative style as head of Brethren Service. During the last years of his leadership of the Brethren Service program in Europe, he was again engaged in a sharp tug-of-wills with his superiors, W. Harold Row and Norman J. Baugher. They insisted that he follow the budget parameters laid down by the General Brotherhood Board and follow accepted policy. He went around them by raising funds from private resources and pushed ahead with projects that they thought unnecessary. So there were many precedents for the struggles that developed between the On Earth Peace program and the Elgin staff.

Creation of the Program

Zigler loved to tell about the inception of the On Earth Peace idea. He gave credit to W. Newton and Hazel Long, for many years active lay leaders in the Baltimore area and among Zigler's most faithful supporters. In September, 1974, Newton Long urged Zigler to see to it that, in addition to the many active programs operating out of the New Windsor center, an intellectual and spiritual focus on peace be developed. Then, as Zigler told it: "One morning at 4 o'clock I recalled Newton Long's concern. Suddenly, the message that came at the birth of Christ "On earth peace and goodwill among men" alerted me. I thought, let the Church of the Brethren implement this message, and search for peace through conferences at New Windsor, Maryland, as a natural thing to do."[1]

After some consultation with New Windsor and Elgin staff, he began to implement the concept, called at this time "Peace on Earth and Goodwill Among Men;" he was later convinced to shorten the name, to fit better on checks and to avoid a sexist image, hence "On Earth Peace." (It was first called "On Earth Peace Conference"—OEPC, later "On Earth Peace Assembly"—OEPA.) His first move was to secure pledges of money for the program, because, in his words, he "knew from experience that a movement should be tested by presenting the purpose of the movement to people of all ranks to measure the general interest and also to discover if the same people interviewed will give resources sufficient to implement a plan for action." He did this by traveling to several states and soliciting money from old friends. The first to donate was Charles Lantz and his wife from Virginia. Within several weeks Zigler had the promise of $30,000. Naturally, he was exuberant at this success. With this backing in hand, he organized planning and business committees.[2]

Along with this initiative, however, began the first complications with church machinery. The World Ministries Commission (WMC), under which New Windsor operated, had begun to work through its staff procedures on the idea of a conference at New Windsor. The initiation of such conferences, in fact, had been one of the proposed functions of Zigler's service at the center as a volunteer. The concept was assigned to Ralph E. Smeltzer, Washington representative of the church, for further development in cooperation with Zigler. Smeltzer had been running a series of church/state conferences in the District of Columbia and saw this as something of an extension of that program. He subsequently drafted a proposal for WMC approval, which then received General Board approval in the November, 1974, meeting. At a planning session on the seminar, however, it soon became evident to Smeltzer that Zigler had something different in mind. He was not developing another conference, he was starting a movement.[3]

The WMC decided internally that Smeltzer would shift his role as liaison to Kenneth E. McDowell, who had direct responsibility for the New Windsor center. In the meantime, Zigler's concept of the On Earth Peace program was expanding. He conceived of a series of meetings at New Windsor, called "assemblies," guided by a "central committee" to create a movement "in process of formation" (all terms imitating the World Council pattern). He foresaw an additional series of smaller vocational groupings dedicated to the pursuit of peace in their respective areas of work—physicians, teachers, farmers, even morticians. In this, the pattern he was following was that of the noted Evangelical Academies in post-World War II Europe; these academies sought to rebuild the shattered ethos and morale of the church by bringing together vocational groupings in retreat centers to discuss what Christian discipleship meant for them. In practice, as On Earth Peace grew, the larger assembly idea and the smaller vocational groupings were often united in the same meetings.

The founding assembly of what came to be called OEPC—On Earth Peace Conference—took place at New Windsor on December 20, 1974, with thirty-three persons attending. Zigler planned the next assembly for March 7-8, 1975. Those who responded to the first call were mostly men and women who had earlier contact with Zigler, many of them former volunteers or Brethren Service staff from Europe. A pattern for the assemblies developed that featured Zigler telling—often at great length— about the vision of the movement, followed by statements from those present on their vision for peace. Some of the later assemblies featured addresses by experts on international relations. Critics of the series noted that there was a strong element of nostalgia present. Zigler brought together those with whom he had formerly worked, such as leaders of the Historic Peace Churches, former World Council of Churches' staff workers, and Gen. Lewis B. Hershey.

There were, in fact, also innovative gatherings. For example, Zigler called together members of the Church of the Brethren who had served in the military and let them discuss their emotions as members of a denomination that discouraged its members from such activity. He brought young people together to introduce them to the peace perspective, at a time when the Brethren had neither an active program for youth nor an extensive peace program. Zigler noticed that thousands of people came through the New Windsor center each year but there was little interpretation of the Brethren peace witness to them. This eventuated in the OEPA bookstore, with emphasis on peace materials.

Acceptance into the Denominational Structure

Zigler was eager to have the blessings of the church on his concept. He used the term "consultative body." Some of his coworkers had reservations. For example, after the first meeting when Zigler pushed for the group to approve a petition to the General Board for incorporation into the denominational program, W. Newton Long commented in a letter: "After leaving our meeting last week, I was concerned that you might feel we were not with you. Well, we are. . . . We were trying to iron out possible difficulties before they occurred. . . . One idea that bothered me some, was the procedure of getting money for expenses from Elgin. I understood they would hold the funds and pay out as authorized by G. B. B. . . . Might that raise some problems?" If Long's counsel had been followed, which was basically to have an independent organization, much annoyance would have been avoided, as Zigler later granted.[4]

Zigler arranged for the proposal to be presented to the spring meeting of the General Board through his WMC liaison, Kenneth E. McDowell. The first step in the process was to present a petition to the Goals and Budget Committee. It is worth quoting for its insight into the plans that M. R. Zigler had for the OEPC program from the beginning:

Petition for Authorization.
ON EARTH PEACE CONFERENCE.

PURPOSE: The aim [of], "On Earth Peace Conference" is to clarify the issues that the Christian Church must face regarding violence with specific reference to war as a method of peace making; and to promote conferences by the Church of the Brethren in search for a better way to settle human conflicts.

This movement does not intend to solve all problems in this area of present day human living. It can do something in the Name of Christ thru the Church of the Brethren by endeavoring to implement the Message that came when Christ was born, "On earth Peace and Good Will Among Men."

[Organizational details follow, here omitted]

CONFERENCES PROPOSED:
>Historic Peace Churches and Methodist.
>Brethren Colleges, Religious Departments and Bethany Theological.
>Lawyer's Consultation.
>Ex Moderators and Ex Board Members.
>World Council of Churches [staff] who worked with me at Geneva.
>Rural Church Secretaries.
>National Interreligious Service Board members.
>Retired Members of the NCC Staff.
>Farmers Consultation.
>Doctors Consultation.
>Conferences when Doctor Potter WCC arrives.
>Orthodox Greek persons we worked with in Greece and in WCC.
>Father Ligutti Catholic Special Interviews.
>General Lewis B. Hershey Special Interviews.
>National Council of Churches Ex Secretaries.
>Ministers Church of the Brethren retired.
>Ministers Church of the Brethren active.

Results to be reported to the General Board through Ken McDowell

MEMBERSHIP: Enlarge the Membership

Office administration located at New Windsor, using the facility and the office administrative procedures and personnel when possible and by agreement.

[Signed:] M. R. Zigler[5]

The Goals and Budget Committee reviewed the petition and defined the conferences as self-supporting and "considered a special project beyond the current budget of the General Board." The committee approved the petition and recommended approval by the General Board, with the understanding that it would be related to the WMC through the office of Kenneth E. McDowell. The General Board did approve, limiting the initial budget to $30,000. S. Loren Bowman, general secretary of the board, communicated the action to leaders of the On Earth Peace Conference and asked for acceptance of the guidelines in order to have a "mutual working agreement."[6]

At the 1975 Annual Conference in Dayton, Ohio, at S. Loren Bowman's invitation, Byron Royer, M. R. Zigler, and Robert Greiner reported to the General Board on the program thus far, plans for the future, and state of the finances. There was some discussion but no action was taken.

Following Zigler's operational style, a steady barrage of written and telephoned communications directed at the church's leadership in Elgin marked this period. His interpretation was that they were dragging their feet; he was eager to have the green light to engage in more solicitation for a much expanded program in future years, which would include many conferences and extensive publications.

S. Loren Bowman, in several letters, tried to spell out the administrative channels for proceeding with the program. Zigler's committees would develop proposals, these would be transmitted through the staff liaison, Ken McDowell, and finally the General Board would make decisions. Bowman's letter in late September, 1975, revealed the frustration he felt after repeated attempts to clarify matters:

> My September 2 letter was an effort to put down as clearly and briefly as possible what I thought had been stated in conversations a number of times. I did this in response to your request and with the hope that you, Ken [McDowell for WMC] and Byron [Royer for OEPC] would deal with these operational matters and come up with mutually acceptable procedures. You just need to keep the two groups in communication with each other so that decisions do not come as surprises or as announced facts before proper clearances are made. I do not feel any of us are expecting perfection in each other but I certainly believe that it is possible to be brotherly in the presence of our failures.
>
> It would be my hope, however, that you would give some thought to the dilemma which we face when we assume certain outcomes in regard to proposals which have not yet been decided by the General Board. . . . I hope that you can put together a clear, concise proposal since the recent OEPC minutes do not put them in a form that is useful for commission or board consideration.[7]

In October, 1975, the WMC reaffirmed the February action of the Goals and Budget Committee and appointed a committee to develop objectives for and evaluation of the OEPC program, delaying the request for a $100,000 budget. A major meeting of staff and OEPC committee members in December, 1975, created a detailed statement of objectives and plans for future work. Zigler was not involved in these discussions, for he said that his presence would inhibit the participation of others. He privately indicated that he "deliberately played dead to see how the machinery would work." The statement was presented to the General Board in the spring of 1976.[8]

In the meantime, the OEPC organization was worked on by the several committees and meetings were held, but money was not raised because of the delay in authorization for this by the General Board and its staff. Elgin staff revealed apprehension that money solicited for this program would be lost to the broader program of the church. Zigler felt this delay keenly and expressed his frustration both privately and publicly.

Growing Tension

During the spring of 1976 tensions grew between Zigler and OEPC on the one hand and the Elgin staff on the other. From the OEPC perspective, they had worked patiently with the General Board through the Elgin staff, trying to relate their programs to the larger denominational program. They felt that the bureaucratic requirements of Elgin were bogging them down, that procedure preempted movement. From the Elgin perspective, Zigler and OEPC would not adhere to arrangements ironed out in lengthy and repeated negotiations. They found themselves giving endless hours to this problem to the detriment of their other work.

An indication of the strain was Elgin's reaction to the OEPC proposal, through regular channels, for time at the next Annual Conference in Wichita, Kansas, for holding meetings with those groups related to it. They particularly desired time for two breakfast meetings and two insight sessions.

The reply they received through Ken McDowell was that no space was available because WMC had received only four slots and these were all taken. They would need to restrict their activities to some informal meetings of eight/ten persons at mealtimes. The justification given was that "the Annual Conference event has become so complicated that very specific procedures have been adopted to limit the number of scheduled events and to give every program of the Board an opportunity for some Conference involvement." He recognized that M. R. would be disappointed, but noted that "none of us are able to get the kind of visibility we would hope to get for our own program" because of this "attempt to provide a balanced program." Also OEPC would not be permitted to report directly to the Board at Annual Conference, although the report from the joint committee was to be dealt with.[9]

Zigler responded in an acquiescent way and then detailed a series of meetings he thought essential for the several vocational groups developed by OEPC. Of particular concern was the group of Brethren theologians, who had begun a process to develop a unified statement on peace. These proposals brought an extremely stiff directive from McDowell, forbidding him to implement his plans for the meetings:

> Your letter would seem to plan for continuous OEPC involvement of persons -without regard for the conference program and this will not be permitted. If OEPC is truly a Board Program it must observe the same freedom and limitations that are shared by all programs. This means that you will not rent a separate room at Wichita for OEPC activities and you will not schedule persons or groups of persons in activities which will inhibit their participation in scheduled conference events.

A similar communication was received from S. Loren Bowman, suggesting that Zigler's planned program looked like "a small Annual Conference" itself.[10]

Proposed Resolution

After considerable discussion and staff work, the administrative staff of the General Board recommended that a full-time staff member (termed the "coordinator") assume responsibility for directing the OEPC program. The OEPC program was designated as a priority for the General Board for 1976-1977. This was subsequently approved by the board in their July, 1976, meeting. The intent of the move was to bring the OEPC program more completely under the Board program. Its funding would be totally integrated into the General Board budget, based on designated gifts for support of the program. The board asked Zigler to stay on as a volunteer member of the OEPC staff with the specific role of fund raiser. A goal of $60,000 was set for the 1977 financial year. The program itself would be directed by the staff coordinator, who, it was contemplated, would be located at New Windsor. This staff member would "maintain a close liaison linkage with the other peace and reconciliation programs and ministries . . . currently a part of WMC." Charles Boyer, formerly a BVS volunteer in Germany and later the Elgin staff worker responsible for the volunteer program, was appointed to the new position.

In a communication to S. Loren Bowman of August 5, 1976, M. R. Zigler indicated approval of the direction but asked that the action be presented to a meeting of the OEPC on September 25 for their approval. By suggesting that the Board action needed approval by the OEPC Assembly, the divided source of authority that had plagued the relationship of the OEPC to the church from the beginning, was extended. A letter by Ken McDowell of August 6, outlined the effect of the decision, pointedly stating that the "actual program will be designed by the new staff person within the guidelines" previously established and "in *consultation* with the OEP Assembly." [emphasis added][11]

S. Loren Bowman picked up the implications of Zigler's letter by pointing out that the Board action superseded any previous agreement. With the integration of the effort, OEPC became an additional component of the Board program on peace. "The Assembly will then need to determine its association with that program but it is not my understanding that the actions of the Board are dependent upon the ratification of the Assembly at its meeting." In effect the assembly would become a consultative and not an executive body.[12]

Charles Boyer clarified his proposed relationship with M. R. Zigler in a letter of November 24, 1976. Zigler would continue to hold the titles of founder and convener of the On Earth Peace Assembly. This entailed planning and hosting semi-annual assemblies, interpreting their meaning, and raising funds for the program. Boyer would act as the administrator, creating budgets, and serving as liaison with the General Board and its staff. He would stay in Elgin for the time being and make periodic trips to New Windsor. Correspondence flowing between New Windsor seemed to presage brighter and less turbulent times ahead.[13]

But that was not to happen. By the summer of 1977, Zigler resigned to protest what he thought were unfair financial decisions at Elgin. One problem had arisen when he accepted an invitation to attend the First World Congress on Religious Liberty, held in Amsterdam on March 21-23, 1977. When he reported his intention to go at his own expense to the OEPC business committee, they voted to cover his costs, in recognition of his donating his time to the program without salary. But this support was blocked by Charles Boyer. After Zigler's return from the trip, which he also used to visit Geneva, Linz, Vienna, Kassel, and Västervik, he commented: "I was not too disappointed that you vetoed it. The only thing that worries me is how you can authorize or veto decisions of the Assembly. . . . I will just live with it for I think that it is so important that the OEP Assembly can be a unit within the church and will have some jurisdiction over its program and finances."[14]

Finances proved to be a real bone of contention. It was Zigler's understanding that the OEPA program had about $30,000 on hand in the fall of 1976; added to this, he believed, was an additional $30,000 raised for the Brotherhood fund through the Elgin staff by a Christmas appeal in the name of On Earth Peace. Based on that assumption, he did no further fund raising in early 1977. An accounting from the treasurer's office in July, 1977, showed only $4,000 remaining for the program. Zigler understood that Boyer had discouraged his raising money for the 1978 program, but Boyer had the opposite opinion. Because of this situation, and because Boyer had committed some OEPA funds without consultation with the OEPA Business Committee, M. R. Zigler indicated in a letter of July 29, 1977, that he "should fade out of On Earth Peace in its total planning."[15]

To his surprise Charles Boyer took him up on this statement and accepted his resignation effective November 1, indicating that he may wish to leave New Windsor soon thereafter but could certainly remain until the first of the year. Zigler's response was to say that . . .

> . . . since December 20, 1974, I have been trying to prove that a minority group can be admitted into the establishment and nurtured as an autonomous entity, rather than organizing as an opposing outside body. You can understand how I feel when I desired to do something in my retirement worthy of the chance to live for the Church of the Brethren. Like a game, I lost and the loser must accept defeat always with a good spirit. I am not mad at anyone. The administration played a good game and won. The game is over and I hope that I can still come to Elgin as my church headquarters where I gave most of my life for which I am very grateful. I had hoped that as an old man I could die working hard for Peace on Earth which I think is the purpose of the Church of the Brethren among the churches.[16]

Not surprisingly, the On Earth Peace bodies did not accept his resignation and asked him to stay on. This he did, making for an anomalous situation. From the point of view of the Elgin staff, he had resigned; from the point of view of the OEPA groups, he remained as convener. Added to the perplexities were a siege of illness and a fall resulting in cracked ribs in January, 1978, which kept him out of action. A letter of February 15, 1978, to Charles Boyer indicated that he was nevertheless "ready to start over" and to raise funds for the On Earth Peace program. A response from Boyer indicated that their leadership styles were so different that they could hardly work well as a team yet also stated that Zigler should continue working with OEPA: "Please understand that I will not try to take away your role with the Assembly." So, with this uneasy *modus vivendi*, the program continued.[17]

OEPA Programs

During the entire time since the initial December, 1974, meeting, the New Windsor operation continued. Despite stormy administrative weather, the OEPA craft continued to float. The seventh On Earth Peace Assembly was held on March 31-April 1, 1978. Smaller meetings of vocational groups persisted, and of course, there were many regular meetings of the business and planning committees. One especially well-organized conference took place on December 19-20, 1978. This was a reunion of Brethren and other personnel who had worked with the World's YMCA in prisoner of war aid during and after World War II. This extensive program had moved beyond material aid to include innovative educational projects, care for families, and spiritual counsel. The proceedings of the conference, which were published, provide a substantial record of this significant chapter in social action.[18]

Later Projects and Developments of On Earth Peace

A bookstore located at New Windsor was decided upon in the summer of 1980 and was operational by November 1. This built on early OEPA success in sponsoring peace-related publications. The most extensive was the documentation of peace discussions held among the Historic Peace Churches after 1935 and also between them and European church leaders after 1955. The book, entitled *On Earth Peace* was published in 1978 by Brethren Press, aided by a subsidy from Dan Raffensperger, former BVS volunteer in Europe and a Zigler supporter. Another volume was a reprint, with a new index, of the classic diary of John Kline, nineteenth century Brethren leader and Civil War martyr. An earlier volume, not directly sponsored by OEPA, was a collection of memoirs of Brethren Service workers in Europe, especially those who were first on the field. Five chapters taken from the unpublished personal history of Brethren Service by M. R. Zigler provided the framework for the recollections. The book, *To Serve the Present Age: The Brethren Service Story* (1975), was also subsidized by Dan Raffensperger.[19]

Zigler had over the years displayed great interest in and concern for the youth of the church. His constant cry had been for a vision of the church for the next thirty years, not as it is but as it should be to serve the coming generations. Therefore, it was entirely in keeping that he shepherded the OEPA movement toward the initiation of weekend retreats held each month, designed to assist young people to think through their attitude toward government and their position on military service. The first such *Academy*, as the weekend came to be called, was held on August 6-8, 1982. Although the monthly pattern has not been held to with complete consistency, since that time virtually every month has seen a gathering of young people with adult resource leaders who have expertise on peace issues. Latterly, some of the academies have been held in the West, Midwest, South, and East, but most have been sited at New Windsor.

In 1981, under the new administration of Robert W. Neff as general secretary at Elgin, a new relationship between the Church of the Brethren and On Earth Peace was established. Neff recommended that OEPA achieve separate incorporation, which was accomplished on August 1, 1981. Subsequently, IRS recognition was obtained, which allowed tax-exempt contributions to be made. The understanding was that OEPA should remain related to the World Ministries Commission but should raise and spend its own funds. This new approach seemed to augur well; in 1982 the donations to the program went over $100,000. However, Zigler and his associates were not content with a separate existence.

A New Relationship

In 1982, OEPA approached the Standing Committee of Annual Conference asking for recognition "as an organization which is related to the Church of the Brethren with permission to solicit funds among churches and church members for the support of its current and future programs." The statement made to the Standing Committee gave its background and present program. In the discussion, an unusual number of Elgin staff members, including Fred Swartz, Ralph McFadden, and Charles Boyer, apparently by prior agreement, urged Standing Committee to reject the appeal; Stewart Kauffman, from the Stewardship Enlistment Team, also spoke on the issue from the floor.

A major concern was OEPA's request for permission to solicit funds. This has always been a neuralgic point for the staff, made responsible as they are for raising a multi-million dollar budget. Another was the problem of duplicate efforts for peace within a small denomination. The Standing Committee directed the General Board and the OEPA Board to find a way of working together. The result was a cooperative arrangement looking toward full integration. An oversight committee, appointed by the Annual Conference, was organized to assist in a complete integration into the program of the General Board, under the WMC. In 1983 M. R. Zigler officially stepped down as OEPA leader, and Harold D. Smith, a university professor who had been vitally connected with the movement from the earliest days, was named as the executive. In January 1984 David Eberly became the coordinator of the Peace Academy. Volunteers assisted throughout with the OEPA program, especially including Linda Logan, Ruth Early, Ida S. Howell, Hazel Peters, David Braune and others.

In the fall of 1984, the On Earth Peace movement looked back over ten years of effort. The gross budget for the year was over $200,000. Despite the administrative tumult, it had sponsored some twenty-eight major assemblies and scores of smaller meetings; more importantly, it had stimulated the peace concern of the Brethren. Thousands had been touched by Zigler's dream of a more peaceful world, with the Christian churches in the vanguard. He, for one, thought the labors and sorrows had been worth it.

Also noteworthy is the fact that M. R. Zigler remained basically supportive of the Elgin staff, however difficult he was to work with. One of his early partisans was C. Wayne Zunkel, a pastor in Pennsylvania. He often spoke with Zigler on the latter's journeys to that part of the country. Of this time, Zunkel wrote: "The picture I got from those long talks in his small hotel room was one of a thoroughly dedicated man, in love with his denomination, yet outside the structure. Frustrated by the dreams he had which were not shared by those in power, yet *always he tried to work within the structure*. And never did I hear him badmouthing those in power. They saw him as a threat and a thorn in their flesh, yet to me he was always supportive of them." [emphasis in original][20]

Beyond the organizational difficulties and tensions, the fact remains that Zigler was able to convey to others his passion for the peace message. He reached out well beyond denominational borders in doing this. A testimony in this regard is given by Presbyterian elder and former Army officer, Joseph B. Yount III, who had worked with Zigler on the Tunker House. He recalls an episode with M. R. Zigler when the latter was passing through Yount's hometown of Waynesboro, Virginia. Yount spent an hour in a local hotel hearing Zigler's vision of On Earth Peace: "Let's just suppose that Jesus were to come right now and say, 'Peace! Peace!' No committees, no discussions, just peace. What a vision!" Admitting that he was not in total agreement with the Brethren peace witness, Yount yet stated that he had felt his "conscience moved on a regular basis ever since that conversation" and that he could truthfully say that "that hour in the hotel struck my conscience as thoroughly as any sermon I ever heard anywhere in the world."[21]

NOTES

1. Million transcript of M. R. Zigler, 9/3-19; M. R. Zigler, "Report No. 1," New Windsor, n.d.
2. Zigler, "Report No. 1."
3. Ralph E. Smeltzer to Joel K. Thompson, Nov. 6, 1974; Smeltzer to H. McKinley Coffman and D. Miller Davis, Nov. 6, 1974; Smeltzer to Thompson, Dec. 23, 1974.
4. W. Newton Long to Bob [Zigler], Dec. 24, 1974.
5. On Earth Peace Conference to Church of the Brethren General Board, Petition for Authorization, Jan. 24, 1975; see also "New Windsor Setting for On Earth Peace Kickoff," *Messenger* (May, 1975): 5.
6. S. Loren Bowman to Byron Royer, Feb. 26, 1975.
7. S. Loren Bowman to M. R. Zigler, Sept. 22, 1975.
8. M. R. Zigler to Harold Smith, March 29, 1976.
9. Kenneth E. McDowell to Ida Howell, March 1, 1976.
10. McDowell to Zigler, June 3, 1976; Bowman to Zigler, June 7, 1976.
11. McDowell to Zigler, August 6, 1976.
12. Bowman to Zigler, Aug. 24, 1976.
13. Charles L. Boyer to M. R. Zigler, Nov. 24, 1976; see also Kermon Thomasson, "Who'll Work on Larry?" *Messenger* (December, 1976): 44.
14. Zigler to Boyer, April 6, 1977.
15. Zigler to Boyer, July 29, 1977.
16. Zigler to Bowman, Sept. 20, 1977.
17. Zigler to Boyer, Feb. 15, 1978; Boyer to Zigler, Feb. 21, 1978.
18. *Brethren Life and Thought*, 26 (1981): 71-121, special issue.
19. D. F. Durnbaugh, ed., *On Earth Peace: Discussions on War/Peace Issues Between Friends, Mennonites, Brethren and European Churches, 1935-1975* (Elgin, IL: Brethren Press, 1978); Benjamin Funk, ed., *Life and Labors of Elder John Kline, The Martyr Missionary* (Elgin, IL: Brethren Press, 1976), reprint of the 1900 original, with index compiled by Edith Bonsack Barnes. (Zigler had raised the money for another reprint of the Kline diary in 1964, the centennial of Kline's assassination.) D. F. Durnbaugh, ed., *To Serve the Present Age: The Brethren Service Story* (Elgin, IL: Brethren Press, 1975).
20. C. Wayne Zunkel to D. F. Durnbaugh, April 15, 1987.
21. Joseph B. Yount III to D. F. Durnbaugh, Dec. 2, 1987; Yount to Geraldine Glick, Dec. 12, 1985.

23

ECUMENICAL RELATIONSHIPS

MORE THAN ANY OTHER person, M. R. Zigler led the Church of the Brethren into ecumenical relationships. He was not the only one, certainly, but he was the main figure. It was therefore quite appropriate that when the first Brethren ecumenical award was given in June, 1980, he was the recipient. But Zigler was also called "Mr. Brethren" and he merited that title, too, because he always linked his strong passion for cooperative relationships with a devotion to his own church.[1]

In the last two decades of his life, he pursued his ecumenical cause with three main foci: the first was inter-Brethren relationships; the second was Historic Peace Church relationships; and the third was the world-wide church relationships. It was part of his genius that he understood that he could only be a good member of the Brethren faith as he invested himself in the activities of sister peace churches and beyond that to the broader church.

Brethren Bodies

One aspect of his ecumenical posture became very evident in the last phase of his life. It was his commitment to work for reconciliation among the divided churches stemming from the original Brethren movement in Schwarzenau, Germany. His first major encounter with all of the "divided brethren" came during his work with conscientious objectors during World War II. At that time representatives of the five larger Brethren bodies often looked to him for counsel and practical assistance. The five groups were his own Church of the Brethren, the Brethren Church

(Ashland, Ohio), the Old German Baptist Brethren ("Old Orders"), the small Dunkard Brethren, and the recently formed Grace Brethren (National Fellowship of Grace Brethren Churches), which emerged in 1939 as a fundamentalist branch of the Brethren Church.

He had enjoyed warm contacts with members of the Brethren Church who pursued talks on unity with the Church of the Brethren in the 1930s and 1940s. Unfortunately, these conversations on merger with some of the leaders of the Ashland group helped, in ironic fashion, to precipitate the bitter division resulting in the Grace Brethren movement. Leaders of the Grace element considered such contact with the Church of the Brethren clear evidence of unwholesome tendencies toward theological liberalism.

This notwithstanding, in later years Zigler attempted to keep lines of communication open with Dr. Alva McClain, the respected theologian of the Grace Brethren, who he had met through the CO work. At one point, Dr. McClain had arranged for an European trip and had planned to travel to Schwarzenau together with Zigler. The McClains did not show up at the appointed time. Zigler later learned that they were about to leave their home in Winona Lake, Indiana, to undertake their trip to Europe when Dr. McClain suffered a debilitating stroke. Years later, when Zigler was traveling through Winona Lake, he contacted the McClain residence to try to make an appointment, only to hear from Mrs. McClain that her husband was ill and could see no one. Overhearing the conversation, McClain ascertained who the caller was and insisted that Zigler come over despite his own weak state. In the long conversation that ensued, McClain expressed his conviction to Zigler that division in the church was wrong.[2]

During the war years Zigler became especially close to Elder Jacob W. Skiles of the Old German Baptist Brethren, who had been named by that church as responsible for counseling their young men of draft age. Skiles was so respected among the Old Order Brethren that he was named the moderator of their Yearly Meeting twelve times. Elder Skiles wrote Zigler in late 1963 at the age of eighty-eight that he had immediately felt a "special closeness" to him when they first met in Zigler's office in Elgin in 1940. He reported that he had told his people many times that "M. R. Zigler did more for the Old German Baptist Brethren on the C.O. work than other person." He recalled a later incident when they met in the train depot in Chicago as Zigler returned from an investigative trip on conditions in postwar Europe. Skiles had repeated often what Zigler had told him on that occasion: "There will be more people die in Europe this winter from starvation and freezing than were killed in the war."[3]

290

Two-and-a-half years later Elder Skiles recalled their meeting again "when I first met you and learned to dearly love you." He had noted that Zigler was slated to speak at the Annual Conference meeting in Louisville, Kentucky, and that church union was a major item on the business agenda. He hoped that the Church of the Brethren would not vote for such a merger, because "too much of the doctrines of Dunkerism would need to be sacrificed." At the age of ninety, he noted that he was one of the few yet living who recalled when all of the Brethren groups worshiped together, that is prior to the divisions of 1881-1883 and afterwards. Zigler deeply appreciated the warmth of this expression; he pinned a note on the Skiles letter stating "I would not take a hundred dollars for this letter from Jacob Skiles of the German Baptist Brethren. M. R. Z."[4]

The Tunker House Meeting

Zigler was not content with nostalgia, although he often relived those hectic but glorious days of World War II. He had the idea of visiting leaders of all of the five Brethren bodies to see if they would be willing to come together simply to "shake hands." As with the onset of the On Earth Peace movement, he gave credit for the inception of the idea to a conversation with W. Newton Long of Baltimore. The Church of the Brethren layman said that he would contribute $1,000 to make it possible.

As time went on the idea evolved, through conversations with Rev. Samuel D. Lindsay, to sponsor a meeting at the venerable Tunker House in Broadway, Virginia. The ancestral home of M. R. Zigler, it had been previously been the residence of a leading Brethren family in the valley of Virginia, the Younts, and then of Peter Nead, outstanding Brethren writer/theologian of the nineteenth century, who had married into the Yount family. Sam and Pauline Lindsay, the new owners of the handsome brick building, had restored it, and secured its status as an historic landmark by both state and national registers.

Sam Lindsay had invited Zigler to give a week-long series of talks at the Tunker House in July, 1972. He was asked to speak of his childhood memories of life at this his birthplace, of the church leaders he had known, of his father, family, and relatives. The gatherings were well-attended and well-received. The talks were recorded and published by Joseph B. Yount III, a descendant of the family that had first used the house. The compilation is one of the best sources of the influences upon Zigler as a youth.[5]

Zigler decided to try to implement Long's idea. The method of this octogenarian was to buy a Greyhound bus ticket, valid for unlimited travel for several weeks, and set off to track down influential figures from each of the bodies to invite them to such a meeting. The Old German Baptist Brethren were most reluctant to promise to come, but he did secure a commitment from an Old Order printer/historian, Fred W. Benedict, to prepare a paper on Peter Nead. Zigler scheduled the meeting at Broadway just after the Old Order Yearly Meeting was to conclude in Virginia, hoping that a number of leaders would come. He invited certain categories from each of the groups—moderator, editor of the church publication, historians and writers, and other interested parties. When it seemed that there was enough certainty that the meeting could be held, Zigler made another swing by bus to develop the program.

The meeting, in fact, did take place at Broadway on June 12-13, 1973, and proved to be historic. Not only was it the first public meeting with attendance (on an informal basis) from all five Brethren bodies, it also started a movement. The shared heritage interest, fellowship, and worship together evoked a warm spirit of friendliness. Many of those attending expressed the wish for additional meetings.[6]

Dr. Joseph R. Shultz, president of Ashland Theological Seminary, invited a number of historians and writers who took lunch together on the second day of the meeting to a meeting at his institution sometime in the following year. This became a reality with a small working conference in April, 1974, on the theme of Brethren history in the post-Revolutionary War period, the so-called "Wilderness period." The Ashland meeting was followed by a conference at Bethany Theological Seminary in May, 1976; in deference to the bicentennial year, this meeting had as its theme the Brethren experience during the Revolutionary era. These historically-oriented meetings were to continue, at irregular intervals, in the following years, as were somewhat larger assemblies of persons from the five Brethren groups.[7]

At the May, 1976, meeting, M. R. Zigler captivated those present with his assessment of Brethren pluralism as the result of the failure to apply the reconciling method of Matthew 18 to church division. In his spontaneous way, he threw out a series of challenges to the groups for greater cooperation. One was that those assembled should work together to gather a large series of historical sources. He said: "Pick up all the rubbish, all the good, and everything everybody can think about in all our Brethren bodies, any little incident and put it in there and index it so if anybody wants to know about a person or an incident, there it is." He gave as examples:

292

"How did we lose the communion, even though we participated in it. . . . Where did we slip? What do the baptismal vows mean?" Each body would produce their own book and out of that "we would probably get a superior one." He suggested that the librarians would be the people to supervise these collections, which would need to be extensive.

This idea did not find great reception among the group, who said that something like an encyclopedia would be better. Out of this discussion, Don Durnbaugh drafted a proposal for a Brethren encyclopedia and circulated it to those attending the meeting. Soon after the Bethany meeting the Brethren Historical Committee met and endorsed the idea in principle. Zigler was soon convinced that this format, which he had at first resisted, would answer the need he had felt and began to promote the concept. In time he came to believe that he was the first to suggest the encyclopedia idea.[8]

At a meeting of the Brethren bodies in New Windsor, Maryland, in December, 1976, with a focus on peace, the encyclopedia was suggested as one way in which the peace message could be carried. It was agreed that another meeting should be held to examine the concept. This took place on July 23, 1977, in the meetinghouse of the first American congregation of the Brethren, at Germantown, now part of Philadelphia. The spirit of the meeting was warm and fraternal; periods of worship were intense and deep. Zigler wrote of it:

> Those representatives present at the meeting will always remember the spirit of the occasion and . . . each one will say the deeper meaning of this day can never be given to others fully by the written word. . . . We first toured the cemetery where our founders rest. Then we learned our names together, we prayed together, and we decided to work together creating an encyclopedia in honor of our forefathers since Schwarzenau. As I send this report to you, I hope you are filled with as much joy as I seem to possess. I know that I love the Church of the Brethren greatly but somehow . . . in my heart and mind, I feel a superior love that we recognize religious liberty to be in five bodies and at the same time, we love the total Brethren family."[9]

Two meetings yet that year completed plans for the undertaking: a conference of writers and historians at Covington, Ohio, on October 21-22 agreed on format, content, and scope; then a smaller group meeting at New Windsor, Maryland, on December 17 arranged for the incorporation of The Brethren Encyclopedia with a board of directors.[10]

Thus it was that a significant effort began which resulted in the production and publication in 1983-1984 of a three-volume encyclopedia on all phases of Brethren belief, life, and practice. Zigler played a key role in the project by acting as convener of the earlier meetings and principally by spearheading the fund raising for the undertaking. Ronald G. Lutz, community worker at Germantown, was his chief lieutenant on finances and publicity. Eventually the targeted amount of $150,000 was raised to cover the costs of producing the manuscript and printing the first volumes. Receipts from sales were allowed to accumulate in order to finance related publications. It was with great delight that the venerable church leader could hold the finished volumes. He had feared that he would die before the complicated project could be completed.[11]

Zigler rightly pointed out that the success of achieving cooperation between members of these separated bodies (all of whom had backgrounds of mutual distance or even strain and antipathy) for such a project was as significant as the actual project. Admittedly, the enterprise had, for the most part, to be carried on by individuals rather than church bodies. At that, the Brethren Church and the Dunkard Brethren officially committed themselves to cooperation. The largest single gift came to the project from the General Services Commission of the Church of the Brethren, which would have officially endorsed the project if it had been asked to do so; this did not happen in deference to the feelings of the other, smaller bodies. Officers of several Annual Conferences of the Church of the Brethren allowed members of the Board of Directors of the Encyclopedia project to present reports of the progress of the publication.

Judging from numerous comments made by Zigler about the success of this effort, this provided him with the happiest moments of his waning years. He garnered appropriate praise for his pioneering achievements in initiating the project. It was therefore fitting that the cover of the *Messenger* containing his obituary article depicted him scanning the completed volumes of the encyclopedia.[12]

Historic Peace Churches

A bright thread throughout the tapestry of Zigler's career had been his association with the Mennonites and Quakers. He acknowledged freely his indebtedness to the American Friends Service Committee as a pattern for the work of the Brethren Service Committee. Over the years he kept in contact by periodic letters and visits with such Friends as Algie Newlin (with whom he had worked in Geneva), E. Raymond Wilson (a co-worker on CPS), Eric Tucker (of the English Friends), and others.

His closest and dearest friend was Orie O. Miller, head of the Mennonite Central Committee, who died on January 10, 1977; Zigler visited this leading layman as often as he could, even when Miller's faltering health prevented direct discourse. He attended Miller's memorial service in Akron, Pennsylvania, on January 15 and testified: "Orie and I represented Mennonites and Brethren for many years. Out of our fellowship, planning, and administrating two programs, I feel we've found a way for churches to work together without organic union, each one enjoying religious freedom." On another occasion he told of the picture of Miller and himself published in Miller's biography, calling it "the highest compliment" he knew of "in ecumenical history" to have a Brethren pictured "along with a Mennonite in a Mennonite book." Zigler also felt very close to Miller's successor at MCC, William T. Snyder. Other Mennonite colleagues included Robert Kreider, Henry Fast, Peter Dyck, and three younger men, Paul Peachey, John H. Yoder and Albert J. Meyer, who had worked so effectively with the series of Puidoux theological conferences.[13]

It is therefore not surprising that in the context of the On Earth Peace program Zigler should turn again to the Historic Peace Churches as participants in the first of the proposed conferences. After beginning the program in late 1974 he attempted to call together many of these friends in late January in New Windsor to discuss, in his words, "how we can eliminate war a method for peacemaking." Because of the illness of several of those invited, this had to be postponed until May 7-8. As the program emerged, it took as its focus the shared experiences of the Historic Peace Churches beginning in the 1930s, with especial attention to the CPS experiment in church/state relations and its implications for the present and future.[14]

Those attending divided basically into two categories, the "elder statesmen," and the younger participants currently active in peace work. In the first category were Zigler himself and L. W. Shultz (Brethren), E. Raymond Wilson (Friends), and Robert S. Kreider and Henry A. Fast (Mennonite)—Orie O. Miller's health did not permit him to attend. In the second category were Charles Boyer, Joel K. Thompson, Warren W. Hoover, J. Kenneth Kreider, Kenneth E. McDowell (Brethren), Stephen C. Cary (Friends), and Albert N Keim, Ted Koontz, William T. Snyder (Mennonites). Also attending were Herman Will, United Methodist executive concerned with peace matters and Lois Teach Paul from the communications office at Elgin. The wide-ranging discussion looked primarily at the way the past cooperative experience could be used effectively to engage current problems. Those attending agreed that the three churches/service agencies should work more closely together; this took the form of reviving the Continuation Committee of the peace churches, which had not been active for some years. One tangible result was the decision to send a joint letter to President Gerald Ford urging amnesty for those US citizens "still alienated from their country because of their opposition to the Vietnamese war." It was signed by Louis W. Schneider (AFSC), William T. Snyder (MCC) and Joel K. Thompson (WMC), as executives for their three churches.[15]

Building on this was a somewhat larger meeting on "Church-State Conversations on Peace and War," organized by the National Interreligious Service Board for Conscientious Objectors and OEPC. This was held at New Windsor on August 8-9, 1975. Members of the Historic Peace Churches and the Fellowship of Reconciliation attended; the major theme of the conference was again learnings from the CPS experience. Gen. Lewis B. Hershey, longtime head of the Selective Service System for the US government, now retired, the featured speaker, reflected on his past relations with the peace churches and the issues of war and peace. Zigler was quite proud of a letter of appreciation that Hershey sent after the conference, in which he wrote, in part: "I count it a high privilege to have been invited to New Windsor on last Friday. . . . The opportunity to see the establishment in New Windsor was an experience I shall never forget. . . . Everyone was most gracious. . . ."[16]

Meeting of World Leaders of the Peace Churches

In January, 1976, the Friends World Committee for Consultation used the New Windsor facilities for a meeting. M. R. Zigler was given the opportunity to recount to them his vision of the On Earth Peace movement. Having also just returned from the WCC World Assembly in Nairobi, Kenya, where peace concerns were given a favorable hearing, he thought the time was ripe for an Historic Peace Church meeting on a world level. He approached the general secretary of the Friends World Committee, William Barton, who expressed openness to such a meeting during his stay in the USA. Through MCC contacts, Zigler found that Paul Kraybill, of the metropolitan Chicago area, was the person responsible for Mennonite world cooperation. Kraybill was willing and able to meet with Barton in late January.

As the Brethren did not have a world organization, Zigler took the line that the Committee on Interchurch Relations (CIR) and the moderator of the Annual Conference represented the Brethren equivalent. He therefore seized the initiative to call DeWitt Miller of the CIR and A. Blair Helman, current moderator, to a meeting in New York, which took place at the Friends House on January 28, 1976.

Zigler realized that this undertaking might be viewed dimly by S. Loren Bowman, general secretary for the Church of the Brethren, whose task it was to coordinate Brethren ecumenical relationships. He therefore described the plans in a letter to Bowman, explaining that the short time the Quaker leader had left in his American stay necessitated the precipitate planning. Bowman replied in a long letter of January 20, explaining the ongoing activities of the Elgin staff with the other peace churches, based on the 1968 Annual Conference statement on conciliar relations. While agreeing that the moderator of Annual Conference had the freedom to consult with other religious leaders, he was concerned that "we will not enhance our WCC and our HPC relationships unless we keep clear the signals and structures of our various groups."[17]

The fact was that Zigler had long dreamed of establishing a Continuation Committee of the Historic Peace Churches on a world level, much as he had been instrumental in doing on a European level during his Geneva years. He saw this as a way to advance the peace cause in the world arena. Even if nothing more developed, it would be worth it to come together as world representatives of the peace churches. "Surely I know that I would [be] watched or checked and maybe rebuked. But that I can't help. I would not have felt good the rest of my life to have failed this opportunity. I deeply feel that 'hunches' like this, the voice of the infinate [*sic*] and how could you stay still." This was vintage M. R. Zigler—seizing the opportunity to push the cooperative peace effort forward, following his inspirations, running ahead of church machinery but still trying to gain approval.[18]

DeWitt L. Miller wrote a perceptive account summing up the meeting's discussion, which deserves quotation. It sums up a great deal of the history of the peace church relationships after 1945:

1. Since World War II, for the most part, the historic peace churches have gone their separate ways: the Friends taking the political route as illustrated by the work of the Quaker House at the United Nations; the Church of the Brethren taking the ecumenical route in cooperation with the National and World Council of Churches; the Mennonites turning to their own cluster of

denominations as the channel through which they make their witness.

2. The growing amount of violence at every level of our corporate life which demands the attention of all who believe in a non-violent approach. (It was pointed out with both satisfaction and humility that the World Council of Churches at its meeting in Nairobi last December gave voice to its concern about the problem of disarmament and violence and instructed the Central Committee to make it one of the top priorities in the coming years. The Central Committee was instructed to "Share the experience of the Historic Peace Churches.") The general consensus was that we should let the Central Committee know that we are eager to be helpful but more importantly should step up our efforts to create more of an awareness of the problem and motivate our respective groups to a sense of mission regarding non-violence and peace.

3. Our mode of operation has changed since World War II days. Partly from necessity and partly because that was largely the way it was done then the cooperat[iv]e activities of the three historic peace churches originated with and revolved around such charismatic personalities as E. Raymond Wilson, Paul Comley French, Orie Miller and M. R. Zigler. Now the peace activities have been integrated into the ongoing and continuing structures of the church. Unfortunately, all too many, at least at the grass roots, are unaware of the many things that are being done unilaterally and cooperatively for the cause of peace. . . .[19]

Although the meeting recognized that it had but an informal character, Zigler hoped against hope that it could continue as an ongoing body. He urged Loren Bowman to move forward with the concept of a world consultation of Historic Peace Churches. However, Bowman pointed out that the Committee on Interchurch Relations was not authorized to pursue such conversations, and that affiliation with a world body would need to be agreed to by the Annual Conference. He made it clear that he would not press forward with Zigler's idea: "I don't think there is any particular value in our continuing our conversations regarding the structures which set forth our ecumenical work."[20]

Zigler could not let the matter rest and tried again typing a letter to Bowman—at 3:00 A.M. :

I thought of our recent correspondence about the potential emerging global encounter of the Historic Peace Churches. . . . I fear that this potential can drop into oblivion if the fire spark is not kindled into flame. I pray that the Brethren will take the lead and unite for one of the greatest efforts we have ever made for united action on the part of our three Historic Peace Churches. Your last letter was not the Loren Bowman production. . . . The last one gave me a sinking feeling that I can't leave without treatment and therefore I felt I should get up and write.[21]

It was a classic example of the kind of conflict which Zigler was continually creating: we see a charismatic figure moving forward to pursue his visions, hardly able to explain them coherently, pushing ahead of the structures to try to initiate new ones; in the process, he ran athwart of conscientious executives, attempting to operate the church's programs in clear and careful ways according to agreed procedures.

Newton, Kansas, and the New Call

The next chapter in Historic Peace Church activity was a meeting at (General Conference Mennonite) Bethel College in Newton, Kansas, to commemorate the landmark conference held there some forty years previously. It is possible that the OEPC meeting of peace church leaders of May, 1975, stimulated the call for the conference, which brought together eighty-five Friends, Mennonites, and Brethren for the day-long consultation on April 10, 1976. Robert Kreider, of the college faculty, interpreted the meaning of the 1935 conference in the perspective of 1976, pointing out that the meeting enabled the three churches to close ranks and prepare for the onslaught of World War II, then already visible on the horizon. Zigler attended the session but did not play a leading role. The meeting, and the articles spun off from it, helped to lay the foundation for a major new cooperative effort, the *New Call to Peacemaking*.[22]

M. R. Zigler clearly gave the impetus for this new movement, when he spoke to Friends at New Windsor in January, 1976. The chief mover in beginning the New Call was Loren G. Heusel, Friends United Meeting executive. In inviting a number of peace church leaders to a meeting at the William Penn House in Washington, D. C., on May 9, he recalled that Zigler's testimony had "deeply moved" the Friends present. "He felt a special burden that the Peace Churches should become prepared to speak with a united voice at the next World Council of Churches Assembly."[23]

The session was called in connection with the third annual Historic Peace Churches Seminar in Washington, D. C., sponsored jointly by the Washington offices of the three bodies. Heusel later wrote to Zigler, thanking him for his "kind notes from time to time." He added:

I recall so clearly those memorable days at New Windsor and my brief though meaningful visits with you. I remember your top form as you shared your

299

observations about the Nairobi Assembly, your assessment of the peace
movement in relation to the churches and your prophetic call to the peace
churches to get ready for the next assembly. I have no doubt whatsoever but
that it was your vision and fervor which created the contagion that finally
spawned the New Call.[24]

A follow-up meeting of the three groups in early July at Elgin agreed
to undertake the New Call to Peacemaking; planners envisioned a large
number of regional conferences culminating in a national gathering in the
fall of 1978. This all took place and resulted in definite quickening of
peace activity and a warming of relationships between many members of
the Historic Peace Churches. After several national conferences the New
Call to Peacemaking extended its interests to the broader sway of denominations with growing peace concerns, including members of the United
Church of Christ, Presbyterians, Roman Catholics, and Southern Baptists.[25]

Consultation on Church Union

The action of the delegates of the Church of the Brethren Annual
Conference in 1966 to remain in its role of observer-consultant to the
Consultation on Church Union rather than to become full participants, was
one of the church's landmark decisions of the twentieth century. No
decision was more thoroughly discussed, more intensely debated, or more
controversial. Many of the leaders of the church thought it marked a retreat
from the ecumenical posture that the church had taken since 1941 and the
decision to enter the Federal Council of Churches.[26]

For all of Zigler's dedication to the conciliar movement, he was
opposed to any action which would have as its outcome the demise of the
denomination. When the COCU proposal was first broached at the 1965
annual conference, he gathered a group of people together at a late night
session. According to one participant, "he shared very fervently about
what the Church of the Brethren meant to him and he felt its continued
existence was essential." Zigler feared that the peace witness of the
Brethren would be lost if were "swallowed up by some mega denomination." Evidently, his position influenced some of those present to move
toward a position which opposed full involvement in the move toward
merger.[27]

Many close friends, such as Harry K. Zeller, Jr., prominent Brethren
pastor, differed strongly on this issue. Some, such as Zeller, believed that

the Brethren were retreating into sectarian isolation. For this and some other reasons, Zeller left the pastoral ministry to become an administrator of a retirement home.[28]

World Council of Churches

M. R. Zigler had attended every World Council of Churches Assembly except Uppsala in 1968. He was eager to attend the Fifth, planned for Nairobi, Kenya, in December, 1975. He therefore wrote to Dr. Philip Potter, WCC general secretary, asking if he could come as a visitor at his own expense. Potter wrote a gracious letter of response, recalling the "happy days in Geneva" when Zigler "represented the Church of the Brethren." He gave permission for attendance as a visitor and sent instructions for necessary steps. Zigler wrote S. Loren Bowman asking for advice about attending the ecumenical gathering. While not advising him not to plan to attend, a list of considerations Bowman suggested had the effect of discouraging attendance. Zigler decided to go anyway, despite some apprehension about traveling alone at the age of 84, and thoroughly enjoyed it.[29]

He seems to have been the oldest person in attendance; a striking photograph exists showing him together with another WCC patriarch, secretary general emeritus W. A. Visser 't Hooft. Zigler took a day from the proceedings to travel with Brethren journalist Howard E. Royer to Mombasa, on the Kenyan coast; the purpose of the trip was to visit the grave of J. H. B. Williams, whose associate he had been in Elgin when he began church work in 1919. Williams had died in Africa in the course of a world trip to investigate areas for new missionary endeavors.[30]

M. R. Zigler was particularly gratified by the WCC Assembly when it placed high priority on the issues of militarism and war. Assembly participants called on the Central Committee to convene a consultation with the goal of reducing the worldwide burden of armaments. A strategy to accomplish this should specifically include sharing the "experience of the Historic Peace Churches." In the debate which produced this resolution, Wanda Will Button, one of the two official Brethren delegates, made a persuasive speech that some observers found to be influential in reaching this conclusion. M. R. Zigler stated that the specific mention of the Historic Peace Churches in the WCC assembly was a first. His long and lonely campaign within the ecumenical movement for greater attention to peace issues was finally bearing fruit. In a letter from Nairobi, he reported:

"It is great to represent OEPC here. The Historic Peace Churches are being recognized more than at other meetings."[31]

The Historic Peace Churches and the IFOR carried on a series of programs as a satellite to the main Assembly program, attracting a large number of delegates, observers, and staff members. Among these were Martin Niemoeller, of Confessing Church fame, and Emilio Castro, WCC staff member and later general secretary. One result of attendance at the Nairobi meeting was that thereafter Zigler pursued cooperation with the American FOR more than previously been the case, working closely with Richard Deats, director of interfaith activities. He was then asked to accept election as a member of the National Advisory Council for the FOR; the executive director stated that it would be an honor for the organization to have his name among other "distinguished members of the board." Zigler accepted although he admitted that he would not be in a position to be very active.[32]

It was not surprising, given this experience, that Zigler angled once again for an invitation to Vancouver, Canada, the projected site for the Sixth World Assembly of the WCC, scheduled for the summer of 1983. In June, 1982, he began writing to WCC leader Philip Potter, asking for an invitation. Potter replied warmly in late August: "I was very touched by your letter of August 24. It brought vivid memories of the years we spent together in Geneva in the fifties. You were always a father to us and my wife remembers particularly the time when you took us for a drive during the Central Committee at Davos in 1955." However, he did not mention the invitation, leading to another request by Zigler in November. He pointed out that he had made arrangements for travel and accommodations but had not yet received clearance. If that were not forthcoming, he would make other plans for that time. He rather poignantly pointed out that he would be ninety-two by the time of the Vancouver conference, and would be ninety-nine if he attended the next one, but felt "very strong" currently.[33]

The invitation did come through, and Zigler did attend and was feted as the oldest person present. He was quoted in the conference newspaper as stating that Nairobi had been a highlight because of the increased presence of the Third World; it meant for him that "while every denomination has a tribal mark, truth breaks out in all languages." He expressed pleasure at the growing importance of peace in the WCC, repeating his old refrain: "If Christians will not participate in war, we can end that type of violence," adding, "Everybody has a pet and mine is peace."[34]

It was to be the last great ecumenical assemblage that he was able to attend. From this time on, physical problems would increasingly hamper his activities.

NOTES

1. *Messenger* (September, 1980): 7.
2. Dale V. Ulrich interview with M. R. Zigler, April, 1984.
3. J. W. Skiles to M. R. Zigler, Dec. 12, 1963. There are many references to Zigler in Skile's autobiographical "Diary of C. O. Labors of Elder Jacob W. Skiles, 1917-1962," (1973), mimeographed.
4. J. W. Skiles to M. R. Zigler, June 3, 1966.
5. Joseph B. Yount III, ed., *Tunker House Proceedings, 1972* (Waynesboro, VA: author, 1973). See also Joseph B. Yount III, "The Tunker House at Broadway, Rockingham County, Virginia," *Brethren Life and Thought*, 33 (Spring, 1988): 112-121.
6. "Brethren Meet for First Time in Century," [Harrisonburg, VA] *Daily News-Record* (June 14, 1973); "Brethren Meeting Results in 'Friendship,'" [Harrisonburg, VA] *Daily News-Record* (June 16, 1973); Mrs. Marshall Williams, "Broadway," [New Market, VA] *Shenandoah Valley* (June 20, 1973); "Homecoming for Brethren: A New Sense of Freedom?" *Messenger* (September, 1973): 5-6; Howard E. Royer, "Reconciliation with our Brethren Kin," *Messenger* (September, 1973): 32. The addresses at the Broadway meeting were published in a special issue of *Brethren Life and Thought*, 19 (Winter, 1974): 2-79, edited by Edward K. Ziegler.
7. Owen H. Alderfer, ed., "The Brethren—1785 to 1860," *Ashland Theological Bulletin*, 8 (Spring, 1975): 1-92, special issue; D. F. Durnbaugh, ed., "Brethren in a Revolutionary Era," *Brethren Life and Thought*, 22 (Winter, 1977): 2-55, special issue; "Brethren Historians Confer at Bethany," *Messenger* (August, 1976): 9.
8. Transcript of M. R. Zigler address, Bethany Theological Seminary, May 15, 1976; Fred W. Benedict, *The Brethren Assemblies—The Brethren Historians and Writers' Conferences—The Brethren Encyclopedia* (Covington, OH: author, 1978).
9. M. R. Zigler, report of the Germantown meeting, July 29, 1977.
10. Benedict, *Brethren Assemblies* (1978); "Historians Group Plans Brethren Encyclopedia," *Messenger* (January, 1978): 4.
11. The story of the encyclopedia is told in several places; see especially: Benedict, *Brethren Assemblies* (1978); D. F. Durnbaugh, "Introduction," *Brethren*

Encyclopedia (1983-1984), vi-xi; Religious News Service, "Long-divided German Brethren Churches Join in Encyclopedia Project," (May 18, 1984); Kermon Thomasson, "An Inside Story," *Messenger* (June, 1984): 10-11; *Brethren Life and Thought*, 30 (Summer, 1985): 132-186—a complete bibliography on the project was included (pages 179-180) in this special issue.

12. *Messenger* (December, 1985), cover.
13. "We Remember with Thanksgiving . . .," *Missionary Messenger* (January, 1978): 7-9. Zigler's letter thanking the journal for a gift of the memorial issue and again expressing his gratitude for the life of Orie Miller was printed, with his permission: "Readers Write," *Missionary Messenger* (May, 1978): 23; Yount, *Proceedings* (1973), 177 The Mennonite publication was Paul Erb, *Orie O. Miller—The Story of a Man and an Era* (Scottdale, PA: Herald Press, 1969).
14. M. R. Zigler to William T. Snyder and E. Raymond Wilson, Jan. 11, 1975.
15. News release, Elgin, May 19, 1975; "Historic Peace Churches Findings," May 7-8, 1975.
16. The proceedings were published as *Church-State Conversations on Peace & War* (Washington, D. C.: NISBCO/OEPC, 1976); Gen. Lewis B. Hershey to M. R. Zigler, Aug. 14, 1975.
17. S. Loren Bowman to M. R. Zigler, Jan. 20, 1976.
18. Zigler to Bowman, Jan. 24, 1976.
19. DeWitt L. Miller, "A personal reaction," [January, 1976].
20. Bowman to Zigler, March 2, 1976.
21. Zigler to Bowman, March 17, 1976.
22. "Historic Peace Churches Renew Acquaintaince, Plan More Cooperation," *Mennonite Weekly Review* (April 15, 1976); Robert Kreider, "How Do Mennonites View the Brethren and Friends," *Gospel Herald* (Dec. 27, 1977): 966-968.
23. Lorton G. Heusel to seven peace church leaders, May 4, 1976.
24. Heusel to Zigler, June 14, 1978.
25. For a general survey, see D. F. Durnbaugh, "Why They Call Them the Peace Churches," [WCC] *One World* (December, 1977); see also Dale W. Brown, "Peace and the Peace Churches," *Christian Century* (March 15, 1978): 266-270, republished in Martin E. Marty, ed., *Where the Spirit Leads: American Denominations Today* (Atlanta: John Knox Press, 1980), 57-67; "The Peace Churches Unite," *Newsweek* (Dec. 4, 1978): 112; "Tax Resistance, Peace Witness Focus of NCP," *Messenger* (December, 1980): 4;
26. *Brethren Life and Thought*, 11 (Winter, 1966), special issue; James E. Weaver, "Brethren Response to COCU," *Brethren Life and Thought*, 14 (1969): 227-247, a bibliographical survey.
27. C. Wayne Zunkel to D. F. Durnbaugh, April 15, 1987.
28. Harry K. Zeller to M. R. Zigler, Oct. 21, 1968.; Zeller to Zigler, March 8, 1969.

29. Philip Potter to M. R. Zigler, Aug. 9, 1975; Sept. 2, 1975.

30. Howard E. Royer, "The Saints Are True Liberators," *Messenger* (February, 1976): 40.

31. M. R. Zigler to "my friends," Dec. 3, 1976.

32. Barton Hunter to M. R. Zigler, April 20, 1976; Zigler to Hunter, April 24, 1976.

33. M. R. Zigler to Philip Potter, Nov. 20, 1982; Potter to Zigler, Dec. 15, 1982; M. R. Zigler to D. F. Durnbaugh, Jan. 14, 1983.

34. Robert Lear, "They Remember World Council in its Yesteryears," [Vancouver Assembly] *Canvas* (July 30, 1983): 4-5.

24

FINAL YEARS AND DEATH

I N SOME PERSONAL correspondence in April, 1978, M. R. Zigler included the following aphorism from the French poet, Claudel: "Some sigh for yesterday. Some for tomorrow. But you must reach old age before you can understand the meaning—the splendid, absolute, unchallengeable, irreplaceable meaning—of the word 'today.'"

This explains much of the tenor of the final years of M. R. Zigler. He was quite conscious of his mortality, talked openly about it, and even joked about the time he had remaining. The coauthor of a book about the experiences of the peace churches in the two world wars in which Zigler was much interested, quotes him as urging: "Get on with the book! I don't have much more time, and I don't know what the interlibrary loan arrangements are in heaven!" His driving urgency, which irritated some, was based in large part on his consciousness of his mortality. He had much he wanted to accomplish and only a short time in which to do it.[1]

His attitude is reflected in a passage in a letter to a long-time friend who had left the Church of the Brethren to join a more conservative Brethren body. Zigler urged that they maintain their correspondence despite the fact that one chose a different road. His intent is clear despite the breathless form in which he dictated it:

> Therefore, I predict that our letters will continue and ought to until "death do us part." I suggest that whoever lands first on the other side to check on this business of the soul that is ahead in the race, eternity, thrust the spiritual influence upon the one that is not yet to come to accomplish the feat of following the will of God as far as insights lead. I pray that we may share our experiences as we live on this earth. There are many good things about it.[2]

306

The deaths of some of his closest associates affected him. He wrote a letter in July, 1982, stating: "But really I am in the period of being afraid to die." He spoke of wishing to exit as did his longtime friend, L. W. Shultz, who died at an alumni dinner at his beloved Manchester College. He also wrote about the deaths of H. Spenser Minnich, an early colleague at Elgin, and of Dr. Robert Burns, a classmate at Bridgewater College. The death of Burns left him as the sole surviving member of both his high school and college graduating classes. "I guess I need to cast out fear. You better help."[3]

He traveled much in these years by Greyhound and told of an experience in the South when a fellow passenger died quietly during the trip. Zigler noticed the occurrence and informed the driver. The latter told him to say nothing to the other passengers and continued the trip. At the bus terminal, the driver callously left the bus, leaving the problem to his replacement. Zigler had visions of dying in the same way, underway to the next appointment. But it did not happen quite that way.

He was able to attend the Annual Conference held at Baltimore, Maryland, from June 28 to July 3, 1983, as it turned out, his last one. At this meeting, an agreement was worked out between the On Earth Peace Assembly and the General Board. The achievement of *The Brethren Encyclopedia*, in the cause of which he had been so active, was given public recognition there. In late November, a large Brethren World Peace Festival was held at Westminster, Maryland, at which he was honored. Early in 1984, however, he became ill, and was hospitalized for four weeks. As he had done so many times, he fought back to regain activity, and spring found him in his Broadway, Virginia, home. He pluckily took his shaky but extensive walks down the long driveway to the road, sometimes even farther, and back, resting as he had to.

He painfully tapped out his letters on his electric typewriter, hitting about as many false keys as correct ones, trying to keep up with his huge correspondence. He had always loved receiving letters and just as equally writing them. Floyd E. Mallott said of him that he was one of "the very few people I've ever known who wrote letters in his leisure time for the sheer joy of it."[4] Because he was a poor typist, he preferred using a stenographer but that was not always possible in his later years. So, he did the best he could himself. In this trait, he was like the great earlier Brethren church-man, Otho Winger.

Celebrations

Sadly, Zigler was not able to attend the celebrative meeting held at Ashland, Ohio, on June 4, 1984, to mark the completion of the encyclopedia project. Two members of the Old German Baptist Brethren community, who had worked closely with him on the task, wrote to him deploring his absence. Wrote one :"You were very much on all our minds at Ashland on June 4. We know that you would have loved to be with us at the 'harvest' meeting for the *Brethren Encyclopedia*. It seemed strange not to hear your voice giving a vision of what we ought to be or giving a benediction on our gathering to share our thoughts and lives."[5]

Another wrote, expressing his own sadness that Zigler's illness prevented his attendance, for "everyone was hoping to see" him there. "It was a meeting of closeness, sharing of feelings and fellowship with all five groups represented. . . . I recently read the book of your life and philosophy, *One Man's Peace*. I greatly enjoyed the book and learned to more greatly appreciate your work. . . . I intend to read it again and perhaps numerous times over the years, as I feel that it is a book that could influence my life for good. I would like to express my great respect for you and your work and your influence on the church and consider it a great privilege having had the opportunity to know you."[6]

Through the offices of his old friend Dr. Calvert N. Ellis, president emeritus of Juniata College, and his new friend, Dr. John C. Baker, chairman of the board of trustees of Juniata , he was awarded an honorary degree, the last of four, on May 27. A younger peace activist, M. Andrew Murray, college chaplain, wrote the tribute, including these apt words:

> Michael Robert Zigler is a man untamed by success or convention or the rigors of a long and active life. After nine decades, the fierce light of his free spirit is still scanning the edges of human endeavor, giving hope, illuminating folly, and providing confidence for a better world. . . .
>
> Conceived and nurtured in the soft womb of the Shenandoah Valley, steeled and sharpened in the dust and mud of Parris Island; educated at Bridgewater, Bethany, Vanderbilt, and Chicago; M. R. has spent his life fighting for peace. For weapons he has used words, money, organization and moral courage. His genius has been to mold cooperative ventures out of separatist roots, calling people to work without solving all theoretical inconsistencies. . . . In his life and work, he has exemplified a rare synthesis of world vision with individual compassion. His eye has always been on the horizon, his hand firmly in the soil. . . .[7]

Previous honorary doctorates were given by Bridgewater (1937), Manchester (1959), and Elizabethtown colleges (1963). His alma mater, Bridgewater College, had also presented him with a special alumni citation in November, 1979; this succeeded an alumni award given in 1947. Many other honors had come to him in these latter years. He was given the Brethren Peacemaker of the Year Award by the Atlantic Northeast District Peace Fellowship for his "lifelong efforts to promote peace and understanding among individuals and nations."[8]

Earlier he had been honored with a portrait, to be hung in Zigler Hall at New Windsor, Maryland. Although he generally deprecated these honors, one he enjoyed was a nomination for the Nobel Peace prize. The nominating material was compiled by Lawrence W. Haynes, a retired professor and volunteer at the Service Center at New Windsor. William G. Willoughby, one of the successors of Zigler as European director of Brethren Service activity, wrote the nominating letter. It was not rewarded with success, but it did many good to hear of the effort. Already mentioned was his recognition with the first Brethren Award for Outstanding Ecumenical Achievement in June, 1980.[9]

Declining Health

The spring of 1984 found his health shaky; he experienced a bad fall when he tried to live alone at New Windsor and had to be returned to Broadway in an ambulance. Nevertheless, when he received an invitation to the Second World Congress on Religious Liberty, to be held in Rome in September, 1984, he wrote back asking for more information. He said "that although he had just had an experience in the hospital" that he "was tempted to say I will try to be with you." The old campaigner simply could not accept that his limitations were increasing. The trip to Huntingdon, Pennsylvania, to receive the honorary degree at Juniata College was almost too much for him, and he suffered a relapse.[10]

He was strong enough to enjoy the tenth anniversary dinner for the OEPA at New Windsor, Maryland, in September. At this time, he wrote one friend that he was following this schedule:

Get up at 7:30. Breakfast at eight. Make up bed and walk to the road down and up hill. Write letter or read a book. Then lunch comes quickly. Mail comes at lunch time when I also read two newspapers, including *Washington Post* and if I have time I write letters. But I go to sleep at three until dinner at five. Then another walk. . . . Then . . . I am writing letters sometimes to midnight and to bed. Hopefully some night[s] at 10:00. Sleeping, eating OK. Don't have to do anything.[11]

He admitted at that point that he had been very discouraged during the spring, when he was quite ill. He was preparing himself for the end, feeling that being nearly blind, almost totally deaf, and unable to walk without assistance, "the end could not be anything but close and desirable." But then his health improved, and he began to worry about what he should be doing "that no one else has done," for he needed "a reason to live." He regretted that he had not kept a good diary nor made a better written record of his life. "My theory," he stated, was to "do a good days work and let it speak for itself."[12]

By the end of 1984 he was admitting to some weakness. He wrote to Harold Smith, who had become the OEPA executive: "Regret I can not feel strong enough to get out and mix with people in order to participate with everyone who needs help. . . . If I had my choice of course I would like to be at New Windsor to observe the drama and take my part of any assignment you and your staff would advise. [But there was] plenty of evidence that I should break this dream and plan to be satisfied to live at Broadway. I am not as strong as I could be by this Christmas time. In spite of what happened I am a very satisfied person hoping to have a joyful 1985."[13]

One of his concerns was to answer all of his mail. As had happened in recent years, the anniversary of his birth was the occasion for floods of mail from well-wishers. The OEPA office aided and abetted the flow of letters, as they urged his friends to contribute one dollar for each year of his life. He had barely struggled to answer these birthday greetings, when the Christmas mail came in.

On the last day of the year, he wrote to the same correspondent, looking forward to 1985—"another year challenges with 365 days made available." He wrote of having 365 days, no more and no less. "We can bet on it." As it turned out, that was a wager he would have lost. He was never to see another Christmas and New Year's eve.

But typically, he used the letter to send on gifts for the OEPA program that had come to him, one from a former colleague in the World's YMCA, two others from the Messiah congregation in Kansas City, Missouri, where he had served as interim pastor. He promised to review his own dwindling finances to see what he could contribute personally in 1985 to OEPA (in earlier years it had been $1,000 and more), before he sent money to other appeals. He supported Bread for the World, the Center on Law and Pacifism, the National Peace Academy, and similar agencies. Zigler was studying the way various organizations were going after his "little contributions." He apologized that his illness in 1984 had made him unable to help at New Windsor but was "inclined to think that it was time for me to move for the good of the cause." He concluded that "maybe some day I will be able to do something magnificent."[14]

By springtime, 1985, he was not able to go far afield from Broadway, Virginia. He continued painfully to type his letters, although he complained that the blurring in his eyes (usually caused by medications) prevented him from seeing what he had written. Even earlier his hearing had so deteriorated that he was forced to communicate one-on-one, with earphones connected to powerful radio transmitters. A bad cold in late spring caused considerable misery. In May, 1985, he wrote to Dale V. Ulrich: "Typing is difficult. Wish [I] could write more as I feel and that I could [focus] my mind [on] one subject long enough. When I read the enclosed letter [which] came I said I must forward it to you and Harold [Smith]. Before I forget I am acting. Great letter for a 15-year-old. . . . Always anxious about OEPA and weep that I can't do anything."[15]

The letter he mentioned that heartened him had been written by young Suzanne Lydic, inspired by the Inez Long biography. Because Zigler had always been concerned about passing on his passion for peace to the young, it is good to know that this expression still reached him. It read, in part:

> Reading about all that you've done has helped me to understand you better. I have seen you at various Annual Conferences, but I never really understood who you were or why you were so special. Well, I definitely know better now! Sometimes I just sit and wonder how you accomplished so much. . . . I really can't put into words how grateful I am for all that you have done for the Brethren denomination and the world. I hope knowing how much you've accomplished that I will be able to reach some of my goals in life.
>
> . . . In the name of the future generation, I thank you eternally for the love and hard work you have given to this world. May we continue to spread peace through the lands.[16]

Death and Memorial Service

In mid-September, 1985, as M. R. Zigler was taking his daily walk, a dog jumped against him, causing him to lose his balance and fall. The result was multiple fractures, including a broken hip. He was subsequently hospitalized in Rockingham Memorial Hospital, Harrisonburg, Virginia, then transferred to the Life Care Center at New Market, where he spent his last three weeks. Visitors found him alert in his mind and eager to leave for home. He died there at 3:30 P.M. on October 25, just fifteen days short of the ninety-fourth anniversary of his day of birth.

A staff worker at the Life Care Center described M. R. Zigler's death to his daughter: "When I last saw your dear Dad on Fri[day] aft[ernoon] about 3:30, he seemed to be talking to himself. His eyes were closed. Then I realized he was speaking to the Lord. . . . He was a true gentleman—even in his awful suffering. He remained calm and patient. Truly I was blessed to have been able to know him even the short time he was at LCC."[17]

Memorial Service

The memorial service was held in the Linville Creek Church of the Brethren at Broadway, where his remains were buried. Many speakers were invited to pay tribute to the departed leader, and others spoke from the congregation. Those invited to speak at the service included: Timothy Snell (local pastor), Donald F. Durnbaugh (Annual Conference moderator), Elaine Sollenberger (chair of the General Board), James K. Garber (representing Robert W. Neff, general secretary), Calvert N. Ellis (president emeritus of Juniata College), Harold D. Smith (executive of OEPA), Wayne F. Geisert (president, Bridgewater College), Fred W. Benedict (president of the Brethren Encyclopedia board), William T. Snyder (former executive secretary of the Mennonite Central Committee), and Dale V. Ulrich (On Earth Peace Assembly).

Members of the congregation were then invited to speak. Among those who chose to speak were a daughter of L. W. Shultz, his long-time friend, who spoke of his completely unexpected but very welcome appearance at her father's funeral service; a young pastor; a senior pastor; a worker at the Brethren Service Center; the daughter of a close associate in Europe; a peace worker from the Brethren in Christ church; a former director of the NSBRO. All in their own way, some with humor, some with pathos, spoke of the impact M. R. Zigler had made on their lives. It was a moving occasion. Afterwards many agreed that with his death, an era had passed.

One of the more incisive observations about M. R. Zigler's life came in a letter after the service, written by Dr. John C. Baker, retired university president and Zigler fan. Calling him the "Brethren Church's Pope John

XXIII," he wrote: "Somewhere in Jewish . . . folklore there is a tradition that the Creator has in every generation 36 anonymous righteous men privileged to see God, and the world exists on their merit. If true it would appear to me that 'M. R.' was one of these rare, select individuals."[18]

Published Memorial Statements

Local newspapers ran extensive obituaries with photos; they included the Harrisonburg, Virginia, *Daily News-Record*, Baltimore *Evening Sun*, and Frederick *Carroll County Times*. Several church publications picked up the news release sent out on October 29 by the director of news services for the Elgin offices. Among these were the *Christian Century*, which printed a paragraph summary; the [Canadian] *Mennonite Reporter*, which printed the entire two-page release; and the [Mennonite] *Gospel Herald*, which printed five paragraphs.[19]

Kermon Thomasson, editor of the Church of the Brethren *Messenger*, had the December issue already at the press in late October but pulled it back in order to feature the late peace activist. The cover showed Zigler perusing the first volumes of the *Brethren Encyclopedia* and read simply: "M. R. Zigler, 1891-1985." His comment: "Zigler's last great achievement was the publishing of the *Brethren Encyclopedia*. It was he who had coaxed the five Brethren bodies together for that joint venture. Our photographer caught him poring over a copy of the 3-volume encyclopedia. Note the cane, a sign of M. R.'s increasing physical frailty. We could have used the photo before, but something told us to tuck it away for another time. That time, sorry to say, has now come."

The well-illustrated tribute, with the headline "Blessed be this peacemaker," began: "In 1971 *Messenger* ran an article titled 'M. R. Zigler at Eighty.' In 1981 the cover article was 'M. R. Zigler at Ninety.' The editor held out the prospect of a similar feature for 1991. But that is not to be." It concluded, with reference to Zigler's hero, the Civil War martyr from Broadway, John Kline: "M. R. Zigler's body now rests near the grave of John Kline. His course, like Kline's was true. His dedication to the making of peace was clear. For many, he incorporated the heart of the Brethren conviction. There will never be another Michael Robert Zigler, but there are scores who have been inspired, directed, and renewed by his life and ministry. Peacemaker, rest in peace."[20]

The *On Earth Peace Newsletter* naturally devoted its columns to the news of its founder's death. The Bridgewater College alumni bulletin devoted two columns to the news of the death of its noted alumnus. *Windsor Winds*, the newsletter of the New Windsor Service Center, had a two-page spread. The editor of the *Brethren Peace Fellowship Newsletter*, C. Wayne Zunkel, for many years a supporter of Zigler, wrote:

> On October 25 at 3:30 P.M., M. R. Zigler passed through his final phase of life on earth. He was within three weeks of his 94th birthday, and he had never retired from his role as a soldier of Jesus Christ and the cause of peace. In 1975 he was named the Brethren Peace Fellowship's "Peacemaker of the Year" for his "consuming conviction that the Church of the Brethren has a special charter, a mandate among all Christians to be wholly dedicated to Christ's call to be peacemakers." May his dream, his passion, his love, his work through "On Earth Peace" and elsewhere never die but live on in us to continue to bless and enrich God's world.

L. William Yolton, executive director of NISBCO, the successor of NSBRO, issued a letter commemorating the life of M. R. Zigler; the envelope contained a photograph of Zigler and his friend Orie O. Miller.[21]

Personal Communications

Given the hundreds of people who considered M. R. Zigler to be a personal friend, it was not surprising that an avalanche of cards, notes of sympathies, and letters of appreciation for his life came to his family. It may be unfair to select from among the outpouring of responses, but a few may stand for the many.

—from Karen Glick Metzler, a grandniece:

> I remember how he opened Grand-daddy Glick's funeral sermon: "I officiated at the wedding that started all of this," and he held his hand out toward where we were all sitting. There was warm laughter and the feeling that we were there to celebrate Grand-daddy's life. That still remains one of the most deeply moving experiences I have had as a part of the Glick family.[22]

—from Jacqueline Richez, a Swiss secretary:

> You know, it took me quite some time to realize that I would never see M. R. Z. any more again. However, he had written me many times, and I know how seriously ill he had been all through 1984. In his January 1985 letter . . . he wrote concerning the birth of Brethren Service, "If anyone thinks that was

easy, he is not aware of the facts. . . ." With M. R.'s death, it is really a friend who disappears, who wrote: "Remember we are always anxious to hear from you." And with his age, he had time and would answer long, wonderful letters.[23]

—from Dr. Kit Colfach, the surgeon in Sweden:

With great confidence in his God and . . . no knowledge about my surgical skill, good old M. R. put his life in my hands and we pulled him through . . . to live another 27 years doing still many, many new spectacular performances for "avant-gardist" projects in the Brethren spirit. His rebellious and wide mind [was] always open to new ideas and thoughts and thus during all these years our friendship and devotion for each other grew stronger, finer, and more serene than one could imagine.[24]

—from Dr. J. Robert Nelson, Methodist theologian:

Our Lord gave your father ninety-four years in which to demonstrate his faith, love and hope. He did this magnificently. And without intending to do so, he left many living monuments to his life in the persons whom he anonymously helped (relief) and inspired (peace) and loved. We knew him first as a co-worker in Geneva from 1953, when we were often with him and your mother. In that high-strung international community, they represented the best in sincere and humane Christianity.[25]

—from Marjorie and Kenneth Morse:

We want to join with the many friends of your family who knew M. R. and valued his friendship and his unique contribution to Christians everywhere, but particularly in the Church of the Brethren. Although our memories go back to our early days in Elgin, we hardly knew him well then, but closer associations (especially in 1958 in Europe) in more recent years helped us gain an appreciation of his dynamic leadership. He can be credited for so many peacemaking accomplishments, but we have been especially impressed with his success in bringing together the various Brethren groups to work together on the *Brethren Encyclopedia*. That publication is only one of the many memorials that will long recognize the achievements of M. R. Zigler.[26]

Tributes

As could be expected, organizations with which M. R. Zigler had been connected, paused at appropriate moments to pay tribute to his memory.

315

The next meeting of the General Board of the Church of the Brethren, meeting in Elgin, Illinois, heard a tribute and spread it on the minutes.[27] One of the most eloquent tributes came from his biographer, Inez Long, given at a peace festival for the Southern District of Pennsylvania on November 10, 1985. Some excerpts:

> A tribute to M. R. Zigler is breathtaking. No matter where or when or how we met him, he was running for peace. We had to catch a second wind to keep up with him. Now he is halted, and we still haven't caught on. . . .
>
> I saw M. R. firsthand in the 1940s as he shuttled back and forth between Elgin, Illinois, and Washington, D. C. in World War II, between the ivory towers of the church headquarters and the iron bastions of the nation's Selective Service offices. . . . Often as I looked out of my third-floor window at the old publishing house, I saw him run across the Fox River bridge to catch the third rail to Chicago. His coat-tails flying, his brief case in hand—with more plans in it than clothes for the next days he would spend away from home—he shuttled from one CPS Camp to another to encourage America's first crop of legalized conscientious objectors to war. Then he ran from one church district to another to gather funds to support them. . . .
>
> He was a man who took risks for peace. He bore those risks with God-given stamina and with the aid of those who knew him, loved him, and trusted him. He broke into high places to register his presence. He believed in going to the top; he never stopped short until he reached the final authority. . . .
>
> He withstood our own Brethren boards and committees who turned aside when he showed up, because they didn't know what to do with him after the church had retired him. They all agreed that he was a great soul, but there was no place for him in their new plans and programs, so he created a program of his own.
>
> It is true that we who are blind stone our prophets while they are alive, and then build stone monuments to them after they die. But peacemakers are not memorialized in stone. They are kept alive through living legends, and M. R. Zigler is one of them. . . .[28]

R. Jan Thompson prepared a long tribute for Zigler for presentation at the March meeting of the Church World Service board. He quoted M. R. on the difficulties he had in interesting the American churches in relief and material aid after World War II. "They believed that they should help mission programs but that relief should be supported through secular non-church related agencies. . . . I have a very clear memory of the struggle that went on before Church World Service was organized." Thompson concluded: "M. R. Zigler was one of those persons who made things happen. If you agreed with him, you felt he was a person of strong convictions. If you happened to disagree with him, you felt he was a bit on the bullheaded side. M. R. Zigler—a dreamer, a planner, ecumenical with his visions, friend to many. . . ."[29]

In the Brethren Revival Fellowship publication, Harold S. Martin wrote a tribute as an introduction to a letter he had received from Zigler:

> M. R. Zigler was an outstanding Church of the Brethren leader who was known for his many efforts in the ecumenical world and for his tireless crusades for the cause of peace. Brother Zigler died on October 25, 1985, just a few weeks before his 94th birthday. . . . Brother Zigler was a man of stature, wisdom, and integrity. He was a personal friend. One day, ten years ago this month, I received a letter from M. R. which expressed his concern about diminishing membership in the Church of the Brethren and his conviction that all the vast efforts for peace (for which he so tirelessly labored) were not really the Church's total mission. . . .[30]

And finally, the actor Don Murray, who had been baptized by M. R. Zigler in the Fulda River near Kassel, Germany, made a special trip to the 1986 Annual Conference of the Church of the Brethren to pay a tribute to his revered mentor. Among other things, he said of Zigler:

> M. R. walked the same walk and talked the same talk with the mighty as he did with the meek. He'd not hesitate to leave the throbbing power center of Geneva to comfort and counsel one individual volunteer. . . .
>
> And perhaps knowing that God looks with particular compassion on those who die young, he kept himself young all those ninety plus years; finally going, whole, all at once, into the grave; not as many do, mouldering away gradually, first good works dead, then faith, then hope. He took more than just an empty garment of man into that untimed hush before the timeless resurrection. . . .
>
> Unlike Caesar, Napoleon, Hitler, M. R. Zigler left no armies, no altered borders, no booty to divide. Unlike Homer, Plato, Shakespeare, Voltaire, he left no great literature as his legacy. He has left only us. Left us to each other. Left us to ourselves. But insofar as he's left an enlightened us, a dedicated us, he has not left children of a lesser god, but children of the Only God.
>
> He has left PEACE-MAKERS.[31]

Memorials

In his memory, the On Earth Peace Assembly created an M. R. Zigler Fund, described as an "endowment to perpetuate a lifetime of peacemak-

317

ing," with a goal of $1.5 million. Further interpretation read: "The life of
M. R. Zigler is an inspiration for many within the Church of the Brethren
and for many others around the world. His example challenges us to
continue working for peace. The income from the Endowment will be used
to continue the life work of M. R. Zigler and to carry out the goals of Jesus
Christ expressed in the New Testament."[32]

An initiative he would have approved, given his keen interest in youth,
was taken by Elizabethtown College in 1985. It established the M. R.
Zigler Peace Essay Competition, with two objectives: (1) "To encourage
students at Elizabethtown College to develop imaginative proposals for a
peaceful world order; and (2) To recognize the historic contributions of
M. R. Zigler and the Church of the Brethren in fostering a peaceful world."
As it happened the first winner was Sharon Ulrich, daughter of Dale V.
Ulrich, a close associate of Zigler on the *Brethren Encyclopedia* and On
Earth Peace projects.[33]

NOTES

1. Albert N. Keim and Grant M. Stoltzfus, *The Politics of Conscience: The Historic Peace Churches and America at War, 1917-1955* (Scottdale, PA: Herald Press, 1988), 15.
2. M. R. Zigler to Floyd E. Mallott, Oct, 26, 1963.
3. M. R. Zigler to Calvert N. Ellis, July 2, 1981.
4. Floyd E. Mallott to Marlin ?, November, 1962.
5. Fred W. Benedict to M. R. Zigler, June 24, 1984.
6. Marcus Miller to M. R. Zigler, June 18, 1984.
7. "Introduction of Dr. Michael Zigler, Juniata College Commencement, May 27, 1984, read by Dr. M. Andrew Murray," typescript; *Juniata College Bulletin* (July, 1984): 12, 13.
8. *Gospel Messenger* (June 13, 1959): 16; *Lancaster* [PA] *New Era* (June 3, 1963): 30; "BC Cites Miller, Zigler," [Harrisonburg, VA] *Daily News-Record* (Nov. 3, 1979): 18; *Bridgewater* (December; 1979); "BC Award to M. Rob't Zigler," [Harrisonburg, VA] *Daily News-Record* [?] (June 2, 1947); "Peace Group Honors a Man 'On a Binge,'" *Messenger* (August, 1975): 5.
9. "Zigler Portrait Presented," *Messenger* (July 16, 1970): 15; William G. Willougby to the Nobel Peace Committee, January 8, 1962; "Honored," *Messenger* (September, 1980): 7.
10. M. R. Zigler to International Religious Liberty Association, March 12, 1984.

11. M. R. Zigler to Joyce Welker, Sept. 20, 1984.
12. M. R. Zigler to Edith Bonsack Barnes, Sept. 18, 1984.
13. M. R. Zigler to Harold Smith, Dec. 17, 1984.
14. Zigler to Smith, Dec. 31, 1984.
15. M. R. Zigler to Dale V. Ulrich, May 19, 1985.
16. Suzanne Lydic to M. R. Zigler, May 13, 1985; the OEPA office published the letter, which had pleased Zigler so much, to the astonishment of the author. He wrote her a fine letter of response, which she answered, telling of the events of her life in high school—Lydic to Zigler, June 23, 1985.
17. Jackie Meadors to Geraldine Glick, Oct. 27, 1985.
18. John C. Baker to D. F. Durnbaugh, Dec. 16. 1985.
19. "Local Nobel Peace Prize Nominee Dies," [Harrisonburg, VA] *Daily News-Record* (Oct. 28, 1985); "Michael R. Zigler," [Baltimore] *Evening Sun* (October 31, 1985); "Michael R. Zigler, 93, of Broadway, Va.," [Frederick, MD] *Carroll County Times* (Oct. 31, 1985); Wendy Chamberlain McFadden, "M. R. Zigler, Ecumenical Leader and Peace Advocate, Dies," (Oct. 29, 1985); *Christian Century* (Nov. 13, 1985): 1026; "M. R. Zigler: Portrait of a Peacemaker," *Mennonite Reporter* (Nov. 25, 1985): 5; "Brethren Leader and Peace Activist, M. R. Zigler, Dies at 93," *Gospel Herald* (Nov. 26, 1985): 843.
20. Kermon Thomasson, "Cover," *Messenger* (December, 1985); Donald F. Durnbaugh, "Blessed Be This Peacemaker," *Messenger* (December, 1985): 12-13.
21. "In Memoriam," *On Earth Peace Newsletter* (November, 1985); "M. R. Zigler Dies," *Bridgewater* (December, 1985): 13; "In Memoriam—Michael Robert Zigler . . .," *Windsor Winds* (Autumn, 1985), no. 5; [C. Wayne Zunkel], "A Giant Dies," *Brethren Peace Fellowship Newsletter* (December, 1985): 1; L. William Yolton to "dear friend," November, 1985.
22. Karen Glick Metzler to Aunt Gerry and Uncle Johnny [Glick], Oct. 26, 1985.
23. Jacqueline Richez to Hazel Peters, December, 1985.
24. Dr. Kit Colfach to Geraldine and John [Glick], Nov. 12, 1985.
25. Dr. J. Robert Nelson to Mr. [Robert] Zigler and Mrs. [Geraldine] Glick, Nov. 3, 1985.
26. Marjorie and Kenneth Morse to "dear friends," November, 1985.
27. D. F. Durnbaugh, "Celebration of the Life and Witness of M. R. Zigler (1891-1985)," Meeting of the General Board, Church of the Brethren, Elgin, IL, March 2, 1986.
28. Inez Long, "A Tribute to M. R. Zigler," Peace Festival, York First Church of the Brethren, Southern District of Pennsylvania, On Earth Peace Assembly, November 10, 1985.
29. R. Jan Thompson, "Tribute to M. R. Zigler," Church World Service, New York, March 12, 1986.
30. Harold S. Martin, "Editorial," *BRF Witness* (January/February, 1987).
31. Donald Patrick Murray, "A Tribute to M. R. Zigler," Church of the Brethren

Annual Conference, Norfolk, VA, June 28, 1986.
32. Brochure, ca. January, 1986.
33. "The Zigler Peace Essay Contest," *Elizabethtown* (Fall, 1986): 43-45.

■ EPILOGUE

H OW DOES ONE sum up the life of a man like Michael Robert Zigler? An anonymous and undated analysis of his signature, found in his papers, reads: "Your handwriting shows a reserved nature. You are good natured and enjoy helping others. You are willing to wait for those things that you want. You are firm and inflexible in your personal decisions. Loyalty is one of your pronounced qualities. An intensely emotional nature is shown in your writing. You sometimes have difficulty in making decisions. Your mind is crowded with unresolved ideas." People who knew him well can register some misses but also some astute guesses in this "appraisal."

M. R. Zigler was a hero to many people and heroes are not in fashion in the late 1980s. In society's drive for equality with its attack on "elitism," the exceptional person is a rarity. The public no longer gives automatic deference to those placed in positions of authority in state and church, especially in the wake of the Vietnam debacle, sleaze in government, and egomania and immorality among televangelists. Society both longs for someone to look up to and lusts after the latest expose of the weaknesses of the celebrated.

A Brethren editor asked, "Now that Anna Mow and M. R. Zigler have died, . . . have [we] run out of heroes?" He answered his own question by observing that he saw no one on the horizon who would faintly match the two named but expected that others would come forth. He later found one such in a Brethren pastor in Florida, devoted to his work in a troubled area, who was killed by a young man of the community he was trying to help.[1]

M. R. Zigler was a great man. Even his detractors would grant that. He thought in large terms, acted boldly, and was never petty. He was a visionary, never satisfied with current achievement, always pressing the church and its members toward better things. At the same time, he was eminently practical, recognizing and forgiving the frailties of the human personality. His attitude was well expressed in the modern hymn "Help Us Accept Each Other" by Fred Kaan, with music by Doreen Potter (who was befriended in Geneva by the Ziglers). The text includes the lines: "Teach us to care for people, for all, not just for some / To love them as we find them, or as they may become."

Caring for people—that is the *leitmotif* that runs all through his life. M. R. Zigler genuinely *liked* people; it would not be too much to say he *loved* people. They sensed it and loved him back. There is ample evidence that he never outgrew childhood playmates, college chums, YMCA friends, church colleagues, pastors he recruited for Home Missions, conciliar leaders he met in New York and Chicago, CPS men on whose behalf he worked during World War II, Brethren Service workers in Europe, ecumenical staff at Geneva, European churchmen and church-women, members of the congregations he served briefly as interim pastor, or retired folks at Sebring. He stayed in close touch with all of them.

His correspondence files bulge with letters of gratitude from those who were remembered. If a Brethren minister he once knew died, he would write a word of comfort to the widow. If someone was appointed or elected to a new position, he would write a letter of encouragement, at the same time prodding the recipient to great accomplishment. One of the most telling proofs of his concern was the care he took to keep in touch with the aides and secretarial staffs of the many organizations with which he was connected. He was concerned about the Swiss, German, and Austrian secretaries with whom Brethren Service staff had worked after 1945. He wrote them, he visited them repeatedly, he made them feel part of the Brethren family. They reciprocated his interest.

It would be impossible to reckon the number of friends of M. R. Zigler. A conservative estimate would reach into the thousands. He had a genius for friendship, for total attention to the person with whom he was involved at the time. He was not abstracted nor distracted nor thinking of the next item on the agenda. He followed up, with calls or letters, to reassure each one of his continued interest.

Some people whose lives he influenced gave witness to that fact by naming their children after him. He took such events more as a cause for sober reflection than as a flattering compliment: "I just received word that another child has come to the LaVonne Ikenberry Grubb home and it shook me [when] they informed me that his name will be Michael Robert. Now I have to be good the rest of my life. I don't know what it means to be named this way. I am not sure how I can play a part in the life of a child."[2]

He was a public person, continually being invited to speak or preach, though always conscious of his limitations as an orator. In part this was of his own doing, as he was eager to spread the message of his current project, and constant communication was necessary. He could be extremely inspiring and he could also be tedious, going on and on in rambling fashion. It is very difficult to outline his messages. But when he was "on" he could have people laughing at a witticism in one breath and nearly crying with the next, as they listened to Zigler's picture of need. He had the gift of orators in sensing how he was reaching the audience. When he spoke at too great length, it was because he realized that he had not made contact, and would keep trying to find something that worked. Noted American Methodist Bishop G. Bromley Oxnam said of him: "He makes the worst speeches I've ever known, but he can move people to action faster than anyone I've ever known."[3]

M. R. was conscious of his inarticulateness and often used others to assist him. When he had an important resolution to offer the church, say at Annual Conference, he would call on a L. W. Shultz or a Paul H. Bowman, Sr., to draft his point. For the sake of easier comprehension, his secretaries often edited his rambling dictation, which often violated the basic rules of syntax, knowing that Zigler would be happy for their aid. A story often told in Brethren Service circles was when he was asked to participate in a distribution of donated cows in Germany under the Heifer Project. He made a "mundane speech in English about how some Brethren in Indiana had decided to share their Herefords" with the refugee recipients. Then Suzanne Windisch, one of the German secretaries at Kassel "translated the speech into a lovely homily about the love and grace of God."[4]

Many persons, on reflection, were struck with his ability to place them in challenging positions, give them the feeling of confidence that they could handle the job, and trust them to do their best. Invariably, people outdid themselves to try to justify the faith placed in them, to avoid letting him down. One way of understanding this gift is to think of M. R. Zigler as a *bishop*. Although Brethren polity did not have the office during his lifetime, that was what he was in functional terms. He recruited people, "ordained" them for service, backed them up when necessary, and, especially, inspired them. He found the material resources they needed, gave them a direction, and trusted that the Lord would guide.

This caring, this love, also helps to explain the power and influence that M. R. Zigler had in the life of the church. There were always people who would respond to his call to service and people of means who would supply resources. More than one has said, at times ruefully, "I can't say 'no' to M. R. Zigler." Straight-line administrators did not always understand this power; or, if they understood it, they tended to resent it. And, on more than one occasion, M. R. Zigler used this influence to go around the set and agreed-upon policy of the church organization to get his own way.

It is said that during World War II, an aide to Marshall Stalin questioned a policy by stating that the pope was opposed to it. "How many divisions has the pope?" shot back the dictator, thus quashing the mild opposition. The fact is that the pope as spiritual leader of millions and arbiter of morals does have his divisions, in the sense of influence and teaching. In the same way, M. R. Zigler had his divisions, made up of the great numbers of friends willing to follow his lead.

Another hallmark of M. R. Zigler was his genuineness. There was no duplicity about his nature. Ecumenical friends noted that quality in his life in Geneva at the center of world Protestantism. The multilingual, cosmo-politan, and sometimes hectic atmosphere might have tempted a lesser figure to adapt his ways to try to fit in better. Not Zigler.

He never learned more than a few phrases in French and German, but was just himself—hearty, friendly, with a passion for peace and service. When it came his time to lead the devotional services held regularly at the ecumenical center, he would open the Bible, read a text, and then speak quite informally about what the text meant for the daily walk. No acute exegesis, no abstract theologizing, just simple exposition and exhortation. There is a phrase in computer talk that fits M. R. Zigler: "What you see is what you get."

But with this, there was a shrewdness, an alertness that revealed that he would not easily be fooled. He read people's faces, watched their manner. He liked to say that he could tell what a person was going to say as that person came into his office. He followed with acuteness the flow of business sessions or conference gatherings and called it a game, with its rules, failures, and victories. He could map strategy to prepare for meetings, so that desired outcomes would occur.

He kept up with the flow of current events and was uncomfortable if cut off from news. Although he liked to pose as someone who did not read, the number of periodicals he subscribed to was many. They covered a range of theological viewpoints, from conservative to radical. He needed to know where the cutting edges of contemporary action and thought were. He bought many books and read them. He continually prodded the Brethren to produce more literature to educate their own people and interpret themselves to others. In this sense, he was truly an intellectual, because of his drive to analyze, to understand.

M. R. Zigler was generous—generous with time, generous with emotions, generous with resources. During all the time he was in Europe, he supported the Elgin congregation, where he and Amy had their memberships, with weekly contributions. Though he never earned more in church employ than $5,000 in a given year, he gave to a host of good causes. In the 1970s there was tension in the Church of the Brethren between conservative and liberal factions. Although personally quite liberal in theological bent, Zigler contributed to the Brethren Revival Fellowship and to William Freed's schismatic Broadfording congregation near Hagerstown, Maryland.

The hospitality of the Zigler's small apartment in Geneva was legendary. It often resembled a hostel, with wall-to-wall overnight guests. In one letter, Zigler spoke of picking up a Swedish hitchhiker on a French highway who was headed for Geneva. He took him all the way to that destination, gave him dinner, a night's lodging, and a hearty breakfast (which he cooked himself) the next morning before sending him on his way.

M. R. Zigler loved to receive visitors to Europe, show them about, take them to his favorite Chinese restaurant in Geneva, all the time filling their ears with the work of Brethren Service and recruiting their support for the program. In some sense it was public relations work, but it flowed from his expansive spirit and never seemed nor was narrowly calculated.

M. R. Zigler was prophetic. He always looked ahead. He was never content with the church as it was but as it could be in the future. He liked to work with young people—as the future of the church—and knew how to get their attention. One device he used was to make them sit on the front benches in the church sanctuary. He liked to ask them what they expected to be in twenty years. After hearing some answers, he would have them turn and face their parents, at which point he would say, "That's what you will be." He then would ask them what kind of a world they wanted for *their* children. And then the discussion would soar.

He liked to say that he "wouldn't give a nickel for the church as it is" but he "would die for the church and its potential." His closest friend was Orie O. Miller, of the Mennonites. A trait they shared, which brought them together, was their vision for what their churches could become. In can be said of both that they were powerful change agents in shaping the future direction of their denominations.

At the same time that M. R. Zigler was prophetic, he was intensely practical. He saw no use for dreams that did not include careful thought concerning how they could be realized. That is why he was always concerned about people and about resources. He maintained that the best test of whether an idea was good or not was whether people would give time and money for it. When he had the vision of On Earth Peace in 1974, he took to the road to see if he could raise money for it. After six weeks he had $30,000 in pledges and was convinced that the concept had wings. All his life he was an administrator, taking ideas and making them work in practice. To do that, he had to be pragmatic, to know what he could do with his people and what he could not do.

M. R. Zigler combined the prophetic with the pragmatic. And that helps to explain the genius of the man. His head was in the clouds but his feet were firmly planted on the soil. He was what he was because he had both the courage of his visions and the canniness of his pragmatism. He had both—he was a pragmatic prophet.

* * * *

M. R. Zigler's best remembered saying was his claim that many wars would never have taken place if Christians had refused to kill other Christians. John Stoner, the executive secretary of the Peace Section of the Mennonite Central Committee, heard of this from Dale W. Brown, of the Bethany seminary faculty, in February, 1984. Stoner was struck by the statement, meditated upon it, and came up with what he called a "Modest Proposal for Christian Unity." He sent this to the WCC periodical, *One World*, the editors of which published it in their May, 1984, issue. Among other things, Stoner wrote:

> Rarely does one find an idea so attractive in its beauty, so compelling in its simplicity and so piercing in its truth. . . . There is a great longing in the church around the world for that unity of the human family which Jesus promised. . . . Some progress has been made, but the world still sees a very divided body when it looks toward the church. Christ's prayer—"May they be brought to complete unity to let the world know that you sent me"—still waits to be

answered. What might the church do to bear unmistakable witness to the love of God in Jesus Christ, in a manner at once relevant to our times and faithful to the received tradition. Here is a modest proposal: *Let the Christians of the world agree that they will not kill each other. . . .*

I claim no originality for this proposal. It has been raised previously. I only claim to hear the voice of God in it, and confess that the Holy Spirit does not allow me to me silent about an action so attuned to the mind of Christ.[5]

The statement was printed as a poster and soon more than 6,000 copies were distributed on five continents. It drew requests from all across the USA and Canada. It caught the attention of a Marine in Chicago, a student at a Southern Baptist seminary, a Ugandan church leader who ordered twenty copies for all of the bishops of the country, and church workers in Central America and Japan.

And so the message of Michael Robert Zigler finds its way across the North American continent and around the world. Who can say when or where it will stop?

* * * *

"People still long for models of wholeness, for evidences that individual lives and choices matter." —Jean Strouse[6]

"The saints are always the true liberators. Their rough and often resented love shakes up a passive and resisting world—and that love does work miracles." —Garry Wills[7]

NOTES

1. Kermon Thomasson, "Have We Run Out of Heroes?" *Messenger* (February, 1986): 32; Kermon Thomasson, "Run Out of Heroes? No Way!" *Messenger* (February, 1987): 24.
2. M. R. Zigler to Kurtis and Gladys Naylor, Feb. 25, 1972.
3. Ruth Shriver to Ernest Kuebler, July 18, 1961.
4. Graydon F. Snyder to D. F. Durnbaugh, July 27, 1987.
5. John Stoner, *One World* (May, 1984): 18.
6. Quoted in Peter S. Prescott, "Lives of the Saints and the Secular," *Newsweek* (October 29, 1984): 118.
7. Quoted in Howard E. Royer, "The Saints Are True Liberators," *Messenger* (February, 1976): 40.

APPENDICES ━━━━━━━━━━

Voices of Those Who Remember M. R. Zigler:

—from Edith Barnes, retired staff worker at Elgin, and volunteer researcher who aided M. R. Zigler with his memoirs:

> When M. R. concluded his work in Europe and returned to America he was in a quandary about a place where he could continue the purposes of Brethren Service, and in a wider, deeper sense the message of Christianity itself. Walking in the General Board offices in Elgin and talking with the persons there, he did not find too much help or encouragement for direction in the days ahead. He concluded finally that his first move should be toward making a written report of Brethren Service under his supervision for several years in Germany and other places in Europe. As a starter for this project, there was an old suitcase full of documents and an outline of chapters for a book. This outline had been prepared by Frances Clemens Nyce before leaving Europe.
>
> The time had come when M. R. knew what he should do when he arrived one morning at the BHLA. "Writing is agony for me," was the way he expressed what he felt about the task before him. . . . One day the urge to get at the disturbing task was overwhelming. "We must get going," he commented as he put papers on the desk and sat down. I was at the table in front of the typewriter ready to catch the words when they came. I never interrupted or questioned, lest I dampen the flow or block the memory or even end the long-awaited outflow. Up from the desk, pacing the length of the room and back seemed to enhance the procedure at times. In time the two chapters on the work in Europe became typewritten copy. . . .[1]

—from Charles Boyer, peace consultant at Elgin and BVS worker:

I have come to regard Bro. Zigler's greatest contribution to mankind as being a visionary, a person who possesses an untold number of ideas as to how our faith in Jesus Christ can be exemplified in acts of serving love. I did not know M. R. personally until after the tragic accident in Sweden. By this time he was no longer a director of Brethren Service, but he continued to visit the Brethren projects and every time he came around it was like a breath of fresh air because he was alive with ideas, ideas of what could be done in the ares we were already serving and ideas of new opportunities for service. . . . There is little place in M. R.'s philosophy for pessimism or discouragement to be vented publicly. I was personally reminded by him that if you are depressed you will not draw others to you nor will you influence others to the degree you can if your actions portray joy and optimism. . . .[2]

—from Clyde Carter, pastor and BVS worker, recounting a meeting with M. R. Zigler and recently arrived volunteers at Brethren House at Kassel:

M. R. appeared tense and intent on getting some very important message to us. He said we were so independent, so much doing things on our own, frequently starting new things, often without permission. He said that he never knew where we were headed and sometimes did not even know where we had been. Then M. R. shifted his weight in the seat, smiled radiantly and said: "And if you were not this way, I would not want you over here." Everyone relaxed and felt especially close in our individuality, as M. R. went on to praise us being self-starters—tough in loneliness, cutting new turf. He instilled us with more courage without neglecting caution and accountability. I've told this often, yet tears again fill my eyes as I recall the huddle at Kassel House with M. R.[3]

—from B. Merle Crouse, church executive and former BVS worker:

M. R. Zigler had an attitude toward the young and often inexperienced workers who entered the European program to which he gave leadership, that was very inspiring and motivational. He trusted the young adults who came into the European program to be highly motivated, to see peace, to love others, and to give of themselves in an uncomplicated way because of their commitment to Christ, to peace and brotherhood. He understood that young workers could be leaders, would make some mistakes, but basically would work through their lack of experience by sheer energy and commitment in a way often not possible for more traditional bureaucratic leadership who had come to be cautious, who knew the rules of protocol and who had lost some of their venturesomeness. . . . M. R. also felt that young persons were less prejudiced and could relate readily to fellow human beings of other cultures and political persuasions without hang-ups, and restricting stereotypes. I believe he was right. He gave me confidence to do things I would never have expected of myself because of his trust in raw talent and high motivation.[4]

—from Leona Row Eller, widow of W. Harold Row, writing of the warmth of the relationship between Row and Zigler despite administrative tensions over the years:

The best example of this relationship was the amount of time M. R. spent with us during the Washington, D. C., days. M. R. was a frequent over-night visitor during Harold's illness (1969-1971). M. R. had returned from Florida to New Windsor, so he was free to come to the city to meet other friends—and he would usually stay with us. The favorite time for both of them was the fruit snack before bed-time. With a plate of fruit, I would peel apples, oranges, or pears, and we would eat together. M. R. would call it our "fruit party." He was like a member of the family when he came.[5]

—from Wayne F. Geisert, president of Bridgewater College:

During my earliest time at Bridgewater College, he confronted me at Annual Conference (in Ocean Grove) and asked me whether I would come to Sebring the following winter to speak during the Bible week there. I explained carefully that I am not a minister. He cut right through that and insisted that it would be good for a layman to be the speaker there. Obviously, I could not decline the invitation. When I arrived in Sebring for the Bible conference, I learned that he had moved temporarily from his very comfortable apartment so that I could enjoy the use of it during my stay. I did enjoy it immensely. He told me that I needed his apartment in order to get some rest, quiet, and relaxation from day to day. As it turned out, the most enjoyable interruptions to the quietness were his regular visits to talk with me concerning whatever was on his mind. From that time on M. R. and I were good friends. While we were not always on the same wave lengths, we seemed always to understand one another.[6]

—from Robert Greiner, CPS man and treasurer of the General Board:

On June 26, 1941, I arrived at Lagro, Indiana, with a group of about 100 inductees to open the first Brethren CPS Camp #6. . . . I soon met Bob, who was also national camp director, Harold Row being employed several months later. We had at least monthly camp meetings, with Bob coming sometimes from Elgin. We had some "radicals" from Chicago, and Bob was very patient while the group debated whether to let him speak, the campers always finally voting to let him do so. . . . Shortly thereafter, while Bob was at camp, he asked me to move to Elgin to handle BSC Camp finances. . . . On Oct. 31, 1942, I was married to Edna in Lancaster, Pa., and Edna came to Elgin with me for a two week "honeymoon," planning to return to Lancaster, since wives could not live with CPSers. Bob supposedly informally cleared with General Hershey her staying, and had publishing house manager. E. M. Hersh, employ her. . . .

During those Elgin CPS days, Amy and Bob had us to their home many Sundays for dinner, and finally the Elgin CPS group grew to 20-25. During those early days, assignee Bill Clannin and I made a number of weekend visits to nearby CPS camps with Bob. For instance, one weekend we drove to Milwaukee, took the boat across Lake Michigan to visit Camp #17, Stronach, Michigan. These trips meant late night travel, and I learned why Bob could keep going: he could quickly fall asleep anywhere; in cars, boats, airplanes, on chairs or floors, etc.[7]

—from Ira Gibbel, pastor and former BSC staff worker in Europe:

The most significant event . . . was M. R.'s visit to Bethany in the spring of '47. I was in my second year as a student there. He had just come back from a visit to Europe and was invited (he probably invited himself) to speak in Chapel. He painted such a picture of the need in war-torn Europe and put forth such a challenge: "We need hundreds of young people to go to Europe to bind up the wounds left by that terrible war." . . . I was caught up by his challenge and so were Henry and Millie Long. . . . [H]is appeal was such that I just had to go. We were duly signed up and assigned to Poland.[8]

—from Glenn and Ethel Harris, active church leaders in Louisiana:

Glenn took a snapshot of M. R. Zigler wading in the Anacoco Creek during the Saturday afternoon break at Texas and Louisiana District Conference held at Rosepine, LA, in the summer of 1946. M. R. Zigler was standing with J. B. Firestone, pant legs rolled up, in the shallow creek. . . . M. R. could talk and deal with military dignitaries and heads of councils of churches, but he also could enjoy wading in the creek with a fellow Brethren minister.[9]

—from Irvin B. Horst, Mennonite scholar and former MCC worker:

My own friendship with M. R. dates from the years of MCC relief work in Europe during the late 1940s. With him I felt fully accepted; he was genuinely interested—not merely curious—about MCC activities. . . . In many ways he was my introduction card to the Brethren. He took a great delight in getting Mennonites and Brethren together.

Later, on my second term during the early 1950s, our friendship became a comradeship. We had many meetings, as well as personal conversations, about peace work and witness. . . . What a challenging task we faced as Historic Peace Churches! The idea of preparing a peace statement for the WCC I am sure was M. R.'s—and the more difficult it became the more he was determined to see it through. . . . In all of this M. R. was the chairman and leading spirit. His genuine friendliness and vision kept us moving ahead. . . .

For me M. R. was a senior brother in the Christian faith with firm convictions about the New Testament way of peace and nonresistance. His loyalty to the tradition was unquestionable. Although he was not a theologian, he was prophetic in his outlook; he never seemed to doubt that the Christian Church was on the road to the rejection of war. M. R. was thoroughly American in his informal friendliness and openness to all persons he met. To some he seemed brash, but the opportunity to meet high officials of church and state never seemed difficult to him. Yet I would say he was a churchman of American allure, a leadership that in the long run paid off.[10]

—from Ida S. Howell, a volunteer aide on the OEPA program:

I thought that M. R. was often lonely. That is understandable, of course, after the loss of his wife. He often just wanted someone to talk to—(or listen)—someone who would understand and share his dreams. He didn't have much patience with just "idle talk" and would quickly change the subject to asking questions about more serious subjects. . . .

He was thrifty in terms of spending money on himself or for his own comfort—like riding the bus at night to save a hotel bill and it was cheaper. He needed to be reminded sometimes that it was time to get new clothes. One of the hostesses at New Windsor was very good at this; she kept his clothes mended and took him shopping when she saw a need. One example I remember was that when he needed hearing aids, instead of buying ones made for him, he used a set for a relative who was deceased. (He did have to give up later and get his own.) Yet he was generous in giving to the church and his favorite charities or projects.[11]

—from Wayne Judd, Church of the Brethren pastor:

The time was the early 1960s at Bridgewater College. Chapel was mostly a time for reading the newspaper. But the opening line by the speaker in the morning caused me to put my paper aside: "I wouldn't give a nickel for the lot of you now, but I would die for what you can become!" I didn't know him at the time but later discovered he was M. R. Zigler.[12]

—from Bernard N. King, pastor and district executive:

When Zigler was Home Missions Secretary at Elgin in 1930 he got me started, fresh out of Juniata College, as a summer pastor in the foothills of Savage Mountain in Western Maryland. I was single, homeless, and without transportation. His regular letters and his newsletters telling of the adventures of all the summer pastors that summer were stimulating.

One Sunday afternoon he suddenly appeared at Deacon Green's farm home, near Lonaconing, presuming that I, too, would be there. He invited me to walk with him. We sat on a rock and chatted for a time in a nearby woods. I was concerned whether he would preach that evening or if he would sit as a judge in a pew. He gracefully excused himself, saying that he had to be on his way west. The memory of that "Elgin" man coming to me when I wasn't sure that I was at the right place, motivated me not only that summer but to continue in part-time ministry that whole year, as I taught high school at Oakland, Maryland. . . .[13]

—from Rufus B. King, CPS man and director of the Castañer project:

There is a tradition that M. R. used to have his "whisker breakfast" at Annual Conference. His party, as I recall, included Elder J. Edson Ulery from Michigan, Elder Reuel B. Pritchett of Tennessee, and Elder I. N. H. Beahm of many parts. These men often vocalized on the floor of Annual Conference. Their support might be crucial in getting backing from segments of the church. These breakfasts would be a clearing ground for M. R. to explain some programs or projects that he felt important to him and to the church. This is an insight in how M. R. got so much effectively accomplished. If one did not agree with him, he could show signs of being disgruntled. But he was a grand person and God, in His wisdom, stretched out M. R.'s life, enabling him to carry on his program to the very end.[14]

—from J. Kenneth Kreider, BVS worker in Germany and Zigler supporter:

When M. R. was scheduled to stay at our home we always stocked up with scrapple. (He always ordered scrapple when in restaurants in Lancaster County.) He was in his 80s and came to our home after an evening meeting. He then learned that he had a ride to Germantown yet that night, rather than stay the night and go to Philadelphia/Germantown by Greyhound the next day. I said, "We have scrapple for breakfast toward morning." He said he would have to eat it tonight. So Carroll fried an entire pan of scrapple, which M. R. ate at 10:15 in the evening—then he left at 10:45 for Philadelphia.[15]

—from John D. Metzler, Sr., longtime associate in relief activities:

When Margaret and I moved to Geneva, MRZ and Amy were anchors, and close friends and helpers in getting integrated. We remained very close, assisting the Ziglers in hosting various Brethren and other groups. Each family bought dishes, a service for twelve of the same pattern, so we could jointly serve groups of 24 with matching dinnerware. . . . Not always did we agree. While our general objectives were very much alike, I do recall one specific item of open disagreement, in regard to the Greek team. MRZ said it would be sufficient if team members would just be nice, loving, friendly people who "hold (the villager's) hand, and say 'I love you,' whether they had any other skills or not." I insisted that we should seek persons who had this social and religious attitude plus technical skills and abilities.

MRZ and Amy, Andre and Magda Trochme [sic], Mr. [Milton] Harder (a representative of the Mennonite Central Committee), and my wife Margaret made a trip to the Eirene project near Ouimes, Morocco, using the Zigler Plymouth. The six passenger car allowed MRZ to take several people, which he liked. It also used a considerable amount of gasoline, and he did not always watch the gauge. So when they ran out of gas in Spain, he flagged down an approaching gasoline truck and tried to use his charm, English, sign language, and other abilities to persuade the driver to sell him some gas from the truck. MRZ seemed to think that his English, "I'm your friend," repeated often enough with gestures, would soften anybody's heart and convey meanings and secure results. But at least this time it did not work, so MRZ was the one who walked to wherever it was necessary to walk to get some emergency gas. While he was gone, Amy shared with the others in the car that she wished she had a dollar for every time in their life together, from courtship days on, that he had run out of gas. His mind was so frequently occupied with the pleasure of people, or with great ideas, that such mundane matters as gasoline supplies often did not intrude.[16]

—from Raymond W. Miller, public relations consultant:

I think it was Kipling who talked about being able to be with ordinary people or walk with kings. Zigler fits that category. I have been with him in the company of some of the most important people in the modern age. He is at home with anybody. I think when he gets to the next world, he will be at home with God in the afternoon. If he dies at night and gets there in the morning, by evening he and God will spend an evening together. Zigler can fit in with anybody who is wholesome minded.[17]

—from Don Murray, former BVS worker in Europe and actor:

M. R. was not an "intellectual." His satisfaction didn't come from discussing and "understanding" things but in doing something about things. He used to get very impatient with the tormented soul-searching of some of his fellow leaders. "Don't sit around studying and talking until you make yourself 'perfect.' There are people out there who are so bad off that just 'good' or even 'fair' seems like perfection to them."

M. R. would sometimes get himself in trouble with the General Brotherhood Board by running off ahead without seeing if anybody was ready to follow. I had sympathy for them. You've got this General Patton of Peacemaking out there conquering territory when you don't have the supply lines in place to hold it. But I had even greater sympathy for M. R.'s view, remembering how he stood up at the World Council of Churches convention and said: "How can there ever be peace in the world when you fellows can't even commit your churches to the promise that you won't go out and kill each other?"

I've hobnobbed with Princess Grace, Frank Lloyd Wright, [and] John F. Kennedy, but the most unforgettable character I've ever met is M. R. Zigler.[18]

—from Howard Schomer, colleague at the World Council of Churches:

Bob was most faithful in participating in the pre-workday devotions at the WCC office, as he was in the workshops and prayer services of the new Ecumenical Institute at Bossey. Often he volunteered to lead our worship, and people from the more formal and stiffer liturgical churches of the Continent were at first a bit surprised and then heart-warmed by his simple Jesus-centered theology, by his intimate way of walking and talking with the Master.

I have never forgotten one self-consciously ecumenical liturgical service in the Bossey chapel, in which Lutherans, Anglicans, Orthodox, Reformed and many others, reading in three languages the mimeographed prayers and responses, in which M. R. Zigler was to bring a brief meditation. As he concluded his refreshing practical remarks he invited the congregation to bow in prayer. He excused himself for not having written his prayer out in advance, ending with that twinkling smile of his, "Anyhow I can't confess my sins in that beautiful language that you Anglicans and Lutherans and the like so easily use. . . . My sins are too ugly and plain to be so elegantly described. And the Lord knows it, and wouldn't believe I was serious. So just bear with me if I talk to him the way I always talk." I sensed he had taught us all an important lesson.[19]

335

—from Chauncey H. Shamberger, Brethren youth director in the 1920s:

> He was not a polished speaker (in a sense he never became one) but in spite of that he always came across with a sense of genuineness. I realized that when he preached in the First Methodist Church of Evanston in the absence of Dr. Tittle, sometime in the 1940s. In spite of the deep affection that existed between Bob and me I had a somewhat queasy feeling as he stood in that pulpit where either Dr. Tittle or in whose absence eminent speakers stood.
>
> By the time he was half way through I had no feeling of apology. I don't think I ever heard Bob speak that he didn't find some place to lambaste the Christian churches for their bloody part in war and prophesying that the churches could go a long way toward establishing peace if they renounced war and refrained from participation in it.[20]

—from Edson Sower, CPS man who left camp to protest cooperation with Selective Service, later Brethren Service worker in Europe:

> I decided to serve out my original commitment of one year [in CPS] and then walk out. I returned my draft card to Selective Service, told them where I could be found and left camp. I ended up in Elgin a few days before Christmas. I attended BSC meetings. I felt that the Church was making a mistake in accepting the responsibility of administration of CPS camps under Selective Service. I was the rebel, kicking over the traces. I talked with Bob, but he was so deeply involved in CPS and we could no place for agreement. Anyway. He asked me what my plans were for [the] next day, Christmas. I had none, and he invited me to their home. It will always remain as one of my life's unforgettable experiences.[21]

—from William Stafford, CPS man and later acclaimed poet:

> M. R. loomed as the personification of the Church of the Brethren for me and the people I knew in Brethren CPS. We felt that in him we had a champion, one who believed in us and our stand, and one who at the same time enjoyed power and status in that world that surrounded us and sometimes seemed a menace.
>
> [As] a young person being managed (inevitably, I know, as we had to be both governed and indulged in order to survive in the strange draft status we had) I sometimes felt overshadowed and treated in a kindly but stern-fatherly way by M. R. and others who ran the program. Not that M. R. was particularly domineering so far as my experience goes, but for his bulk and sway in meetings, and his leverage on committees and such, he had to endure some of the barbs from people held in camps and feeling put upon by the system. He

336

couldn't free us; he couldn't indulge us more than the government would allow. And as a consequence he was sometimes a lightning rod in times of stress. I always felt he was a great one, a leader in the only kind of sense I felt like being a follower, someone with moral authority and a sense of fellow-feeling with all human beings.[22]

—from Eric Tucker, English Quaker and pacifist:

What first struck me about M. R. from the beginning was his ease of association. I was Eric to him from our first introduction. He seemed always at ease whether he was talking with people who were famous in their walk of life or with the newest young C.O. working in a totally unfamiliar surrounding. The fellowship conferences continued for some years. They were never dominated by M. R.; indeed, he was always thrusting others into positions of leadership. He had a great belief in trusting others to do what he was most fitted to do himself.

His generosity of spirit was another characteristic. I recall an occasion of a meeting of the Continuation Committee of the HPC which used to meet on the Continent about twice a year. He was staying in a reasonable but comfortable hotel with the Mennonite representative. I was staying in the far less comfort at that time of the Quaker Centre (this was in Paris). M. R. suggested that it would be better and more convenient if I moved in with them, and when I demurred on grounds of cost, he insisted on making himself responsible for the hotel charges.[23]

—from Roy White, on a Home Mission visit by Zigler in Alabama:

The first forenoon after he spent the night with us, he walked from the G. W. Petcher home downhill to the still where I was working in the cooper shed making barrels to hold our next charge of hot rosin. He greeted me as I worked at shaping a barrel to ready it for fitting in a bottom. Then his eye was caught by a huge gallinippper doing its dance aerially in a quiet corner. Watching the inch-or-more, mosquito-shaped insect with bulging eyes, Bob asked reverently, "Roy, what is that?"

Straightening and looking, I quipped, "That, Bob, is an Alabama mosquito. A young one. If an adult mosquito takes after you, then you must get a club and defend yourself." . . .

The dinner call sounded so we walked back the path, past the country store, and in the back door, through the kitchen and into the dining room. After washing, seating, and Bob blessing the food, Bob looked up the table to my girl, Ruth Wine. . . . "Ruth," Bob queried, "are you going to marry this fellow?" After exchanging a look with me, Ruth nodded. So Bob continued. "Well, do you believe everything he tells you?" "Sure do," Ruth replied. Then

337

she studied me and added, "If he is serious." "Well, how can you tell?" demanded Bob. Ruth considered, "Oh—if he looks at you, he means it. But if he is grinning and his eyes are dancing, he may be pulling your leg." Bob had a cautious swallow of coffee, then spoke as he set his cup down," Well, he sure tried to pull mine awhile ago."[24]

—from Harper Will, well-known Brethren pastor:

The genius of M. R. was in his capacity for friendship. He was at home wherever he was, on the road, in camp, in Europe, among soldiers, or with whomever his fellow-travelers happened to be. He knew, as did Jesus, his Mentor, the necessity of a circle of disciples. He had limitations in administration, but genius in gathering friends, and no hesitation in requesting their assistance in realizing his dreams. To a lot of Brethren M. R. was unofficially a bishop.[25]

—from Pastor Wilfried Warneck, Church and Peace, West Germany:

Many members of the Church of the Brethren are not aware of how important the Church of the Brethren has been for the development of the ecumenical movement. That's true for the foundation of the World Council of Churches as such, but it's particularly true for the whole area of service and ecumenical help and interchurch aid. This dimension of the ecumenical movement wouldn't have been started so early and with the same drive had it not been for Brother M. R. Zigler and other Brethren representatives to the ecumenical movement in Geneva.[26]

—from Leland Wilson, pastor and director of the Washington office:

I remember an evening when M. R. had come to dinner, and after dinner . . . M. R. and Bruce, my second son, continued to talk. Bruce was then in college. M. R. asked him something about the church. Bruce answered: "I don't know. Anyway, M. R., I'm an atheist." "A what?" "An atheist, said Bruce. "Oh. I didn't know that you were so smart! Tell me about being an atheist. I might be one myself." There followed a really profound discussion about religious belief and faith—an area where Bruce did not often venture in those days. But this religious giant took seriously the claim to atheism and the basis for religious dialogue was established. He was a believer whose belief was not threatened by other belief or unbelief.[27]

—from Suzanne Windisch, German secretary at the Kassel House:

> I was asked one day to write a letter for Dr. Zigler. I was rather nervous for fear I would not be able to do my task right. I shall never forget the natural human kindness with which he helped me to overcome my fear. Never before had I met a person in Dr. Zigler's position who was so little "boss-like" as he was. Something else I noticed during his stay at Brethren House: he had a very easy and natural way of establishing contact with other people and especially with young people. For him every individual seemed to be important notwith-standing social status, education or religion. . . . When Dr. Zigler was already in his eighties he visited Kassel twice. All he would carry with him was a small suitcase with his personal belongings. He lived still the "simple life" like the boy he had been and who, as he once told me, went to school without wearing shoes.[28]

A Letter from M. R. Zigler:

Steve Hoover, the young son of Warren and Ruth Hoover, had heard M. R. Zigler speak about peace. When he asked his mother how M. R. got started on peace, his mother replied: "Steve, I am not sure. That is a very good question, so why don't you write and ask him?" Somewhat later, the child reappeared with this handwritten letter, covering a page: "Dear M. R. How did you get started in Peace Love Steve Hoover." This is M. R. Zigler's reply:

November 26, 1976

Dear Steve:
    You should have had a letter from me sooner but I have been away and now before I go again this afternoon I will try to answer your wonderful question. I guess you know that I am 85 years old and that is a long time since I was a little boy your age. I can remember those days when I used to ask questions of older people and I am glad that you felt like asking me how I got started in peace.
    First, I was born in a home where they believed killing was wrong and they were against war as a method of settling problems.
    Second, the church I attended as a boy helped me to understand that war was wrong and that I should not participate in violence, even little fights on the school ground or other places. It seemed fun for awhile until anger developed, then fight.
    Third, it was understood in my family that I should love everybody and help them in every way possible to have a good life, especially when children

339

needed things. At age 10 I decided to join the Church of the Brethren. When I was baptized, several questions were asked. Among these was, "Will you promise not to participate in war or learn the art of war?" This I promised and I feel as long as I am a member I must do this or leave the church.

Fourth, I attended a college that helped me as a young man to keep my vow never to go to war.

Fifth, during World War I, I was a YMCA secretary and observed young men joining the Marines in training for war. For three years I lived with this and every day I thought that the greatest injury to our nation was the waste of the lives of young men all physically well and intelligent.

Sixth, with my training of not participating in war, I decided that another war should not occur, but it did and we had World War II. The suffering beyond the battle scene after the war was over was terrible: refugees, starving people, homeless families, lost children, burned out property leaving so many dead people and the living having trouble finding places to sleep because the buildings were destroyed.

After this, one cannot help hoping that war will never come again. It is the business of Christian people to prevent wars.

You will see that I have gone beyond your question how I got started in peace making, but I thought you would be interested. If you do not understand this letter, next time you see me let's talk more about how I got started in peace.

It has given me much joy to write this letter and I hope that we will meet many times in the future. I hope that you will be a person who will talk and write to others about bringing peace in the world.[29]

M. R. Zigler,
Convener of ON EARTH PEACE ASSEMBLY

NOTES

1. Edith Bonsack Barnes to D. F. Durnbaugh, April 10, 1987.
2. Charles Boyer, statement prior to M. R. Zigler's visit to Bethany Theological Seminary, November, 1962.
3. Clyde Carter to D. F. Durnbaugh, April 11, 1987.
4. B. Merle Crouse to D. F. Durnbaugh, April 27, 1987.
5. Leona Row Eller to D. F. Durnbaugh, May 2, 1987.
6. Wayne F. Geisert to D. F. Durnbaugh, April 13, 1987.
7. Robert Greiner to D. F. Durnbaugh, May 10, 1987.
8. Ira W. Gibbel to D. F. Durnbaugh, May 25, 1987.

9. Glenn and Ethel Harris to D. F. Durnbaugh, April 22, 1987.

10. Irvin B. Horst to D. F. Durnbaugh, June 30, 1987.

11. Ida S. Howell to D. F. Durnbaugh, April 20, 1987.

12. J. Wayne Judd to D. F. Durnbaugh, [May, 1987].

13. Bernard N. King to D. F. Durnbaugh, May 22, 1987.

14. Rufus B. King to D. F. Durnbaugh, Aug. 12, 1978.

15. J. Kenneth Kreider to D. F. Durnbaugh, Nov. 3, 1987.

16. John D. Metzler, Sr., to D. F. Durnbaugh, June 12, 1987.

17. Harold D. Smith interview with Raymond W. Miller, Dec. 17, 1984.

18. Don Murray to D. F. Durnbaugh, May 4, 1987.

19. Howard Schomer to D. F. Durnbaugh, May 7, 1987.

20. Chauncey H. Shamberger to D. F. Durnbaugh, April, 1987].

21. Edson Sower to D. F. Durnbaugh, May 30, 1988.

22. William Stafford to D. F. Durnbaugh, April 15, 1987.

23. Eric Tucker to D. F. Durnbaugh, May 1, 1987.

24. Roy White to D. F. Durnbaugh, May, 1987.

25. Harper Will to D. F. Durnbaugh, April 22, 1985.

26. Pfarrer Wilfried Warneck, church bulletin, 1983.

27. Leland Wilson to D. F. Durnbaugh, July 13, 1987.

28. Suzanne Windisch to D. F. Durnbaugh, May 21, 1987.

29. M. R. Zigler to Steve Hoover, Nov. 26, 1976.

SOURCES

F OR YEARS, friends insisted that M. R. Zigler should write his memoirs. They knew that he alone possessed information about peace causes and relief efforts that had never been chronicled. The requests started coming, in fact, as he lay stricken in his hospital bed in Västervik, Sweden, in the autumn of 1958. He was then for a time employed to do so by the General Brotherhood Board of the Church of the Brethren when he returned to the USA late in 1958. Off and on, interrupted by numerous speaking engagements, M. R. Zigler devoted time to the project. He made several trips to Europe to collect materials, aided by capable research assistance in the persons of Frances Clemens (Nyce), Suzanne Windisch, and Marlene Boehme. In Elgin, retired Brethren staff worker Edith Barnes came to his assistance. The eventual result was a manuscript, which, however, he never released, with the expectation that it would be revealed after his death. Five chapters of this work, however, were published as the first section of the book of memoirs of pioneer Brethren Service workers, titled *To Serve the Present Age* (1975). At the time he gave permission for the use of those chapters, he indicated that he had slowed work on the manuscript at the suggestion of Norman J. Baugher and W. Harold Row, both of whom stated that Row intended to write a history of Brethren Service.

Because Zigler found it so difficult to get his thoughts into organized written prose, his many admirers pressed him to dictate his recollections. This he attempted to do on many occasions, most completely in 1982 when Romelle S. Million, a professional verbatim reporter, transcribed his reflections. Other lengthy interviews were conducted by J. Kenneth

Kreider, Vernon F. Miller, Donald F. Durnbaugh, Lawrence W. Haynes and Donald W. Rummel, and other Brethren. A number of taped interviews were made in Sebring, Florida. Grant Stoltzfus, Mennonite scholar, taped Zigler's memories about the Civilian Public Service program and the NSBRO, as did two scholars of military history, John J. O'Sullivan and Edgar L. Money, Jr. Harold E. Fey taped an interview with M. R. Zigler in the course of collecting material for his history of Church World Service. Some of M. R. Zigler's public addresses were caught on tape, and, in part, transcribed. Additionally, from time to time M. R. Zigler wrote unpublished essays on different parts of his life and work, such as his memories of the Zigler farm and the fateful accident at Västervik. His daughter, Geraldine Zigler Glick, helped him in organizing this material.

Unfortunately, in these interviews, as well as in his writings, his characteristic rambling narrative approach makes them very difficult to use. He generally found it necessary to begin dealing with any current situation by relating his life as a boy in Broadway, Virginia, and his experiences as a YMCA worker on Parris Island. It seemed impossible for him to speak at length on any single point without ranging over the whole of his impressively lengthy and active career. There is great redundancy in all of these materials.

Trying to respond to the pressure to write his memoirs, M. R. Zigler, in his later years, began to write lengthy letters to his correspondents, in which he reflected on his experiences. He also ransacked his files to find what he considered significant documents, which he stamped with the notation *Biographical* and sent to those interested.

All of these materials, along with hundreds of folders of his collected correspondence, are found in his papers. Unfortunately, these papers are in chaotic condition. Never kept in truly systematic fashion, they are hopelessly disorganized. The son and daughter of M. R. Zigler have graciously placed the papers in the Bridgewater College Library, Bridgewater, Virginia, where they may, in good time, be placed in order. Other Zigler papers are to be found mixed with the files of the On Earth Peace Assembly at New Windsor, Maryland.

The central repository for Church of the Brethren records is the Brethren Historical Library and Archives, Elgin, Illinois. Because of Zigler's extended tenure as a church executive, from 1919 to 1948 in the USA and from 1948 to 1958 in Europe, thousands of documents exist there written by him, to him, or related to his work. In addition, his activities with the On Earth Peace movement from 1974 to his death in 1985, as well as his contacts with other Brethren bodies, have created other records. The BHLA has biographical files about church leaders, notably including M. R. Zigler.

A score of other libraries and archives in this country and abroad also contain data on Zigler and his endeavors. They are mentioned in the following list. The potential biographer, therefore, does not have the problem of too little material but of too much disorganized material. It is not hard to see why most of those who thought of undertaking a biography of M. R. Zigler decided not to pursue it. The exceptions are Inez Long who wrote *One Man's Peace* (1983) and the present effort.

List of Archives and Libraries Consulted

(Note: All unpublished letters and documents listed in the chapter notes without locations are taken from the M. R. Zigler Papers, now deposited at the Bridgewater College Library, Bridgewater, Virginia.)

District of Columbia:
National Archives and Records Administration, Washington (Selective Service Records)

Illinois:
Bethany Theological Library Archives, Oak Brook (Rufus D. Bowman Papers, Albert C. Wieand Papers)
Brethren Historical Library and Archives, Elgin (Biographical Files, Brethren Service Committee/Commission Files, Christian Education Files, Home Mission Files, Ministry Files, miscellaneous files)
Department of Special Collections, University of Chicago Library, Chicago (Kermit Eby Papers)

Indiana:
Special Collections, Manchester College Library, North Manchester (Otho Winger Papers)
Mennonite Historical Archives, Goshen (Mennonite Central Committee Files, Harold S. Bender Papers, Orie O. Miller Papers, Peace Problems Committee Papers)

Kansas:
McPherson College Library, McPherson (Historical Collection)
Mennonite Historical Library and Archives, Newton (H. P. Krehbiel Papers)

Maryland:
On Earth Peace Assembly, New Windsor (M. R. Zigler Papers, OEPA Records)

New Jersey:
Rutgers University Archives, New Brunswick (American Council of Voluntary
Agencies for Foreign Service Records)

New York:
Rare Book and Manuscript Library, Columbia University, New York (Andrew W.
Cordier Papers)
Union Theological Library, New York (Special Collections, A. L. Warnshuis
Papers)

Ohio:
Ashland College and Seminary Library, Ashland (Special Collections)

Pennsylvania:
American Friends Service Committee Archives, Philadelphia (AFSC Files,
Clarence Pickett Diary)
Elizabethtown College Library, Elizabethtown (Special Collections)
Haverford College Library, Haverford (Rufus Jones Papers)
Presbyterian Historical Society, Philadelphia (Federal Council of Churches
Papers)
Swarthmore College Peace Collection, Swarthmore (NSBRO Records, Paul
Comley French Diary)
US Army Military History Institute, Carlisle Barracks (Selective Service Files,
Gen. Lewis B. Hershey Papers)

Switzerland:
Brethren Service Commission, Geneva (BSC Files)
World Council of Churches Library and Archives, Geneva (Inter-Church Aid and
Service to Refugees Files, Historic Peace Churches Papers)

Virginia:
Bridgewater College Library, Bridgewater (Special Collections)
Menno Simons Historical Library and Archives, Eastern Mennonite College,
Harrisonburg (Grant Stoltzus Papers, Agnes Kline Papers)

List of Informants

In the spring of 1987 a large list of friends of M. R. Zigler were asked if they would be willing to share remembrances of the Brethren leader for the purpose of this biography. Many responded positively, sending in anecdotes, copies of letters, and in a few cases, extensive manuscripts. They were of great assistance in the writing process, even if not all were specifically quoted or cited. The gratitude of the author is expressed to the following persons who responded to the query or gave assistance in other ways:

John C. Baker (New Jersey)
Edith Barnes (Illlinois)
Fred W. Benedict (Ohio)
Desmond W. Bittinger (California)
Marlene Boehme (Austria)
Harold Z. Bomberger (Pennsylvania)
S. Loren Bowman (California)
Dale W. Brown (Illinois)
Wayne F. Buckle (Virginia)
L. Clyde Carter (Virginia)
Stephen Cary (Pennsylvania)
McKinley Coffman (Maryland)
Dante Cricca (Italy)
Ed Crill (Pennsylvania)
B. Merle Crouse (Florida)
A. Stauffer Curry (New York)
Byron E. Dell (Oklahoma)
Ruth Early (Florida)
Leona Row Eller (Florida)
Calvert N. Ellis (Pennsylvania)
Harold D. Fasnacht (California)
Earle Fike, Jr. (Pennsylvania)
Glenn J. Fruth (Kansas)
Dennis Garber (Austria)
Merlin E. Garber (Virginia)
Wayne F. Geisert (Virginia)
Ira W. Gibbel (Pennsylvania)
G. Wayne Glick (Pennsylvania)
Geraldine Zigler Glick (Virginia)
Robert Greiner (Illinois)
Warren F. Groff (Illinois)

Glenn and Ethel Harris (Louisiana)
Mildred E. Heckert (Illinois)
A. Blair Helman (Indiana)
Esther Mohler Ho (California)
Irvin B. Horst (Pennsylvania)
Ida S. Howell (California)
Jacob S. Huffman (Virginia)
J. Wayne Judd (Virginia)
Alice Kachkachian (Switzerland)
Max M. Kampelman (Washington, D. C.)
Bernard N. King (Pennsylvania)
Rufus D. King (Indiana)
Paul W. Kinsel (Ohio)
J. Kenneth Kreider (Pennsylvania)
Robert S. Kreider (Kansas)
John A. Lapp (Pennsylvania)
Samuel D. Lindsay (Virginia)
Inez Long (Pennsylvania)
Ercell V. Lynn (North Carolina)
Kenneth E. McDowell (Maryland)
Jefferson Mathis (California)
Gerald Mease (Indiana)
John D. Metzler, Sr. (Oregon)
John Mischitz (Illinois)
Ira W. Moomaw (Florida)
Kenneth I. Morse (Illinois)
Baxter M. Mow (Virginia)
Joseph B. Mow (West Virginia)
Don Murray (California)
James F. Myer (Pennsylvania)

Kurtis F. Naylor (Missouri)

Robert W. Neff (Pennsylvania)

Hubert Newcomer (Florida)

Gerry Pence (California)

Hazel Peters (Virginia/Maryland)

Raymond R. Peters (Florida)

Ronald D. Petry (Maryland)

Dan Raffensperger (Pennsylvania)

Jacqueline Mueller Richez (Switzerland)

Donald W. Rummel (Pennsylvania)

Roger E. Sappington (Virginia)

Howard Schomer (New Jersey)

Chauncey H. Shamberger (Idaho)

Harold D. Smith (Maryland/Virginia)

Graydon F. Snyder (Illinois)

William T. Snyder (Pennsylvania)

Edson Sower (Arizona)

William E. Stafford (Oregon)

Kermon Thomasson (Illinois)

R. Jan Thompson (Maryland)

Eric Tucker (England)

Dale V. Ulrich (Virginia)

M. Guy West (Virginia)

Harper Will (Indiana)

Leland Wilson (Washington, D. C.)

Robin Wilson (Pennsylvania)

Suzanne Windisch (West Germany)

Ronald E. Wyrick (Virginia)

John Howard Yoder (Indiana)

Joseph B. Yount III (Virginia)

Robert S. Zigler (Washington, D. C.)

C. Wayne Zunkel (California)

Charles E. Zunkel (Indiana)

BIBLIOGRAPHY OF ███████
M. R. ZIGLER'S WRITINGS

Articles:

(Abbreviations: *GM* = *Gospel Messenger*; *MV* = *Missionary Visitor*; *BLT* = *Brethren Life and Thought*. Listed in chronological order by articles and books.)

"Spanish-Speaking Americans," *GM* (November, 13, 1920): 683
[MRZ], "Opportunities in the Homeland," *MV* (November, 1920): 299-308
"A Conference on Negro Work," *GM* (January 21, 1921): 36
"Home Missions and the Annual Conference," *MV* (May, 1922): 146
"Meeting of District Mission Boards June 6 and 7," *GM* (June 3, 1922): 340
"Meeting of District Mission Boards at Winona Lake, Ind.," *MV* (August, 1922): 320-322
"Our Italian Challenge," *GM* (December 23, 1922): 803
"Nineteen-Twenty-three," *MV* (January, 1923): 18
"Unauthorized Solicitations," *GM* (January 13, 1923): 19
"'Wearever' or Christ?" *GM* (February 24, 1923): 116
"A Noble Life [Anna A. Swigart, Germantown]," *MV* (March, 1923): 77-79
"Christ and Retrenchment," *MV* (October, 1923): 370-371
"Conference for Country Church Leaders," *GM* (December 15, 1923): 789
"A School for Rural Pastors," *MV* (January, 1924): 20
"The School for Rural Church Leaders," *GM* (February 23, 1924): 124 also published in *MV* (March, 1924): 76, 80
"Home Mission Notes," *GM* (May 3, 1924): 277
"Thanksgiving and Home Missions," *GM* (November 20, 1924): 746
"Home Mission Number," *MV* (November, 1924): 385-386
"Is America on Your Heart?" *MV* (November, 1926): 353-354

"Let Us Walk with Christ," *MV* (February, 1928), insert

"Paying the Price," *MV* (October, 1928): 305-306

"Is America Christian?" *MV* (November, 1930): 402

"Pastoral Conference Program," *GM* (February 21, 1931): 21

"Our Home Mission Work," *GM* (November 21, 1931): 5-6

"Meeting of the General Ministerial Board," *GM* (January 2, 1932): 12, 20

"Schools for Rural Church Leaders," *GM* (February 20, 1932): 21

"Camp Mack Training School and Bible Conference," *GM* (June 11, 1932): 27

"Report of the Meeting of the General Ministerial Board at Anderson, Indiana,"
     GM (July 2, 1932): 12

"Answers Concerning Our Home Mission Work," *GM* (August 27, 1932): 14

"Annual Report of Congregations for the Yearbook," *GM* (September 10, 1932):
     17

"Trending Toward Christianity," *GM* (November 5, 1932): 5-6

"The Present Ministerial Situation," *GM* (November 26, 1932): 14-15

"Meeting of the General Ministerial Board," *GM* (January 14, 1933): 24

"Membership Increase," *GM* (March 25, 1933): 18

"Strength in Tennessee," *GM* (May 20, 1933): 5

"Southern Virginia," *GM* (August 19, 1933): 11

"Meeting of District Ministerial and Mission Boards," *GM* (September 2, 1933):
     11

"Policy on Ministerial Placement," *GM* (September 9, 1933): 18-20

"Ministers' Conference [Bethany]," *GM* (September 9, 1933): 21, 24

"Bethany Ministers' Conference," *GM* (September 23, 1933): 24-25

"The Statistical Report 1932-33," *GM* (October 14, 1922): 6-7

"Bethany Ministers' Conference," *GM* (October 21, 1933): 11

"The Meeting of the General Ministerial Board," *GM* (November 18, 1933): 9-10

"Evangelistic Work," *GM* (November 18, 1933): 19

"Sectional Conferences for Ministers and Other Church Workers," *GM* (May 26,
     1934): 12

"Bethany Ministers' Conference," *GM* (September 29, 1934): 24

"Home Life in the Church of the Brethren," *GM* (October 6, 1934): 3

"Men and Home Missions," *GM* (November 24, 1934): 5-6

"To Ministers and Superintendents," *GM* (April 13, 1935): 18

"Trends in Home Missions," *GM* (June 1, 1935): 47-50

"Meetings of the General Boards," *GM* (November 30, 1935): 8-9

"Peace Action Program for the Church of the Brethren, 1936-1937 (includes Letter
     to Churches)," *GM* (April 11, 1936): 21-23

"Our 1937 Easter Offering," *GM* (March 6, 1937): 8-10

"Our Ministry," *GM* (April 10, 1937): 8-9

"Flood Relief [in Ohio Valley]," *GM* (May 29, 1937): 20-21

"Concerning Ministerial Placement," *GM* (July 3, 1937): 16

"A Message from the Oxford Conference to the Christian Churches," *GM* (August 21, 1937): 5-7

"The Oxford Conference Closes and the Edinburgh Conference Begins," *GM* (August 18, 1937): 15, 21

"Church, Community and State," *GM* (September 11, 1937): 13-15

"The Church and the Economic Order," *GM* (September 18, 1937): 6-7

"The Church and War and the World of Nations," *GM* (September 25, 1937): 6-7)

"Schwarzenau Today," *GM* (October 2, 1937): 5-6

"Sweden and Denmark," *GM* (October 9, 1937): 5-6

"The World Conference on Faith and Order," *GM* (October 16, 1937): 6-8

"Peace," *GM* (December 18, 1937): 21-22

"Matching Sacrifice [on relief giving]," *GM* (January 8, 1938): 5-6

"Materials for Local Church Workers, 1938-39," *GM* (September 3, 1938): 19

"Bethany and Our Demands," *GM* (September 10, 1938): 5

"A Real Co-operative," *GM* (March 18, 1939): 22

"The Church at Work in Teaching—Evangelism," *GM* (March 25, 1939): 22-23

"The Church Work Through Passion Week," *GM* (April 1, 1939): 21

"The Church Looking Forward to Pentecost," *GM* (April 8, 1939): 20

"Annual Conference," *GM* (April 15, 1939): 21-22

"The Minister and Annual Conference," *GM* (May 13, 1939): 18

"Every Child Is the Concern of Us All," *GM* (August 19, 1939): 21

"Religious Education Work," *GM* (September 9, 1939): 20-21

"Home Missions and Human Need," *GM* (February 17, 1940): 15, 21

"A Revitalized Membership—Through Christian Education," *GM* (March 16, 1940): 10

"The Selective Training and Service Act of 1940," *GM* (October 5, 1940): 17

"Meeting of the General Ministerial Board," *GM* (November 23, 1940): 21-22

"Meeting of the Council of Boards," *GM* (November 23, 1940): 22

"Church Architecture," *GM* (January 4, 1941): 22-23

"Brethren Service Committee Meeting," *GM* (September 6, 1941): 19-20

"Our Brethren Colleges and Rural Heritage," *GM* (November 1, 1941): 15

"A Call to the Church—A Time for Sacrifice," *GM* (December 20, 1941): 17

"Brethren Service in Our World," *GM* (January 3, 1942): 13

"To the Laity of the Church," *GM* (February 7, 1942): 19-20

"Our Part in Religious Liberty," *GM* (February 21, 1942): 10

"Home Missions in the Church of the Brethren," *GM* (April 11, 1942): 18-22

"Council of Boards," *GM* (May 16, 1942): 13

"Brethren Service Committee," *GM* (May 16, 1942): 16

"General Ministerial Board," *GM* (May 16, 1942): 16-17

"Items Concerning Ministerial Interests," *GM* (August 15, 1942): 22-23

"Report of September Brethren Service Committee Meeting . . .," *GM* (October 17, 1942): 10-11

"Guarantee . . .," *GM* (October 24, 1942): 5-6

"Regional Policy Adopted by Annual Conference," *GM* (October 24, 1942): 13-14

"The Church Today," *GM* (November 7, 1942): 26-27

"General Ministerial Board," *GM* (December 12, 1942): 8-9

"Brethren Service Committee," *GM* (December 12, 1942): 9-10

"Council of Boards," *GM* (December 12, 1942): 10-11

"Fulfilling Our Privilege in 1943 . . .," *GM* (January 2, 1943): 18

"Report of January Brethren Service Committee Meeting . . .," *GM* (February 13, 1943): 12

"Looking Ahead," *GM* (March 6, 1943): 14-15

"Relief Work in Puerto Rico," *GM* (April 10, 1943): 10

"Report of the Brethren Service Committee Meeting . . ., " *GM* (July 24, 1943): 11

"Brethren Service in 1944," *GM* (January 1, 1944): 14-15

"A Letter to the Brotherhood," *GM* (May 20, 1944): 10-11

"Resources for the World Task," *GM* (November 11, 1944): 5

"Guest Editorial," *GM* (November 10, 1945): 3

"Europe Suffers—Will the Christian Church Respond?" *GM* (November 10, 1945): 7-8

"Statement Before the Senate Military Affairs Committee," *GM* (June 1, 1946): 6

"The Angels Sang, 'Peace . . . Goodwill,'" *GM* (December 22, 1945): 6-7

"Three Things We Must Do," *GM* (April 20, 1946: 7-8

"Where Lies Our Task?" *GM* (November 2, 1946): 5-6

"Crisis Appeals," *GM* (March 20, 1948): 11-12

"M. R. Zigler Accompanies [CROP] Abraham Lincoln Friendship Train," *GM* (March 20, 1948): 10

"Thoughts at Schwarzenau," *GM* (October 2, 1948): 7-8

"The Christian's Response to Europe's Need," *GM* (November 6, 1948): 8-9

"One Great Hour and the Way to Peace," *GM* (March 19, 1949): 6-7

"Let Us Prove Ourselves," *GM* (July 9, 1949): 8-9

"Peace Through Acts of Charity," *GM* (March 4, 1950): 10-11

"A Challenge to the Church," *GM* (June 10, 1950): 8-9

"A Firm Vow," *GM* (March 3, 1951): 3, 12-13

"P. G. Bhagat Tours Europe," *GM* (May 5, 1951): 19

"Christmas—Palestine—and You," *GM* (December 20, 1952): 18-19

"Our Peace Witness in Europe Will Help to Scatter the Darkness and Misery," *GM* (February 28, 1953): 3-4

"Central Committee of the World Council," *GM* (May 9, 1953): 12-13

"Finding Footprints in India," *GM* (May 16, 1953): 8-9

"New Era Begins at Summit Conference," *GM* (September 17, 1955): 14-15

"The Report of the Central Committee," *GM* (September 24, 1955): 12-13

"Responsibility Inescapable," *GM* (October 13, 1956): 9-11
"Refugees 1956," *GM* (December 15, 1956): 14-15
"Reconciling the Churches," *GM* (May 11, 1957): 9-10, 28
"My Hope for Our Future Witness: In Pacifism and Nonviolence," *GM* (April 26, 1958): 24
"Supreme," [text of bulletin back cover] (July 4, 1959)
"Divine Insights," [text of bulletin back cover] [1959]
"World Council Meetings," *GM* (October 10, 1959: 10-12
"Youth Lead Again," *GM* (May 4, 1963): 21
"Dialogue Saved the Church from Division," *GM* (June 1, 1963): 8-10, 16
"No Photograph But a Life," *GM* (October 26, 1963): 12-13
"The Press Was There in 1879," *GM* (June 27, 1964): 18-21
"Elder John Kline—Churchman," *BLT*, 9 (Summer, 1964): 3-20
"Cottrell Memorial Nursing Home," *GM* (September 19, 1964): 24-25
"The Meaning of the Life and Work of Harold S. Bender: A Symposium," *Mennonite Quarterly Review*, 38 (1964): 209-210
"Tribute to Clarence Pickett," *Reporter For Conscience' Sake*, 22 (May, 1965): 1, 3-4
"To Work for Peace Through the Churches," *Messenger* (November 21, 1968): 2-5
"Twenty-Nine Years to Go, Or the Year 2000," *BLT*, 17 (Winter, 1972): 17-23
(with Hazel Peters), "M. R. Zigler at Eighty," *Messenger* (March 1, 1972): 14-17
(with Edward K. Ziegler), "The Assembly of the Brethren," *BLT*, 19 (Winter, 1974): 6-7, 11, 15, 33-35
(with C. Wayne Zunkel), "Interview with M. R. Zigler—May, 1973," *BLT*, 19 (Summer, 1974): 167-177
"The Cooperation of the World's YMCA and the Brethren Service Committee in the Prisoners of War Program During World War II," *BLT*, 26 (Spring, 1981): 84-86
(with Micki Smith), "M. R. Zigler on being Brethren Today," *Messenger* (November, 1981): 14-15
"Originating the Brethren Encyclopedia Project," *BLT*, 30 (Summer, 1985): 135-136

Books and Chapters in Books:

(MRZ and Don E. Smucker), *America's Pacifist Minority, A Comprehensive Survey of the American Conscientious Objector and His Problems Based on the Chicago C.O. Conference of Nov. 15, 1941: Revised and Rechecked, May 4, 1941* (Chicago: Mid-West Fellowship of Reconciliation, 1942), 111pp.
"Introduction," in Roger E. Sappington, *Courageous Prophet: Chapters From the Life of John Kline* (Elgin: Brethren Press, 1964), 9-10

"Before CROP," in *Community Compassion: The Story of Crop* (1967), [5-6]
"Vision for Peace," in David S. Young, ed., *Study War No More* (Elgin: Brethren Press, 1971), 75-88
(MRZ and others), *Tunker House Proceedings: 1972* (Harrisonburg, VA: 1973), 215pp.
(MRZ and others), *To Serve the Present Age: The Brethren Service Story*, ed. D. F. Durnbaugh (Elgin, IL: Brethren Press, 1975), 224pp.
"Brethren," in *On Earth Peace: Discussions on War/Peace Issues Between Friends, Mennonites, Brethren, and European Churches, 1935-1975*, ed. D. F. Durnbaugh (Elgin, IL: Brethren Press, 1978), 13-14

Unpublished Manuscripts

"Future Pacifism—And the Service of the Conscientious Objector" (unsigned, undated manuscript)
"The Creation of Brethren Service," [May, 1960]
"[History of Brethren Service in Europe]," [ca. 189pp.], [ca. 1963]
"People I Met Along the Way Beyond the Family and Public School Teachers and Passing by a Large Number of Church Members, My Home Being Very Close to the Linville Creek Church and Always Open to Guests, We Generally Entertained Church Leaders Visiting Our Congregation, Evangelists, Solicitors, Tramps, School Teachers," 16pp. [ca. 1972]
[Transcript by Romelle S. Million of Zigler's Memoirs], [246pp.], [1982]
"Ministry of the Church of the Brethren," 11pp., "Understanding the Catholics," 3pp.; "Statement Concerning the Automobile Accident at Västervik, Sweden, August 16, 1958," 6pp., [ca. 1979]
[Transcripts of M. R. Zigler's Memoirs,] Sebring, Florida, [34pp.], [n.d.]

BIBLIOGRAPHY OF WRITINGS ABOUT M. R. ZIGLER

(Abbreviations: *GM* = *Gospel Messenger*; *BLT* = *Brethren Life and Thought*. Listed in chronological order by articles and books.)

[Obituary of Mary Zigler], *GM* (February 6, 1904): 95

Jesse Ziegler, with Daniel P. Ziegler, *The Ziegler Family Record* (Royersford, PA: author, 1906)

"Kingdom Gleanings," *GM* (December 13, 1919): 702

[Edward Frantz], "Echoes from Sedalia Conference," *GM* (June 19, 1920): 356 (on first address by MRZ at Annual Conference; one of first of many references to MRZ in *GM*—mention of travels, addresses at conferences)

W. Arthur Cable and Homer F. Sanger, eds., *Educational Blue Book and Directory of the Church of the Brethren, 1708-1923* (Elgin, IL: General Education Board, 1923), 413

[Obituary of Michael Zigler], *GM* (February 6, 1926): 94

Religious Leaders of America (1941-1942), 2: 1145

Rufus D. Bowman, *The Church of the Brethren and War* (Elgin, IL: Brethren Publishing House, 1944); reprinted, with an introduction by Donald F. Durnbaugh (New York: Garland Publishers, 1971)

"Church Leader Tells Plight of Low Countries," *Chicago Daily Tribune* (November 24, 1945): 12

Rufus D. Bowman, *Seventy Times Seven* (Elgin, IL: Brethren Publishing House, 1945)

"BC Award to M. Rob't Zigler," [Harrisonburg, VA] *Daily News-Record* (?) (June 2, 1947)

Edwin T. Randall, "'He Is Not Ashamed to Call Them Brethren,'" *GM* (October 11, 1947): 10-11 (originally published in *New Century Leader*)

Rufus D. Bowman, "Called to Serve Christ in Europe," *GM* (December 6, 1947): 17

Howard Sollenberger and Wendell Flory, "History of the UNRRA-Brethren Service Unit," [Elgin, IL: 1947]

"Zigler Goes to World Council," [Harrisonburg, VA] *Daily News-Record* (?) (June 4, 1948)

Leslie Eisan, *Pathways of Peace* (Elgin, IL: Brethren Publishing House, 1948)

"Dr. Zigler To Be Feted At Dinner," *Elgin* [IL] *Daily Courier-News* (ca. March, 1948)

"Honor Dr. M. R. Zigler At Farewell Dinner; Leaves May 18 for Europe," *Elgin* [IL] *Daily Courier-News* (April 10, 1948), 1, 3

Ralph E. Smeltzer, "The History of Brethren Service in Austria: From Its Beginnings (November, 1946) to July, 1949," class paper, Bethany Biblical Seminary, November 28, 1949

Melvin Gingerich, *Service for Peace: A History of Mennonite Civilian Public Service* (Akron, PA: MCC, 1949)

"Broadway High Class of 1910 in Reunion," [Harrisonburg, VA] *Daily News-Record* (?) (June 7, 1950): 2

Lorell Weiss, *Ten Years of Brethren Service: 1941-1951* (Elgin, IL: BSC, 1951)

Merlin G. Shull, "History of the Brethren Service Commission in Austria, with special emphasis on the span from the summer of 1950 to the summer of 1953," class paper, Bethany Biblical Seminary, November, 1953

Kermit Eby, "Unto the Least of These," in *The God in You* (Chicago: University of Chicago Press, 1954)

"Festtag fuer ganz Schwarzenau: Die Einweihung der neuen Schule," *Aus der Wittgensteiner Heimat* (September 11, 1956)

Lorell Weiss, "Socio-Psychological Factors in the Pacifism of the Church of the Brethren During the Second World War," PhD dissertation, University of Southern California (1957)

"European Director Fills Many Roles," *GM* (March 8, 1958): 12-13

"Aufbauen, dienen, lieben: Zum 250. Geburtstag der 'Church of the Brethren,'" [Kassel] *Evangelischen Sonntagsboten* (August 3, 1958)

"Mrs. M. R. Zigler Is Killed in Swedish Crash; Husband Hurt," *Elgin* [IL] *Daily Courier-News* (August 18, 1958): 1-2

"Brethren Lost in Accidents," *GM* (August 30, 1958): 17

Eleanor Williamson, "Brethren Service in Austria, 1947-1958," mimeographed paper, June, 1958

"European Conference [250th anniversary]," *GM* (September 20, 1958): 8-13

"Kingdom Gleanings," *GM* (September 27, 1958): 16

Paul H. Bowman, ed., *The Adventurous Future: A Compilation of Addresses, Papers, Statements, and Messages Associated with the Celebration of the Two-Hundred-Fiftieth Anniversary of the Church of the Brethren* (Elgin, IL: Brethren Press, 1959)

"20 Employees Are Honored at Brethren Headquarters," *Elgin* [IL] *Daily Courier-News* (April 10, 1959): 20

"Dr. Zigler To Speak Tonight," *Elgin* [IL] *Daily Courier-News* (April 10, 1959): 15

"About People," *Christian Century* (October 8, 1959): 1166

Edgar H. S. Chandler, *The High Tower of Refuge: The Inspiring Story of Refugee Relief Throughout the World* (New York: Frederick A. Praeger, 1959)

Inez Long, "Unbroken Soldier for Peace," *Christian Living* (October, 1960): 16-17, 39

Edith Barnes, "An Apostle of Brotherly Love—Michael Robert Zigler, 1891—" in *Brethren Trailblazers*, ed. Mary C. Garber (Elgin, IL: Brethren Press, 1960), 176-181

Inez Long, "Amy Zigler: The Woman Who Stayed Behind," *GM* (June 25, 1960): 14-15, 18; reprinted in *Faces Among the Faithful* (Elgin, IL: Brethren Press, 1962), 169-173

Roger E. Sappington, *Brethren Social Policy* (Elgin, IL: Brethren Press, 1961); based on "The Development of Social Policy in the Church of the Brethren: 1908-1958," (PhD dissertation, Duke University, 1959)

"NSBRO Marks 20th Anniversary," *Reporter for Conscience' Sake*, 17 (December, 1960): 1

—Berget, "Dr Zigler har vigt sitt liv at att hjaelpa de foertryckta," [Swedish newspaper, ca. November, 1961]

"Churchman's Antidote to World War-Service," [Portland] *Oregon Journal* (April 7, 1962)

"Dr. Zigler Tells Local Brethren of War Danger," [Nampa] *Idaho Free Press* (May 4, 1962): 4

Bethany Biblical Seminary, "Who Is M. R. Zigler?" autumn, 1962

Anna Geesaman, "The Peace Worker," class paper, Manchester College, December 21, 1962

"International Church Leader To Speak at Union Bridge Church of the Brethren." [Frederick, MD] *Carroll County Times* (January 31, 1963)

"Biographical Sketch: Dr. M. R. Zigler," newspaper release, February, 1963

LaVonne Grubb, "M. R. Zigler—Peacemaker," *Horizons* (May 12, 1963): 18-21; also in *Friends* (March 24, 1963): 12-13

"130 Students Graduate from E-town College," *Lancaster* [PA] *New Era* (June 3, 1963) [MRZ given DHL—photo]

"Brethren Leader for Institute Service Sunday," *Decatur* [IL] *Review* (March 7, 1964?): 1-2

"'I Remember Well,' Say 1910 Broadway Graduates: All Six Attend Reunion," [Harrisonburg, VA] *Daily News-Record* (October 22, 1964): 12

"Cottrell Nursing Home Admits Five Patients," *Sebring* [FL] *News* (Dec. 24, 1964

Eileen Egan and Elizabeth Clark Reiss, *Transfigured Night: The CRALOG Experience* (Philadelphia: Livingston Publishing Company, 1964)

[John Eberly], "Co-Founder [Clarence Pickett] of NSBRO Dies," *Reporter for Conscience' Sake*, 22 (May, 1965): 1, 3

"Brethren Churches of Country to Honor Sebring Churchman Sunday," *Sebring* [FL] *News* (September 23, 1965): 18

[bulletin], "M. R. Zigler," (September 26, 1965)

"Zigler Speaks at CPS-1W-BVS Luncheon, June 24," *Brethren Service News* (May, 1966): 1

Harold E. Fey, *Cooperation in Compassion: The Story of Church World Service* (New York: Friendship Press, 1966)

Lenore Wallace, "Attainment of Peace Seen Responsibility of Church: Retired Minister Visits Pomona," [Pomona, CA,] *Beacon* (June 3, 1967)

CROP, *Community Compassion: The Story of CROP* (Elkhart, IN: CROP, 1967)

Ken Baker, "Teams—An Ecumenical Adventure," *Newsletter: Division of Inter-Church Aid, Refugee and World Service, WCC* (March, 1968): 1-10; "It All Began In Greece," (March, 1968): 11-12

M. R. Zigler, "To Work for Peace Through the Churches," *Messenger* (November 21, 1968): 2-5

Donald F. Durnbaugh, "The Puidoux Conferences: Ten Years of Theological Peace Discussion Among Members of the Historic Peace Churches and Others," *BLT*, 13 (Winter, 1968): 30-40

Paul Erb, *Orie O. Miller: The Story of a Man and an Era* (Scottdale, PA: Herald Press, 1969), 11, 222-223

"Portrait of Zigler Given To Brethren Center," [Frederick, MD] *Carroll County Times* (May 14, 1970): 10B

Donald F. Durnbaugh, ed., *The Church of the Brethren: Past and Present* (Elgin, IL: Brethren Press, 1971)

Lawrence W. Shultz, *People and Places, 1890-1970. An Autobiography* (Winona Lake, IN: Life and Light Press, 1971)

Michael Shultz, "Center Founder Returns: Humanitarian Now 80," [Baltimore] *Evening Sun* (February 10, 1972): 1, 10A

Hazel Peters, "M. R. Zigler at Eighty," *Messenger* (March 1, 1972): 14-17

Ben Gamber, "Tunker House Recalls Broadway's Past," [Harrisonburg, VA] *Daily News-Record* (July 25, 1972)

"Dr. Zigler speaks Sunday at Black Rock Brethren," [?] *Daily Record* (December 2, 1972)

M. R. Zigler, *Tunker House Proceedings*, ed. Joseph B. Yount III (Waynesboro, VA: author, 1973), 215pp.

Evelyn Johnson, "Written for the La Verne *Messenger*," January, 1974, typescript

C. Wayne Zunkel, "Interview with M. R. Zigler," *BLT*, 19 (Summer, 1974): 167-177

"Church of the Brethren celebrates anniversary," [Nampa] *Idaho Free Press* (November 15, 1974)

357

"Long-time ministers share thoughts on anniversary of Nampa church [of the Brethren]," [Nampa] *Idaho Free Press* (November 16, 1974)

Edward K. Ziegler, "The Assembly of the Brethren," *BLT*, 19 (Winter, 1974): 5-36

M. R. Zigler and others, *To Serve the Present Age: The Brethren Service Story*, ed. D. F. Durnbaugh (Elgin, IL: Brethren Press, 1975); see review by Florence Z. Sanger in *BLT*, 21 (Winter, 1976): 61-62.

"M. R. Zigler: Peacemaker of the Year," *Reporter for Conscience' Sake* (June, 1975): 3

C. Wayne Zunkel, "M. R. Zigler: Rebel With a Cause," [Manchester College] *Bulletin of the Peace Studies Institute*, 6 (August, 1976): 1-4

"[Monsignor Ligutti] Home Again," [Des Moines, IA] *Catholic Mirror* (June 7, 1977)

"Brethren center appoints new officials," [Frederick, MD] *Carroll County Times* (November 21, 1977)

Albert N. Keim, "Service or Resistance? The Mennonite Response to Conscription in World War II, " *Mennonite Quarterly Review*, 52 (1978): 141-156

Richard L. Benner, "Off the Record," *Bedford* [PA] *Country Press* (July 21, 1978)

Ida Shockley Howell, "A History of the 'On Earth Peace Conference,'" *BLT*, 23 (Winter, 1978): 13-15

Mary Jo Bowman, "Lessons for Peacemakers: M. R. Zigler Remembers," *BLT*, 23 (Winter, 1978): 16-17

Donald F. Durnbaugh, ed., *On Earth Peace: Discussions on War/Peace Issues Between Friends, Mennonites, Brethren and European Churches, 1935-1975* (Elgin, IL: Brethren Press, 1978)

Glee Yoder, *Passing on the Gift: The Story of Dan West* (Elgin, IL: Brethren Press, 1978)

Dawn Chase, "War: It's a Silly Road to Peace, Brethren Minister Says," *Richmond* [VA] *News Leader* (February 24, 1979)

Ellen Layman, "BC Cites Miller, Zigler," [Harrisonburg, VA] *Daily News-Record* (November 3, 1979): 18

"College Cites Dr. Miller, Dr. Zigler," *Bridgewater* (December, 1979): 1, 16.

"Brethren Honor H. [*sic*] R. Zigler," [Baltimore] *Evening Sun* (November 25, 1980)

Donald F. Durnbaugh, "M. R. Zigler at ninety: Still chafing at the status quo," *Messenger* (November, 1981): 13-15

Micki Smith, "M. R. Zigler on being Brethren today," *Messenger* (November, 1981): 14-15

Kermon Thomasson, "[untitled,] *Messenger* (November, 1981): 1

Raymond W. Miller, *Monsignor Ligutti: The Pope's County Agent* (Lanham, MD: University Press of America, 1981)

Joe Baker, "Pacifist Priest: Cure to man's inhumanity simple: Stop the killing," *Rockford* [IL] *Register Star* (February 4, 1982), B6

"Brethren leader to mark 91st year," [Baltimore] *Evening Sun* (Nov. 5, 1982)

Debbie McDaniel, "Striving for Peace at 91," *Carroll County* [MD] *Times* (November, 8, 1982): 1

Gail Cissna, "Although the prize went to others . . . New Windsor pacifist was nominated for Nobel Peace Prize," *Frederick* [MD] *News-Post* (November 8, 1982)

Nancy Frye, "Peace Advocate Speaks in Midway: 'War Is A Perishing Thing,'" [Lebanon, PA] *Daily News* (February 2, 1983)

John Billmyre, "The Story of M. R. Zigler," [Frederick, MD] *Carroll County Times* (June 29, 1983): C1-C2

Robert Lear, "They Remember World Council In Its Yesteryears," [WCC Vancouver Assembly] *Canvas* (July 30, 1983): 4-5

Bob Krummerich, "700 gather for peace," [Frederick, MD] *Carroll County Times* (November 7, 1983)

Donald F. Durnbaugh, "Zigler, Michael Robert," *Brethren Encyclopedia* (1983), 2: 1398-1399

Inez Long, *One Man's Peace: A Story of M. R. Zigler* (New Windsor, MD: OEPA, 1983), 153pp.; unpublished review by Patricia K. Helman

Eileen Eagan, "When Church and State Go Abroad: Refugee, Immigration and Relief Work," (New York: Council on Religion and International Affairs, ca. 1983), mimeographed

"Zigler honored," [Frederick, MD] *Carroll County Times* (June 8, 1984)

Donald F. Durnbaugh, "Decade of Daring," Sept. 29, 1984, New Windsor, MD, on tenth anniversary of OEPA, typescript

Donald F. Durnbaugh, "Blessed be this peacemaker," *Messenger* (December, 1985): 12-13

"Local Nobel Peace Prize Nominee Dies," [Harrisonburg, VA] *Daily News-Record* (October 28, 1985): 5

Shawn Perry, "NISBCO Celebrates 45th Anniversary," *Reporter for Conscience' Sake*, 42 (October/November, 1985): 2

"Deaths," *Christian Century* (November 13, 1985): 1026

"M. R. Zigler: Portrait of a peacemaker," *Mennonite Reporter* (November 25, 1985): 5

"Brethren leader and peace activist, M. R. Zigler, dies at 93," *Gospel Herald* (November 26, 1985): 843

"In Memoriam," *On Earth Peace Newsletter* (November, 1985)

"Church of the Brethren to pay tribute to former leader at peace festival," [York, PA] (?), (November, 1985)

"In Memoriam: Michael Robert Zigler: November 9, 1891– October 25, 1985," *Windsor Winds* (Autumn, 1985), no. 5

"A Giant Dies," *Brethren Peace Fellowship Newsletter*, 19, no. 4 (December, 1985): 1

359

Elizabeth Clark Reiss, *The American Council of Voluntary Agencies for Foreign Service: Four Monographs* (New York: ACVAFS, 1985)
Donald F. Durnbaugh, ed., *Church of the Brethren: Yesterday and Today* (Elgin, IL: Brethren Press, 1986)
Shawn Perry, "CPS Independence Had a Price Tag," *Reporter for Conscience' Sake*, 43 (January, 1986): 3-4
Henry Cline Eller, *Time Flies! Lest I Forget at 85: An Autobiography*, revised (Harrisonburg, VA: Campbell Coty Center, 1987), 38
Milton Hostetter, "Formulating a Response: Mennonite Accommodation to the Demands of Government in America's Wars," class paper, State University of New York, Stony Brook, May 13, 1987
Donald F. Durnbaugh, "M. R. Zigler: Pragmatic Prophet," November 3, 1987, address at Elizabethtown College
Joseph B. Yount III, "The Tunker House at Broadway, Rockingham County, Virginia," *BLT*, 33 (1988): 112-121
Albert N. Keim and Grant M. Stoltzfus, *The Politics of Conscience: The Historic Peace Churches and America at War, 1917-1955* (Scottdale, PA: Herald Press, 1988)
Cynthia Eller, "Moral and Religious Arguments in Support of Pacifism: Conscientious Objectors and the Second World War," PhD thesis, University of Southern California, 1988

Brethren Bodies/Brethren Encyclopedia

"Brethren Meet for First Time in Century," [Harrisonburg, VA] *Daily News-Record* (June 14, 1973)
"Brethren Meeting Results in 'Friendship,'" [Harrisonburg, VA] *Daily News-Record* (June 16, 1973)
Mrs. Marshall Williams, "Broadway," [New Market, VA] *Shenandoah Valley* (June 20, 1973)
"Homecoming for Brethren: A new sense of freedom?" *Messenger* (September, 1973): 5-6
Howard E. Royer, "Reconciliation with our Brethren kin," *Messenger* (September, 1973): 32
Edward K. Ziegler, "The Assembly of the Brethren," *BLT*, 19 (Winter, 1974): 5-36
[Kermon Thomasson], "Brethren historians confer at Bethany," *Messenger* (August, 1976): 9
Donald F. Durnbaugh, "Introduction to the Historical Issue," *BLT*, 22 (Winter, 1977): 2-55
Fred W. Benedict, *The Brethren Assemblies. The Brethren Historians and Writers Conferences. The Brethren Encyclopedia* [Covington, OH: 1977]

"Historians group plans Brethren encyclopedia," *Messenger* (January, 1978): 4

"Brethren approve grant for encyclopedia fund," *Messenger* (May, 1978): 9

"Proposed Brethren Encyclopedia," *Brethren Roots and Branches*, 2, no. 2 (June, 1978): 8

Kermon Thomasson, "A sign of reconciliation," *Messenger* (October, 1978): 40

Donald F. Durnbaugh, "Creating an encyclopedia," *Messenger* (November, 1978): 23

Edward K. Ziegler, "The Brethren Encyclopedia," *BLT*, 24 (Winter, 1979): 60

Fred W. Benedict, "Planning the Brethren Encyclopedia," *BLT*, 24 (Winter, 1979): 60-61

Donald F. Durnbaugh, "The Proposed Brethren Encyclopedia," *BLT*, 24 (Winter, 1979): 62-63

Religious News Service, "Long-divided German Brethren churches join in encyclopedia project," (May 18, 1984)

Kermon Thomasson, "An inside story," *Messenger* (June, 1984): 10-11

"Members of five Brethren groups meet to celebrate printing of encyclopedia," *Brethren Evangelist* (July/August, 1984): 24

[Special issue on the Brethren Encyclopedia], *BLT*, 30 (1985): 132-186

Donald F. Durnbaugh, "Confessions of an Encyclopedia Editor," *BLT*, 30 (1985): 163-169

Kermon Thomasson, "At Ashland, 'we and them became us,'" *Messenger* (June, 1987): 12-14

Dale R. Stoffer, "When Brethren view mission, what do they see?" *Messenger* (July, 1987): 19-22

"Members from Five Brethren Groups Meet for Conference on Mission," *Brethren Evangelist* (May, 1987): 20

Michael Zigler, father of M. R. Zigler, at a blacksmith shop near Broadway, Virginia, ca. 1900.

M. R. Zigler's parents, Michael and Mary Jane Knupp Zigler, at their Broadway, Virginia, home, ca. 1900.

The first known photograph of Michael Robert Zigler, ca. 1892.

Robert Zigler's first trip to Bridgewater, Virginia, ca. 1910; he is in the middle of the last row, wearing a white hat (photographer, J. M. Hill, Bridgewater).

Pupils of the Broadway High School; Zigler is hatless and seated in the middle of the front row.

Roy Hoover, Suzie Arnold, Amy Arnold, and Robert Zigler, ca. 1915.

Robert Zigler (on right) and other Bridgewater College students, ca. 1915.

M. Robert Zigler at Bridgewater College,
ca. 1915.

Amy Arnold at Bridgewater College,
ca. 1915.

Robert Zigler and Amy Arnold on an outing in Virginia, ca. 1915.

Robert Zigler and Amy Arnold as engaged couple, Bridgewater, Virginia, ca. 1915.

Robert Zigler (on left) and Amy Arnold (on right) with college friends on a bathing excursion, ca. 1915.

M. Robert Zigler's graduation photograph,
Bridgewater College, 1916.

Scene from a temperance play at Vanderbilt University, 1917; Robert Zigler
is on the far left.

M. R. Zigler (fourth from left) at a YMCA training camp in Black Mountain, North Carolina, ca. 1916. The famous evangelical leader, William Jennings Bryan (with a bow tie), is near the bottom of the steps. Second from the right on the lower row is R. H. King, who was Zigler's superior in the YMCA work on Parris Island.

M. R. Zigler in a YMCA uniform seated on a trench at the training grounds at Parris Island, South Carolina, ca. 1917.

M. R. "Zig" Zigler as a YMCA worker at the Marine training camp on Parris Island, South Carolina, ca. 1917.

Headquarters area, Marine training base, Parris Island, South Carolina, Zigler's place of work in 1917-1919.

The Zigler family in Elgin, Illinois, ca. 1929: Geraldine, Amy Zigler, Robert, M. R. Zigler.

Amy and Geraldine Zigler at Elgin, Illinois, ca. 1929.

Amy and M. R. Zigler at
Elgin, Illinois, 1937.

H. Spenser Minnich and
M. R. Zigler at the Annual
Conference held in Calgary,
Canada, June, 1923.

371

Elgin staff members ca. 1925: (from left) H. Spenser Minnich, Clyde Culp, M. R. Zigler, Chauncey Shamberger.

M. R. Zigler (second from right, back row) with colleagues from a conciliar movement, later 1930s.

Church of the Brethren delegates to the Federal Council of Churches in the early 1940s: (from left) Paul H. Bowman, Sr., W. Newton Long, C. Ernest Davis, M. R. Zigler, J. Quinter Miller.

M. R. Zigler and W. Harold Row (seated at the end of the table) with directors of Brethren-administered Civilian Public Service Camps, October 20, 1942.

Meeting of the Town and Country Committee of the Rural Life Commission, at the Brethren headquarters, Elgin, Illinois, 1944; M. R. Zigler is at the left of the bottom row.

M. R. Zigler with other employees of the Brethren Publishing House and General Boards recognized for serving more than twenty-five years, March, 1945.

Dan West, Mahlon Harvey, M. R. Zigler, and Earl Smith in front of the Quaker center in Paris, September, 1937.

M. R. and Amy Zigler with the J. F. Graybill family, visiting Pastor Karl Pabst (on right) and children at Schwarzenau, 1937.

The first full Brethren Service Committee, August 15, 1941: (from left, front row) H. F. Richards, M. R. Zigler (executive secretary), L. W. Shultz, Florence Fogelsanger Murphy; (from left, second row), Leland S. Brubaker, Paul H. Bowman, Sr., J. I. Baugher, Andrew W. Cordier (chairman), Paul Kinsel (secretary).

Recognition dinner for M. R. Zigler, April, 1948, prior to leaving for Geneva: (from left, seated) Andrew W. Cordier, M. R. Zigler, Amy Zigler; (from left, standing), John F. Schaefer (local pastor), Raymond R. Peters, Roscoe S. Cartwright (principal of the Elgin high school), Calvert N. Ellis (photo by the *Elgin* [Ill.] *Daily Courier-News*).

Meeting of members of the National Service Board for Religious Objectors during World War II: Orie O. Miller (left), M. R. Zigler (second from right, chairman), Paul Comly French (far right, executive secretary).

377

M. R. and Amy Zigler
leaving Germany
for the USA, June, 1954.

M. R. Zigler during his
inspection trip in China,
summer, 1947.

Amy and M. R. Zigler, n.d.

M. R. and Amy Zigler at Schwarzenau with the family of Pastor Karl Pabst, 1949; also present: (back row, left) Edson Sower, BSC worker, (back row, third from left) Heinz Renkewitz, Moravian scholar.

379

M. R. Zigler and his author friend,
Marcus Bach, clowning in
Geneva, ca. 1955.

Amy Zigler visiting German school, 1949.

Jacqueline Mueller Richez (Swiss secretary), Kurtis F. Naylor, and M. R. Zigler, in the Brethren Service office at the World Council of Churches, in Geneva, 1948.

M. R. Zigler, Helena Kruger, unidentified, Stewart Hermann, at the World Council of Churches offices, in Geneva, 1948.

The dedication of the Alexander Mack School, Schwarzenau, Germany, in 1956; M. R. Zigler is the speaker.

Distribution of animals in Germany through the Heifer Project; M. R. Zigler, center of first row; to his left Wendell Rolston, BSC volunteer worker.

Brethren House, Kassel, Germany.

At the dedication of the Brethren House, Germany, December 13, 1953: (from left) Jacob Dick, M. R. Zigler, Hylton Harman, Don Snider.

Brethren House, Linz, Austria (photo by U. S. Information Service, Vienna).

At the dedication of the Brethren House, Linz, Austria, February 18, 1951: (from left), Lutheran church official, M. R. Zigler, Byron P. Royer (BSC Germany), W. W. Peters (BSC Austria), government official (photo by US Information Service, Vienna).

384

At the Thalham Tubercular Sanatorium, St. Georgen, Austria, established with the help of Brethren Service, summer, 1958; (from left) Harlan Mummert (BSC Austria), M. R. Zigler, Dr. Reiter, Austrian, Desmond W. Bittinger (moderator of Annual Conference).

The Zigler family, ca. 1948. M. R. , Geraldine, Amy, and Robert.

Allen Weldy presents book of congratulatory letters to M. R. and Amy Zigler, Kassel, Germany, August, 1958.

Scene of the tragic accident south of Västervik, Sweden, on August 16, 1958.

387

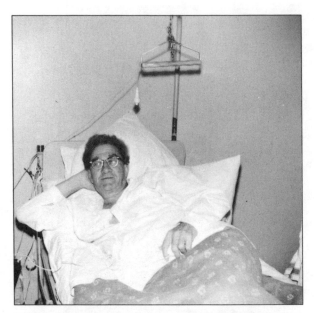

M. R. Zigler in the Västervik hospital, fall, 1958.

At the Västervik hospital, fall of 1958; M. R. Zigler and nurse.

Reunion at Bridgewater College, Virginia, 1969.

Apartment in the Manor, Sebring, Florida, ca. 1965.

389

Meeting of members of the Rotary Club, aboard the S. S. Statendam.

Planning meeting of representatives of five Brethren bodies at the Germantown Church of the Brethren, July 23, 1977, which decided to publish the Brethren Encyclopedia.

W. Harold Row and M. R. Zigler.

Andrew W. Cordier and M. R. Zigler.

M. R. Zigler and Dr. Kit Colfach, Swedish surgeon, in Washington, D. C.

M. R. Zigler and W. A. Visser 't Hooft, general secretary emeritus of the World Council of Churches, Fourth Assembly of the World Council of Churches, November/ December 1975.

M. R. Zigler at a meeting of the On Earth Peace Assembly, New Windsor, Maryland, 1980s.

Geraldine Zigler Glick at a meeting of the On Earth Peace Assembly, New Windsor, Maryland, 1980s.

M. R. Zigler at the celebration of the ninety-second anniversary of his birth, November, 1983.

An On Earth Peace Assembly meeting, 1980s. Friends.

M. R. Zigler in 1984.
Photo by Jim Bishop.

Last photograph known of M. R. Zigler, spring/summer 1985, in his room at
Broadway, Virginia.

Michael Robert Zigler
November 9, 1891—October 25, 1985

INDEX

415